Landmark Visitors Guide

Undiscovered
France

Judy Smith

D0493644

Published by
Landmark Publishing
Ashbourne Hall, Cokayne Ave, Ashbourne,
Derbyshire DE6 1EJ England

Dedication

To Eric – husband, companion, advisor, proof-reader and provider
of second (and sometimes first) opinions, you could not have
given me more encouragement with this book.
Thank you.

Acknowledgements

Thanks to the very helpful staff of Llangollen Library, to Offices de Tourisme throughout the length and breadth of France, and to the many friends at home who offered us their advice, experience and ideas.

While working on this book we were involved in an unfortunate road accident near Paray-le-Monial in Burgundy. We are very grateful for all the help we received and would particularly like to thank Marieke, Franck, Tristan and Emilie for their immeasurable kindness at a time when we really were in need.

Opposite: Looking over the Gorges de Nouailles.

Landmark Visitors Guide

Undiscovered
France

Judy Smith

Contents

Above: Pointe de St. Mathieu. [Chapter 1]

Right: le Conquet. [Chapter 1]

Coastal path near Trégana. [Chapter 1]

'Four-à-goémon (seaweed oven) at Porspaul. [Chapter 1]

House of purple schist, St Malon-sur-Mel. [Chapter 2]

Château de Fougères. [Chapter 2]

Chapel with oak tree, le Tertre-Alix.
[Chapter 2]

Trompe l'Oeil wall in Fougères.
[Chapter 2]

Bay of Ecalgrain. [Chapter 3]

Fort on Tatihou, St Vaast-la-Houge. [Chapter 3]

Above: Port Racine at low tide. [Chapter 3]

Left: Borne 0 (Milestone 0), Ste Mère-Église. [Chapter 3]

Commanderie at Arville. [Chapter 4]

Above: Étang de la Herse.
[Chapter 4]

Right: Basilica at la
Chapelle Montligéon.
[Chapter 4]

Manoir de Courboyer. [Chapter 4]

Right: Harfleur. [Chapter 5]

*Below: Cathedral at Amiens.
[Chapter 5]*

Port d'Aval and l'Aiguille at Étretat. [Chapter 5]

Horloge du Grand Marionnettiste, Charleville-Mézières. [Chapter 6]

Neptune's fountain, Place Stanislas, Nancy. [Chapter 7]

Louis Pasteur's house. [Chapter 8]

Boats at Port-Titi, Lac de St Point. [Chapter 8]

Beside the Lac de Settons. [Chapter 9]

Traditional Loire boats at Gien. [Chapter 10]

Site de Mantelot. [Chapter 10]

15

Left: Beside the Creuse at Argenton. [Chapter 11]

Below: Angles-sur-l'Anglin. [Chapter 11]

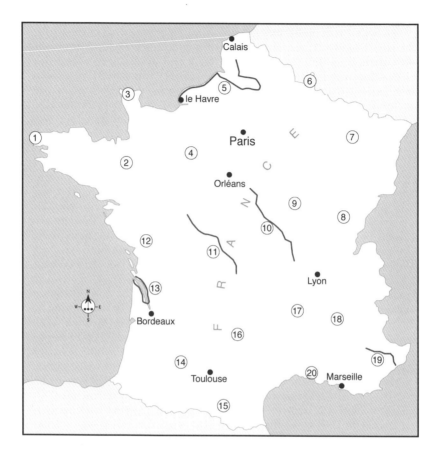

France, the envy of its European neighbours, seems to be a country that has it all – an amazing diversity of landscape; a couple of thousand miles of varied coastline; a climate, that, even in the north, is an improvement on our own; a reverence for history, culture and gastronomy; vineyards producing wines for all tastes and occasions; and an ambiance, style and joie de vivre unparalleled elsewhere. No wonder it attracts so many holiday-makers from all around the world. Around 75 million of them descend on France every year and added to that, 90 per cent of French people recognise the merits of their own country and take their holidays at home. It does mean that, at certain times and in certain places, things can feel a little crowded. But is it possible to find your own quiet corner of the real France: a beach with few people; your own personal tour of a historic monument or cave; a beautiful village that is not merely a showpiece; a restaurant where the other customers are all locals; a family park or playground where the other visitors are French? It certainly is – but it is all a matter of when and where.

The 'when' part of the question is the easiest. Basically France surges into life to greet the 14 July (Bastille Day), parties for around six weeks, and then retires into its shell again at the end of August. If it is Paris you want to see, this is the time to go because everyone has left for the countryside or coast. Elsewhere it is going to be busy, or at least, busier than at other times. Timing your holiday is all-important – even St. Tropez will feel very quiet in January!

Having said that, many of us for reasons of work or family, have no choice about 'when' and need most of all to consider 'where?' For you – and indeed for everyone who loves France and wants to explore pastures new – this book has been written. It describes 20 not-so-well-known holiday-sized areas – effectively 20 potential holidays with a difference, 20 places you might not think of (or even have heard of), all of which offer a taste of authentic French life with plenty of interest as well.

Choosing the areas for this book was a fascinating challenge. Some of the most appealing places were out of the frame immediately because even with the imagination at full stretch, they could not be considered 'undiscovered' – the Côte d'Azur resorts, the banks of the Dordogne, the château-country of the Loire. And of course, it is the coastal regions that attract the most summer visitors of all, yet it would be unbalanced to ignore them completely. The quietest areas of north, south and west have found a place here.

Finally, different people want different things from a holiday and enjoy different types of scenery – the selection had to reflect that and had also to be distributed across the whole country. With all those constraints there were still more than enough contenders for a slot in this book and what you have here is a personal 'Top 20'. If you know France just a little, you are sure to be saying 'But you haven't included ...'. You may be right and if so, I am sorry.

So what of the final choice? Five of the 20 are in fact journeys, and are offered as potential projects for a travelling holiday – for example, following the ancient pilgrim trail through the Lot valley or the very beautiful River Creuse from its confluence with the Vienne to its source in the mountains. A third 'tour' encircles the wide mouth of the Gironde, a fourth tracks the Loire and its canals through Burgundy, while the fifth is more eccentric in attempting to follow in the steps of Henry V on his march to Agincourt. Another chapter describes a potent-ially car-free holiday, exploring the scenic route of the little Train des Pignes that runs from Nice into the mountains.

The 14 chapters that remain portray areas that each have some very special appeal. For some, like the coast of the Cotentin, the Diois or the valleys of the Loue and the Lison, it is simply the very fine scenery; for others there is an individual theme such as exploring the pre-historic cave art in the Pyrenees, dipping into the rich mythology of Brittany, seeking out the source of the Loire high in the Cévennes or discovering Art Nouveau in the back streets of Nancy.

Each chapter in this book ends with practical information about places of interest to visit and Tourist Offices that could be contacted before you go. All of these will be able to give you help with accommodation and will happily send you a screed of detail about the attractions of their area. A particular feature of this book is that this section also includes suggestions for good walks – and since we ourselves enjoy nothing more than a good ramble when on holiday, they really do come with personal recommendation.

The same cannot quite be said about the cycle rides, because there are simply so many possibilities and, for mountain bikes, so much variation in difficulty, but we have attempted to explore as much as possible, and include details of the relevant maps. With families in mind, there is also information on water-sports facilities, a catalogue of lake and sea beaches where swimming is possible, and places where pedalos and canoes can be hired. And no self-respecting Frenchman would consider his investigation of a region complete without a dip into its gastronomic possibilities – you can have fun trying to track down just the few specialities that have been listed.

Finally I could not resist adding a personal note – the features or events we ourselves had found 'most memorable' in visiting each area. Sometimes they are a bit obscure and you will probably come away with a completely different list of your own!

In conclusion I would like to say what enormous pleasure we have had in researching and writing this book. We have visited France for over 30 years, but devoting ourselves to 'Undiscovered France' provided a new adventure every day; we found ourselves in some curious situations and we met some fascinating people. It has all added up to a guidebook that is very different, but I trust that with its help, you also can enjoy some exciting holidays in these less-frequented corners of France.

Judy Smith

1 Rough Seas and Calm Waters –
The Abers of Finistère

The region known as the Abers is in the north-west of Brittany, at the tip of Finistère – the very end of 'Land's End'. And the landscape fits the bill. There are no dramatic cliffs here, but Brittany certainly does not 'go gentle' into that ocean. Instead, long fingers of dark raw granite reach into the foam of the white-flecked sea, and reefs and islands stretch to the horizon, the land's last protest before finally being swallowed up by the waves. Seen on the map, this rugged coastline shows three clear breaks, deep slashes that are the *abers* – the word is the same as the one in Welsh, meaning the mouth of a river. But the abers of Finistère are not river estuaries like those found on the north coast. Instead they are technically *rias*, long tidal inlets formed when sea levels rose to flood existing river valleys at the end of the Ice Age. The tranquil waters of the abers are at their most beautiful at full tide and in the evening, when, facing west, they reflect the rays of the setting sun. So this is a place of contrasts, rough seas and calm waters – and it is also one of the most remote, beautiful and atmospheric places in France.

Strangely some guidebooks play down the merits of this coast and are lukewarm in presenting this as a place worthy of your summer holiday. Certainly the visitor attractions are not immediately obvious, but this is a land of enormous character, tracing its history back to a time when it was the last refuge and stronghold of the Druids as Christianity swept through Brittany. Even today strong Catholicism goes hand-in-hand with pagan belief and there is plenty of evidence of both, especially in the colourful *pardons* and fêtes that take place throughout the summer months. This north-western peninsula goes by the name of Léon (the *Lyonesse* of the Arthurian legends) and the area is steeped in its folklore – Tristan and Iseult landed here, Ste. Haude wanders round with her head in her hands, Ankou, the grim reaper, creaks by in the night. Each village has its little grey church, sometimes with an elaborate parish close, and not far away you will possibly find a well or spring said to have magic powers. Drink or bathe in the waters, whatever your malady there will be a *fontaine* somewhere that can do something about it. And then there are the prehistoric standing stones, the menhirs – more than 50 of them scattered throughout the area. So commonplace are they that they seem to attract little local attention – farmers simply plough and sow their fields around them. The tallest standing stone in France is here – Kerloas at 31ft (9.5m) – but there are bigger ones that have fallen down. Much interest has been invested in these menhirs. Are they set at ancient crossroads? Are they in straight lines? Or at what angle to each other? Are they at high points where they can be seen? No-one knows for certain – your theory is likely to be as valid as that of anyone else.

Le Conquet and around

This may be a rugged coastline but it still has family appeal, because in and among all the rocky outcrops, there are beaches of fine white sand. One of the best of these is the 1.2 mile (2 km) long Plage des Blancs Sablons at le Conquet – and since **le Conquet** is the most attractive place on this coast, an unspoilt fishing port on a little aber of its own, with splendid coastal walks and the possibility of boat trips to the islands of Molène and Ouessant, there could not be a better place to base your holiday. Despite its lack of sophistication, le Conquet boasts two or three hotels and a large but pleasant camp-site tucked into the dunes behind the beach.

Le Conquet's history includes a spell under Roman occupation, a devastating raid by the English and Dutch in 1558 and a couple of hundred years as a commercial port (transhipping wine and salt) before more ruin with the Revolution. The fishing industry began only about 150 years ago, with the arrival of immigrant fishing families from the north coast of Brittany, but today there is certainly plenty of activity around a harbourside that is piled with nets and lobster pots. This is obviously the heart of the town – and it is also the place to catch a ferry to the islands or take off for a little under-sea exploration in a glass-bottomed boat. The setting of it all is idyllic, backed by grey-stone merchant houses from the days of commerce (note the outside stair-cases), and overlooked by the bracken-clad peninsula of Kermorvan across the estuary.

Crowning the town above the harbour is the stone church that was built here in the 19th century (although it has windows and carvings from much earlier), and which now contains the tomb of Dom Michel de Nobletz, a Breton missionary priest who died in le Conquet in 1652. The house where he died (in a narrow street near the harbour) has been converted into a chapel, and contains an exhibition about his life and the hand-painted tableaux (*Taolennou*) he produced to teach his illiterate parishioners the scriptures. From the church, the narrow streets leading down to the harbour are lined with some excellent eating-houses, along with shops selling seafaring necessities, local produce, and plenty of fresh fish. Campers who shop in town can make their way home over a specially constructed footbridge spanning the estuary, thus avoiding the use of a car (and a drive of about 3 miles [5 km]). The same footbridge can be used to access Kermorvan with its splendid coastal path, and the lovely sheltered beach of Blancs Sablons (approx. half a mile (1 km) from town this way).

The three most renowned abers are all to the north of le Conquet, but before going to explore them we should go out to the islands – and before even that, it is worth having just a quick look around the corner to the south. The first place reached in this direction is the **Pointe de St Mathieu** – and no-one could pretend that it was 'undiscovered'. There are plenty of visitors to this promon-tory with its monastery and light-house, two buildings that are not so much juxtaposed as entangled with each other. The monastery was founded here in the sixth century by the Breton St Tanguy, at the site where St. Matthew's skull was said to have been brought ashore by sailors who had carried it from Ethiopia. The roofless walls standing today date from the 12th or 13th century – and you wonder how they could have survived so long in this exposed spot. A little museum telling the abbey's story welcomes visitors and the lighthouse (163 steps) does the same in high season. The other prominent structure on the site faces the sea, and is a memorial to French sailors lost in World War I. At its summit, the sculpture by Réné Quillivic is of a Breton woman weeping – and well she might, for the passage she overlooks has seen many a wreck of its own. Out there are the Pierres Noires, jagged rocks that form the fringe of the Molène archipelago, while to their right, the more gentle shores of Béniguet conceal a sea pierced with rocky islets all the way out to distant Ouessant. Far away to the south, the vista extends past the Crozon peninsula into the Bay of Douarnenez – perhaps backed by the misty silhouette of the Pointe du Raz. An orientation table points out every feature.

There may be a few people at the point, but their number soon dwindles if you take to the coastal footpath starting beside the chapel. The seascapes are magnificent, and in about half an hour you reach a rocky cove overlooked by the houses of the hamlet of Vaéré, a cove where seaweed was once harvested commercially. If you look at the edge of the cliff here you will see several examples of a *davied* (a Breton word), a stone with a hole that once held a pulley used for hauling the seaweed up the cliff. Back at the Pointe de St Mathieu again, you could now head east on the road to Plougonvelin – and in 500m or so, pass the Gibets des Moines, two ancient menhirs that have been 'Christianised' with the addition of a cross. Farther along, you can turn right to reach the seaweed cove with its *davieds* by road.

In **Plougonvelin**, follow signs to the Fort de Berthaume, a citadel on a rocky island that protects a natural harbour, and guards the entrance to the Brest Channel. There has been a fortress here for many centuries, but not surprisingly, the current model, linked to the land by a bridge, was the work of Vauban. Now open to visitors, it offers a scenic walk around its ramparts, a room of changing exhibitions, and a summer evening *son et lumière* that adds some rather unexpected colour to the scene. Anyone simply looking for a photogenic view of the fort can take the coastal path to the right of its entrance. From Berthaume you can descend past a pretty bay and then continue along the seafront to the fashionable Plage du Trez Hir. The coastal path will take you on to the cove of Porsmilin and then Trégana, with yet another glorious beach (by car you will need to loop inland to reach the same point). Here we should probably call it a day, but this coastal trail is becoming addictive – wild flowers at your feet, seagulls wheeling overhead and a view across the turquoise waters to the Pointe de Penhir on the Crozon peninsula, with the conical rocks of the Tas de Pois (literally Heap of Peas) off its tip. Just 15 minutes more of this splendour and you will pass an old stone customs officers' hut on the slope above you – and as far again will bring you to the narrow **Cove of Déolen** that was the departure point of the first transatlantic telephone cable in 1879 and a second in 1898. Cable can still be seen among the stones of the beach and the yellow building on the left of the valley was once the headquarters of the *Compagnie Française des Câbles*. The scenic path winds on into Brest, but you must retrace your steps (or find a route inland with the aid of a map), pick up the car, and return to le Conquet. It is time to take a trip out to the islands.

OFF TO THE ISLANDS

Two maritime companies are based at the quayside in le Conquet, Pen ar Bed and Finist'mer – the latter operate high speed vessels, making the direct crossing to Ouessant (not calling at Molène) in about half the time. But maybe it is not speed you want – the trip is an experience in itself, with the boat threading its way through a sea scattered with jagged rocks, marked by buoys and the occasional lighthouse. The slower boat docks first at Molène, where the rocks stand like sentries in a line guarding the entrance to the harbour. **Molène** is definitely the off-the-beaten-track option – only a fraction of the passengers disembark here. But Molène is tiny. Its perimeter path, all of 4km, can be walked in an hour – although it is worth lingering and looking a bit longer because there are both grey seals and dolphins to be seen in the waters off Molène, as well as a great variety of seabirds. But since the boats only call two or three times a day at the most, other diversions are necessary. The tiny island boasts three museums – a sea rescue museum, an environmental museum exploring the local flora and fauna, and a museum telling the sad tale of the British liner Drummond Castle that fell foul of the notorious rocks known as the Pierres Vertes in 1896.

From Molène the boat crosses the Fromveur Channel to Ouessant – and you can be reassured that the Pierres Vertes are far away at the its other end. Even so you cannot help wondering what rocky reefs lie beneath you and just how far down they are. **Ouessant** (its anglicised version is Ushant) is the largest island of the archipelago, and at something like 4.5x2.5 miles (7x4 km), is just too big to walk around in the time available on a day trip. The boat puts into the deep Bay of Stiff on the island's east side and as soon as you land, you see the answer – hundreds upon hundreds of bikes for hire, equipped with child seats, carriages and the rest, all stashed on the roadsides around the harbour. Ouessant on a fine summer's day vies with the morning rush hour in Amsterdam – bikes are flying in all directions. Things are very different if it rains. Then most people opt for a mini-bus ride into the 'capital' of Lampaul, 1.9 miles (3km) away on the opposite coast, to browse around the handful of shops and, of course, the restaurants. And if the sun should come out – well, there are more bikes for hire in town.

Bike it or walk it, the two eco-museums of Ouessant are both within easy reach of Lampaul. The first of these, the **Maison du Niou** (about a third of a mile [500m] west of town), is simply two traditional cottages and their surrounding yards, but it will give you a very clear idea of what life was like here in the 19th century.

The menfolk of Ouessant were merchant seamen, and away from home for maybe several years at a time. Left behind, the women were self-sufficient, growing vegetables and rearing sheep and other livestock on the rough ground. Life was subject to the elements, summer droughts, autumn fogs or winter winds – and there was always the prospect of the loss of a son or husband at sea.

Religion and superstition formed the background to everyday life – the doors and windows of the grey granite houses of Ouessant were traditionally painted blue to ensure the protection of the Virgin Mary. At the Maison du Niou not only the shutters but the furniture inside is blue, and it serves to divide up the living space – there are no interior walls. All is neat and tidy, with colourful box beds, scrubbed wooden tables and baubles hanging from the ceiling to represent the absent menfolk. Other aspects of island life dealt with in the museum are the severe black dress of the women (in later years changed to white) and the ceremony of the wax Proëlla cross that was given to a woman when she was told that one of her family had perished at sea. The Proëlla cross represented his body – it was taken to a funeral service and later lodged with other crosses in a monument in the cemetery. If you have time, you can find the monument of the Proëlla crosses in the middle of the cemetery at Lampaul.

The second eco-museum is at the lighthouse of Creac'h, just a little farther down the road from the maison du Niou. The **Musée des Phares et Balises** has a wide range of optical exhibits dealing with the evolution of lighthouses, and offers a film (French only) detailing the particular perils and warning systems of this wild west coast. There is quite a lot to be seen and on a wet day, a couple of hours could happily be spent here.

After the lighthouse, most of the other attractions of the island are natural ones – with perhaps the exception of the windmill you have probably already passed and the curious star-shaped sheepfolds scattered across the islands (look carefully at the sheep – they are traditionally tethered in twos between February and September). But maybe the most impressive sight is right in front of you at the lighthouse – the sharp-toothed rocks of the north coast appear like the spines of so many prehistoric monsters rising from the deep. A footpath will take you out beside them, and this is where you wish you hadn't got the bike, because these grassy paths that encircle the whole island are out-of-bounds for wheels of any kind. The footpath could take you all the way round the coast to the harbour at Stiff – it is about 6 miles (10km), depending on how many headlands you take in – but you might prefer to pass up on the physical activity and return to Lampaul for a lazy afternoon on its sandy beach (just past the harbour) instead. If you have a bike you could take a look at other beaches, Yusin in the north and Penn Arlan in the south-east, but their isolation and rocky surrounds can make them seem less friendly.

TO THE NORTH OF LE CONQUET

Back on the mainland again now, and at long last it is time to head for the abers – but do not be in too much of a hurry, there are a couple of places to call in at on the way. If you look at a map casually, you may think that le Conquet and the Pointe de St Mathieu are the most westerly places on the mainland of Brittany – but not quite. By a hair's breadth, that distinction belongs to the **Pointe de Corsen** just to the north (best accessed via the D28 and Ploumoguer), making it effectively the 'Land's End' of 'Land's End'. But Cornwall eat your heart out – this is what a land's end should be, a lonely elemental place to be discovered quietly, not one decked with all the trappings of mass tourism. Here, 164ft (50m) above the foaming ocean, there is only an artistic tiled orientation table pointing out the islands of the archipelago, and yet another monument to souls forfeited to that savage sea. Behind you, the centre of CROSS-Corsen (Centre Régional Opérationnel de Surveillance et de Sauvetage) was installed here after the terrible disaster of the oil tanker *Amoco-Cadiz* in 1978 and it has the role of monitoring shipping by means of satellites, co-ordinating sea rescue operations and checking pollution levels along the coast.

The lighthouse you can see from Corsen is that of **Trézien**, sited about a kilometre inland. If you drive past it (but pause if it is open, because it offers the best possible views of the islands) and continue along the road in the direction of Plouarzel, you can turn left into the village of Trézien to meet the first of the many *fontaines* of this region. Picturesquely situated in a small field opposite the church, the *fontaine* of Notre-Dame-de-Trézien holds waters that are said to be beneficial for childhood maladies.

Beyond Trézien the road returns to the coast and the first place you reach is **Porspaul**, with yet another curiosity. The road bearing left to Beg ar Vir runs along an isthmus between harbour and sea and on each side of it is the stone-ringed trench of an old *four-à-goémon* – a seaweed oven. These two ovens have been preserved and an information panel tells you how they were piled with pre-dried seaweed, which was then burned slowly. The block of soda that was produced was taken to a local factory for the extraction of iodine. The *fours-à-goémon* have not been used for the last 50 years or so – but if you walk the coastal path along here you will be able to pick out several

of them in the dunes.

Today the seaweed industry is still important along this coast but is more mechanised – and just along the road at the harbour of **Porscave**, you can get a glimpse of how it is done. Porscave faces the strange outcrop of the Rocher du Crapaud (Toad Rock) across the entrance to the first of the abers, Aber Ildut. On the opposite shore is Lanildut, a port solely devoted to seaweed, and moored in the channel are boats that carry a *scoubidou*, a huge folding arm like a bottle-opener that scoops the seaweed from the sea bed. Lanildut clearly merits a visit, but there is no direct road taking you to the head of the aber (although there is a magnificent footpath). So let us reserve Lanildut for another day, and from here return to le Conquet – calling in at a menhir and a viewpoint on the way.

Leaving Porscave via Plouarzel (where the Office de Tourisme stages a menhir exhibition) and keeping ahead on the D5, a sign directs you right to the **Menhir of Kerloas**, the tallest standing stone in France. Thick as well as high, it is well-nicknamed *le Bossu* (the Hunchback). Up close you can see a couple of protuberances at about waist-height on its side where, according to tradition, newly-weds would rub their bellies – he in the hope of begetting a son, and she in the hope of ruling the household. Lots of other stories are told about this great giant, and those in the know about such things get very excited about its distance from certain crucial points like churches and other menhirs. As the crow flies, Kerloas is in fact situated about half a mile (500m) from the highest point in this area (466ft [142m]).

Just a little lower and just a little

to the west, another summit is crowned by the **Belvédère of Keramézec**, which is well worth a visit, but once again the road journey is a lot longer that that on foot. Keep ahead, turn right on the D67, right again and then right to the village of Lamber and you will be almost back where you started. From Lamber the road is signed – and it comes as a surprise after driving through such barren countryside to find a fine orientation table accompanied by many hedge-sheltered picnic tables. The panorama is splendid, encompassing the abers, le Conquet, the Pointe St Mathieu, the islands, the Crozon peninsula and a lot more. When you come down again, devote a few moments to **Lamber** itself. The lovely church dates from the 11th century, its plain interior complemented by the beautiful colours and designs of the very modern stained glass windows depicting the life of St Peter. In front of the church a *fontaine* miraculously trickles water from a mound of moss-covered rocks isolated in the road.

If you return to le Conquet on the D67, there could be just one mini-diversion before home. The village of **Trébabu** (on the right just before le Conquet) has another beautiful church in a wooded valley. You have probably already noticed the open bell walls in the churches of this area, and this is a fine example, if not a grand one. An outside rocky staircase gives access to the bell from the roof behind. Just outside the church grounds (to the south-west) a tree trunk bears a fine carving of the Virgin and Child. And if you want one more curiosity before going home, take a look in the angle of the road as you rejoin the D67. The old milestone dates from pre-Revolutionary days and carries its measurement in *toises* – units of about 2.2 yards (2m).

NORTH OF THE ABER ILDUT

The next day you must set out for Lanildut – the D28 will take you through Ploumoguer and Plouarzel (note the balconied bell-tower) to Brélès near the head of the Aber Ildut. Horse-lovers will probably want to take instead the minor road to the east via **St Eloi** – the waters of the *fontaine* here are said to protect against all equine maladies, so a bottleful to take home wouldn't come amiss (pour it on the rump, as they do at the annual *pardon* here). But whichever way you go, **Brélès** is your destination. In fact it is just off the road that leads to Lanildut, but you might like to divert to take a look at its church. Here is a not too elaborate example of a parish close – at least there is a triumphal arch leading into the cemetery. Other items present within the enclosure should be an ossuary and a calvary clustered with carved biblical figures. The best nearby examples of parish closes are Gumiliau, Lampaul-Gumiliau and St Thégonnec, just off the N12 to Morlaix, but there are lesser ones all over Finistère, and for the moment you must make do with humble Brélès. The inside of the church here is adorned with various angels playing Breton instruments and there is a curious *trompe l'oeil* on the back wall. The spire is pierced with playing card symbols, hearts, clubs, diamonds, spades – a feature that is not entirely unique around here.

On at last to **Lanildut** with its fascinating port. The boats with their *scoubidous* are moored all around and there are many other smaller boats obviously used for harvesting. You may be lucky enough to watch the unloading, but beware – the quayside is slippery with all that spilled seaweed! The colourfully-painted Maison de l'Algue alongside tells you all about it, but is only open in high season. From Lanildut we could continue up the main road to Porspoder, but this is the area with the greatest density of menhirs. Why are they gathered here? It is all a mystery, but there are certainly quite a few you could home in on. The tallest menhir of all (36ft [11m]) is at **Kergadiou**, but unfortunately it has fallen down. A lesser one stands beside it, but both are over a high hedge in a field of crops. Nevertheless signs have recently appeared, so they expect visitors – head north from the road that links Brélès and Lanildut and turn on to an earth track.

Your menhir-hunting will be most successful if you can equip yourself with the relevant map (Top 25 – 0416 ET). Other nearby menhirs worth seeking out are those at Kerhouézel and St Gonvarc'h, but they receive no publicity. If you do seek them, you might also find your way to **Larret**, where, behind the little grey church (continue down the road and look left), there is perhaps the most attractive of all *fontaines*. Soon though it will be back to Porspoder and heading north past the white sands of the Anse de Penfoul, an attractive bay popular with surfers. From here the road follows the coast closely and passes the lovely stone **Chapel of St Samson**, perched scenically above the reef-strewn sea. Down on the coastal path here there is a *fontaine* with powers over rheumatism, and beside it, a stone cross.

This particular section of wild coast is home to one of Brittany's most famous legends, that of Tristan and Iseult. The star-crossed lovers are said to have landed at **Trémazan**, and as you round the headland you can see on the right the ivy-clad ruins of an ancient keep, in whose walls a little imagination will help you to perceive a heart-shaped hole.

Legend of Gurguy and Haude

Gurguy and Haude were the children of a sixth-century Lord of the Manor in Trémazan and were brought up by their 'wicked stepmother'. Gurguy ran away from home, and on returning 10 years later was deceived into thinking that Haude had been banished for her intolerable behaviour. Rushing after her, he found her beside the local *fontaine*, and promptly cut off her head. When he returned home, Haude appeared carrying her head in her hands and the lying stepmother was immediately struck dead by a thunderbolt. Haude replaced her head (clearly she was a saint!) and a penitent Gurguy followed her example of piety, becoming St Tanguy, the founder of the monastery at St. Mathieu.

The other legend belonging to Trémazan is that of Ste. Haude, and to pursue it, the next place to visit is the **Chapel of Kersaint**, just a little farther down the road. Here the story is told in stained glass and a statue of Ste Haude, head in hands, peers down on the gathered congregations. The church is interesting in itself, with an extra side aisle said to be helpful for dealing with the crowds at festival time, and the recent addition of a very modern window, filling its corner with brilliant blue light. The *fontaine* that was the scene of the decapitation can be visited (follow the not-too-obvious signs from the church), and it is said that the circular basin was formed by Haude's falling head.

Beyond Trémazan the road bends into **Portsall**, and on a headland overlooking the harbour (park by the *crêperie* before the village and follow the white on red Grande Randonnée marks) you can find the **Dolmen of Gulligui** with a calvary alongside. Dating from 6000BC, this dolmen is one of the oldest in Brittany – and its view is unsurpassable. A quote reads:

> When the narrowness of life causes you pain you should go and stand on Guilligui headland with your back to a dolmen and your eyes fixed on the open sea to gain strength from the ocean air that flows into your lungs.

Portsall harbour is indeed a beautiful spot, yet sadly it was here that the *Amoco-Cadiz* foundered on the rocks one March evening in 1978. The huge ship's anchor is kept on the seafront as a reminder of the devastation. To the immediate north of Portsall, the vast sandy beaches look out to the Île Carn and its huge tumulus that was excavated some 50 years ago. Within its three chambers were found pottery, jewellery and other funereal objects made of stone.

Time now to head south through Ploudalmézeau (where, if the hour is right, the panoramic *crêperie* at the top of the water-tower might appeal) to explore some of the curiosities inland. Beyond Ploudalmézeau (on the D168) is **Lanrivoaré**, with its attractive parish close and 'Cemetery of the Saints'. The latter is right beside the church, an enclosed area said to be the communal grave of 7,847 Christians, massacred for their beliefs in the fifth century. It is presided over by the tiny figure of St Hervé and his eight stones. The story goes that St Hervé, weak and ill, approached a farmer to beg some of the bread he was baking. The farmer refused – and when he went back to his oven he found the loaves turned to stone. St Hervé was actually a blind hermit living with a wolf in the nearby woods – you can visit the site by returning towards Ploudalmézeau and turning right to Tréourgat. Just before the village an inconspicuous sign on the right directs you down a rough track to the **Hermitage St Hervé**. At the edge of the woods there are obvious signs of habitation, a chapel, a tiny cell, and, of course, a *fontaine*

At this point you begin to feel confused between reality and myth – and if from Lanrivoaré you head west to the stern Château of Kergroadès, hiding behind its long road of gnarled oak trees you will feel sure you are in the land of fairly sinister fairy tales. This is the moment to return to the safety of le Conquet – or maybe you should stay in this area, because there's more to explore in the north tomorrow.

ABER BENOÎT, ABER WRAC'H AND THE NORTH

Let us start this next journey at Ploudalmézeau and head north to **Lampaul-Ploudalmézeau**, where the church has a lantern tower above the belfry, and an exterior balcony from which there are wide views of the coast. North from here the dunes of Corn-ar-Gazel look out across the mouth of the Aber Benoît and a sea scattered with islands. Turning inland the road reaches **St Pabu** and you can descend to its picturesque Port Stellac'h and gaze enviously at all those boats bobbing on the tide. From here the main road runs along the south side of the Aber Benoît – not that you can see it for most of the time, and the best way to do just that is to abandon the car, and take to the footpath that follows this shore from Trégoniou. Those who have not had enough of menhirs can follow signs from the main road to that of **Lannoulouarn** (6.5m) – you should find the menhir without too much difficulty, but there is a fair chance of getting lost on the way back!

Back on the main road, Aber Benoît is crossed on the long bridge at Trégloniou, after which you can head for the tip of this promontory between two abers. The superbly well-appointed campsite here (prosaically called *The Abers*) has one of the best views on the coast and beside it, footpaths head out into the lovely dunes of Ste Marguerite. The dunes extend to the mouth of the **Aber Wrac'h**, a channel peppered with islets, guarded by the Fort Cézon (on its own island) and watched over from a distance by the lighthouse of Île Vierge. This coast is incredibly beautiful, and the road curves round the blue waters of the Baie des Anges (Bay of Angels) to reach the port of Aber Wrac'h itself.

To get the very best view of this aber, head now towards Lannilis, but turn left towards Plouguerneau and cross the bridge, the Pont du Paluden. As the road climbs, there is a pull-in viewpoint on the left – and you are definitely going to need the camera, because this is a shot appearing in many travel guides and brochures. Beyond the viewpoint, a turning on the left (signed) takes you very quickly to a beautiful little church surrounded by hydrangeas in a pretty valley. The 16th century parish close of Notre-Dame-du-Val reveals some delightful carvings – on the triumphal arch, on the calvary (the work of two Italian brothers), on the bell-tower, and even on the roof of the church.

Just a couple of minutes up the road, **Plouguerneau** itself has an interesting church in which you can see the 'little saints' carved by 17th century villagers in thanks for their escape from the plague and now carried triumphantly on their poles in feast day processions. Plouguerneau is also home to the eco-museum **Musée des Goémoniers** (just off the D32 north). Breton appears to be the first language here, with French offered in translation – no English, of course. But this is a genuine little museum and with film, photographs and a few models, it tells you all you need to know about the past and present seaweed industry of this coast. Seaweed is particularly used in cosmetics and there are plenty of examples on sale – but you may (or may not) be tempted by more unconventional products like seaweed beer.

The coast to the north of Plouguerneau is full of interest. The lighthouse of **Île Vierge**, 271ft

(82.5m) high and the tallest in France, rises like a dull grey finger from its own offshore island. In summertime boats taking visitors to the lighthouse leave from the harbour of Perros to the west, but those wanting simply a good view can drive on through Lilia to the end of the road. On a fine summer's day the blue sea, islands and brightly coloured boats make a pretty scene; in foul weather there is something menacing about it all.

To the east of the Île Vierge viewpoint, the little village of **St Michel** is worth a visit – but you will have to return almost to Plouguerneau to get there. Entering the village, a road to the left leads to the ruins of **Iliz-Koz**. These are effectively the remains of the parish close of a village known as Tremenac'h that became engulfed by the dunes early in the 18th century. Church and ossuary can be seen, but most intriguing are the tombs with their various carvings depicting the profession of the occupant. If from Iliz-Koz you turn towards the sea, the attractive little chapel of St Michel has fine modern stained glass windows and houses a permanent exhibition on the life and work of Michel le Nobletz (the one you met in le Conquet). The dunes behind the chapel conceal modern sculptures, bronze-age relics, *fours-à-goémon* and more – to sort out what you want to see, consult the map at the car park.

Beyond Plouguernou, the road continues to le Grouannec with its fine parish close and then le Folgoët, where each September, its 15th century

---

The Breton language

Around half a million people speak Breton and the language is being revived with formal teaching in schools and signs appearing in Breton as well as French. Most native speakers live near this western coast. Place names here are almost exclusively Breton in origin and confusingly, very many are prefixed by *plou* (parish), *lan* (monastery or hermitage) or *ker* (town, village). *Ker* particularly appears frequently in surnames – just look in the cemetery at Trébabu for a classic example.

Breton is of course a Celtic language and Welsh speakers will find many words whose similarity they instantly recognise:

white = *gwyn* (Welsh), *gwenn* (Breton);
head = *pen* (Welsh), *penn* (Breton);
and the words black (*du*), sea (*mor*) and house (*ty*) are identical in the two languages.

But in many ways the languages are also very different – for example, the letters 'k' and 'z' that crop up so frequently in Breton do not even appear in the traditional Welsh alphabet.

Other words you might like to know are *aven* (river), *beg* (point or summit), *men* (stone), *trez* (beach) and *pors* (port). The Breton flag is called the *Gwenn ha Du* (White and Black) and Bretons refer to their country as *Breizh* and to Finistère as *Penn ar Bed*.

basilica is the focus of one of the largest *pardons* in Brittany – but now it is time to leave the abers. For your last look at them, return through Plouguerneau, and follow the narrow road inland along the north bank of the Aber Wrac'h. In a few kilometres you reach the tiny ancient church of **Prad-Paol**, which makes a fitting end to this tour. In its grounds are three springs which were definitely created by St Pol Aurelian – but whether he did this by tapping his stick three times on the ground, or whether it was the head of the dragon that he slew which bounced three times is a matter of debate. Also in the grounds of the church are four crosses along with two pagan steles, and just along the road is the **Devil's Bridge**, a partially sunken ford of stones across the aber – which of course, the devil was tricked into building in return for a soul (he actually got that of a cat). Religion, pagan belief, mythology, history and legend, all combined in a truly beautiful setting – the essence of the abers.

Offices de Tourisme

The south of this region, up as far as the Aber Benoît, is known as the Pays d'Iroise (the western sea being the Mer d'Iroise), while in the north, it is the Pays des Abers. Tourist offices tend to offer information relating only to their own area, so if you want it all, try, for example, both le Conquet and Plouguerneau.

Le Conquet
Parc de Beauséjour
29217 LE CONQUET
☎ 02.98.89.11.31

Ouessant
Bourg de Lampaul
29242 OUESSANT
☎ 02.98.48.85.83

Ploudalmézeau
BP 31
29830 PLOUDALMÉZEAU
☎ 02.98.48.12.28

Plouguerneau
Place de l'Europe
29880 PLOUGUERNEAU
☎ 02.98.04.70.93

PLACES OF INTEREST

Pointe de St Mathieu

Abbey Museum
Open July and August 10am-12.30pm, 2-7pm (except Sun morning); June and September 2.30-6.30pm every day except Tuesday; rest of year weekends and Wednesdays only 2-6pm (April and May 2.30-6.30pm).

Lighthouse
Open all day every day in July and August; in April, May, June, September and October, weekends only 2.30-6.30pm.

Plougonvelin

Fort de Berthaume
Open July and August every day 10am-7pm; April, May, June and September 2-6.30pm (closed Mondays).

Molène

SNSM. museum (sea rescue)
Open in July and August 11am-1pm, 3-5pm.

Le Maison de l'Environment Insulaire (environment museum)
Open every afternoon in July and August, weekend afternoons in June and September.

Drummond Castle Museum
Open afternoons from April to October.

Ouessant

Maison du Niou
Open April to September 10.30am-6.30pm, rest of year 1.30-5pm approx. (but all day in school holidays).

Musée des Phares et Balises
Hours the same as the Maison du Niou.

Trézien

Lighthouse
Open July and August, 2.30-6pm.

Château de Kergroadès
Open 10am-12noon, 2-6pm, 4 July to 22 August.

Plouguerneau

Musée des Guémoniers
Open 2.30-6pm every day in July and August and weekends only in June and September.

Île Vierge
Visits every afternoons in July and August.

St. Michel

Iliz-Koz ruins
Open from mid-June to mid-September every afternoon except Monday 2-6pm.

Chapelle Saint-Michel
Open 2-5pm in July and August.

LOCAL HIGHLIGHTS

Best walks

- There are not enough superlatives to describe the coastal path (once used by customs officers) that goes all the way around these western shores. It is now a Grande Randonnée (the GR34), very well waymarked, and very easy to follow. Suggestions for the best bits are difficult, but – walk east from Trégana for gentle seascapes, north from Porspoder for wild seascapes and along the south of Aber Ildut (from Pont Reun) for a contrast. Maps are not strictly needed, but all the above paths are marked on IGN Top 25 0417ET.

- For a good look at menhirs without negotiating a labyrinth of narrow lanes in your car, take the 10 mile (16km) Circuit des Menhirs, which takes you past St Gonvarc'h, Kerhouézel and Kergadiou, as well as the *fontaine* at Larret. OT at Ploudalmézeau should be able to find the route for you on request – otherwise you will need to resort (at some very justifiable expense) to the Topoguide *Le Pays d'Iroise à pied*.

- Circular routes in the north of the area are described (with English translation) in the inexpensive booklet *Randonnée – Circuits du Pays des Abers* available from OT at Lannilis or Plouguerneau.

For cyclists

- Road cyclists should ask at any OT for the Pays d'Iroise guides, four fact sheets describing circuits from 25 to 93 km using minor roads.

- Mountain bikers will find that 12 circuits of varying difficulty have been designated in the Pays d'Iroise. Again ask any OT.

Watersports

- This beautiful coast offers plenty of opportunity for swimming from sheltered beaches. Where beaches directly face the Atlantic, surfing is often more appropriate. There is a particularly fine indoor sea-water swimming complex at Plougonvelin (*Treziroise*).

- There are six main sailing centres on this coast (Plougonvelin, Portsall, Argenton, Tréompan, Lanildut and Porsman) and they also offer opportunities for canoeing or sea-kayaking. Boats and kayaks may simply be hired or tuition provided. Access the website www.nautisme.pays-iroise.com for more details.

For the palate

- First and foremost, seafood. Fresh fish and anything else that has come straight from the sea. And yes, that does include seaweed – it is incorporated into all sorts of products from bread, cakes and biscuits to beer.

- This is Brittany, so you must have a meal of savoury buckwheat *galettes*, followed by a sweet *crêpe* – all washed down with a *bol* (large open cup) of cider.

- There are dozens of other Breton specialities – *Kouign Amann* (buttercake), *Far Breton* (if made traditionally, a very exotic rich pudding), and *Chouchen* (mead – and very powerful!) are just a few.

And the most memorable

- High seas on the crossing to Ouessant – and the French families around us discussing in detail the menu for the five-course lunch they had reserved!

- Standing in what certainly appeared to be a one-time hermitage in the woods near Tréourgat and wondering what happened to the boundary between fact and fiction.

- Simply the magnificent sight of the Aber Wrac'h at sunset (from the road above the Pont du Paluden).

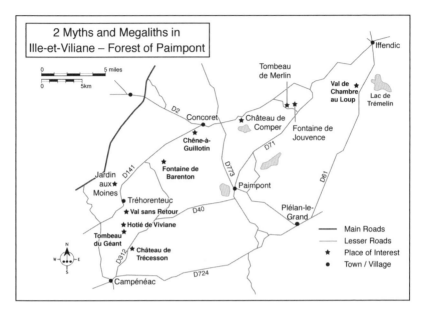

2 Myths and Megaliths in Ille-et-Viliane – Forest of Paimpont

0   5 miles
0   5km

Iffendic

Tombeau de Merlin

Val de Chambre au Loup

Lac de Trémelin

Concoret

Château de Comper

Fontaine de Jouvence

D2

Chêne-à-Guillotin

D71

Jardin aux Moines

D141

Fontaine de Barenton

D773

Paimpont

D61

Tréhorenteuc

Val sans Retour

D40

Plélan-le-Grand

Hotié de Viviane

Tombeau du Géant

Château de Trécesson

D312

Main Roads
Lesser Roads
★ Place of Interest
● Town / Village

N W E S

Campénéac

D724

The familiar images of Brittany are those of granite cliffs and lighthouses, sandy coves, fishing villages, rock pools and family holidays on the beach. Added to that are the megaliths, the standing stones (menhirs), dolmens and gallery graves (*allées couvertes*) so liberally sprinkled across this ancient countryside. Prehistoric man left more evidence of his occupation here than anywhere else in Europe. But above all Brittany is a Celtic country, a country of fervent religious beliefs side-by-side with deep-seated superstition, an enchanted land rich with legend and folklore. Brittany is set apart from the rest of France as much culturally as it is geographically – and you might expect that this 'Celticness' would increase as you travel west. Well, to some extent it does – the most classic legends of Brittany,

those of the drowned city of Ys and the saga of Tristan and Iseult, both largely relate to the west coast. But you will not be in any doubt that you have hit a land of magic as soon as you reach the most easterly *département* of Brittany, Ille-et-Vilaine.

Fougères, just 12.4 miles (20 km) from the Normandy border, says that its history is 'engraved in the stones' and so it is. In the forest outside the town there is a long line of standing stones, a huge dolmen, the remains of a gallic oppidum, a cross marking the site of a tree where rituals were performed to procure recovery from illness – and a mischievous forest goblin. In the surrounding villages you can find a rock that bears the imprint of a saint's knees and one that was scored by the shoe of a horse as it made a fatal leap, rocks that hide treasure and get up and walk on

Christmas Eve, trees that heal and menhirs that bring bad luck to any who gaze on them, a rock where smoke rises as the devil fries his pancakes and lots more.

Fougères is just the start of things, but if it gives you a taste for these stones and stories you could head south from here to the Roche-aux-Fées, one of the largest gallery graves in France – and there is some folklore here, too. Thence, you could continue to St. Just where on a windswept moorland, prehistoric man has left a veritable exhibition of every kind of megalith grouped together. Ranked second in importance only to Carnac's standing stones, this site is much less visited, and is much more atmospheric in its loneliness. Going north again now, the extent of the site at Monteneuf has only just become evident and there are thought to be more than 400 stones still to be uncovered.

Leaving the megaliths for the myths, there is one more scene in Ille-et-Vilaine that cries out to be explored – the Forest of Paimpont, which is said to be Brocéliande, the scene of the stories of King Arthur and the Knights of the Round Table. Today Paimpont is a beautiful forest of oak and beech, particularly fine in burning autumn colours. In its depths are hidden many designated sites associated with the legend, some much easier to find than others – Merlin's tomb (a megalith) is well signed and just off the road, but finding the Fountain of Barenton, where Merlin met the fairy Viviane, needs both leg-work and a little inspiration. At the site of the Château

of Comper (where Sir Lancelot was raised in a crystal palace by the Lady of the Lake) there is a permanent Arthurian exhibition – and the church at Tréhorenteuc has stained glass windows (and much more) blending Christianity with the legends.

So here is a sort of mystery tour of Ille-et-Vilaine. Of course you can return to reality from time to time with a little sidetracking – the medieval châteaux of Fougères and Vitré, the beautiful floral gardens at le Châtellier, the pretty lakeside village of Paimpont, all merit your attention as you pass. And the bonus is that you won't find many of Brittany's visitors stopping in inland Ille-et-Vilaine – they're all in a hurry to get to that marvellous coast. So let us go back to **Fougères** and take a brief look around the town before investigating farther.

FOUGÈRES

To the delight of today's tourist office, Victor Hugo once penned the words 'I should like to ask everyone, have you seen Fougères?' At the time of writing he was lodging in the town while working on his novel *Quatre-Vingt-Treize*, a tale of the Breton anti-Revolutionary uprising of 1793 in which Fougères and its forest played an important part. You will understand Hugo's enthusiasm once you have caught a glimpse of Fougères' splendid château, the epitome of medieval military architecture with solid walls, moat, drawbridge, and a host of pepper-pot towers, some sprouting lesser pepper-pot towers, like so many sharpened pencil ends all pointing to the sky. So let us begin this tour of Fougères at the place with the very best view of the château – the terrace of the Jardin Botanique, below the Église St Léonard (it is at the west end of the town near the Hôtel de Ville – follow the signs). The scene is most dramatic when the château is floodlit at night – and if you can add a little autumn mist swirling up from the river, it is spine-chilling.

From the terrace a path zig-zags through the steeply sloping gardens to the oldest part of the town immediately below. At the Place du Marchix with its colourful half-timbered buildings you can bear right towards the château – but maybe make a detour to the left first, because the slate-spired Église St Sulpice harbours an unusual 12th century statue of the Virgin suckling the Child, said to have been retrieved from the depths of the château moat (where it had been flung by inconsiderate English invaders); and at the same time you can make your acquaintance with the Fairy Melusine who is featured in a stained glass window.

Melusine was apparently an ancestor of the Lusignan family, one-time barons of Fougères. Her story is a sad one, but she is now thought to protect Fougères, and gives warning of impending disaster with a high-pitched cry as she flies across the town. It was apparently last heard before a heavy air-raid in 1944.

From St Sulpice, a walk beside the moat brings you to the château entrance, guarded by the square tower of La Haye-St-Hilaire. Inside is the forecourt, and beyond it the fortress itself, ringed with ramparts and yet more towers. This is the sort of place children will love – you can walk all around the ramparts and climb any number of dark spiral staircases up the towers; from their summits you can peer down on all the activities of the town below, and from slits in the thick walls fire an imaginary arrow or two. Fougères is one of a line of castles established to defend the borders of Brittany, and certainly it seems well equipped to do the job. Nevertheless it has been taken and re-taken half a dozen times since its building in 1166 (when it replaced a wooden fortress that had already been razed to the ground by the English King Henry II). The château has little in the way of added contents (an exhibition of the town's long-standing shoe industry and a tribe of free-range pet rabbits are the most notable), but its classical layout with inner and outer baileys is interesting, and the towers of Gobbelins and Melusine offer excellent views of the town on its ridge above.

Leaving the château, the Rue de la Pinterie climbs directly up the hill behind – and you can pause for a last photogenic view from the small garden on the right hand side half way up. At the top of the hill there are restaurants and *crêperies* on all sides and the Office de Tourisme stands on the corner. This is the moment to pick up any items you may need later – do not miss out on a map of the forest, at the least. Now you can head back along the Rue Nationale, one of the finest streets of the *haute ville*, lined with elegant granite façades. On the right a short road leads to the *beffroi*, built in 1397, a time when the commercial and artistic life of the town was thriving. The names of important citizens were engraved on the bells.

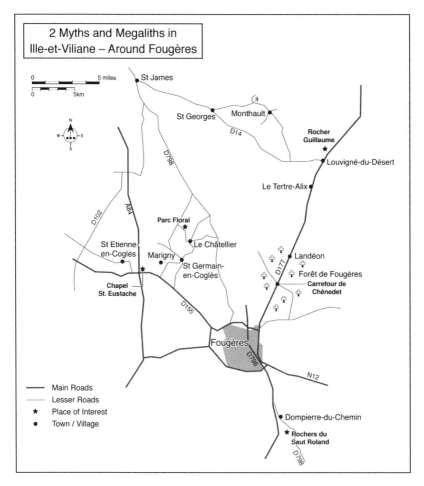

2 Myths and Megaliths in
Ille-et-Viliane – Around Fougères

On the opposite side the half-timbered building overhanging the road on granite arches houses a museum of oils and sketches by Emmanuel de la Villéon, the Breton landscape artist who was born in Fougères in 1858.

From the museum it is a short stride back to the solidly gothic Église St Léonard. Inside, the windows are surprisingly bright and modern (with notable exceptions), and at certain times it is possible to climb up to the belfry for what has to be the supreme view of the town and château. This should be the – literally – high point on which to leave Fougères, but nearby is a curiosity well worth an extra 5-minute walk. Facing the roundabout on the Avenue François Mitterrand (descend from St Léonard past the square with the equestrian statue) there is a remarkable *trompe l'oeil* wall. It is quite difficult to see where reality begins and ends (you might drive past without noticing it), but the centre section cleverly includes the most notable features of Fougères and is strangely topped with a replica of a painting by de la

Villéon. Take your life in your hands and stand on the roundabout to admire it!

FROM THE TOWN TO THE FOREST

Now it is time to leave Fougères and the first place to go is the forest, which stretches out on either side of the D177 to the north of the town. The **Forêt de Fougères** is packed with history and legend, but is also a lovely place in its own right, a thick woodland of beech and oak, criss-crossed by many meandering paths. Families will want to head for the western part of the forest (turn left off the D177, following signs to Chênedet), where there is a swimming lake with sandy shore, playground equipment and a small restaurant open in summertime. The parking lots for this lake are set well back in the trees, and from near them, a broad track through the woods will take you to the enormous dolmen known as the Pierre Courcoulée (this is where the map comes in – the path is marked with bars of white on red, but you need to be sure you are going in the right direction). The massive top stone of the dolmen has broken in two, and the twelve legs have sunk into the ground a little under the weight, but it is still impressive.

From the dolmen you could turn left on the track and then cross over the tarmac road to the track opposite. In about 220yd (200m), a cross marks the former site of a much-revered beech tree, the Fouteau du Poulailler. To ensure recovery from illness, peasants once danced around the tree sweeping the ground with a holly branch, and placed an egg between its roots.

Pieces of bark then taken from the tree effected the cure. If you care to carry on up the same hill, the remains of a Roman hill-fort (oppidum) can be found in the undergrowth on the left hand side.

Back again at the crossroads (Carrefour de Chênedet) on the D177, a track on the opposite side of the main road leads to the Pierre de Trésor, a dolmen said to conceal hidden treasure. It is less remarkable that it might have been, as it collapsed when someone clumsily tried to seek his fortune underneath. Nearby another forest track leads past the Cordon of Druids, an alignment of some 50 quartz menhirs of differing sizes. And farther along, the same forest road passes a lake beside which a wealthy Franciscan abbey once stood – a long-lost golden statue of St Francis is rumoured to lie beneath the waters.

Heading north on the D177, a cross at the limit of the forest (Croix de la Recouvrance) marks the place of the first encounter of the Revolutionary forces with the Breton opposition. These local reactionaries were known as the Chouans, their name deriving from *chat huant*, the cry of the screech owl, which they used in signalling to each other – and they were not so much Royalists as a people opposing the new mass levies and the laws against priests. In addition to the narrations of Victor Hugo, their story is told by Balzac in his novel *Les Chouans*. If you pause to look at the Croix de la Recouvrance, you might also look in the forest on the western side of the road, where the barred-up entrance to the Cellars of Landéan can be seen. They date back to the 12th century when Raoul II, Baron of Fougères, needed a safe place to conceal his possessions from the marauding English.

NORTH OF FOUGÈRES

The Forest of Fougères retains quite enough folk-lore, but things get even wilder as you head out into the villages. The D177 continues north to Louvigné-du-Désert, but just before you reach that town, look to the right as the road runs uphill through the village of **Tertre-Alix** – an inconspicuous sign points to *La Chapelle*. Just down the track here, a tiny oratory and an enormous ancient oak tree are juxtaposed. The story goes that a certain Sire Alix was one day chased by wolves, and on praying to the Virgin, found refuge in the branches of an oak tree. He built an oratory on the spot and lived there in piety for the rest of his days. The bark of the great oak is said to cure fevers.

Louvigné itself has another enigmatic site, which is more difficult to find. On the hillside above the hamlet of Bas Monlouvier (turn left off the D177 on the northern outskirts of Louvigné just after the school), a strange group of rocks apparently served as a refuge for St Guillaume over seven years, during which time he sent his donkey into the village every day to fetch his bread. On the rocks you can pick out where St Guillaume slept, the bowl from which he ate and the marks made by his knees as he prayed – but you will need the walk leaflet *Circuit St Guillaume* (from OT Fougères) to locate the place and a large dose of imagination thereafter. And yet all this is not quite as fanciful as it sounds, because the suffix Désert (Louvigné-du-Desert, Bazouges-du-

Désert) signifies a place where a hermit once lived.

Just west of Louvigné, the hill near **Monthault** (off the road to St Georges) is the scene of yet another fantastic ensemble of boulders. As you climb towards the chapel on the summit, the first rock you see is the Pierre Écriante, a huge 43ft (13m) long block of stone polished smooth by young girls who would slide down it naked in the cherished hope of finding a husband within the year. The top of the hill has more interesting rocks – a Pierre au Diable, marked with the claws of the Devil who dropped it en route for St Michel, a stone with hollows on its upper surface, said to have been a sacrificial site, and a 'monk's stone', where the religious retired to do penance. Unlike other sites, the hill of Monthault is being developed as a picnic spot (it is also a fine viewpoint) and signposts are being installed to identify the rocks.

To the south of Monthault, the area known as the *Coglais* has many a tale to tell. At **St Etienne-en-Coglès**, your first visit must be to the Chapel of St Eustache – you will need to take the D155 in the direction of Fougères to cross the *autoroute*, and then double back to the left. This 17th century chapel has been left stranded between modern highways and an industrial site, but take a look at the huge block of granite to the right of its doors. Many are its attributed powers! Young girls would climb it after the Good Friday service, balance for a second on its summit, and throw a quick glance over the crowd to pick out a future husband. After sunset on St Eustache's Day (20 September), young women who were slow to conceive would rub their bare breasts upon the stone in the hope of soon becoming mothers. And apparently there is some very valuable treasure underneath that slab, but those who set eyes on it will die within the year, and so far there have not been that many willing to dig.

After St Eustache, the next turning off the D155 will take you to **Marigny**. The old grey château beside the lake was once a place of rendezvous for the leaders of the Chouan movement and Balzac refers to it in his novel under the name of Château de la Vivetière. The lake itself conceals a village drowned long ago – but even so you can hear the bells ringing in the night. Past the church overlooking the water, a track leads over the hill to a pile of granite boulders known as the Rochers des Couardes. It is said that when the bells ring for midnight Mass at Christmas, the top rock climbs down from his perch to drink in the stream below, and that you have just the time it takes for the clock to strike twelve to seize the great riches hidden beneath. But the rock moves swiftly, and if you are in its way, you will be crushed.

Immediately to the north-east of Marigny, the village of **le Châtellier** sits on top of a conical hill. This is again a place of magic. On the slopes of the hill is a huge rock (Roche au Diable) from whose cleft, at certain times, a spiral of 'smoke' is seen to rise. Do not for a moment think atmospheric conditions have any bearing on this – it is clearly the Devil frying his pancakes. In this place also he forges the money to buy the souls who make a pact with him. To find this impressive rock – which is one among many – you will need to skirt around the left side of the church and follow white on red waymarks down through the wood, or alternatively,

descend the steep road to the north, turn left at the bottom and follow the same waymarks uphill. If the Devil should not be at home you might like to test the other story associated with this rock. Once again it is to do with finding a husband, a subject that must have weighed heavily on the minds of Breton maidens. Below the Roche au Diable is a cave, and from there a narrow passage runs underneath – all those who cross that passage before Trinity will marry within the year.

There are more curious stories in le Châtellier, tales connected with the building of the steep road to the church and the Devil's part in that particular enterprise – but to give the imagination a rest for a while, you could spend a few pleasant hours in the magnificent surroundings of the **Parc Floral de Haute Bretagne**, just a kilometre to the north. In the grounds of the Château de la Foltière there are perhaps a dozen beautifully laid out imaginative gardens – a Persian garden, a Japanese garden, a Cretan labyrinth, a 'lagoon' comprising only blue flowers, a children's garden with long tunnel and maze, a 'Poets' Valley' and more. An English text guides you round, and at the end of the day there are plants for sale and refreshment on offer in the tearoom.

SOUTH OF FOUGÈRES

Fougères is certainly a region steeped in legend, and some 50 miles (80km) away on the far side of Rennes, the Forest of Paimpont is yet another. Taking the long way round, some of the best megalithic sites in Brittany can be visited on the way. The first of these is the gigantic dolmen of la Roche aux Fées to the south – but heading in that direction, it is possible to squeeze in just one more of Fougères' legendary sites first. The **Rochers du Saut Roland** (5 miles [8km] from Fougères, just off the D798 near Dompierre-du-Chemin) are two enormous outcrops of rock about a hundred metres apart on either side of the valley of the St Blaise. Roland, a 9th century Prefect of the Breton Marches, apparently challenged himself to jump the gap on horseback three times. The first leap, dedicated to le 'Bon Dieu', was successful, and the second for the 'Bonne Vierge' was similarly so. The third leap he pledged to his 'Dame', and this time his horse's foot slipped and he plunged to his death in the valley below. The horse's hoof scored the rock on this fatal jump and you can find its imprint – but it is not a complete horseshoe, of course, because the foot was slipping.

In the valley below the outcrops, a boulder magically drips water into a hollow of rock, said to be the tears of Roland's beloved, crying until Judgement Day. And nearby, another boulder closes the entrance to an underground cavern of treasures – it can be opened only by using a hazel stick on the morning of St John's Day, and even then, the entrance is guarded by a dragon. How much of all this you identify is up to you (there are no signs), but the walk into the valley is beautiful in itself. From the little car park, follow the broad marked track until it swings right, and then keep straight ahead on the descending path.

At last it is time for the Roche aux Fées. Keep south on the D178 through Vitré (worth a pause for its really splendid old town, its medieval château and its culinary speciality *roulade* – so much appreciated by visitors that OT hands out free recipes) and then turn west on the D47 after la Guerche-de-Bretagne. Beyond Rétiers the dolmen is signed to the north, but considering its importance, it does not get a lot of publicity.

A FEAST OF MEGALITHS

The **Roche aux Fées** stands on an open site away from any habitations. Consisting of more than 40 massive blocks of red schist, it is by far the largest dolmen in Brittany, the only similar ones being found farther south in the Loire Valley. The nearest source of this particular stone is a seam some 2.5 miles (4km) distant, and you have to wonder how these boulders were transported from there to this elevated site. Naturally the job was said to have been done by the fairies, who carried the rocks in their aprons, and even dropped one on the way (the menhir of Runfort). However the rocks came here, the dolmen is known to date from some 4500 years ago (the end of the Neolithic period) and was used as a burial chamber and possibly as a sacred place. It was carefully positioned, with portico, ante-chamber and main chamber aligned so that the rising sun's rays would pass directly through on the day of the winter solstice. And naturally a site like this has acquired a little Breton wedding mythology! Engaged couples should walk round the dolmen in opposite directions counting the stones. If their numbers tally, the future looks rosy!

Some 31 miles (50km) to the south-west of the Roche-aux-Fées (via Bain-de-Bretagne and Pipriac), the **Moorland of Cojoux**, just west of

St Just, is one of the most mysterious and beautiful sites in Brittany. The collection of megaliths here is quite amazing – menhirs, *allées couvertes* (gallery graves), barrows, and dolmens are strung in a long line through a landscape of gorse, broom and heather. Naturally some of the megaliths have legends attached to them. The Three Demoiselles, three large quartz menhirs, are said to be three maidens who were turned to stone because they went to play on the moors rather than attend vespers. The Château-Bû, a huge dolmen with chambers and corridors, is rather more sinister – it is certainly a sacrificial site, but that the traditional offering was a young virgin is hopefully a myth. At the Croix St Pierre, an ancient cross-roads, there are several dolmens and tumuli, and here were found two vases dating from about 5000BC.

Perhaps most fascinating of all, though not so impressive to look at, is a semi-circle of rocks known as the Tribunal, which is actually a prehistoric calendar. The rocks mark the points at which the sun rises and sets at different times of the year when viewed from one distant rock, and the tallest rock of all indicates the point of sunset at the winter solstice. The lives of the primitive Neolithic farmers who built these monuments were entirely governed by the sun, and it is thought that they would have gathered from miles around to celebrate the solstices on this wild moorland.

A short walk of about 2 miles (3km) from St Just will take you out to all these megaliths. For those with time to spare, it is worth continuing for a few minutes to the edge of the moorland, where a scenic path overlooks the waters of the Étang du Val, snaking through the deep valley below. And you could consider going on to see the splendid *allée couverte* on the wooded ridge at Tréal, just over a mile (2km) to the north-west (just east of the D67).

Anyone who has developed a taste for menhirs might think of continuing to Langon (about 9 miles [15km] south-east) where there are about 30 of them scattered on the moorland on the northern fringe of the village. These smallish quartz blocks are much less exciting than the varied arrays of St Just, but the village itself is of interest, having a tiny brick-and-stone Gallo-Roman chapel at its heart. The ancient frescoes inside reveal that this was a chapel dedicated to Venus, but their unique character means that they can only be viewed at certain times – apply to OT in the village.

Heading north from St Just towards the Forest of Paimpont, your route will pass very close to yet another superb megalithic site, near the town of **Monteneuf**. The site (beside the D776 to the west of Guer) is not actually in Ille-et-Vilaine, but just over the border in the neighbouring *département* of Morbihan. Nevertheless, all devoted megalith-hunters will want to stretch a point to visit it. Before 1989 only three menhirs were to be seen at this location. Since then, excavations have uncovered more than 400 more, and it seems that they were probably standing until around a thousand years ago, when religious orders demanded their destruction. Around 40 of these great stones have now been re-erected. The site at Monteneuf is thought to date from 4000 to 2000BC, and spreads over an area of about 17.3 acres (7 hectares). Beyond the first group of menhirs (known as the Pierres Droites), footpaths lead to other local features, including several *alleés couvertes* and a rocking stone (*Pierre Tremblante*) beside a sacrificial stone slab. Latter day mythology has it that any young girl who sets the stone rocking will – yes, marry within the year!

Unlike the other megalithic sites, the one at Monteneuf seems to have embarked on a grand public relations exercise. Anyone can wander around it at any time, but in addition there are guided visits, demonstrations of how to erect a menhir, light a fire or create Neolithic pottery, mystical night walks, and even a prehistoric weapon-throwing competition, all geared to increase your under-standing of the lives of our Neolithic ancestors.

THE FOREST OF PAIMPONT

Just north of Monteneuf lies the vast Forest of Paimpont – and the Breton storytellers of the Middle Ages identified this forest with one of the most famous legends of all time. The forest became Brocéliande, the scene of the court of King Arthur and the Knights of the Round Table. Fact, legend and fantasy are well-mixed here, so to try to get a handle on things, head first for the little town of Paimpont, situated on a natural lake at the heart of the forest. You might consider taking the less obvious route via the D161 to the north, because then you could call in at **Campénéac**, which is very proud of the little imp figure carved on its pulpit. Just north of Campénéac, this route also passes the romantic 14th century **château of Trécesson**, set in its own pool, and said to be haunted by a lady in a white bridal gown (an alarming tale goes with this one).

After entering the forest, the road then reaches **Paimpont**, which can offer you accommodation with a couple of small hotels and a neat campsite. It is a strange and simple little place, having just one long street of terraced houses, almost like those you might find in a Yorkshire village. The difference is that these are built of deeply-coloured purple schist, and

The Megalith-builders

The multitude of megaliths are obvious signs of Brittany's early occupation, but not a lot is known of the people who built them. Most megaliths date from 5000 to 2000BC. The east-west orientation of alignments and the discovery of primitive 'calendars' suggest cults based on worship of the sun and perhaps other astronomical features. Men at this time were primitive farmers, for whom it would have been important to predict the seasons. They were also fascinated with the afterlife, having notions of a goddess-mother who protected the dead. The huge dolmens they constructed for burial were often covered with earth or with stones. Excavations of the latest of these dolmens (from the Bronze Age, 1800 – 600BC) have yielded jewellery, decorated pottery and other artefacts, now to be found in the museums at Vannes and Rennes.

the street is entered by an archway at one end. Nearby the lake laps silently around a promontory on which stands a large pale-stoned abbey, said to have been founded in the 7th century by St Judicaël. Today the old abbey church with its fine statues has become the parish church of Paimpont and the remaining buildings form the town hall and the sacristy, where the abbey treasure is housed. The latter most notably includes a silver hand reliquary containing a finger of St Judicaël and a 17th century ivory Christ on an ebony cross. A delightful footpath skirts the north shore of the lake and leads to a shrine on the spot where St Judicaël once had a vision of the Virgin Mary, a present-day place of pilgrimage.

Once you have seen the abbey and lake at Paimpont you will want to get out into the mysteries of Brocéliande. Before leaving the town, call in at the little tourist office beside the abbey and, among the wealth of literature on offer (much of it in English), at least take advantage of their free map of the forest sites. If you want to do any walking, you could invest in a copy of the magnificent Topoguide *Brocéliande à pied* – even if you understand not a word of the French, the maps, routes chosen and photographs are superb.

Thus equipped, it is time to go, and the most exciting place to start is **Tréhorenteuc** on the west side of the forest (D40 for 3 miles [5km] and turn north where signed). In the middle of the 20th century, the priest at Tréhorenteuc was one Henri Gillard. He was so absorbed by the Arthurian legends that he began mingling Christianity and mythology in his church. The stained-glass windows have several representations of the Holy Grail – and are those the disciples at the Last Supper, or the knights of Arthur gathered at the round table? The Stations of the

The legend of King Arthur

The model for King Arthur was probably a much-loved 6th-century Romano-British leader who bravely defended his people against Saxon invaders. When the Britons were finally pushed west into Wales and Cornwall, and thence into Brittany, they took with them tales of this great ruler. By the 12th century, minstrels and troubadours were carrying such stories from court to court as they entertained. In Brittany, the most famous storyteller was one Chrétien-de-Troyes, and it was he who located the tales of King Arthur here, in the Forest of Paimpont, which became the Brocéliande of the legend. Chrétien-de-Troyes was also apparently responsible for the first appearance in the story of the Holy Grail, the cup from which Christ drank at the Last Supper, and in which Joseph of Arimathea collected a few drops of Christ's blood, after the Crucifixion. In Brocéliande, Arthur and his knights pursued the Holy Grail – but even so, the Forest of Paimpont seems to have more connections with Merlin, the son of the devil and a woman who was magician at Arthur's court, and lived outside the court in the forest.

Cross have Arthurian themes (one even has Jesus falling at the feet of the wicked fairy Morgane, dressed in a flimsy red robe), while Celtic mosaics and pictures of legendary creatures decorate the walls. Sadly for Gillard, his unorthodox ideas were not viewed favourably and he was asked to leave. He was, however, loved by his parishioners and returned frequently, finally requesting to be buried in the church. This was granted – but how things have since changed! The church has become a place of curiosity, attracting many visitors, and a tourist office has been set up opposite. They organise guided tours – although out of season you can have the key to look for yourself. And most incredibly, a statue of the Rev. Gillard has been erected in front of the main door!

After Tréhorenteuc, the next place to visit is the **Val sans Retour** – the Valley of No Return. The story here is that Morgane, half-sister of King Arthur, was betrayed in love, and in revenge imprisoned all the faithless lovers who entered this valley. They were condemned to wander for ever in this place, the entrance to which was guarded by red rocks (Rocher des Faux Amants) on which sat the fairy herself. Just think before you go any farther! But if you decide to risk it, drive down the Campénéac road to a car park just out of Tréhorenteuc and walk up a track to the left. In a few minutes you will reach the lake (the *Mirroir aux Fées* – Fairy Mirror) in the depths of the Val sans Retour. The red rocks where Morgane sits are high on the left – and also on the left is the Arbre d'Or (Tree of Gold), a sculpture by François Davin, commissioned to commemorate the terrible forest fire of 1990. It incorporates the Christian-mythological

symbol of antlers to represent new life arising from the flames. A path leads up beside the stream through the Val sans Retour, and makes a pleasant short ramble. And if you continue on this path up to the north rim, you can find a rock known as Merlin's Seat, where Merlin would sit at sunset, meditating as he watched the long shadows creep across the valley.

There are several other sites worth visiting in the vicinity of Tréhorenteuc. The **Hotié de Viviane** (Viviane's House) is in fact a Neolithic burial place, in a wild and beautiful moorland setting, high above the valley. The **Tombeau du Géant** is another legend-invested megalithic site a little to the south. Both these can be reached from the far end of the path through the Val sans Retour, by following the signposted GR37. If you think of doing this, ask for the free leaflet *Landes de Gurwan* from the tourist office in Tréhorenteuc, or follow the same route described in the Brocéliande Topoguide.

Before leaving this area, call in to the **Jardin aux Moines** (north off the D141) – this curious prehistoric rectangle surrounded by blocks in alternating colours is in reality thought to be a funeral barrow, but legend has it that a local lord took a monk hostage and then went hunting on All Saints Day. During vespers a mighty storm broke, and later that day this rectangle was found – the whole hunt had been turned to stone.

The one place you must visit in Brocéliande is the **Fontaine de Barenton**. Drive about 2 miles (3km) north from Tréhorenteuc to the village of Folle Pensée and park in the designated area on the edge of the forest, just beyond the village.

From here take the footpath on the right into the forest. Barenton has never been well signed (perhaps deliberately) but in about a kilometre you should reach a stone-edged spring of crystal-clear water, in which rising bubbles of nitrogen give the appearance of boiling. It is the early descriptions of this spring that confirm the location of Brocéliande in the Forest of Paimpont. Legend has it that it was at the stone slab beside the *fontaine* that Merlin first met his beloved fairy Viviane, and here that she imprisoned him in nine magic circles of air, to keep him in the forest forever. It is also said that if you accidentally spill water from the spring on that stone, a huge storm will arise immediately. This appears to be so well authenticated that even the established church attempted to use its powers in the drought of 1835. There seems to be no record of what happened next, but a more recent Arthurian congress is certainly claiming success – so if you take a drink, beware!

The other area of forest that has most legendary connections is in the north-east, beyond the classically purple-schist town of **Concoret**. If you go that way, you could take a right turn just before the town to visit the **Chêne-à-Guillotin**, one of those gnarled oaks old enough to warrant preservation, with support for aged breaking boughs. This one is thought to be around a thousand years old, and apparently gave shelter to a priest named Guillotin in the post-Revolutionary Reign of Terror.

Beyond Concoret is **Comper**, whose original château was said to be the birthplace of the Fairy Viviane, dearly beloved of Merlin. Below the waters of its lake he built for her a crystal palace, and here, as the Lady of the Lake, she brought up Sir Lancelot, delivering him to the court of Arthur in his 15th year. Few people are allowed to see that crystal palace, and even then, for no more than a second. To find out if that privilege will be yours, you will need to come in the summer time when the present château is open – in winter all you can see is the crumbling turret and overgrown moat of a former edifice dating from 1100. Today's château houses the Centre de l'Imaginaire Arthurien, an exhibition of tableaux and videos relating to the legends and the forest.

Beyond Comper, you will want to visit **Merlin's Tomb** and the **Fontaine de Jouvence**, from which he drank to preserve his youth. Both can be reached by turning right off the D31, about 2 miles (3km) east of Comper – but unfortunately, neither is as impressive as it ought to be. Merlin's tomb is the meagre remains of a Neolithic gallery grave, and is often adorned with offerings from cult-followers. The path leads on from here to the Fountain of Youth, a rather uninviting brick-lined muddy hole tucked beneath a forest fence. Fortunately you are not expected to drink from it. Apparently gazing into the waters for just one minute is sufficient to remove wrinkles – provided you have bare feet at the time! A nearby board offers another explanation for its name by telling you that at one time, all children born within the year were brought to this *fontaine* to be registered at the summer solstice.

At this point you have seen just about all the sites associated with the King Arthur legends, but there is one more nearby place of magic worth a visit. If you continue to Iffendic and turn south on the D61, you will pass the **Lac de Trémelin**, a huge forest lake. Just beyond the turning to this lake, a road on the opposite side leads to the valley of the **Chambre au Loup** – you can park below the dam that holds back a long lake. If from here you follow the white on red marked path alongside the lake and over beside a second lake at a place known as Ozanne, you will be in a deep valley, whose sides are outcrops of purple schist. The largest of these outcrops is said to be the roof of the Château des Guenâs, the door of which is at the foot of the rocks above a nest of yellow vipers. The Guenâs, the inhabitants of this château, are tiny purple elves. They are there all right – if you cannot see them, it is purely because they blend with the rock...

OFFICES DE TOURISME

Fougères
1, Place Aristide Briand
35300 FOUGÈRES
☎ 02.99.94.12.20

Rennes
11, Rue Saint Yves
35064 RENNES
☎ 02.99.67.11.11

Ploërmel (for Monteneuf)
5, Rue du Val
56800 PLOËRMEL
☎ 02.97.74.02.70

Paimpont
5, Esplanade de Brocéliande
35380 PAIMPONT
☎ 02.99.07.84.23

PLACES OF INTEREST

Fougères

The Château
Open every day mid-June to mid-September 9am-7pm; April to mid-June and latter part of September 9.30am-12noon, 2-6pm, rest of year (except January) 10am-12noon, 2-5pm.

Musée Emmanuel de la Villéon
Open every day 10am-12.30pm, 2-6pm, mid-June to mid-September.

Bell-tower of St Léonard
Hours as the Musée Emmanuel de la Villéon.
A joint ticket (with considerable saving) may be purchased to include the above three visits and a tour of the town.

Le Châtellier

Parc Floral de Haute Bretagne
Open every day from July to mid-August 10.30am-6pm; mid-March to June and mid-August to September 2-6pm (10.30am-6pm Sundays and Bank holidays); early March and October to mid-November 2-5.30pm every day (times given are for ticket purchase – the park closes approx. 1 hour later).

Monteneuf

Megalithic site –
free entry at all times
Animations take place at the Pierres Droites site every afternoon except Monday in July and August. There are guided visits every Sunday afternoon from June to September, and a guided walk around the whole Megalith Circuit (8.7 miles [14km]) on Sunday afternoons in July and August.

Comper

Centre de l'Imagination Arthurien
Open July to September 10am-7pm every day except Wednesday; May, June and October, 10am-5.30pm every day except Tuesday and Wednesday.

LOCAL HIGHLIGHTS

Best walks

· Walks in the Forest of Fougères. Four individual routes, each around 3.7 miles (6km) in length, have been waymarked. Do them all and you will have visited every feature in the forest (almost!).

· Walks starting from the Pierres Droites site at Monteneuf. Four short circuits have been marked out using different coloured signs – if you do not want a long hike, make sure you stick to one colour! Seasoned walkers might like to visit everything by taking the 8.7 miles (14km) well-signed *Circuit des Megalithes*. OT at Monteneuf has free maps.

· There are so many fine walks in the Forest of Paimpont. Quite possibly the best is the walk up the Val sans Retour and on to the Landes de Gurwan. A route of about 10 miles (16km) (which can be shortened), it includes the Hotié de Viviane, Tombeau du Géant and the Château de Trécesson. Free maps from OT Tréhorenteuc.

For cyclists

• Four VTT routes are marked out in the Forest of Fougères.

• The Voie Verte (Green Way) is a 36 mile (58km) stretch of converted disused railway line, extending from Mauron (just north of Tréhorenteuc) due south to Questembert. Cyclists, roller-bladers, walkers and joggers are well-catered for. Ask for the leaflet *Découvrir la Voie Verte* from Offices de Tourisme (in Morbihan only – i.e., near Monteneuf).

Watersports

• The lake in the Forest of Fougères has a good swimming beach and canoes for hire.

• Canoes may be hired on the lake at Paimpont in summertime, although swimming is not allowed.

• The Lac de Trémelin has it all – swimming, sailing, canoeing, electric boats and pedalos for hire. Also on-site are VTT hire, tennis, mini-golf and a whole lot of other amusements – most of them confined to high season.

For the palate

• Prehistoric man would have probably had (at best) roasted boar with gathered berries, Arthur and his knights might have enjoyed roast venison, unleavened bread and mead – how near can you get to that?

• More prosaically, this is Brittany and you cannot leave without having had a meal of pancakes – a savoury buckwheat (*sarrasin*) one to begin with, followed by a sweet crêpe.

• Make sure that the pancakes are accompanied by **Breton** cider. If you feel adventurous, you can always follow with a *chouchen* (Breton mead) and propose a toast to King Arthur!

And the most memorable

• Our first sight of the Château of Fougères on a November night some years ago. The floodlit pepper-pot turrets shone an eerie green through eddying waves of white river mist.

• Looking out over the Val sans Retour as the evening shadows lengthened and filled it. Here Merlin once sat…

• The haunting blend of Christianity and mythology in the church at Tréhorenteuc. There can be nothing like it.

3. The lonely coast of the Cotentin

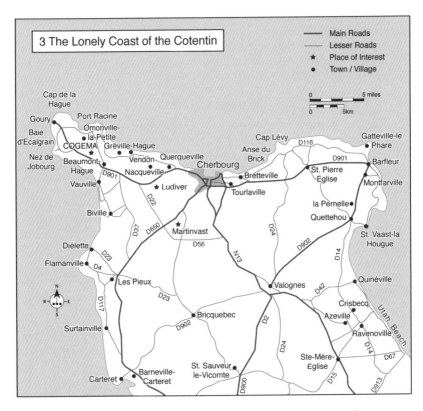

Cherbourg sits right on the end of the Cotentin peninsula – and all those arrivals on the car ferry cannot wait to get away on the N13 and head south just as fast as they can go. This peninsula has some of the wildest and loveliest shoreline in France yet there it sits, close at hand but undisturbed, and well short of the quota of admirers such vistas might reasonably expect. In the Cotentin, you can walk all day on the most scenic of coastal paths without meeting a soul, or sit on a fine sandy beach with only a handful of French families for company.

A splendid coastline it does have,

but the Cotentin has another asset – its climate. The peninsula is low-lying, particularly in the south, and a rise in sea level of a mere 33ft (10m) would be sufficient to convert it to an island. Beware global warming! As it is, having the sea on three sides is enough to moderate extremes of temperature and produce ideal conditions for the many parks and gardens that thrive here. With the warm Gulf Stream washing its western shores, winter is mild and spring comes early, yet summer days are rarely too hot for comfort.

Geologically speaking, the Cotentin is an extension of the same Armorican

Massif of which Brittany is formed – and so it shares with Brittany its skeleton of hard granite rock and something of the ruggedness of its Atlantic coastline as well. The wildest corner is without doubt the Cap de la Hague in the north-west, where the gorse-clad granite cliffs slope steeply to the foaming dark sea beneath. On the bare moorland of the cliff-tops, grey houses and stunted churches crouch low against the westerly winds – their view no more than the Atlantic mists and, on a good day, the off-shore islands of Alderney and Guernsey. Surrounded by all the austerity of this area, the lovely sandy bay of Ecalgrain is a haven of peace with sunsets never to be forgotten.

South of Ecalgrain the wild scenery continues for a while with the rocky promontory of the Nez de Jobourg (and a breath-taking path along the cliffs), but farther south still the seascape is softened to huge dunes sheltering nature reserves. Beyond, there are sandy beaches with safe bathing for families and one or two small resorts before the relative sophistication of Barneville-Carteret.

The north-east corner of the Cotentin is rather lower in relief with little in the way of cliffs and many offshore reefs. Gatteville lighthouse, the second tallest in France, guards the tip of the peninsula beside the pretty fishing port of Barfleur, one of the exclusive *plus beaux villages de France*. Farther south, St Vaast-la-Hougue likewise brings in its fish, but it is more famed for its oysters.

Beyond St Vaast the long wide stretch of sand retains the code name given to it some 60 years ago for the D-Day landings – Utah Beach. Museums at each end of the beach tell the story of the occupation and of the landings themselves. Inland too the towns have their memories – at Ste-Mère-Église a model paratrooper still hangs from the church spire as did John Steele that June morning. Cherbourg, the valuable port at the heart of the mission has almost re-invented itself, and well repays a few hours spent wandering in its old streets or visiting its own wartime museum in the Fort du Roule. On the very edge of the harbour, the brand new state-of-the-art *Cité de la Mer* will bring you right back to the 21st century with a few well-chosen submarines, virtual and otherwise. But let us now leave Cherbourg to the end of this chapter – you have to come back there anyway – and first of all, head west.

CAP DE LA HAGUE

From Cherbourg the D901 traverses the spine of the peninsula to reach the Cap de la Hague at its tip. The coast road is far more interesting, but before you turn off (at Hameau-de-la-Mer) it is worth mentioning something just a couple of miles on down the main road – the planetarium '**Ludiver**'. A centre of scientific discovery located here on account of the clear unpolluted atmosphere, the main building includes a planetarium, weather station and exhibitions on the 'Big Bang' while outside there is an observatory with telescopes, an exhibition of time, picnic areas and lot more. But let us reserve Ludiver for a rainy day (or perhaps a starry night, when live observations are possible), and get down to the sea again.

As you turn on to the D45, the village of **Querqueville** looks down from its hillside on the left. If you decide to investigate, take a look at its 10th century Chapelle St Germain, possibly the oldest such building in Normandy – and from nearby, the view extends over this northern coast from Point Jardeheu in the west to Cap Lévy in the east. A couple of minutes farther on down the road, the same hillside shelters the **Château of Nacqueville**, a lovely grey turreted building whose origins go back to the 16th century. Its gardens, landscaped in the 1830s, are brimming over with rhododendrons, azaleas and hydrangeas, all set around a stream with waterfalls and a lake.

Beyond the turning to the château, the D45 soon has you at the coast again. The village of Urville-Nacqueville is proud of its beautiful beach of fine sand, ideal for the family – and just beyond the village, the attractive **Manor of Dur-Ecu** has increased its own family appeal with the annual addition of a 'Maize Maze' in the fields opposite. From here the road leaves the coast and climbs to the pretty village of **Gréville-Hague**, whose outlying hamlet, Gruchy, was the birthplace of Jean-François Millet. The eldest son of a local peasant family, he spent his youth in the village before going to study in Cherbourg. Although his talents later took him far afield, he frequently returned to Gruchy and painted many nearby scenes.

In recent years the cottage owned by the Millet family has been restored and filled with such humble furniture as might have been there at the time of his birth (1814). Unfortunately there are not a lot of personal items relating to the great man's life, but the many sketches and studies that were preludes to his finest works are interesting, and an introductory video fills you in on the finer details. When you leave the museum, it is worth walking down the village street and continuing along the footpath to the **Rocher du Castel Vendon**. After no more than 10 minutes you reach a bench at a viewpoint – way below you is the sea, and ahead the mounting ridge of granite that seems to have haunted Millet, and certainly inspired several of his paintings.

From Gréville-Hague the road descends again to **Omonville-la-Rogue** with splendid views of the sea and of the Point de Jardeheu with its signalling station. Beside the calm waters of the Anse St Martin, a road leads up to **Omonville-la-Petite**, a beautiful village decked in geraniums and fuschias, where the 20th century poet Jacques Prévert made his home. If you want to visit it, you will need to park near the church (where he is buried) and walk up the narrow road for a few minutes. Back on the D45 again and soon you are beside the breakwaters of **Port Racine**, claiming, not unreasonably, to be the smallest harbour in France. Up and over the hill from here, the road passes through St Germain-des-Vaux and then descends to Goury.

Goury is the only safe haven on that most treacherous of sea passages, the Alderney Race. To sea, a light-house stands on reefs lashed by the waves, while the few houses of the village are clustered around the port with its octagonal lifeboat station. The surprising addition to all this is a first-class and very popular seafood restaurant.

THE WEST COAST

Restored by the maritime delicacies of Goury, it is time to head down the west coast. From Auderville, take the coast road (D401) towards the Nez de Jobourg, which descends past the very lovely and remote **Bay of Ecalgrain**. At Dannery you can turn to the **Nez de Jobourg** – at least, that is what the signs say, but in fact the road goes to the next promontory, the Nez de Voidries. Here the only intrusion on the natural scene is the little Auberge des Grottes (named from the caves in the cliff beneath) – and what a view it has. Walking out on to the headland you can look south across a shingly cove to the bare rocky hump of the Nez de Jobourg, or north to the sweeping Bay of Ecalgrain backed by moorland, gorse and heather. Out to sea the Channel Islands emerge from the mist – nearby Alderney, and far, far away to the south-west, Guernsey and Sark together. There are likely to be quite a few people around (the Nez de Jobourg has a certain appeal), but take a walk along the coastal path from here and very soon you have that wild beauty all to yourself. The path to the south, past the Nez de Jobourg, is the most exciting, and there is even the possibility of meeting the herd of wild goats that range these cliffs. But if you have no head for heights, make sure you go the other way!

The village of Jobourg is directly inland from the Nez and on the main road (D901) again – its church dates from the 11th century. Turning right here you are immediately beside something that seems quite out of place – the pale pastel-coloured blocks of **COGEMA**, a huge **nuclear waste recycling plant**. Before throwing up your hands in horror at the apparent violation of this wild place, pause for a few minutes and take a closer look. A building near the entrance welcomes visitors with personal attention, a wealth of displays and a video in English, making sure you understand what really goes on here – and a free coach trip demonstrates the care taken at certain environmentally sensitive places in the vicinity. Public relations are clearly high on the agenda (the early history of this plant included a skirmish with the Greenpeace ship *Rainbow Warrior*) and the centre will furnish you with lots of literature to ponder over at home.

The employees of COGEMA mostly live in Beaumont-Hague, a pleasant place and the only one of any size in these parts. You need not go into the town, but instead turn down to the coast again and the village of Vauville. On the hillside above you, a prehistoric gallery grave, the **Pierre Pouquelée**, has an enviable position amid the gorse and bracken with views along the length of the coast (to reach it, leave the car by the sign on the roadside and climb for about 20 minutes, finally taking a track on the left just before reaching the plateau). The village of **Vauville** is lovely – old houses with roofs of local blue schist, a little stream through the streets and a fine grey stone 17th century château with palm trees peeping over its walls. The château grounds form a **Jardin Botanique** that has been painstakingly created by the owners, and they are unusual in that the accent is on the different shades and textures of the evergreen vegetation rather than flowering plants. The proximity of the Gulf Stream ensures the survival of a host of subtropical species, most evidently the palm-trees. From Vauville the road runs above the Mare de Vauville, a long lake that is now an ornithological reserve, and then rises to a belvedere above the village of le Petit Thot. From here the whole lonely Bay of Vauville is in view, from the Nez de Jobourg in the north to Flamanville in the south. The Channel Islands are dim shapes on the horizon – and, given that the hour is right, you could just be lucky enough to watch the sun sinking into the western sea between them. A little way down the road, the same splendid panorama can be admired from the Calvary of the Dunes at **Biville**, a viewing point reached by a footpath starting near the church. The church itself houses the remains of the Blessed Thomas Hélye, priest and missionary, who died in 1257. Below the church the road descends to the dunes themselves, a far-stretching alien world of mighty sand-heaps, each with its fragile covering of vegetation.

And now it is time to go on again, to head briefly inland before returning to the coast and dunes at Siouville-Hague. Beyond is the lively port of Diélette. The main road continues uphill to **Flamanville** here, but the road beside the port goes out to the tip of the peninsula, now occupied by a nuclear power station. More horror? Well, yes, but once again the trouble-shooters are there, welcoming you to the excellent exhibition room and happy to spend time discussing the issues involved. A series of videos – in English – gives yet more detail.

Beyond Flamanville the road follows the untamed coast – past le Rozel, Surtainville and Baubigny with campsites that are bigger than the villages themselves and on to the

unexpected civilisation of **Barneville-Carteret**. As its name would suggest, this is a resort in two parts. To the north is Carteret, clustered around the foot of a rocky headland. Its busy port is used by both fishing vessels and pleasure craft, and is the terminus for a frequent ferry service to Jersey. From the lighthouse on the clifftop above there is a clear view of the island, which seems surprisingly close. Paths lead from the lighthouse to the Sentier des Douaniers (Customs Officers' Path) that skirts the cliffs and joins Carteret's two very different beaches. The town of Barneville lies inland across the estuary – but interest here centres on its beach a mile away, a genteel sort of place bordered by elegant villas and boasting not even a shop never mind a candyfloss stall. There are pleasant views to Carteret across the estuary and a way-marked discovery trail through the low dunes.

THE EAST COAST

Despite its slightly time-warped air, Barneville-Carteret marks the beginning of the main holiday area for this west coast. Let us leave it here and, ignoring everything on the way, cut across the peninsula to visit the east coast instead. The first town of any note you are going to reach is **Ste-Mère-Église**, and it certainly is not 'undiscovered' – although it might have been, but for the events of the early hours of D-Day. Under cover of darkness, troops of the American 82nd Airborne Division were parachuted into the area to support the first troops landing at dawn on the nearby beaches.

All hung up

An unfortunate young man by the name of John Steele found his parachute caught up on the church steeple and was obliged to dangle there for two and a half hours tortured by the continuous tolling of the bell until he was cut down and taken prisoner. His effigy still hangs there to this day, and the church below has been given new stained glass windows commemorating the landings.

Today in buildings shaped like parachutes, the **Musée des Troupes Aeroportées** displays a glider and C-47 (Dakota) plane along with other documents and memorabilia relating to the occasion. And in front of the *Mairie* (in the main street) stands 'Borne 0', the first of 12,000 symbolic milestones on the 'Road of Liberty', the route followed by the American troops as they marched through France to Bastogne in Belgium.

This whole area can never forget its central role in that momentous day, but if you want to break away from it all briefly, on the outskirts of Ste-Mère-Église (head north and follow signs) there is the little **Ferme Musée du Cotentin**. The impressive old buildings grouped around the courtyard include such Norman necessities as a cider pressing room and butter-making chamber. Stock reared on the farm are particularly of local breeds – Cotentin donkeys and brown-faced Roussin sheep from la Hague.

From Ste-Mère-Église the D67 takes you to the sea at Utah Beach and from here to Quinéville both coast and inland are laden with memories. Museums and monuments are many – this is a place to linger.

After Quinéville the road turns inland, and the wartime scene is left behind as you head north towards Quettehou. The road gives fine views across the bay to St Vaast de la Hougue and its fort – the town of Quettehou invites you to enjoy the same view from its churchyard. Beyond Quettehou the road runs east to **St Vaast-la-Hougue**. That St Vaast (pronounced 'Va') is a place with history might be guessed from the twin fortresses guarding its bay. The saga dates back to 1692, when the French fleet set sail for Britain with the aim of restoring the Catholic James II (deposed by William of Orange) to the throne. The English and Dutch fleets arrived in greater numbers, battle was engaged, and many of the damaged French ships were forced to take shelter in the harbour of la Hougue – where the English were less than chivalrous and promptly set fire to them all. Louis XIV decided to guard against similar occurrences by arranging for Vauban to install forts on the islands of Tatihou and la Hougue. Each was equipped with a tower and canons – which have never been used to this day.

St Vaast is a popular place but has in no way been spoilt by its visitors, it remains a genuine fishing port with fishermen going about their business, sorting their nets, and unloading their catches to be sold on the quayside. Beyond the harbour-home of the fishing fleet is a pleasure port, and then the long sandy Réville Bay, devoted to *ostreiculture*. St Vaast is the oyster capital of the north and

Continued on page 59

Utah Beach and the D-Day landings

The theatre for the Allied invasion was chosen a year in advance. The Calais coast was too well defended and the cliffs too difficult to negotiate – it had to be more distant Normandy, where the wide sandy beaches backed by dunes offered safer landing. Utah was the most westerly of the five designated beaches and, along with neighbouring Omaha, destined to be the landing ground of the American forces. In the early hours of the 6 June 1944 the first invaders arrived, American paratroopers of the 82nd and 101st Airborne Divisions, on a mission to capture Ste-Mère-Église and secure the roads leading from the beaches. With skies heavily overcast, the planes had trouble finding their targets and most of the drops were well wide of the mark. More than 30 men landed in Ste-Mère-Église itself and were quickly captured or killed. The town was nevertheless taken before daybreak.

With low tide at dawn the assault on the beach began – first the heavy air and sea bombardment and then the troops themselves. Utah was under the command of Brigadier General Theodore Roosevelt, cousin of the President. He too found his landing place to be off-course, about a mile to the south of his intended destination. He decided to stay put and take all his forces down the one road accessible to them. The German batteries guarding Utah put up little resistance and the landing was eminently successful in that allied losses were only around 200 men. At Omaha, just around the corner, they were almost 20 times that number.

At the southern end of Utah Beach, near the village of la Madeleine, the newly restored **Musée du Débarquement** looks out over a sea that was once black with ships. Inside, every detail of the story is told with film, models, weapons and equipment galore. The site itself contains several memorials to the various divisions involved and also 'Borne 00', an extension to the Road of Liberty. The Musée du Débarquement attracts many visitors, but most are left behind as you travel north. The road follows the long sandy beach, although the only break in the dunes that will allow you to see it comes some two and a half miles (4km) from the museum, where there is a monument shaped like the prow of a ship, accompanied by a tank. This was the point at which General Leclerc later came ashore with his 2nd French Armoured Division. Still the road hugs the coast, and after Ravenoville Plage a sign invites you to turn left to the **Batteries of Crisbecq and Azeville**. Crisbecq comes first, two concrete shelters jutting from the hillside with views over a sea now empty but for the dark smudges of the Marcouf Islands. This was the most important battery in the protection of Utah Beach and it was surrounded by minefields. The site is quite extensive and includes several restored shelters and trenches. Azeville is farther on and higher up still, a huge complex of concrete chambers that have been opened to the public. A trip through the underground passageways and a film on

Rommel's 932 mile (1500 km) 'Atlantic Wall' are features of the tour. From Azeville it is worth returning to the coast road to reach **Quinéville**, a little town that is now something of a holiday resort. But Quinéville too has wartime memories and right beside its fine beach stands the **Musée de la Libération**. This is a museum with a difference, concentrating on the compelling story of life in occupied France – the poverty and lack of food, restriction of movement, forced labour, propaganda, collaboration and heroic resistance. No weapons are displayed. Documents, posters, newspaper cuttings, photographs, ration cards and an hour-long film (in English) are offered instead, and there are some good tableaux, including that of an entire street.

when the tide falls, a cavalcade of tractors can be seen heading out to tend the black rows of beds that fill the bay. The oysters are said to have an unusual nutty flavour, probably due to the local plankton.

Across the bay is the island of **Tatihou** – you can go out to it by amphibious vehicle (its starting point depends on the tide) or chance your luck on the Rhun, a raised passage that is said to be safe at low tide when the tidal coefficient is greater than 50. It cannot be as dangerous as it sounds – the Maritime Music Festival (*Traversées de Tatihou*) held every August sees long processions of people making the crossing on foot to join in the fun on the island. But however you get there, Tatihou is a must. A museum houses a miscellany of relics recovered from ships lost in the Battle of la Hougue and an exhibition on the seafaringly-inspired stained glass windows of Normandy. Temporary exhibitions are also staged. Outside there are gardens of salt-loving plants and a path out to the lookout tower (Tour Vauban) at the end of the island. The large area maintained as an ornithological reserve is out-of-bounds, but an observatory is located above the *poudrières*

(powder house) and there are free guided visits in summertime.

The second fort at St Vaast is currently a military establishment not open to visitors. Its island has been joined to the mainland by a causeway that now backs the town's main beach.

VAL DE SAIRE

St Vaast is the gateway to the particularly delightful north-eastern corner of the Cotentin known as the **Val de Saire**. This is a triangle of typical Normandy bocage – high-banked lanes, green fields grazed by 'bespectacled' Normandy cattle, stone farmhouses and scattered woodland. Wild flowers grow in profusion, and in springtime every bank here is scattered with celandines, wood anemones, violets and above all, primroses. Surprisingly this was once an industrial area. Head north-west from Quettehou to le Vast if you want to see something of the many mills that were powered by the Saire in the 19th century. Otherwise it is time to head north to Barfleur – but just out of Quettehou, do not miss the turning to la Pernelle, from where you can enjoy the very best view of this coast.

The road to **la Pernelle** climbs past a shrine in the rocks, from where you can reach the viewpoint directly (via steps) or continue up the road. A fine ceramic *table d'orientation* points out the distant scene from Gatteville lighthouse in the north to the Marcouf Islands in the south, and on a good day includes the Grandchamp cliffs on the north Normandy coast. A restaurant offers diners the added benefits of its vista. Back down on the main road (D902) again, there is another diversion before Barfleur – the pale grey granite church in the village of **Montfarville**. There are some fine statues here, particularly that of a 12th century Virgin and Child, but its greatest treasures are a series of paintings by the local artist Guillaume Fouace. In the 1870s the Abbé Goutière of Montfarville made a visit to the Sistine Chapel in Rome, and thus inspired, engaged Fouace to adorn the roof vaults of his church with paintings depicting events in the life of Christ. It took him two years to complete his task, and many village people of the time were used as models. Currently these 18 individual works are undergoing restoration, and have been listed as historic monuments.

Just beyond Montfarville, **Barfleur** is one of the most attractive places on the Cotentin coast – the picture of its squat granite church beside a long harbour wall lined with fishing smacks is one that graces many a tourist guide. In the Middle Ages, Barfleur was the most important port in Normandy, but, historically speaking, its defining moment came a little earlier with the building of the *Mora*, the ship that brought William the Conqueror to English shores. Etienne, a local *Barfleurais* was at the helm. Today Barfleur sleeps quietly in the sun, and its old quays, dotted with nets and lobster-pots, seem to attract few visitors – although the tourist office at the end of the line tries hard enough and the assortment of daily information it chalks on the board by its door is worth a detour in itself.

The other place that merits a visit in Barfleur, the **Maison de Julie Postel**, gets little publicity and there are no obvious signs to direct you. Tucked away in the hamlet of la Bretonne on the far side of the harbour, this is not a grand museum, but rather the humble home of a local ropemaker's daughter who took holy orders, ran a school for local girls and, as Sr Marie-Madeleine, founded the Sisters of the Christian Schools of Mercy. When the Revolution brought religious persecution, she arranged for priests to be smuggled to England and for covert celebrations of Mass to be held in her own home. The 'warden' who lives next door is proud to show you the place where she hid the sacrament and the window at which she was able to receive secret signals. If you find the French too much (although she speaks very slowly), the whole tale is retold in the stained glass windows of the church next door, which was erected in her memory. Soeur Marie-Madeleine was canonised in 1926.

From Barfleur, a lovely coastal path (approx 2 miles [3 k]m) leads past the harbours of Crabec and Flicmare to Gatteville lighthouse. Look out to sea as you walk – some half a mile (800m) from the shore is the reef known as the Rocher de Quillebeuf, on which foundered the White Ship carrying the two sons and heirs of Henry I (and half the English nobility) back to England in 1120. Apparently Henry never smiled again after this tragedy – but later ensured the succession by marrying his daughter Matilda to Geoffrey of Anjou (nicknamed Plantagenet from the sprig of broom (*genêt*) that he wore in his cap), thus founding a ruling house in England that lasted nearly 300 years.

Gatteville lighthouse stands on more reefs at the very tip of the land – by road it can be accessed via the village of Gatteville-le-Phare, whose 13th century bell tower can be seen for miles around. The lighthouse, at 233ft (71m) the second tallest in France, was clearly designed by someone with an obsession for the calendar as it is said to have 365 steps, 12 floors and 52 windows. In practice the last step is numbered 349 (what happened?) and even if you continue up the few scary metal steps to see the revolving light the numbers do not quite tally. Nevertheless both view and breeze are breathtaking up here, and you may need to hold on tight as you peer down the whole length of the Cotentin coast.

From Gatteville the D116 heads west to Cherbourg, with many good views on the way – you might consider diverting to **Cap Lévy** with its fortress, which is now owned by the Conservatoire du Littoral and accessible at all times. The prettiest spot is possibly the sandy cove of the **Anse du Brick**, furnished with a very discrete but first-class campsite and a nearby auberge. Taking the only road to the left here, you quickly climb to a splendid viewpoint (a couple of minutes off the road on the right hand side) where a well-painted *table d'orientation* identifies every point along the coast. You might like to make another diversion at Bretteville, where the D320 soon has you beside a very well preserved *allée couverte* (gallery grave).

CHERBOURG

Back into **Cherbourg** now, and as you reach the main road, the suburb of Tourlaville is on your left. The château on its outskirts (**Château des Ravalet** – follow signs from Tourlaville centre) seems to be a weekend bolt-hole much in favour with the urban population of Cherbourg – and no wonder. Entry to this lovely 16th century blue schist château and to its extensive grounds is entirely free. With a lake of swans, masses of colourful flowerbeds, changing exhibitions in the château, and a play area for children, it is an ideal place to take a little family exercise before retiring for coffee and gâteau in the restaurant.

Families looking for more high-tech entertainment can head for Cherbourg and the **Cité de la Mer**, in the former railway station by the harbour. Its theme is the depths of the ocean, and you can enjoy submarines through time, a visit to *Le Redoutable*, a little virtual piloting, and some huge aquaria displaying the flora and fauna you find when you get down there. If the Cité de la Mer is not for you, at least take a stroll beside the harbour where exuberant floral displays surround the equestrian statue of Napoleon. He was responsible for the transformation of the humble fishing port on this site to a transatlantic terminal. His curious declaration that he would 'recreate the wonders of Egypt' here is recalled on his statue – but quite what he had in mind is not obvious!

Across the road from the statue, the **Basilique de la Trinité** is worth a look for its altar-piece, carvings and flying buttresses – and from here you can meander through the back streets into town, or walk along the main road and follow signs to the Parc Emmanuel-Liais to escape the urban scene in a profusion of tropical vegetation. If town is your choice, do not miss the **Musée Thomas Henry** where (among many others) you can enjoy a fine collection of Millet's paintings, and also works by Fouace, of Montfarville fame.

More war history – particularly that relating to Cherbourg – is on offer at the hilltop **Fort du Roule** (accessed via the road to Valognes, just south of the port) – and with it, the most splendid view of Cherbourg and its harbour. And of course, for anyone returning to Britain, the Auchon hypermarket a couple of kilometres on down the same road has its attractions! But the

parting shot in this chapter has to be the **Parc Floral of the Château de Martinvast** (3.7 miles [6km] south, off the D650), which is again a popular retreat for the people of Cherbourg. The neo-gothic château itself can sometimes be visited, but the vast park is the main attraction. Six different rambles of varying lengths have been marked out allowing you to enjoy meadows and woodland, streams, lakes and waterfalls, a water-mill, a dolmen, an Italian garden, and most of all the abundance of magnificent rhododendrons and azaleas that thrive so well in the climate here – a lasting memory of the Cotentin to take back across the Channel.

OFFICES DE TOURISME

Comité Départemental du Tourisme de la Manche
Maison du Département
50008 SAINT-LÔ Cedex
☎ 02.33.05.98.70

Cherbourg
2, Quai Alexandre III
50100 CHERBOURG-
OCTEVILLE
☎ 02.33.93.52.02

La Hague
BP 45
50400 BEAUMONT-HAGUE
☎ 02.33.52.74.94

Barneville-Carteret
10, Rue des Écoles BP 101
50270 BARNEVILLE-CARTERET
☎ 02.33.04.90.58

St Vaast-la-Hougue
1, Place du Général de Gaulle
50550 SAINT-VAAST-LA-
HOUGUE
☎ 02.33.23.19.32

St-Mère-Église
6 Rue Eisenhower
50480 SAINTE-MÈRE-ÉGLISE
☎ 02.33.21.00.33

PLACES OF INTEREST

Ludiver
Times are complicated, but basically the museum area is open all day every day in July and August. Outside those months, it is closed on Saturday and Sunday mornings and

for an hour each lunchtime. There is at least one planetarium show every day, with a designated English show on Wednesday at 11.30am in summer.

Urville-Nacqueville

Château et Parc de Nacqueville
Guided visits at 2, 3, 4 and 5pm
every afternoon with exception of
Tuesday and Friday from Easter to
September.

Manoir de Dur-Ecu
Open daily in July and August,
11am-1pm and 2-7pm.

Gréville-Hague

**Maison natale de
Jean-François Millet**
Open every day in July and August
11am-7pm; June and September
11am-6pm; April, May and school
holidays 2-6pm.

Omonville-la-Petite

Maison de Jacques Prévert
Same opening hours as the Maison
natale de Jean-François Millet.

Beaumont-Hague

**COGEMA nuclear
reprocessing plant**
Open to visitors from April to
September, weekdays 10am-6pm
(coach trips at 10am and 2pm),
Saturdays and Sundays, 1-7pm
(coach trips at 3pm).

Vauville

Jardin Botanique
Open May to October, Tuesdays
and Sundays 2-6pm (Saturdays
also in June, July and August).

Flamanville

**Centre d'Information du Public
(at the nuclear power station)**
Open from Tuesday to Saturday,
mid-June to mid-September,
10.30am-12.30pm, 2-6pm; outside
those months, 2-6pm only.

Ste-Mère-Église

Musée des Troupes Aeroportées
Open every day from April to
September 9am-6.45pm; February,
March, October and November
9.30am-12noon, 2-6pm
Ferme Musée du Cotentin
Open July and August, 11am-7pm;
June and September 11am-6pm;
April and May, 2-6pm.

Utah Beach

Musée du Débarquement
Open May to September, 9.30am-
7pm; April, October, and
weekends from November to
March 10am-12.30pm, 2-5.30pm
(6pm in April, Oct).

Batterie de Crisbecq
Open May to September 10am-
7pm; April 10.30am-12.30pm, 2-
6pm; October and November, as
April but with 5pm closing.

Batterie d'Azeville
Open July and August, 11am-7pm;
May, June and September, 11am-
6pm; April and October 2-6pm.

Quinéville

Musée de la Liberté
Open June to September 9.30am-
7.30pm; Mid-March to May and
October to mid-November 10am-
6pm.

St Vaast-la-Hougue

Island of Tatihou
The island is accessible from April
to October 10am-6pm (7pm in
July and August) and on weekend
afternoons only in winter.
Crossings depend on the tide and
tickets should be bought in
advance from the Billeterie on the

quayside (not from the terminus on the harbour wall) as numbers on the island are limited. Tickets for entry to the Musée Maritime can be bought at the same time.

Barfleur

Maison de Julie Postel
Open all year round approx 10am-5pm (later in summertime). No charge.

Gatteville-le-Phare

Lighthouse
Open every day throughout the year except mid-Nov to mid-Dec; 10am-12noon, 2- 4pm (5pm March and Oct, 6pm April and Sept, 7pm May to August).

Cherbourg

Château des Ravalet
Open every day throughout the year. Times will vary, but 8am-7.30pm in July and August.

Cité de la Mer
Open mid-September to May, 10am-5pm; rest of year 9.30am-6pm.

Musée Thomas Henry
Open May to September 10am-6pm (except Sunday and Monday mornings), October to April 2-6pm (except Monday and Tuesday).

Fort du Roule
Open July and August daily 11am-6pm; May and September 10am-12noon, 2-6pm except Sun and Mon mornings; rest of year 2-6pm, except Monday and Tuesday.

**Château de Martinvast
(Parc Floral)**
Open daily 10am-12noon, 2-6pm (closed weekend mornings and all day Saturday from November to March).

LOCAL HIGHLIGHTS

Best walks

A long distance path (known as the Sentier des Douaniers – Customs Officers' Path) skirts the entire coast of the Cotentin peninsula. Any section would make an excellent ramble, and the whole route is well-marked in bars of white on red. These are merely a couple of suggestions.

· The spectacular cliff path around the Nez de Jobourg and its less demanding follow-up beside the Baie d'Ecalgrain. If you want to convert this to a 6.2 mile (10km) circular walk, get the leaflet *Jobourg* in the *Découverte de la Hague à pied* series (ask OT Beaumont-Hague) and follow the map and excellent waymarking.

· The short walk to Gatteville lighthouse from Barfleur takes in a particularly pleasant and easy section of the coastal path.

· And if you want a change from the seascapes, take a walk in the Val de Saire – OT at St Vaast-la-Hougue can provide routes and recommendations

For cyclists

- To really do things in style, mountain-bikers should get hold of the relatively expensive publication *La Manche à VTT*, which covers the area to the south as well as the Cotentin (all the *département* of Manche). 50 routes of varying length are described (French only), but there is a good map with each. Available from Comité Départemental du Tourisme de la Manche.

- Those wanting to stay on tarmac are less well served in the Cotentin in terms of designated routes, although there are facilities for cycle hire in Cherbourg, Carteret, St Vaast, Ste-Mère-Église, Gatteville and elsewhere. The publication *Découverte du Val de Saire* includes three suggested routes for road-bikes.

Watersports

- The Cotentin is well blessed with beaches of fine white sand, most of which are suitable for swimming. There are also indoor pools at Cherbourg, Beaumont-Hague and Tourlaville.

- Facilities for other watersports – sailing, rowing, diving and sea-kayaking – are plentiful. Contact the Tourist Committee of la Manche for all details.

For the palate

- Seafood of all sorts. Make sure you check out the 'nutty' flavour of oysters from St Vaast.

- This is Normandy, so do not miss out on the dairy products – butter, crème-fraîche and those powerful (at least to the nose) cheeses, Camembert, Pont l'Évêque, Livarot and Neufchâtel.

- Think Normandy, think orchards – cider, poiré (the same thing made from pears), calvados and pommeau (matured apple juice with calvados).

And the most memorable

- Walking through the sunken lanes of the Val de Saire in March, when every green bank was bursting with primroses.

- Among the wealth of information in the Musée de la Libération in Quinéville, reading that the Nazis thought the French habit of eating freshly-baked bread too self-indulgent, and therefore decreed that bread must not be eaten before it was 24 hours old – a glimpse of the utter madness underlying it all.

- A spring evening at the Belvédère du Thot when sky and sea were streaked blood-red as the sun set far out in the Bay of Vauville.

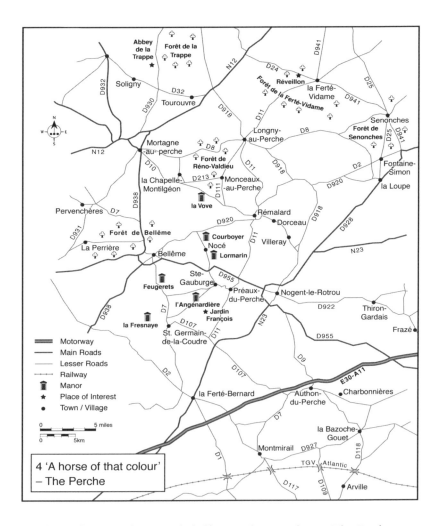

4 'A horse of that colour' – The Perche

Map legend:
- Motorway
- Main Roads
- Lesser Roads
- Railway
- 🏠 Manor
- ★ Place of Interest
- ● Town / Village

0 ___ 5 miles
0 ___ 5km

At the southern tip of Normandy, half way to nowhere and not on the route to anywhere in particular, there is a fairly well circumscribed region of rolling farmland known as the Perche. If you have heard of it at all it will probably have been in connection with its eponymous product – a horse. The Percherons are workhorses, not as heavy as the Shires or Clydesdales, but still sturdy and muscular, and very useful on the farm on account of their willing nature. Intelligent and gentle, they have evolved from over a thousand years of breeding on the fertile pastures of the Perche and can still be seen in its fields today.

The Perche is truly traditional country, originally a province that was created in the 12th century by the fusion of three baronies. The landscape here is a mix of oak forests, low hills, sweeping pastures, lakes and woodland; of ancient manors and fortified farmhouses, watermills, grey abbeys and hilltop towns with crumbling ramparts. An unassuming land, it is also one with a rich heritage. Generally it is considered to be in two parts – the northern Norman Perche is more forested and hilly, while the Perche-Gouet in the south is flatter with smaller farms, high-banked lanes and patchwork fields. In 1998 almost all the original area of the Perche was included in a new Natural Regional Park in which its long-established ways of life are respected and its traditional agriculture and rural crafts are encouraged to thrive.

So what about this region appeals enough to spend a holiday here? Like avocado or asparagus, the Perche is an acquired taste – its charms are not immediately revealed with the first bite, but are more subtle, growing on you steadily until you are hooked. The Perche is the sort of place you may find yourself wanting to return to again and again, because there is far more tucked into these country lanes than you could possibly discover on first acquaintance.

For a start, there are the manor houses, all 300 or so of them, liberally sprinkled across the countryside. When the French kings and their associates were moving out of the capital to the Loire valley, the lesser nobility were moving to the Perche, an area half way between the two. The manors they built are in all styles from the early austerity of Manoir de la Vove to the elaborate late 16th century Manoir de l'Angenardière. Naturally most of them remain private properties, but a few now open their doors to the public in summer time and yet more invite

The Percheron

Percherons originally developed from the heavy Flemish horses in this region. In the 8th century these local horses were mated with Arabian stock and the resulting progeny were lighter, more agile and more suitable for riding. Over the centuries, Spanish and even English blood was introduced, but in 1820 two grey Arab stallions were brought in by the Royal Stud at le Pin. One of their offspring, a stallion with the human-sounding name of Jean le Blanc, became the one horse from whom all present-day bloodlines can directly trace their ancestry. Thus Percherons are usually grey in colour, although blacks and browns are acceptable. Today's horses stand around 17 – 18 hands high and weigh in the region of 2204 lb (1000kg). Intelligent, good-natured and eager to work, they are useful both on the farm and as carriage horses.

visitors into the grounds. A day's manor-spotting can be fascinating, but you will need to equip yourself with a good map and a lot more time than you think to navigate the network of winding lanes in these parts. In addition to the manors, the Perche is blessed with a fair scattering of châteaux in various states of repair and (particularly in the east) an assortment of fortified farmhouses, dating from a time when ownership of this territory was constantly in dispute. The region is also well endowed with ecclesiastical buildings, abbeys and priory churches, some of which have now been turned over to more secular uses, while others like the Abbey of la Trappe, are still home to a community of monks.

Complementing its ample endowment of fine buildings, the Perche is not lacking in natural beauty. In times past, forest covered the whole area and it was known to the Romans under the name of *Sylva Pertica*. Several particularly large tracts of woodland remain to this day – notably those of Bellême, Réno-Valdieu, la Trappe, la Ferté-Vidame and Senonches. The trees are almost entirely oak and beech and of course they are particularly glorious in autumn colours. Each forest has its prized specimens, most of them oaks more than 400 years old. Around Bellême the forest is especially renowned for its fungi. If the season is right you can join the local population on their forays of *ramassage* – and if, unlike them, you cannot immediately distinguish between edible and inedible, the pharmacy in Bellême readily dispenses free advice.

Finally, what about the children? There are no Disney-Land-type theme-parks in the Perche – although if you do want to break away from the 'off-the-beaten-track' atmosphere you can reach Paris in an hour and a half by train. But the Perche is very well-equipped for the more unsophisticated pleasures, and there are several lakes where swimming is supervised in summertime, and where pedalos and rowing boats can be hired. At the park headquarters in the old Manoir de Courboyer, the Percherons can be admired in action, and other farms in the area offer visits and the chance to ride in a horse-drawn carriage. The forests are all well marked out with walks and off-road cycle tracks – and of course, finding and collecting mushrooms and other fungi can be enjoyed by all the family. The Perche is a place to appreciate simple pleasures, and the words 'unspoilt' and 'undiscovered', often used too lightly, genuinely apply here.

NOGENT-LE-ROTROU

The confusion over which town is the capital of the Perche is probably due to the fact that it extends into two *départements* – the two-thirds or so that is in the north and west is in the *département* of Orne, while the remainder to the south and east belongs to Eure-et-Loire. There is no doubt that back in the Middle Ages Mortagne-au-Perche was the original capital. Its role was later taken over by Bellême – that is, as far as the people of Orne are concerned. In Eure-et-Loire, the capital of the Perche is most definitely **Nogent-le-Rotrou** – and this is certainly the biggest town by far, with a population of around 11,000. Having several hotels and a small camp site, you could well make Nogent your holiday base, but you may prefer a more rural location in one of the many gîtes in this area.

Let us anyway begin this exploration of the Perche in the town of Nogent, whose houses sprawl beneath a hill that was once the site of a Gallo-Roman oppidum. The Château St Jean crowns the hill today, its 12th century keep fronted by twin pepper-pot towers reached by a bridge across the empty moat. The upper rooms of one tower are home to the Musée du Perche, a small but well-presented collection of items of local life – and the modest entrance fee is worthwhile for the view from the windows alone. The old town is immediately below the château and to explore it you can head down the steps (the Ruelle des Marches) just outside the entrance gate.

The most interesting street is straight ahead at the bottom of the flight – among the varied old houses of the Rue Bourg-le-Comte you will find the grey-stoned 16th-century Maison du Bailli (now a college) with its original inscription over the door and a *colombage* (half-timbered house) with mullioned windows dating from the same time, now given a new life as a bistro. The main town of Nogent-le-Rotrou stretches west of the château and is gathered around the Place St Pol with its fountains and floral displays. If you stop here to shop or eat, you could pop across to the Église Notre-Dame to see its 500-year-old crib scene of terracotta figures or seek out the marble statues on Sully's tomb (he was financier to Henri IV and the region's big landowner) in a courtyard at the heart of the Hôtel-Dieu, which is now a hospital (a hint – there's no need to go through the hospital, just head up the road alongside it and look for the courtyard entrance)

WEST OF NOGENT

Feeling acquainted with the 'capital' it is now time to set out into the countryside – and the best place to start is at the **Manoir de Courboyer**, the scene of the Park headquarters. Leave Nogent on the D555 in the direction of Bellême and then turn north towards Nocé. Just before you reach the village, glance across the fields on the right to see the dark pointed towers of the Manoir de Lormarin – it is one of those whose grounds can be visited in summer. The Manoir de Courboyer is signed from Nocé and stands beside the D9, about a mile and a half (2km). to the north.

The Park Headquarters, once housed in the manor house, has recently moved to some of the restored outbuildings, where there is also an exhibition of local produce. Though the manor house is photogenic, it does not have a lot of real interest inside. The grounds however will provide some very pleasant short walks – and they are home to a friendly team of Percherons who give displays and draw carriages for the visitors on high days and holidays. All the literature that you could possibly wish for on this region is to be found in the Manoir de Courboyer and well-produced as it is, you will realise straight away that absolutely none of it is in English. Well – you wanted to be in 'undiscovered' France! Even if you know no French at all, it is worth spending a couple of euros on a superbly-produced folder of leaflets entitled *Routes Tranquilles du Perche* – contained within are suggested drives that between them will take you to just about every hidden corner of this region.

After Courboyer, the other local establishment setting the scene of life in the Perche is the **Ecomusée du Perche** in the Prieuré Sainte-Gauburge. Head south from Courboyer through Nocé, cross the main road and continue on the D9 to Preaux-du-Perche – from where **Sainte-Gauburge** is signed on the right. The eco-museum is housed in a building alongside the priory, while the priory itself is used for temporary exhibitions – which, depending on the theme, may seem strangely out of place in such a hallowed setting! The eco-museum itself is well put together, concentrating on traditional crafts, skills and past industries of the region – and again there is a fund of literature on offer.

The area around Sainte-Gauburge, roughly that between Nogent and Bellême, has the highest density of the region's famous *manoirs*. Before leaving Sainte-Gauburge you might like to check out the Ferme de la Chaponnière (on the right as you came into the village) and then go back past the priory and turn left to the find the impressive **Manoir de l'Angenardière** still hiding behind its ancient defences. The road passing the manor leads on to Gémages, but where the route takes a right turn you could consider stopping for a few minutes to follow a well-signed path through the forest (a quarter of a mile [400m]) to a huge rock known as the Pierre de la Procureuse. As its name would suggest, this ancient dolmen (2500BC) has a reputation for procuring good luck and good health for everyone that touches it – it has to be worth a try!

At this point you could take a break from the manors and head a few kilometres east to the little hamlet of la Guinière and the celebrated **Jardin François**, a not large but very artistically planted garden that blends perfectly with its setting – and, as a bonus, there is a cider farm down the road at l'Hermitière. But back on the manor trail again, whichever way you go you will soon reach St Germain-de-la-Coudre. From here it is only a short drive on to the **Manoir de la Fresnaye**, a characteristic 14th – 15th century manor that allows visits to the interior in summer. To find it, cross the main road (D7) in St Germain and take the D211 in the direction of Marcilly – after about two and a half miles (4km) signs direct you to an uphill track on the right. The manor sits resplendent at the summit of the rise, with commanding views on all sides.

For more manor-hunting you could make your way back to the D7 and head north – about 4 miles (6km) south of Bellême, the beautifully proportioned 16th century **Domaine des Feugerets** stands on the hillside on the right. Its grounds may sometimes be visited, while on summer weekends it hosts a very popular *son-et-lumière* horse show. And for those who still have energy for such things, there is one more manor that should be included with this list of classics – the **Manoir de la Vove**. It is a little distance away to the north-east of Bellême and can probably be best reached via the D5 and Mauves-sur-Huisne. This old feudal manor seems more foreboding than most, with a 12th century keep and detached chapel.

No doubt this journey has also offered you glimpses of other manors that have not been mentioned – the whole countryside is dotted with them. If you want to go on, there is a château down the road at Maison-Maugis and there are four more manors to the north of Rémalard (Verger, Vaujours, Boiscorde and Voré). And you have only explored a small corner of the Perche as yet! The best map for locating all these manors is the one entitled *Parc Naturel Regional du Perche* in the IGN *Culture et Environnement* series. But now it must be time to venture farther afield and we can first turn our attention to the west and Bellême.

BELLÊME AND AROUND

Bellême is a lovely hilltop town of whose original fortifications only an archway flanked by two restored towers remains. Below the archway is the market square (Place de la République) and on its far side, the Église Saint-Sauveur with its richly patterned interior. On the other side of the arch, the Rue Ville-Close is renowned for its well-preserved 17th – 18th century houses with wrought iron balconies. At the bottom of the Rue de Ville-Close, the elegant façade of the Hôtel de Bansard des Bois overlooks a lake that was once part of the château moat, and on the opposite side of the road, the well-stocked Office de Tourisme must be the friendliest in the Perche.

You cannot come to Bellême without dipping into its forest, which is particularly beautiful. Generations of oaks and beeches line every path and between and among them are holly, holm oak, silver birch, spruce, Douglas fir and the rest. Most remarkable is its wealth of fungi, and every September sees a mycological congress in which the world's experts and the general public are invited to share.

Many signed walks start from Bellême and probably the best of them leads to the **Étang de la Herse** at the heart of the forest. La Herse is a magical spot, a lake whose still waters reflect perfectly the beauty of the surrounding trees. If you cannot manage the 6.2 mile (10km) walk, drive north on the D958 Mortagne road (on the way you could consider a diversion to pretty St Martin-du-Vieux-Bellême with its priory) and park in the well-concealed site almost opposite the Auberge de la Herse. From here you can easily walk down to the lake and enjoy lunch at one of the picnic tables or stroll around the circumference in 15 minutes or so.

Mineral spring

Before leaving La Herse, it is worth crossing the main road (with great care) to the field beside the Auberge de la Herse, which has a tale to tell. Here you will find a spring surrounded by stones with strange Latin inscriptions invoking Aphrodite, Mars, Mercury and Venus. Nothing is known about its origins, but in the 17th century a doctor declared its iron-rich waters to be good for just about every affliction and a constant supply was subsequently transported to Bellême by a team of donkeys. But Bellême's heyday as a spa town was short-lived – and a latter-day caption reads *Eau non Potable*!

Returning to Bellême from la Herse, the first road on the right is signed to la Perrière – and it is a beautiful forest drive all the way, winding through the dappled light of the beech woods. About a kilometre before reaching la Perrière, a turn on the left leads down to the **Chêne de l'École**, an oak more than 300 years old. Tall and straight with no lower branches, it illustrates perfectly the way in which these woods are managed. Here the oak is king – the beeches are planted merely to give the oak shade in its early years and so to encourage a long knot-free growth of the trunk. **La Perrière** itself merits a few minutes of your time. The village boasts some splendid old stone buildings, among them a château, a priory and a one-time bishop's residence. From the terrace around the church the fine view across the rolling fields and forests of the Perche is said to include 17 church spires. Stroll around the village at your leisure, or if you really want to test your French (and your sense of direction), get hold of the little leaflet that describes the village tour from the local Office de Tourisme.

The Chêne de l'École may be old, but at **Pervenchères** (just to the north), an oak known as the **Chêne de Lambonnière** is older. Beginning life some 500 years ago, this much-venerated specimen is said to be the oldest tree in the Perche (this must mean in Orne, because there is one near Senonches that trumps it con-vincingly) and has consequently been given lifetime protection by a local group who have bought up the field in which it grows. A sign in the village street will direct you to the tree by car but it is also possible to reach it on foot in about half an hour by a pleasant if sometimes muddy signed

path that starts from the road beside the Plan d'Eau. Returning to Bellême from Pervenchères, take instead the road south via Montgaudry, where you can drive up the hill to the church for a final long view of this western part of the Perche.

NORTH-WEST OF NOGENT

Back to base at Nogent again now, and the next excursion could be to the north-west and the area around Mortagne-au-Perche – but there are so many interesting diversions on the way to this one, the day may have ended before you get there. Never mind – you can always pick up the trail again tomorrow! If you set out north from Nogent on the D918, you can turn off at Condé-sur-Huisne and take the road to Rémalard through the valley of the Huisne – and here the diversions start. The village of **Villeray** (just off the road on the left) is a real gem, a cluster of lovely warm-stone flower-decked houses topped by a château in the same mode, and a photogenic mill (now a restaurant), complete with wheel, on the banks of the gurgling river. Continuing up the main road again (the D10) it is worth returning to the river at **Dorceau** – the mill here is quite different, idyllically set in riverside greenery with a peaceful picnic site opposite.

Rémalard itself is a pleasant small market town – by-pass it now, and continue north (by whichever road) to reach Monceaux-au-Perche and the **Manoir du Pontgirard.** You have seen enough *manoirs* already? Well, yes, but this one's glory is its garden – waterfalls, fountains, topiary hedges, and medicinal plants. Open to the public only at weekends, the pale stone manor and its floral surround make a pretty enough picture from the roadside at any other time.

From Monceaux, continue to **la Chapelle-Montligeon** – and make sure you take the D213, followed by a turn to the north. It is important to arrive by the right road, because rounding the final corner, you will get the full impact of the enormous ornate grey-stone church dominating the valley ahead. What is this vast neo-gothic edifice doing in a remote place like this? The story is that back in 1878 a new curate, l'Abbé Paul Buguet, arrived in la Chapelle-Montligeon, which at the time had only a modest church at the heart of the village. He found the rural community depressed and becoming depleted on account of the lack of employment in the area. Wanting to do something to help, he first created workshops producing knitwear, then lace and gloves. All failed. But he surely was a true entrepreneur because, praying as he usually did for souls in purgatory, he then had the idea that he could pray for other souls from outside his community for a small consideration. He started a printing press, sending out leaflets offering this service and naming those prayed for – and soon he had employment for more than 150 local people in the print shop, clients from all over the world and enough money to build this fine chapel to welcome pilgrims. Started in 1896 and finished 15 years later, the interior has some fine mosaics, but most impressive are the beautiful stained glass windows by local master-craftsmen. Alongside the basilica, the printing works still serve their original function, but now also produce packaging for the pharmaceutical industry.

From la Chapelle-Montligeon you could go directly to Mortagne, but if you have by now developed an interest in the forest trees, there are some very fine specimens at the heart of the **Forêt de Réno-Valdieu**. Head north from la Chapelle-Montligeon (the road you want is the only one off the main street opposite the basilica) and continue through the forest. On reaching the D8 you can pick up signs for the *Série Artistique* and follow them into the depths of the forest (remember which way you came – there are no signs going back). The whole 'series' comprises about 400 oaks and 250 beeches, preserved from exploitation on account of their great age. A gravelled path leads you around four of the trees, tall straight oaks, each of them with its own dedication (including the Universities of Oxford and Aberdeen) and each accompanied by a plaque bearing its vital statistics – age, height, etc. Back at the D8 you can soon reach Mortagne – unless, of course, you have been lured aside by the signs to the Abbaye de Valdieu, of which only a few vestiges of the original building remain.

MORTAGNE-AU-PERCHE

Having finally arrived in **Mortagne-au-Perche**, you might wonder why you came here. It is certainly not 'undiscovered', having a busy main road running right through the centre. Nevertheless, you can find a quiet corner (if you manage to park the car), by making your way downhill to the back of the Église Notre-Dame where an arch of the old town gateway remains, flanked by a turret housing the Musée Percheron and the library incorporating a museum relating to the life of the philosopher Alain. The church itself has a window dedicated to one of the Perche's first emigrants to Canada (about 150 families from this region crossed the Atlantic in the latter half of the 17th century) – but you may be concerned about the ethics of his fight with the native Indians in the lower section!

Back in the town, Mortagne's culinary speciality is immediately obvious – black puddings top the menu of every eating house. But if that is not what you fancy for lunch, there are quiet gardens behind the *Mairie* where scattered benches offer a fine view to be enjoyed with a picnic. Before leaving Mortagne you might like to check out its other curiosity, the *cadrans solaires* – sundials. The town boasts more than 20 of them, but in truth they are widely distributed throughout the Perche, and anyone interested in seeking them out should ask at OT for the well-produced little booklet *Cadrans Solaires du Perche*

Having come as far as Mortagne, you cannot go home without a visit to the **Forest of la Trappe** – and in particular to its abbey, from which the Trappists (Cistercians of the Strict Observance) take their name. Head north through the little village of Soligny and then continue for a further two and a half miles (4km) to the **Abbey of la Trappe** at the edge of the forest. The 'white monks' here have taken a vow of silence, and it is not possible to do more than peer through the gates at the impressive buildings within. The first monastery on this site was founded in 1140, but the buildings you see today date from the end of the 19th century. The monastery shop alongside is usually open for visitors and another room offers an audio-visual presentation of the history of the abbey and the life of the monks. Beside the shop, the Fontaine St Bernard pours out its

clear waters, which are said to be particularly pure after filtering through the forest. There must be something special here, because there are often long queues of devotees waiting to fill their bottles. Get a taste if you can get near!

Beyond the abbey is the forest, its narrow roads radiating like spokes from the central Carrefour de l'Étoile. Walking and cycling routes are there in plenty, and on the western edge (off the D930) a forest lake (the Étang Neuf) offers opportunities for swimming and boating. This well-managed small complex could not have a more attractive setting and with sandy beach, waterslide and play equipment, provides perfect family entertainment for a hot summer's day. And now it is time to go home, perhaps calling in to **Tourouvre**, where there is a small museum about the Canadian emigration and yet more church windows on the theme, and maybe at the same time visiting the cheerful little museum entitled *l'Épicerie d'autrefois* (The Grocer's shop of olden days), which is currently (2005) being moved to Tourouvre from nearby Lignerolles.

NORTH-EAST OF NOGENT

Another excursion now, this time heading north-east to the neighbouring towns of la Ferté-Vidame and Senonches, each flanked by its own forest. The towns are very different. At **la Ferté-Vidame**, the classically wide main street leads straight to the imposing gateway of a château in a wide expanse of green parkland – but glancing through, you can see that no more than a skeleton of the original building remains.

The château of la Ferté-Vidame was built by the Duc de Saint-Simon in the 17th century, and enlarged and elaborated by the Marquis de Laborde when he acquired it a century later. At the beginning of the Revolution a château of enormous proportions stood here – five years later it was in ruins as it is today, its treasures and even its stones pillaged by all and sundry. Ten years later the political dust had settled and the land and ravaged building were bought by Louis-Philippe, Duke of Orléans and future King of France, who thought to restore them, and began by renovating the 'petit-château' in the grounds for his own habitation in the meantime. His grand plans never got farther than the drawing board and the château remains in its post-revolutionary misery, but surrounded by parkland with lakes and moats where you can wander freely at any time. In the street behind the Petit-Château, the Église Saint-Nicolas dates from the original building project in 1659 – and you might also like to visit the small museum beside the château gates.

The best views of the château are undoubtedly from the D24 to the west, where two formal lakes flank the original entrance road edged by limes . From this distance the eye and even the camera are deceived. A parking area alongside the D24 (the Rond Montpensier) gives access to the lakes. It is also the starting point for some marked forest walks and a quarter mile (400m) mountain-bike circuit, ideal for real beginners. Farther along the D24 (one and a half miles [3km]), the lovely steep-roofed **Chapelle de Réveillon** is another jewel in Louis-Philippe's domain – the fine 16th century wall paintings are designated historic monuments.

Seven and a half miles (12km) south-east of la Ferté-Vidame, **Senonches** is a small market town engulfed by its forest. Its most notable buildings are an iron-stone 12th century keep and the edifice that is now the Hôtel de Ville, an elaborate amalgamation of patterned turrets, peaked windows and bell-tower, not much more than a century old.

South of Senonches, the straight forest road leads to the little village of **Fontaine-Simon** with a fine lake-side swimming complex and camp-site. At this point, you're definitely on the way home, but first turn west on the road to Manou, and then south on the D15 towards la Loupe. Standing in open fields, the large walled building on the left is now an auberge, but was once the fortified farm of **la Grand'Maison**. The four-sided tower, walls and moat date back to the 12th century. If you care to wander further afield, other fine examples of fortified farms are to be found beyond la Loupe (and outside the Perche) at Pontgouin in the east and Montlandon in the south.

On south again now, and there is just one more stop. Reaching the busy D920 you will see a big tree on the opposite side of the road. The **Gros Chêne** was apparently planted in 1360. It was fortunate to survive the Revolution because by then it was sheltering a statue of the Virgin in one of the hollows of its trunk. Legend has it that when men arrived to cut down the tree, their axes were miraculously blunted. Whatever happened, it is still there today, and looking pretty good for its 600+ years – you just wish it had a more peaceful spot in which to enjoy old age.

PERCHE-GOUET

Finally it is time to visit the Perche-Gouet. From Nogent you could head directly south to the pretty little town of **Authon-du-Perche** – but first you might like to travel east to **Thiron-Gardais** with its huge abbey-church. The building is disappointingly bare inside though, and its most fascinating features are the faces carved on the misericords, dating from the 14th century. The grounds outside recreate the monks' garden. If you have strayed this far, you could go on to **Frazé**, whose curious but appealing château is a jumble of pepper-pot turrets, keep, chapel and watch-towers, scattered in landscaped grounds.

Back to Authon now, and for another château (a glimpse only, since it is private) you might first leave via the D13 and turn off in a couple of kilometres to **Charbonnières** – its gleaming white fairy-tale façade greets you at the entrance to the village. Travelling on south from here the landscape becomes flatter as the Perche approaches the cereal plains of the Beauce. By the time you reach **la Bazoche-Gouet** there is not a hill or even a bump to be seen – and the town itself, though pleasant, is as undistinguished as the landscape. Traffic rumbles through its main street, shaking the foundations of the Église Saint Jean-Baptiste, which after all has some fine stained-glass windows to preserve. On the opposite side of the road is a 17th century water-mill, restored by its enthusiastic owner, who proudly shows off its internal workings on designated days.

The Perche-Gouet markets itself as a weekend retreat for Parisians weary of the hurly-burly of city life. It may only be an hour and a half by train, but nowhere could be farther from city life that the area around la Bazoche-Gouet. Here you could be a century back in time – half-timbered farms with muddy yards and tumble-down barns, farmers wives in black feeding scrawny chickens from an aluminium bucket. This is genuine working countryside – and perhaps that is what refreshes the Parisian soul. La Bazoche-Gouet surprisingly offers more waymarked walks than most small towns. If you can take one of them, you will get a feel for an area that is very decidedly 'undiscovered'.

Lastly, if you have come this far, you must step out of the boundaries of the Perche to visit the unusual and most attractive **Commanderie at Arville**, 6 miles (9km) south of la Bazoche-Gouet. Founded here by the Templars in the 12th century, this is the best preserved such group of buildings in France. The Templars were both monks and soldiers, and their aims were to protect the Holy Land from the Muslims and to care for knights on pilgrimage to Jerusalem. The *Centre d'Histoire des orders de Chevalerie*, housed in one of the outbuildings, tells the story of the Templars and evokes the epoch of the Crusades with a variety of tableaux. And when you leave Arville to return, you can get right back to the present day when you cross the lines of the TGV Atlantique. Choose a bridge on a quiet road rather than the D921 and you can watch them flash beneath you at 187 miles (300km) an hour (there is said to be one every five minutes). It seems an unfitting end to a sojourn in a place as peaceful and timeless as the Perche, but the children will love it!

OFFICES DE TOURISME

Nogent-le-Rotrou
44, Rue Vilette-Gaté
28400 NOGENT-le-ROTROU
☎ 02.37.29.68.86

Bellême
Blvd. Bansard des Bois
61130 BELLÊME
☎ 02.33.73.09.69

Mortagne-au-Perche
Halle aux Grains
61400 MORTAGNE-au-PERCHE
☎ 02.33.85.11.18

Senonches
34, Place de l'Hôtel de Ville
28250 SENONCHES
☎ 02.37.37.80.11

La Bazoche-Gouet
Mairie
28330 LA BAZOCHE-GOUET
☎ 02.37.49.23.45

PLACES OF INTEREST

Nogent-le-Rotrou

Château St Jean
Open every day except Tuesdays May to October 10am-12noon, 2-6pm, November to April 10am-12noon, 2-5pm.

Nocé

Manoir de Courboyer
Open 10.30am-7pm daily throughout the year with the exception of weekdays in November and December.

Sainte-Gauburge

L'ecomusée du Perche
Open every day throughout the year except Tuesdays, 2-6.30pm in summer, 2-6pm in winter.

Jardin François
Open every day throughout the year 10am-7pm – and until 11 p.m. on Friday evenings in summer, when it is illuminated.

Sundry manors
It is impossible to give details for all these. Ask at your local Office de Tourisme who will happily check out if and when each manor is open.

Monceaux-au-Perche

Manoir du Pontgirard
Gardens are open 2.30-6.30pm, weekends and public holidays only from May to September.

Mortagne-au-Perche

Musée Percheron
Local exhibitions, every day except Monday from mid-June to mid-September.

Musée Alain
Closed Sunday and Monday. Otherwise open every morning and also Wednesday and Saturday afternoons.

Soligny

Abbaye de la Trappe
Audio-visual presentation on request.

La Ferté-Vidame

The Château
Grounds open every day April to
October 9am-7pm, November to
March 9am-5.30pm.

Musée Saint-Simon
Open Wednesday to Sunday 2-
7pm in July, and weekends and
bank holidays from May to
September 2.30-6.30pm.

La Chapelle de Réveillon
Guided visits at 3pm on designated
days from June to September.
Contact the Office de Tourisme at la
Ferté-Vidame for more information.

Thiron –Gardais

Abbey open every day throughout
the year. Park open only by
appointment.

Frazé

The Château
Grounds only open 3-6pm Sundays
and Bank holidays only from Easter
to end of September.

La Bazoche-Gouet

Le Moulin d'Eau
Open Saturday and Sunday 2-6pm
from Easter to 1 November.

Arville

Commanderie d'Arville
Guided tour of the buildings and
separate admission to the *Centre
d'Histoire*. Open 10am-7pm every
day from May to September, and
2-6pm in March, April, October,
November.

LOCAL HIGHLIGHTS

Best walks

- The 6 mile (10km) hike through the Forest of Bellême to the Étang de la Herse – no. 4 on a leaflet of local walks (including a good map) from the Office de Tourisme in Bellême. The very best way to see this lovely forest and its lake.

- Every tiny village in the Perche has its own walk leaflet – how can you choose from so many? But the walk from Rémalard has the highest concentration of manors (5), with some fine forest and a few good viewpoints thrown in. It is rather long at 14.3 miles (23km) – but short cuts are possible.

- Those who like a challenge should get hold of the book *Promenons-nous dans les forêts du Perche*. One of a series, it will take you to the depths of any of the region's forests with the aid of maps (useful), diagrams of junctions (baffling) and oak leaf logos nailed to trees (not enough of them).

- Finally, there is a discovery walk (*sentier de découverte*) that all the family will enjoy in the forest just west of La Ferté-Vidame. Much of it is on boardwalk raised above the moss and lichen-clad forest floor. A booklet (*La forêt humide des Mousseuses*) is available from the Park HQ and most OTs – if you cannot decipher the French, at least it will tell you where to start and from there you can follow the green dots on the trees. Let the children lead you!

For cyclists

- For the ordinary cyclist, nothing could be better than the Perche. Stay off the main roads and you have a lattice of minor ones to wander at will. The region is more hilly in the west (although nothing too severe); around La Ferté-Vidame in the north and in the Perche-Gouet in the south, you will never need to leave the saddle. Cycles may be hired from the Tourist Office at Bellême among other places.

- All forests are marked out with mountain-bike routes and all tourist offices can offer maps of the local circuits. For a first try, go for the easy 'blue' circuit of 9.6 mile (15.5km) through the Forest of Bellême (although it does cross a main road at one point). OT at Bellême stocks the map (*VTT en forêt dominiale de Bellême et alentours*) and when you get the hang of following the signs, you can progress to one of the longer routes. VTT hire is widely available in the Perche – ask at any OT.

Watersports

- The attractive Etang Neuf in the forest near Soligny has a beach area (swimming supervised in July and August), pedalos and rowing boats for hire, mini-golf and children's playground. Open from 1-8pm every day in July and August, and Sundays and Bank holidays from Easter onwards.

- The Parc Aquatique du Perche at la Fontaine-Simon has a more open setting. An imaginitive covered swimming pool (useful in bad weather) overlooks a lake with sandy beach where swimming is supervised in July and August. There are kayaks and pedalos for hire and, on shore, plenty of games for the children. The Parc Aquatique is open in July and August 10am-12.30pm, 2-7.30pm, with the pool and other indoor facilities open at similar hours throughout the year. The tidy little campsite alongside should appeal to anyone with a family of water-babies in tow.

For the palate

- This is the place to enjoy dairy produce of all kinds – cheeses, unsalted butter, crème fraîche, even milk jam (*confiture du lait*).

- Mortagne-au-Perche is famed for black pudding (*boudin noir*)– and varies it with the addition of onions, nuts, plums, Calvados and more.

- Cider. And if you want to find out if Perche cider is different from that of the rest of Normandy, visit l'Hermitière, near St Germain-de-la-Coudre (open April to October 10am-12noon, 3-8pm).

And the most memorable

- The colours of autumn trees faultlessly reflected in the dark waters of the Étang de la Herse.

- 'Talking' to three Percherons early one morning at the Manoir de Courboyer.

- The excitement of two small boys as a streak of blue and silver TGV shot under their feet at 187 miles (300km) an hour on the bridge at Arville.

5. Marching to Agincourt

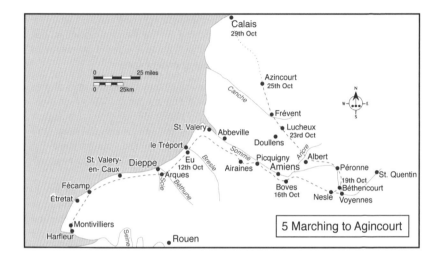

Calais
29th Oct

0   25 miles

0   25km

Azincourt
25th Oct

Canche

N
W · E
S

Frévent

St. Valery   Abbeville
          Lucheux
          23rd Oct

le Tréport
       Doullens

Somme

St. Valery-   Dieppe   Eu   Picquigny   Albert
en- Caux   12th Oct   Airaines   Amiens   Péronne
           Arques   St. Quentin

Bresle   Arc/re   19th Oct

Fécamp   Boves   Béthencourt
Étretat   Scie   Béthune   16th Oct   Nesle   Voyennes

Montivilliers

Harfleur   Seine   Rouen

5 Marching to Agincourt

That Agincourt is one of the best-known battles in English history is perhaps more thanks to Shakespeare than to the history books. The site of the famous conflict is near the village of Azincourt (Agincourt seems to be just an English mis-spelling), some 25 miles (40km) south of Calais and there is now an excellent state-of-the-art museum telling the whole story, while the battlefield itself is decked with appropriate information panels. But Henry V and his army did not just arrive at the scene fresh from Calais or from the nearest suitable shore. In fact they landed near le Havre and marched along the north coast of Normandy and through the valley of the Somme before turning north to arrive at the battle-site.

Following the route Henry took to Agincourt gives us an excuse for visiting some of the most fascinating parts of northern France – the white-cliffed Alabaster Coast, the city of Amiens, the battlefields of the Somme

and finally the very rural 'seven-valleys' of western Pas-de-Calais. So you could embark on this journey for its historical content or simply for its own sake, but be sure to leave yourself plenty of time to cover the 150 miles (241km) or so involved here. Henry and his armies made it in less than three weeks but they were not sightseeing – you may want a little longer. And before you start it is probably worth a recap on the history!

HISTORY OF AGINCOURT

The year was 1415. For almost a century there had been battles over the English-claimed territories in France and since the time of Edward III a question over the rightful heir to the French crown itself. Henry V was newly on the throne of England and wanted to establish his position – and probably to gain some respect at home in doing so. Negotiations with France were begun, but even while they were taking place, Henry was gathering his army, building ships and making weapons. He would take control of the Seine, important for shipping, and move on through Normandy to Paris and then Bordeaux.

In the event, it took more than a month to take the port of Harfleur (now merely a suburb of le Havre) and in the process he lost a third of his men with dysentery. With forces now unfit for the task he originally had in mind, Henry decided instead to march north through the territory he believed rightfully belonged to him, Normandy and Picardy – and thence to return home via Calais. In making this choice he played right into the hands of the French, and was finally trapped by their armies at Azincourt. With his men sick, depleted in numbers and weary through marching, Henry tried first to avoid conflict by offering prisoners. The French refused – and the following day's battle was a resounding victory for the smaller English army. Henry marched on to Calais and returned in triumph to his native shores – and nearly 200 years later Shakespeare produced the play through which most of us have learned of these events. Even if Shakespeare's account is not entirely historically accurate, 25 October, the day of Sts Crispin and Crispinian, has been engraved on our hearts from schooldays.

The Hundred Years War

The English King Edward III held a more-than-tentative claim to the French throne. This arose when Charles IV of France, the last son of Philip IV, died without heirs in 1328. At the time, Philip IV had a surviving daughter, Isabelle, who had married Edward II of England 20 years earlier. Their son was Edward III. However, in 1316 France had decreed Salic Law, under which no female could accede to the throne. On the death of Charles IV, the French crown was therefore given to Philip of Valois, a nephew of Philip IV. Henry V was the grandson of Edward III and had inherited from him the genuine feeling that the French crown was his birthright.

Lending weight to the succession argument, much of south-west France was under English control, having been acquired when Eleanor of Aquitaine married the future Henry II of England in 1152. The strengthening of the French-Scottish alliance and the clash over trade with wealthy Flanders finally set the stage for a long war. The Naval battle of Sluys (1340), and the land battles of Crécy (1346) and Poitiers (1356) all went in favour of the English. France later rallied and by the end of the 14th century, only Calais, Bordeaux and Bayonne were in English hands. Agincourt in 1415 was a much-needed English victory. The tide turned in favour of the French again when Joan of Arc raised the siege of Orleans (1429) but the war continued until 1453, by which time Calais was the only remaining English possession in France.

LE HAVRE TO DIEPPE

So let us now go back to the beginning – in the Solent where the English fleet was assembled early in August 1415. On 11 August an army of around 9000 men set sail, of which something like 6000 were archers. Two days later they were anchored off the French coast near the mouth of the Seine, from where they went ashore to set up camp at a place known as **Ste-Adresse**, at the northern tip of the estuary. Today Ste-Adresse is an up-market suburb of le Havre, its steep cliffs lined with terrace upon terrace of fashionable villas, all of them looking out over the blue horizon and the stream of shipping entering and leaving the second busiest port in France. The star-studded roll of past residents here includes Gabriel Fauré, Sarah Bernhardt, Claude Monet and Raoul Dufy. If you are going to play the game of following Henry faithfully, this illustrious suburb must be your first port of call – it is immediately to the west of le Havre and if you arrive via the car ferry, you can surprise all the other traffic by turning left rather than right when you reach the first main road (N15).

There is not a lot of excitement in Ste-Adresse (although it is popular with locals on a summer weekend) but if you drive along the beach road and then up the fairly steep hill beyond, you can stop at a viewpoint looking out to sea – and picture the English fleet out there. More views are to be had from the lighthouse at the top of the cliff (Cap de la Hève), and if you get this far, you could try descending past the (signed) Pain de Sucre, a rather bulbous white pillar erected in memory of one General Lefèbvre-Desnouettes, lost at sea in 1822. Higher up the narrow road, the Chapelle Notre-Dame-des-Flots has many ex-votos given by mariners in thanks for their safe return.

Henry did not stay long in Ste-Adresse but moved east to **Graville** from where he could besiege the desired port of Harfleur. Graville today is a fairly undistinguished sprawling suburb – seek it out if you will (its priory with a museum of religious art could merit a visit, and there are good views of the river), but a stop at **Harfleur** is mandatory. If you make your way back to the N15, the town is clearly signed from one of its roundabouts towards the eastern side of le Havre. Situated at the mouth of the River Lézarde, Harfleur was a busy port until the 16th century, when that river became silted up and the action moved to a new port built by Francois I, the present-day le Havre. Today the best view of Harfleur is from the old quays on the Lézarde, where the tall crocketted spire of St Martin's church can be seen looking down on the town square and a bridge garlanded with flowers. It was to this church (or at least its forerunner) that Henry came to give thanks after the final surrender of Harfleur on 22 September, a gruelling six weeks after he had set up the siege.

The busy roads of **le Havre** may make you long to get 'off the beaten track', but it is worth forgetting the Henry connections for a moment and devoting a few thoughts to the city itself. There is virtually no old building in le Havre – all was destroyed by the bombs of 1944. Invited to reconstruct the place, the Parisian architect Auguste Perret enjoyed a field day in his favourite medium, reinforced concrete. Credit for the classic Hôtel de Ville and the gigantically-towered Église St Joseph belongs to Perret. The prominent 'volcano' (yoghourt pot, elephant's foot, or what have you) at the end of the Bassin de Commerce is the work of another architect, the Brazilian Oscar Niemeyer, and serves as a cultural centre with theatre and cinema inside. At the entrance to the port, yet another modern building and one that perfectly fits its role, is the glass and metal museum of fine art (Musée André Malraux). Its collection of works by Dufy (a native of le Havre), Boudin, Corot and Pissaro are a good incentive to spend just a little more time in le Havre.

Eventually, as with Henry, it must be time to move on. The army, now decimated by dysentery and numbering barely 6000 men, left Harfleur on 7 October and set off north through the valley of the Lézarde to Montivilliers. **Montivilliers** today is an unprepossessing sort of place, almost a suburb of le Havre, but it does have at its heart the very fine Église St Sauveur on the site of a monastery founded here by St Philibert in the 6th century. The lantern tower surmounting the transept crossing dates from the 11th century, so that at least must have been seen by Henry's army as it passed by the town. From Montivilliers the army moved rapidly north-east to Fécamp, and you should do the same – but that would be to bypass Étretat, and if you have not visited before, it just has to be worth the diversion.

The high white cliffs, arches and needles of **Étretat** form one of the best-known coastlines in France, a scene that appears on many a tourist brochure. The reality is just as impressive as the photographs. From Étretat's shingle beach you can look east to the low arch of the Porte d'Amont, while to the west is that most famous of seascapes, the arch

of the Porte d'Aval with the tall white *aiguille* beside. As you might expect, there are some splendid walks along the cliffs in both directions. On the eastern side, a giant cliff-top finger pointing to the sky commemorates two French aviators who in 1927 were the 'first to dare' the crossing of the Atlantic by plane. They were last seen over Étretat and a small museum nearby now tells their story. Back in the town there is lots more of interest.

The elegant villas were mostly built by the rich and famous of Paris, who in the *belle époque* made Étretat their summer watering place. One of the villas, the Château les Aygues, was for many years a holiday residence of the Queens of Spain. Another belonged to the composer Jacques Offenbach. Other famous names to be associated with Étretat are of course those of the impressionists – Corot and Courbet were soon followed by Boudin and Monet in coming to capture the dramatic coastal scenes on canvas. Writers were here too – Maupassant lived in Étretat in his childhood, Dumas built a villa in the town, André Gide and Victor Hugo were frequent visitors. Most evidently remembered is the novelist Maurice Leblanc, who created the appealing character of Arsene Lupin, the 'gentleman-thief' – Leblanc's villa, the Clos Lupin, now welcomes visit-ors who come to solve a classic Lupin-type mystery.

Étretat is a fascinating place, but now it is time again to follow Henry to **Fécamp**. In fact he never quite reached the town, because by this time the French had gathered up a force there to oppose him. Trouble was averted by quickly passing Fécamp on its eastern side – but you do not have to do likewise, and if you have not previously made the acquaintance of the liqueur Benedictine, this is the moment to do so. Fécamp is a pleasant seaside resort in its own right, and a place whose fortunes for many centuries depended on its fishing industry. Historically, the town was founded where a bottle said to contain drops of Christ's blood from the Crucifixion was washed up on the shore and these relics are still venerated in the 13th century Abbatiale de la Trinité. Despite all this, Fécamp's fame rests chiefly on Benedictine.

The story goes that in the early 16th century, one Brother Vincelli began to distil a blend of herbs and spices in his monastery in Fécamp. With the Revolution all details of this potion were lost – but in 1863 a wine merchant named Alexandre le Grand miraculously found the recipe again. By the end of the century the liqueur was being produced from a monstrously flamboyant Gothic/ Renaissance/Art Nouveau 'Palais Bénédictine' at the heart of the town. Visits to the building today begin with several rooms of fine art treasures before a final descent into the herb room, followed by the distillery and cellars. The tour ends in the bar with a glass of the magic liquid – and of course there are opportunities to purchase.

Agincourt is still a long way ahead and it is time to get back on the trail. The next time we hear of Henry's army is near Dieppe and there's more than enough opportunity for diverting on the way to this one – the popular resort of St Valéry-en-Caux, the lesser and perhaps prettier Veulettes-sur-Mer, the charming but seasonally overcrowded Veules-les-Roses with the 'shortest river in France' (1200yd [1.1km]). Each retains a turn-of-the-century air, a shingly beach with rows of white bathing huts and the ever-

present high chalk cliffs. But all these places can be busy, and in quest of a peaceful summer swim, you would do better to head for the lesser resorts – the little village of Les Petites Dalles (on the D79, seven and a half miles (12km) east of Fécamp) with its tiny beach would fit the bill perfectly!

Henry however kept just inland, marching across the high plateau of the Caux, now a vast expanse of arable land. Reaching the **Château d'Arques**, four miles from Dieppe, the army was fired upon from the walls, but by threatening to set fire to the place, they were finally allowed to pass unheeded and even supplied with bread and wine. The remains of the Château d'Arques can today be reached by a signed turning off the D548 south of Dieppe. More famous for a later battle (Henry IV of France defeated the Duke of Mayenne here in 1589, hence the name 'Arques-la-Bataille'), it seems to have been allowed to crumble as nature intended, making it now too dangerous to wander around the stonework. Instead there is a very pleasant path along the encircling rampart, from which there are good views of the town, forest and river valley below – and you probably will not find a soul there, even in the height of summer.

FORWARD TO AMIENS

From Arques, Henry's march continued as before, parallel to the coast, but if you want just one more glimpse of that remarkable shoreline, opt for Criel-sur-Mer – or Criel Plage to be accurate, since Criel Bourg is a couple of kilometres from the sea. The white chalk cliffs to the west of Criel rise 328ft (100m) above the foaming sea and are said to be the highest in France, although there are one or two other places that make the same claim! If you have time, follow the footpath (a well-marked Grande-Randonnée) along the cliff top and listen to the waves grinding the pebbles way below – but do not go too near the edge!

Back again to the army. On 10 October, the next day after the confrontation at Arques, they were 20 miles (32km) on and south of the town of Eu at the mouth of the Bresle. Once again they were challenged, once again the threat to fire worked and once again they were given supplies. Confidence must have been growing as they trudged upriver to find a crossing. Before following them, it is well worth sparing a few hours for Eu, and maybe for its next-door-neighbour, le Tréport, as well.

The pleasantly stylish old town of **Eu** thinks itself 'undiscovered' even by the French, adorning its town brochure with the slogan *Eu, c'est où?* (Eu, where's that?). Nevertheless the town has two magnificent buildings at its heart, an elegant red-brick château and an enormous Collégiate church. The impressive château was begun some time in the 16th century and has undergone lots of alterations since. Sadly there is nothing left of an original much earlier building, although a plaque recently placed in the square tells you of its greatest moment, the marriage of William the Conqueror and Matilda, here in 1050. Today's château was built by the Guise family, passed into the hands of the Dukes of Orléans, and became a favourite residence of Louis-Philippe, the last king of France – it was from Eu that he fled to his exile in England in 1848. The Musée Louis-Philippe gives access to part of the château and allows you to visit nine rooms maintained as they were in his time. The grounds of the Château of Eu are always open and comprise a formal garden with some of Louis-Philippe's chosen statues and an extensive parkland beyond. Among the beeches to the rear of the château is one veritable Methuselah. Known as *le Guisard*, it was planted in 1585.

The Collégiale at Eu is dedicated to Notre Dame and St Lawrence (or Laurent) O'Toole. The latter may start ringing some confused bells with you, but in fact he was an Archbishop of Dublin who arrived in Eu in 1180, en route to meeting Henry II on neutral ground to discuss the thorny problem of Irish taxation. Old and sick at the time, he died four days later – and was canonised in 1225. The Gothic-style church was begun six years after his death and is most impressive for the graceful lines of its high-arched interior. In the crypt you can view a recumbent effigy of O'Toole himself, thought to be one of the oldest such surviving in France.

Just down the road from Eu (and accessible by tourist train that serves the two towns) is the port and resort of **le Tréport**. Flanked by the now familiar white cliffs, the town has a long pebbly beach that reveals sand at low tide, and a most exciting harbour busy with fishing boats. Beyond is a commercial port area where cereals, fertilisers, salt and clay are transhipped. Three hundred and sixty-five leg-aching steps take the fittest visitors to Les Terraces, a cliff top viewpoint looking over the bay, the town and the distant mouth of the Somme – and at the foot of the steps is the former fishermen's area known as the Quartier des Cordiers, the most unusual and fascinating part of le Tréport. In the *belle époque*, embellishing a house with a name or slogan in ceramic was greatly in vogue along the Normandy coast and later the fashion spread to Paris. Many of the high terraced houses in this quarter of le Tréport still bear their original decorative ceramic plaques. The Tourist Office (by the harbour) offers you 20 to 'spot' in its Town Guide, but there are many others – an excellent diversion for all the family on a dull day.

Time is passing, and with the army, you must find the crossing of the Bresle. The road to the south of the river (the D49) has views over the many lakes that fill the valley. After Incheville, the **Forest of Eu** stretches uphill on your right hand side and there are some first-class walks and cycle rides to be had in its leafy depths, not to mention a Gallo-Roman site (Bois l'Abbé) with vestiges of a temple and a theatre. Finally (just before Gamaches) you reach the few houses of **Gousseauville** – and this point, we are told, was Henry's crossing place. Leave the D49 by the road on the left into the village and turn left again to cross the railway. Beyond is a concrete bridge over an attractive stretch of shallow river, the scene of the original ford. From this point Henry hurried north to the Somme, and we hear of him again in the town of Friville-Escarbotin – to get there yourself, continue from the bridge past the old château that is now a riding school, to meet the main road. Turn left, and then turn right in the village of Beauchamps. From Friville the army continued north towards the mouth of the Somme, intending to cross at the low-water ford known as Blanque-Taque. But Henry had made a miscalculation – he had sent forward only a small force to guard this vital crossing. Now his heralds

were returning with the news that the causeways across the marshes to the ford had been destroyed (or 'spiked' as some versions have it) and that the French armies were gathered on the far side. They would have to turn away and find another crossing upstream.

The mouth of the Somme today presents a very different scene from that of 600 years ago. In 1835 the river itself was canalised and in recent times the sand beds in the bay have been gradually rising in height. The nearest you can now get to the old Blanque-Taque crossing is probably **St Valéry-sur-Somme**, from where you can look out across the greening mud-flats of low tide to the silhouetted buildings of le Crotoy on the far side. A walk up into the medieval Haute Ville of St Valéry will give you the best views of the marshy estuary, and the little Tourist Train of the Somme that crosses it must take a route not too different from that of the Middle Ages. St Valéry is forever famed as the port from which William the Conqueror left for England in 1066. It is a place to linger, a delightful town with old streets of brightly painted houses and a long pleasant boardwalk along the waterfront. If you have a few extra moments to spare here, devote them to the exceptional Ecomusée Picarvie in the main street. One man's private collection over the past 40 years, it displays past life in the region in a series of life-like tableaux – the family at home, the blacksmith's shop, the schoolroom, the hunting scene, and a lot more, all with remarkable attention to detail.

This dallying in 21st century resorts is all very well, but again we need to go back a few hundred years to find that crossing of the Somme. Henry and his dispirited army turned back south-east, and we hear of them passing through Airaines en route for the next ford at Picquigny. It is not easy to follow them exactly, but you might well take the D173 for most of the way. The country you will be driving through (that between the Bresle and the Somme) is known as the Vimeu – rolling agricultural land with wooded valleys and tiny farming villages. At last you are truly off-the-beaten-track! **Airaines** puts you firmly on it again. A town at a busy cross-roads, there is not a lot to hang around for – although you might, by following the signs, take a peep at its 12th century Church of Notre-Dame (there is not much inside except a carved stone 11th century font) and the twin Tours des Luynes, vestiges of a 17th century château.

Fifteen miles (24km) to the east of Airaines is **Picquigny**, a medieval fortified town, at that time well-known for its ford across the Somme. When Henry's army arrived they found the French waiting on the far side of the river, and again no crossing was possible. Picquigny today is a pleasant small town with some interesting half-timbered and painted buildings in its main street. The château and ramparts that were there in Henry's time (11th century originally, but modified in the 14th) can still be seen above the town and summertime tours are on offer. At other times you can wander through the imposing archway and admire the ruins beyond, with the 15th century Collégiale St Martin alongside. The Somme now passes through Picquigny in two parts – the canal with its lock for the barges and the rushing river popular with canoeists. Starting from the road crossing the canal, you can pick up a footpath along the banks and walk past Trève Island where, in 1475, the Treaty of Piquigny was

signed by Louis XI and Edward IV of England, thus officially bringing to an end the Hundred Years War.

Yet another diversion presents itself at Picquigny, a venue where you can delve yet farther into the past. **Samara** (just across the river and a couple of kilometres to the east) is an exhibition park devoted to life between the Paleolithic and Gallo-Roman eras – said to be 600,000 years of history. Dwelling places throughout the ages have been recreated and there is lots more detail of daily life in the exhibition pavilion. An arboretum and botanical garden have been thrown in for good measure.

AMIENS

But back to Henry and his troubles in crossing the Somme. Having found no joy in Picquigny, he turned south and is said to have given **Amiens** a wide berth. But as he walked on the high ground to the south of the town he must have been able to see in the distance that magnificent cathedral, which had already been in place almost 200 years. In present times, the city's other readily distinguishable landmark is another of Perret's exuberances in reinforced concrete, an apartment block unimaginatively known as the Tour Perret. Forget the latter, but if you have not explored the cathedral before, this is an excellent opportunity because at Picquigny you are in the very best position for accessing the city.

The N235 takes you alongside the river with minimum hassle to arrive right beside the cathedral itself and there is ample parking nearby. The rich detail of the cathedral's western façade is breathtaking. Above and around the three doorways are gathered hundreds upon hundreds of perfectly carved figures – the focus of the central doorway is the 'Beau Dieu', his hand raised in blessing, flanked by the apostles, and with all the severity of the Last Judgement ranged on the tympanum above his head. The left doorway is centred on St Firmin and the right on the Virgin Mary, both attended by a multitude of Biblical characters and saints. Higher up, the kings of Judah stand in line beneath a glorious rose window and above it all are two ornately decorated towers of oddly unequal height. With the recent removal of centuries of grime, all the figures have revealed traces of early polychrome tints – presumably every one was originally decked in multiple colours. A laser projection show held every evening in summer recreates these medieval colours, and for just 45 minutes, allows you to see how stunning this must have been.

The interior of the cathedral is rather a contrast, a place of space, height and light. On the floor is a marble 'labyrinth' – more a meditation spiral really, as there are no blind endings. The one contorted path eventually leads to the centre, where are engraved the names of the cathedral's original architects, Robert de Luzarches, Thomas de Cormont and his son Renaud. Carvings are here again, but less obvious. Look for the story of St Firmin on the south side of the chancel and that of John the Baptist on the north. Both date from later than the façade (around 1500) and their detail is masterful. The misericords of the choir stalls manifest yet more exceptional carving – everything from Old Testament heroes to characters from 16th century life in Amiens. Before leaving the cathedral you might like to visit the towers for

a fine view of the needle-like spire and of the whole town.

Walk down the steps from the cathedral and you will be in the Quartier St Leu. Once the town's slums and heart of Amiens' textile industry, it has metamorphosed to an attractive area of cobbled streets, subtly painted houses and burgeoning outdoor restaurants along the canal-like arms of the Somme. A lively scene by day or night, the Quartier St Leu is also home to a Puppet Theatre, for which Amiens has been famous for over 200 years. Walking from the cathedral in the opposite direction (Boulevard Victor Hugo, then Rue des Otages), you will soon reach the one-time home of Jules Verne who lived in the town from 1871 until his death in 1905. His prophetic assertion 'Amiens in 2000, an ideal town' has now been put to the test.

While in Amiens, there is just one more visit you must make – and if you arrive on a warm summer's afternoon you will see that everyone else has had the same thought. Les Hortillonages are a curiosity, an extensive area of private market gardens developed on the marshes of the Somme and now intersected by a network of narrow canals. Perhaps by reason of inducements from the Tourist Board, the vegetables have in many cases been replaced by riotous floral displays. This is Amiens' answer to Venice, and the traditional boats (*barques à cornet*) that take 12 passengers a time are vaguely gondola-like in shape, although usually (but not always!) propelled by an almost-silent engine rather than a pole. A French commentary is given by the 'gondolier', but if you do not understand a word of it, it does not matter – this is a pleasantly relaxing way to spend an hour or so at the heart of an otherwise busy town. Les

Hortillonages can be reached on foot from the cathedral in about 10 minutes – walk down to the riverside, cross the bridge and turn right on the path along the far bank which soon skirts the Parc St Pierre. At a road bridge, a fingerpost directs you to the embarkation point, about 220yd (200m) up the road. Rather more limited views of the gardens can be had by continuing along the towpath on foot.

THE SOMME AND ITS BATTLEFIELDS

Amiens has a lot more to offer, but it is time to catch up again with Henry who by now has arrived at the southeast of the city in the village of **Boves**. The story goes that here the weary troops found much wine, and had to be prevented by Henry from drinking the cellars dry. Boves is not much of a place today, and makes little of its one-time château, which was probably the scene of the drinking bout. If you want to try to find it, take the D116 to the south of the town, pass the cemetery and turn up the next field track on the left. Leave the car, continue on foot and look left – two gigantic pieces of broken wall can be seen towering above the trees. A path through the wood will take you to the site, but in its crumbling state, that château has to be dangerous.

From Boves, Henry turned southeast again and marched as rapidly as he could across the flat plains, thinking to gain the upper reaches of the Somme. Today the town of **Nesle** is ringed by trees and seems like an oasis in this flat wilderness, even if it is dominated by the steaming bulk of 'Amylum France'. It was to Nesle that Henry came and it appears that its residents were so keen to get rid of

the invaders that they suggested the fords at nearby **Voyennes** and **Béthencourt** might be passable. With the aid of a few doors and masonry taken from neighbouring villages this proved to be the case, and by nightfall on 19 October, the army had crossed the Somme. If you go along to the site now, you will find the river wandering gently enough through Voyennes and prettier-than-most-around-here Béthencourt – and you can almost imagine the one-time ford.

Back to 1415 again, and the French were not ignorant of Henry's movements – they were already camped in Péronne, just a few miles north of Béthencourt, when they heard news of the crossing. Next day they decided to offer a formal challenge to the English, and sent heralds to Henry telling him that they would engage him in battle some time in the next few days. Henry seems to have accepted this news as inevitable (Shakespeare has him say 'we are in God's hand, not in theirs'), and continued with his march north, passing near Péronne himself the next day. The French army had already left, but traces of their recent passing indicated that they were indeed a huge force.

From Béthencourt you too must head for Péronne – and texts tell us that Henry went via Athies, which should be no problem to you as it directly on the route. **Athies** again is a village of red-brick, its greatest asset being the 13th century carvings above the church door. **Péronne** surely warrants a longer pause. It is a town well-acquainted with conflict. In 1536, a violent assault by Spanish troops here was rebuffed by the strong leadership of one Marie Fouré, a townswoman whose statue now stands in the square. Again in 1870, the Prussians besieged the town for almost two weeks. At the forefront of the Battle of the Somme in 1916, the portals of Péronne's 14th century château now lead to the Historial de la Grande Guerre, a modernistic museum. High rooms of bright white concrete set the scene for the outbreak of war in 1914, and then take you through its various developments with maps, uniforms, weapons and other artefacts. Multiple small screens show archive footage for which English translation is available by means of handsets. There is no film of the worst day of the Battle of the Somme (1 July 1916, when 19,000 were killed), but the English version of surrounding events shown in the cinema (backed by Britten's War Requiem) is probably as near to the horror as you can get.

Outside its war museum Péronne does not obviously have great appeal, but it is in fact a town surrounded almost entirely by lakes. The Tourist Office can offer you a waterside route right around the town passing ramparts, market gardens and the old Porte de Bretagne, but if you just want a quick glimpse, turn right outside the château entrance down the Rue de la Résistance. In a few paces you reach the pleasant Étang du Cam and a glance behind will reveal that that museum is actually teetering on thin pillars rising from its waters. Not content with its lakes and river, Péronne is also situated on two canals – the Canal de la Somme and the Canal du Nord meet just to the south of the town. The site is just off the N17 (signed Port de Plaisance) – water-ways enthusiasts might care to take a look.

From Péronne Henry marched first towards Albert and then north to cross the Ancre at Miraumont. What atrocities this land would later know would have been impossible to contemplate. Stark cemeteries are now tucked in every corner. **Albert** itself houses the Musée des Abris, a long underground air-raid shelter accessed from the side of the church. Down below are many tableaux of trench scenes, lots of history (in both French and English), and a section simulating the sounds of battle in a trench. So much war debris remains in this area that an assortment of rusting (and otherwise) memorabilia are offered for sale at the end of the tunnel. Out in the light again, you can look up to the golden statue of the Virgin and Child on the top of the Basilica of Notre-Dame de Brébières. It was hit by a grenade in 1916, but though seriously listing, managed to hold on to its lofty perch throughout the war and was said to have been an inspiration to the soldiers.

After Albert, the road on to Miraumont is flanked by memorials. Keep south of the Ancre to visit **Thiepval** – its gaunt majestic arch, designed by Sir Edwin Lutyens, is visible on its hilltop for miles around. Thiepval was created to commemorate the 73,367 who have no known grave, and the enormity of that figure is given reality when you get right up to the memorial and see their names engraved on the white stones, and the occasional cross or poppy left by a grandchild. Most, of course, have no successors to pay them homage. More reality comes in the new exhibition centre giving access to the memorial, where hundreds of portrait photographs are displayed. From Thiepval it is a short trip on the D73 to the **Memorial Park at Beaumont-Hamel** – and on the way (just out of Thiepval) you pass the Ulster Tower, a replica of one near Belfast, a memorial to the casualties of the 36th Irish Division.

Beaumont-Hamel commemorates

the action seen by the Newfoundland Division on that dreadful first day of the Battle of the Somme. The memorial site comprises acres of trenches, watched over by a huge statue of a Caribou, the regiment's emblem figure. Almost all of the Newfoundlanders lost their lives and a visitor centre nearby tells the story of these brave men.

ON TO AGINCOURT

There are many other sites and memorials to explore in this otherwise pleasant rural corner of France – a route touring the battlefields (The Circuit of Remembrance) can be picked up from any Office de Tourisme in the region, as can a free and very informative Visitor's Guide. But we must step back in time once more, and follow Henry's armies west through the farming villages of **Forceville** and **Acheux** and across the rolling agricultural plains to the larger settlement of **Beauquesne**. At this point in the journey the French were shadowing Henry's forces just a few kilometres to the east. Neither army apparently knew the exact whereabouts of the other, which given the bare nature of the land today seems surprising.

At Beauquesne, Henry turned north to cross the Authie near **Doullens** – a place to pause again. The town's most prominent building, the brick-built *beffroi* with its slightly-out-of-line grey topping dates from 1363, and so should have witnessed the army's passing. The older-looking ramparts of the Citadelle, to the south-west of the town, in fact originate only from the 16th century. Doullens also boasts a couple of interesting churches and a rather grand-looking museum housing the paintings and the Egyptian

memorabilia of a well-travelled one-time citizen (Lombart) – but the place you should really get a look at is the town hall. In a room on its first floor one of the most important documents of World War I was signed. Giving unique control of the French and British forces to General Foch, it led directly to the conclusion of hostilities. The room with its original table can be visited when the building is open and has been invested with wall paintings and a stained-glass window commemorating its finest hour.

Beyond Doullens Henry continued north to cross the Grouche near Lucheux – and by now you like Henry will be desperate to get on to the north and the point of all this. But **Lucheux** is a curiosity, a little medieval village not even getting a mention in the guidebooks. Its belfry-entrance-gate was erected in the 13th century (Joan of Arc passed through soon after Henry) while its twin-towered château and keep date from a hundred years or so earlier. There are finely arcaded defensive walls and a Grande Salle with ornately sculptured windows. The church dates from 1140 and the carved capitals amusingly depict the sinful temptations of the monks of the day. All can be visited in the summer on guided tours, for which an English translation is provided.

And now it really is time to travel – through **Bonnières** and brick-built **Frévent** (both rebuilt after wartime), across the Canche and north to **Blangy** on the Ternoise. And all the while the French were there to the east, following along the right bank of the river. On the morning of 24 October a few of their number were sighted near Anvin – and later in the day, when Henry's army reached the summit of the long hill out of Blangy they could see the whole French force directly ahead coming out of the valley between Azincourt and Ruisseauville to confront them. Battle was inevitable. Henry and his army spent the night in the village of **Maisoncelle** and it is recorded that he attended three Masses in the church there. His troops also made their confessions – the French army outnumbered them by at least three to one. All night it rained heavily and in the morning the opponents faced each other for four long wet hours before either side made a move. Success that day was due to the superiority of the English longbows, to the boggy saturated ground in which the heavily armoured French were unable to manoeuvre, and to the inspirational and conscientious leadership of Henry V.

If you travel north on the D104 from Blangy, you will actually cross the battlefield (passing a monument on the left hand side) before arriving at the village of **Azincourt** where the excellent museum is situated. There are likely to be a lot more English cars than French outside! But the whole story is told dispassionately in both French and English, using videos and animated characters. Children particularly will enjoy the chance to feel the weight of real armour, pick up a sword or two, swing a club, look through the narrow slit of a visor or test the power needed to fire a long-bow – a surprising insight into the strength needed for medieval war-fare. Leaving the exhibitions you are offered a map to tour the battle site itself, a two and a half mile (4km) ride identifying the positions of the armies on that day. There has been no ex-ploitation of the site, which makes it all seem more real – and no doubt the locals are used to English cars crawling along the lanes, their occupants emerging from time to time to drool over the bare turnip fields!

In this quiet corner of rural France this journey must end. From Agincourt Henry marched on to Calais, crossing the Channel on 16 November and being received by cheering crowds in London a week later, when he went to give thanks in Westminster Abbey. Chroniclers report that the king himself appeared particularly sober on that day – Agincourt, though a great victory, was only a small step in his ambition for France.

OFFICES DE TOURISME

Comité Départemental de Tourisme de Seine-Maritime
6, rue Couronné BP 60
76420 BIHOREL
☎ 02.35.12.10.10

Fécamp
113, Rue Alexandre le Grand
76403 FÉCAMP
☎02.35.28.51.01

Eu
41, Rue Bignon
76200 EU
☎ 02.35.86.04.68

Le Tréport
Quai Sadi Carnot
76470 LE TRÉPORT
☎ 02.35.86.05.69

Amiens
6 bis, Rue Dusevel
80000 AMIENS Cedex 1
☎ 03.22.71.60.50

Albert
9, Rue Gambetta
80300 ALBERT PAYS DE
L'ANCRE
☎ 03.22.75.16.42

Doullens
Le Beffroi BP 69
80600 DOULLENS
☎ 03.22.32.54.52

Hesdin
Hôtel de Ville
Place d'Armes
62140 HESDIN
☎ 03.21.86.19.19

PLACES OF INTEREST

Le Havre

Musée du Prieuré de Graville
Open every day except Monday and
Tuesday, 10am-12noon, 2-6pm.

**Musée des Beaux Arts
Andre-Malraux**
Open daily except Tuesdays,
11am-6pm (7pm at weekends).

Étretat

Le Clos Lupin
Open April to September, daily
10am-7pm; October to March Fri,
Sat and Sun only, 11am-5pm.

Fécamp

Palais Bénédictine
Open July and August 10am-6pm;
outside those months opening
times vary slightly, but 2 hours
lunch-break (10-12) is taken and
closure may be as early as 5pm.

Eu

**Château d'Eu
– Musée Louis – Philippe**
Open mid-March to 1st Sunday in
November. No times given.

**Collégiale de Notre-Dame et St
Laurent-O'Toole**
Open daily 9am-12noon (Sundays
10.30am-12.30pm), 2-5pm.

Gallo-Roman site of Bois l'Abbé
Guided tours Tuesdays at 2pm,
mid-June to mid-September.

St Valéry-sur-Somme

Ecomusée Picarvie
Open April to November 2-7pm.

Picquigny

Château et Collégiale
July and August, guided visits
Tuesday to Saturday at 11am, 3
and 4.30pm; Sundays and holidays
3 and 4.30pm. Some visits at other
times – ask at OT in the main street
(☎ 05.22.51.46.85).

Samara
Open mid-March to mid-November.
Hours vary slightly (later closing
time in June, July and August), but
approx. 9.30am-6.30pm every day,
with no break for lunch.

Amiens

Towers of the Cathedral
Guided tours every day (ask at OT
for times). Unaccompanied visiting
2-6pm every day in July and August;
Saturday and Sunday, April, May,
June, September.

Théâtre de Marionnettes
Performances every evening
except Monday at 6pm. Free entry
to exhibition every day except
Monday 10am-12noon, 2-6pm.

La Maison de Jules Verne – 2, rue Charles-Dubois
Open Tuesday-Friday 9am-12noon, 2-6pm; weekends 2-6pm.

Les Hortillonages
Frequent excursions every afternoon (from 2pm), April to October.

Péronne

Historial de la Grande Guerre
Open every day from 10am-6pm, with the exception of Mondays from October to March. Closed mid-December – mid-January.

Albert

Musée des Abris (also called Musée Somme 1916)
Open February – mid-December 9.30am-12noon, 2-6pm. No lunchbreak taken from June to September.

Doullens

Citadelle
Guided visits at 3 and 4.30pm every day in July and August, weekends and holidays in May, June and September.
No times are given for the Musée Lombart (closed for renovation at the time of writing).

Lucheux
Guided visits to the sites at 2.30 and 4.30 pm every day in July and August starting from the Tourist Office (by the belfry entrance).

Azincourt
Centre Historique Médiéval
Open April to October, 10am-6pm every day; November to March, 10am-5pm every day except Tuesday.

LOCAL HIGHLIGHTS

Best Walks

· Footpaths along the cliffs of the Alabaster Coast. The coastal path, the GR21, follows it all the way and is clearly marked with bars of white on red. But each Tourist Office also has its own leaflet of circular walks, and these too are well marked on the ground and easy to follow.

· Walks in the Forest of Eu. A circuit of 7 miles (11km) starting from Incheville is marked in yellow – for this and for other details of the forest paths, ask OT at Eu.

· The pleasant undulating countryside just west of Azincourt is crossed by several rivers and has adopted the name 'Pays des 7 Vallées'. There are many well-marked walking routes here (and cycle and VTT routes) – ask OT at Hesdin for maps and details.

For Cyclists

· There is a marked cycle route on minor roads all the way along the Alabaster Coast from Le Tréport to Le Havre, a distance of 107 miles (172km). The route (in 4 stages) is obtainable from any of the local Tourist Offices.

- For circular routes in the same area, get hold of the *Topoguide Vélo* produced by the Comité Départemental du Tourisme in Seine-Maritime (try www.seine-maritime-tourisme.com) – 34 routes, good maps, and some of it even translated into English.

- The departments of Somme and Nord/Pas de Calais both have many marked cycle routes. Ask at any Office de Tourisme for details.

Watersports

- Swimming, sailing, sea-canoeing and fishing are on offer all along the Alabaster Coast. Get the booklet *Loisirs de Plein-Air* from the Comité Départemental du Tourisme of Seine-Maritime (see above) for all details.

- Canoe-kayak enthusiasts will find themselves well catered for at Amiens (descent of the Somme, etc.) and on the bay of the Somme at St Valéry. The '7 Valleys' region has a base at Beaurainville, just downstream from Hesdin.

- Those wanting to do it in style can hire a *pénichette* (barge) at Cappy (SE of Albert) to explore the Canal of the Somme from Péronne to St Valéry. (Locaboat Holidays, ☎ 03.22.76.12.12).

For the Palate

- Picardy specialities include chocolate wafers and heavy, rich macaroons from Amiens. On the savoury side, try Paté de Canard en Croûte – a sort of pastry-enclosed duck paté.

- The Somme is famous for its eels, caught in special traps. Try smoked eel washed down with the local Colvert Beer, brewed in Péronne.

- Sea-food is plentiful in the restaurants of the Alabaster Coast – or you can buy it freshly caught at any time (depending on tides) at the quayside in le Tréport.

And the most memorable

- Étretat on a sunny day – brilliant white cliffs, arches and needles rising from a turquoise sea.

- The stunning spectacle of Amiens cathedral at night. The recreated colours truly feel medieval.

- Seeing a bent and wizened old lady searching intently among the names on Thiepval Memorial. Was one of the 73,000 her father?

- Reaching the top of the hill after Blangy and seeing the vast French army emerging from the valley ahead. Well, with a little imagination – at any rate it would have been memorable for Henry!

The route taken by Henry V's army has been derived from many sources, in particular *Henry V and the invasion of France* by Ernest Fraser Jacob and *The Island Race* by Winston Churchill.

6· Ambling through the Ardennes

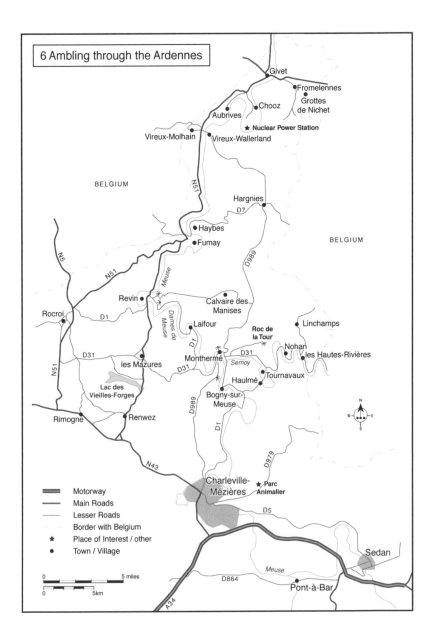

The Ardennes? Surely that is a range of hills in Belgium? Well, yes and no. Certainly the region known as the Ardennes is largely in Belgium, but it also extends south into France and farther east into Luxembourg. And in France it is more of a plateau than a range of hills. Through that plateau the meandering rivers (the Meuse and the Semoy) have cut deep wide gorges – and so it seems that crossing the Ardennes you are either following a river valley or forever going up and down hill. There are summits to be sure, but on the whole they are insignificant. Far more impressive are the many rocky viewpoints along the rims of gorges from where you can look down on the towns and villages below and marvel at the tortuous course of the rivers as they make their way north to the sea.

This strange landscape was determined more than 500 million years ago, at the time when the great Hercynian fold brought to the surface a mixture of hard rocks such as schist and soft calcareous rocks. Over the millenia the rivers have skirted the former and cut deeply into the latter to achieve their present day convolutions – and it all makes for some breathtaking scenery, which is made all the more attractive by a dense covering of deciduous forest. Visit this region in autumn for an unforgettable display of russet colours – but remember also that the Ardennes is traditional hunting country, and on autumn weekends, certain sections of the forest may be closed while *la chasse* is in progress.

The part of the Ardennes that lies in France has some of the finest scenery but being pushed against the border, and not being on the way to anywhere, it is little visited even by the most committed of Francophiles. So what can be found in the Ardennes that might lure you to divert to this neglected corner? First of all the outstanding landscape – this is wonderful country for walkers, nature lovers and anyone who enjoys a fine panorama. The woodland of the high plateau, the viewpoints into the gorges and the more open countryside in the north are all served by a well-laid out network of paths, all splendidly signed. Any bookshop or tourist information can offer you a plethora of guides and leaflets from which to choose walking routes – and the railway that follows the course of the Meuse can be a bonus for getting you home at the end of a day on the heights.

The forests are also home to a rich variety of wildlife. Deer are plentiful and the wild boar, their numbers once decimated by hunters, are well on the increase again. The boar are both shy and nocturnal and in fact you are more likely to meet them on your plate than in the forest, but if you are desperate for an encounter you can always try the local ploy of putting out potatoes and waiting!

The Ardennes is genuinely a natural paradise, but it has a lot more to offer. The towns here are confined to the valleys and are often, like Revin and Monthermé, wrapped around by coils of the winding rivers. Industry has left its mark and passed on. Slate was quarried from the 13th century until about 30 years ago and the story of that particular enterprise is recalled in the museums at Fumay and

Rimogne. Forestry still thrives and the first-class Museum of the Forest at Renwez will give you some insight.

Being a border country, this land has seen plenty of conflict – the town of Rocroi is a star-shaped citadel characteristically fashioned by Vauban, the Château of Sedan is said to be the largest such in all Europe, and at the tip of a long finger of French territory extending into Belgium, the 16th century Château of Charlemont at Givet solidly crowns its spur above the river. Finally, the Ardennes is a land of fairytales and magic. Forests are the breeding grounds of legends, and folklore has survived here into the 21st century with tales of Pie-pie Vanvan who will lead you astray in the forest and the *nutons* who will come out to mend your shoes at night. Every craggy outcrop of the landscape is invested with a story – the Roc de la Tour is the ruins of a château built by the devil in one night; the crests of the Dames de Meuse are ladies turned to stone for being unfaithful to their betrothed; Mont Malgré Tout (in spite of everything mountain) is where a man once built his house in a night.

The most celebrated legend (with perhaps a little truth in it) is that of the Quatre Fils d'Aymon. In a tale of murder and intrigue, these four brothers fell foul of the Emperor Charlemagne who pursued them through the forest for many years, but (largely thanks to their powerful horse Bayart) was unable to catch them. An episode in their story is now told every hour beneath a clockface at the heart of Charleville-Mézières, the regional capital – a city that is well-worth investigating on several other scores, including the fine Florentine architecture of its Place Ducale and the pleasant riverside nearby.

So where should you start in exploring the Ardennes? First of all, it is important to realise that the *département* that includes the French part of the Ardennes massif has been named *Ardenne* – so if you get tourist literature on this area it will include not only the wooded plateau in the north of this *département*, but also the gentler countryside to the south of Charleville-Mézières. This, too, is well off the beaten track and worthy of your attention, but for the moment, we are going to confine ourselves to the more dramatic north where Monthermé, at the confluence of the Meuse and the Semoy, makes a good base.

MONTHERMÉ TO CHARLEVILLE

Monthermé, like the other settlements of this region, is not instantly the most inviting of towns, although its grey slate-roofed buildings are very much brightened by the addition of bright red geraniums in summertime. Monthermé's appeal is all about location. The Meuse, already a meandering river, doubles back on itself as it reaches Monthermé, curving with admirable geometric precision around the old town quarter with the medieval fortified church of St Leger rising at its heart. All this is best seen not from the riverside, but from the steep hillside above, where two splendid rocky balconies give aerial views. Both are reached from the D989 to Hargnies (turn left at the top of the hill, just out of Monthermé).

The first viewpoint, the **Roche à Sept Heures**, is an easily-accessed outcrop of rock beside the road. The view of Monthermé from here is good but a little oblique. If you then continue to the end of the road and walk on for about 15 minutes (keep to the widest track – although they all lead to the same place) you arrive at one of the most stunning viewpoints in all the Ardennes, the **Longue Roche**. Far below you the river makes a great sweep around the town, people walk the streets like so many ants and vehicles in miniature cross the river bridge – the scene is somehow reminiscent of a model railway setting. And yet the railway that is ever present beside the Meuse does not pass through the town of Monthermé.

The railway station serving Monthermé is actually just upriver at **Bogny-sur-Meuse** – and industrial Bogny, formed from the amalgamation of three riverside villages, is just about as visually appealing as its name might suggest. Indeed, Bogny is best approached from the air – or at least from the high rocky peaks of the Quatre Fils d'Aymon that dominate the town. Up at those heights,

paths roam through a landscape of beech and gorse, silver birch and heather, and the particular trail that comes over from Monthermé offers some splendid views, even if the going does get a bit rough in the vicinity of the rocks themselves. From here the descending path into Bogny passes a huge grey statue of the Aymon brothers and their remarkable horse, stonily gazing over yet another twist in the river.

The scenic forest path from Monthermé to Bogny is part of a designated circular walk (the *Boucle des Sept Roches* – see Best Walks) that continues by crossing the river bridge at Bogny and then offers two options for the ascent on the other side – steep or very steep. The latter ascends a sheer cliff-face and is marked 'dangerous' – forget it. But the softer option (which is still not so soft) leads up through a very interesting part of town. As the road begins to climb, you can see on the left a stone arch-

Les Quatre Fils d'Aymon (The Four Sons of Aymon)

The tale of the four sons of Aymon is one of many legends and romances that developed around the inspirational figure of Charlemagne. Charlemagne of course was real enough – great warrior, statesman, patron of the arts and intellectual, he became both King of the Franks and, in 800AD, Holy Roman Emperor.

The story here has several different versions, but it seems that Aymon, Duke of Dordogne, had a brother who was killed by the supporters of Charlemagne. Either before or after this incident, depending on which side ayou believe, a son (or nephew) of Charlemagne was himself killed by the Aymon family. The four sons of Aymon (Renaut, Allart, Guichart and Richart) were well implicated in all this, and Charlemagne's troops pursued them into the Ardennes forest. Thanks to the speed and agility of their horse Bayart (whom they all rode together) they escaped and secretly built a castle on the hillside above the Meuse. There they were found, and the forest chase continued for another three years (thus engendering many more tales) until they finally escaped to their father's fortress in the south – and more adventures.

way engraved with the words 'Joseph et Maré'. This was once an entrance to the *Grosse Boutique*, an iron bolt-making factory that in the latter half of the 19th century employed over 1000 people. A complete community in itself, it offered housing, shops where workers could spend the tokens that were part of their wages, and a crèche for the young children. The *Grosse Boutique* was demolished in 1970 and a secondary school now stands on its site. Some of the workers' accommodation can be seen farther up the hill where two long lines of tall terraced houses face each other across an impossible slope. This is the Cité de l'Echelle (Ladder Estate), and it looks like an overgrown version of a northern mill town.

Unfortunately (for those following the walking trail) your way lies up it. Just to the right at the top of the Echelle, a broad track leads to another viewpoint, the **Roche Fendue de l'Hermitage**, from which the whole of Bogny can be surveyed. It is as well to spend a few moments on the seat here because the path gets even more precipitous later as it climbs through the woods. Eventually it descends to yet another viewpoint, the **Roche aux Sept Villages** from which, as you might expect, seven villages can be seen – along with the nearby profile of the ridge with the rocks of the Quatre Fils d'Aymon. From the Sept Villages viewpoint traffic descends the gentle slope into Monthermé, but those on foot face a track that is scarcely less dramatic than its earlier part to arrive back in the old town.

The *Boucle des Sept Roches* is a ramble that gives a very good feel for this part of the world – viewpoints, industry, forest and river – but it should definitely be reserved for seasoned walkers! Everyone else will be pleased to know that both the viewpoints are accessible by road (the Hermitage from the Rue Bernisseaux leaving the end of the river bridge at Bogny, and the Roche aux Sept Villages from the D989 to Charleville-Mézières), and that there is a car park just below the statue of the Quatre Fils d'Aymon in Bogny.

Whether or not you took the *Sept Roches* walking route, you are going to need to return to Bogny because there is more on offer. The place to find out about the Grosse Boutique is the Musée de la Métallurgie, which is interwoven with the Office de Tourisme beside the D1 on the right bank of the river. The whole story is told with the aid of working machines and videos, and there are other strange relics of the age of metal such as the forge and its dog-powered wheel.

Elsewhere in Bogny (back towards Monthermé), the Centre d'Exposition des Mineraux et Fossiles des Ardennes displays rocks, minerals and fossils from the Ardennes on its ground floor, and goes world-wide in the space above. And finally, there's Woinic. This 50-tonne metal wild boar with a 2-tonne tail lives in a shed at the back of an otherwise rather run-down metal-worker's yard not far from the station (that is, Bogny station, not Monthermé). It took 12,000 working hours to fashion this gigantic beast, which is hardly recompensed by the modest entry fee.

On the way back to Monthermé you might like to pause at the **Abbaye de Laval-Dieu**, not far from the scarcely noticeable confluence of the Semoy and the Meuse, just on the outskirts of the town. The Premonstratensians established the abbey here in the 12th century, and the square tower dates from that time –

although the brick façade is very much later. When the abbey church is open in summertime you can admire the interior woodwork and 18th century mural.

CHARLEVILLE-MÉZIÈRES

At this point it is time to take a look at the main town of the Ardennes, **Charleville-Mézières**, sitting on a particularly contorted section of the Meuse to the south of Monthermé. The southern part of the town, in and around its own loop of the river, is Mézières, the administrative capital, while Charleville to the north is the commercial town, and the more interesting to visit. Its centrepiece is the 17th century Place Ducale, designed by Clément Métézeau, younger brother of Louis, who designed the Place des Vosges in Paris. The two have similarities. The vast cobbled Place Ducale with central fountain is flanked by fine Louis XIII buildings with slated mansard roofs (sloping on sides and ends) and arcaded galleries at street level. If you want peace to admire it all, come on a Sunday, when the town is empty and you can park in the square itself. For more action, lively markets are held here on Tuesdays, Thursdays and Saturdays.

Charleville-Mézières' idiosyncratic claim to fame lies in the world of puppets. Originally the home of an amateur puppet theatre, since 1961 it has been staging the three-yearly *Festival Mondial des Théatres de Marionettes*, a 10-day bonanza in which puppeteers from all over the globe descend on the town (next to be held in September 2006). Courses in the making and performing of puppets are held at the Institute International, to be found in the Place

Winston Churchill, immediately to the south of the Place Ducale – and alongside is the famous Horloge du Grande Marionettiste. On the hour, every hour, this giant automaton pulls the strings for an episode in the saga of the Quatre Fils d'Aymon, and the whole story is re-run on a Saturday evening.

If you want to see the workings of the Horloge, then all is revealed in the adjacent Musée des Ardennes, which has a window looking into the back of the marionette theatre, and a miniature model for closer examination. The museum actually extends over several buildings with connecting ramps and bridges, and has so much in the way of content (Roman coins and jewellery, weapons, pottery, paintings, sculptures, regional life and industry) that you will have to keep moving to get round it all in an afternoon. Incongruously scattered throughout the academia are items of the most off-beat modern art.

A couple of minutes walk from the Place Ducale (down the Rue du Moulin), the other main scene of interest in Charleville is the riverside, where an over-elegant 17th century watermill now houses the Musée Arthur Rimbaud. Rimbaud, one of France's greatest poets, was born in Charleville in 1854. He apparently did not think much of the place, and spent much of his youth trying to run away from home. Nevertheless the town pays him homage with this collection of photographs, sketches, mementoes and writings, and does not shirk from detailing some of the more bohemian aspects of his lifestyle. And there is a little modern art thrown in, of course (look out for Ophelia in the water below)

Beside the Musée Rimbaud, a footbridge crosses the river to a tree-clad mound grandly known as Mont Olympe. A municipal campsite enjoys a privileged position beside the river here, and farther on, a fine swimming complex overlooks a marina offering overnight stays for the many pleasure boats plying the river. This is the place to stroll, jog and feed the ducks – and you can add extra exertion by climbing to the flat grassy summit of Mont Olympe.

That is probably all you want to see of urban Charleville, but on its outskirts is a splendid animal park that seems to draw half the families in the Ardennes on a Sunday afternoon. The **Parc Animalier de St Laurent** (off the D979 to the east of town) is a vast woodland where native species roam in semi-freedom. This is the ideal place to see wild boar – the ones here run up to see if you are bringing food (although notices warn against it). Whatever their diet, they look well and they must be considerably better off than their cousins in the wild at the mercy of all those avid hunters. Other animals that can be seen from the paths include wild goats, mouflon and majestically-antlered roe-deer that can only be glimpsed among the trees.

THE RIVER MEUSE

At last its time to explore the Meuse heading north from Monthermé – and you might seriously think boat! It makes a peaceful alternative to the busy riverside road, and the hire-base at Pont-à-Bar (near Sedan) tells you that you can easily make Givet and back in a week. So by road (D1), river, or even the railway that follows them both, the first spectacle north of Monthermé is the **Dames de Meuse**, three densely forested incredibly steep

hills with their feet on the riverside. The story goes that these were the three daughters of a local lord, betrothed to the sons of the lord of Hierges in the north. When the youths all went off on crusade, the girls found themselves other gallant company – and on the day on which Jerusalem was taken, were punished for their infidelity by being transformed into these impressive slopes. From Laifour it is possible to climb to the summit of the Dames des Meuse, an ascent of 853ft (260m). There are superb viewpoints and information panels up there, but reaching them is hard work!

Next downstream, **Revin** is a town completely entangled with the loops of this capricious river. Every road seems to lead to the riverside – which, in spite of there being a lot of it, is not always attractive. But the port area beside the Parc Rocheteau is pleasant, as is the riverside campsite, and the Quai Edgar Quintet has some fine old buildings, including the 16th century half-timbered Maison Espagnole. The latter is now home to the Office de Tourisme, but its upper floors are given over to a museum of local life, with a reconstruction of a home of the 1920s, and an exhibition of the town's former iron-work industries. Revin is in some ways a grey town (and in the past must have been even greyer) but it appears to have inspired Georges Sand, who came here in 1869 hoping to recover from a bout of 'writer's block'. Just a few days after arriving she was writing her new novel *Malgré–Tout* – named after the particularly steep crest that overlooks Revin from the north.

Mont Malgré-Tout itself refers to the tale of a man called Merquin who, being legally forbidden to build a house on this wild mountain, got all his friends together, and 'in spite of everything', built the house in one night. Of course the mountain has splendid views, and you can reach it by turning off the D1 in Revin, just on the town side of the railway.

The Résistance in the Ardennes

The road that climbs Mont Malgré-Trout passes the Monument des Manises, dedicated to the local *Résistance* groups who met clandestinely in this forest. There is a fine view of Revin from here, and an even better one from the (signed) Belvédère a little higher up the road. If you then continue for about 3 miles (5 km), you reach the Calvaire des Manises, one of the most moving memorials to the *Résistance* in all France. A collection of bare mass-graves, each topped only by a cross, lies at the end of a path deep in the forest. A board tells the terrible story and the tricolor flutters damply nearby.

Back down below, river, road and railway continue north to their next destination, Fumay. **Fumay** was a slate town – in fact perhaps the most important slate town of the region, on account of the quality and range of colours of its product. The last slate quarry closed in 1971. Now Fumay has an exceptionally pleasant riverside area to attract visitors and passing boats – and just off the quay, in the former buildings of a Carmelite convent, a little slate museum in the basement of the Tourist Office. Here a few important relics of the mining

days have been preserved and the details are filled in with a video. If all this inspires you to find out more about the slate industry, OT has the folder *Sentiers et Circuits en Ardennes* (French only) to guide you and there is even a collection of walking routes that explore the nearby quarries (*Au fil de l'Ardoise*). But for the moment, go on to the adjacent town of Haybes, renowned for its 'pink' slate – and as you cross the river bridge, look back for one of the finest views of the quays of Fumay, backed by the town, the yellow-stoned church and the arc of hills behind.

Haybes is less industrial than Fumay, and again boasts a charming riverside. A road ascending from the top of the town takes you out to the viewpoint of la Platale, overlooking Fumay – although perhaps better views are to be had from the high ridge on the other side of the river, accessible by footpath from Fumay itself (ask at OT for the circuit entitled *Le Chemin des Eaux*).

On north goes the river, and its valley begins to open up after Haybes. The village of **Vireux-Wallerand** makes a photogenic scene on the far bank – that is, if you can ignore the two enormous white plumes of steam in the background. But the **Chooz** nuclear power station prefers not to be ignored. France derives 77 per cent of its power in this way and establishments like Chooz are always falling over them-selves to build good public relations. Chooz is reached via a turning about 3 miles (5km) farther up the main road, has a picnic table by its main gate (who would want to dine here?) and goes on to welcome visitors warmly with a recently-updated first-class exhibition centre (on the left near the gate – signs are not obvious). All the facts are here and there are lots of working models; button-pressing youngsters are well-catered for, and you will leave with an armful of literature. And while you are here, look out for the wall sculpture *Ex-Nihilo Nihil* by local artist Georges-Armand Favaudon. You can see more of his work on the riverside at Aubrives (just past the power station) – and, back in Fumay, there is a recently-commissioned fresco by the same sculptor entitled *Les Scailleux* (The Slate-Quarriers)

At this point let us forget Chooz and return to Vireux Wallerand to look on the opposite side of the road. The twin village of **Vireux-Molhain** has a *Collégiale* church with a 9th century crypt, ancient tombstones and some fine statues, including a 16th century entombment. Overlooking the road and river, Mont Vireux is the site of a Gallo-Roman fort, with information boards explaining the details. And the next village, **Hierges**, is one of the prettiest around with an interesting ruined castle.

The Belgian border is now closing in on the river, and all that lies ahead is **Givet**. The *Trois Fontaines* quarry on the approach to the town yields a blue limestone known as *Bleu de Givet*, in the past used for house building, for baptismal fonts and even for certain bridges in Paris. Beyond the quarry the massive bulk of the Fort de Charlemont hugs the hill. The original was built in 1555 by the Holy Roman Emperor Charles V, who needed to defend his territory from the French. A century later it came into French hands and the fort and its counterpart on the opposite bank (Fort du Mont d'Haurs) were together part of Louis XIV's scheme to fortify this northern border and protect the river crossing at Givet.

Needless to say, both forts owe their present design to the redoubtable Vauban.

Beyond the fort, the riverside takes on a more light-hearted air with pavement cafés spilling along the quayside. The 14th century round Tour Victoire, once a castle keep, is now a summertime exhibition centre and nearby the Centre Européen des Metiers d'Art displays some fascinating craft-work along with the finest gastronomic products of the Ardennes. At the port, a cheerful *bateau mouche* loads visitors for the trip upriver to Dinant. The river bridge itself groans – or rather vibrates – under the weight of traffic, but nevertheless offers the best views of the town, with fort, tower and church in the frame. The church too was designed by Vauban, and its bizarre tower provoked Victor Hugo to comment

'the architect took a priest's or a barrister's hat, on this he placed an upturned salad bowl, on the base of the salad bowl he stood a sugar basin, on the sugar basin a bottle, on the bottle a sun partly inserted into the neck and finally on the sun he fixed a cock on a spit'.

From Givet it is just a few kilometres to Fromelennes and the **Grottes de Nichet**, pushed up against the Belgian border to the east (off the road to Beauraing). The caves are worth visiting for their setting alone – on a hillside looking over Givet and the Meuse valley there are woodland paths, picnic tables under the oaks and beeches, a children's play area, a fitness course and a little snack restaurant. The underground chambers themselves are quite extensive – and although their limestone formations are not the most remarkable, there is no doubt that these caverns are the home of the *nutons* and you will get a warm welcome.

THE RIVER SEMOY

Having explored the Meuse, we should now turn east along the Semoy, which, if anything, is even more convoluted – although its wildest swings are over the border in Belgium (where it is known as the Semois). Leaving Monthermé on the D31, you could start the day by forgetting the river and taking the left turn (on the outskirts of town) signed to the **Roc de la Tour**. The road climbs through a beautiful wooded valley and past a picnic site that is the starting point of several inviting short walks. At the top of the hill a track on the right leads to the Roc de la Tour, a strange ensemble of quartzite blocks perched on the rim of the densely wooded valley of the Semoy. The huge boulders look as if they had just tumbled down from somewhere, and the tale that these are the ruins of a château the devil attempted to build in one night (for a soul, of course) does not seem that fanciful. Suffice it to say he did not finish his task (the cock crowed early) and he knocked the lot down in a fit of pique. Whatever you make of it all, this is a beautiful spot enhanced by the colours of the surrounding beech trees and the views are magnificent.

Back down below, the D31 follows the curves and twists of the Semoy. After a few kilometres you could leave it to turn down to **Tournavaux**, a pretty village in a plain of water meadows. From here a pleasantly wooded path follows the river upstream to **Haulmé**, which with its neat buildings of grey slate, must be one of the most attractive villages around. A campsite enjoys a rather favoured setting on the far bank, and in its other role as a leisure activities centre, offers canoe and mountain bike hire.

From Haulmé, those on foot can return to Tournavaux on a track across the meadows or extend the riverside walk and return from Thilay across the hill. Eventually though, it is back to the D31, and beyond Thilay the road again picks up the river. After the bridge at **Nohan**, there are some interesting ironwork sculptures along the bank. The last town in France is **les Hautes-Rivières**, a sprawling rather anonymous place, but the starting point of many good walks and cycle rides. The viewpoint at the Croix de l'Enfer is easily accessible on foot (ask OT for directions) and anyone wanting to get even farther off-the-beaten-track can take the D13 up the valley to Linchamps (and beyond).

OF WOOD AND SLATE – WEST OF MONTHERMÉ

Back to Monthermé again now, and on another day you could explore the area to the west of the river valleys. Leaving Monthermé on the Charleville-Mézières road and then taking the D31 to les Mazures and turning south, you will cross the end of a long stretch of water, the **Lac des Vieilles Forges**. The lake was created as part of a hydro-electricity scheme, and has been endowed with a splendid leisure area – a long sandy beach (supervised swimming in summer), a sailing school and an excellent campsite tucked discretely into the woodland behind. In summer a *friterie* serves impromptu meals under the trees on the shore.

There are many walking trails in the forest around Les Vieilles Forges, and the campsite also operates a shuttle service to the nearby **Forest Museum at Renwez**. Opened in the summer of 2003, the museum has instant appeal as a forest peopled with little log men, all going about their business in various tableaux. But this is not just fairyland – rather it deals thoroughly with every aspect of the forest, its plants and animals, the people who worked here over the centuries and the uses of the wood. In addition to the woodland circuits there are exhibition rooms, videos and a puppet theatre – and English visitors are catered for with their own headphone translation.

If from Renwez you go south to Lonny and then turn up the N43, you will soon reach **Rimogne** – a town remarkable for nothing other than its Maison de l'Ardoise, a slate museum on the site of a former mine. The interior here is in semi-darkness, thus recreating the feel of the mine (it always looks closed from the outside!). Rooms of original working machinery, equipment and film footage lead you on to peer at last into the draughty cold dampness of the original shaft.

Just to the north of Rimogne, **Rocroi** is a border town whose original fortifications were the French King Henry II's answer to the stronghold of Charlemont. It was later improved by Vauban, whose star-shaped ramparts still shelter the town. And Rocroi needs shelter, because it sits at the heart of a bare plateau and in winter, nowhere could be more bleak. But in summertime Rocroi is pleasant enough, and visitors can appreciate its substantial double-layered ramparts from an orientation table near the main gate (Porte Royale). Starting from the same place, a footpath fo-

llows the walls on the north side. The other attraction is the tiny informal little Musée de la Bataille de Rocroy. In 1643 the plateau outside the town was the scene of a battle in which the invading Spanish forces were soundly trounced. A video details the strategic movements of both sides ('baddies' and 'goodies' are helpfully colour-coded), after which you are free to admire the splendid tableaux of lead soldiers in various stages of combat and a few other memorabilia.

SEDAN

If military history such as that at Rocroi interests you, there is one more visit you must make. Some 9 miles (15km) to the east of Charleville-Mézières, the fortress at **Sedan** is acclaimed as the largest in Europe. Built by the powerful local family of la Marck (who became the Princes of Sedan) in the 15th century, the huge brooding château is as imposing today as it ever was. It is said to comprise seven floors – although once you start to wander along corridors, up and down ladders and flights of stairs, through tunnels, out into the open, down into dungeons and even into the 17th-century world of the adjoining Palais des Princes, you soon lose track of what level you are on or even where you are at all. Odd corners are filled with lifelike wax-work figures and one section houses the town museum with everything from military paintings to archaeological specimens. An audioguide in English is available to take you through it all.

Spread out beneath the great château, the town of Sedan is far less impressive. Once the centre of a thriving cloth industry, the tall houses that were the workshops are falling into disrepair, giving the town a neglected feel. Only **Dijonval**, a classically-styled 18th century building that once housed a high-class woollen cloth factory is in a state to be admired. One workshop that is still operating is that of **Point de Sedan** – a firm who from a cold half-empty room with 19th century equipment, manufacture carpets to grace the floors of some of Europe's most prestigious households. Both Dijonval and the Point de Sedan are signed from the roundabout outside the Palais des Princes – and it is well worthwhile tracking them down!

With Sedan and its industries this tour of the Ardennes must end. There is more of course, if you have time and want to travel farther. To the west are the fortified churches of the Thiérache, to the south the lakes and forests, and to the east the fortifications along the border. The *département* of Ardenne has designed six themed itineraries (you have already met the one relating to the legends of the Meuse and the Semoy) to cover all its diversity – and each of them very firmly belongs to 'undiscovered France'.

OFFICES DE TOURISME

Monthermé
Place Jean-Baptiste Clément
08800 MONTHERMÉ
☎ 03.24.54.46.73

Fumay
Rue Martin Coupaye
08170 FUMAY
☎ 03.24.41.10.25

Charleville-Mézières
4, Place Ducale BP 229
08102 CHARLEVILLE-MÉZIÈRES
☎ 03.24.55.69.90

Givet
10, quai des Fours
08600 GIVET
☎ 03.24.42.03.54

Revin
Maison Espagnole
2, rue Victor Hugo BP 63
08500 REVIN
☎ 03.24.40.19.59

PLACES OF INTEREST

Bogny-sur-Meuse

Musée de la Métallurgie
Open July and August every day 10am-12noon, 2-6pm; June and September 2-6pm.

Centre d'Exposition des Minéraux et Fossiles des Ardennes
Open mid-June to August, every day except Monday and weekends in September 2-6pm.

Woinic
Ask for viewing times at the Office
de Tourisme.

Charleville-Mézières

Horloge du Grande Marinettiste
Episodes are shown every hour
from 9am-10pm and the 12 scenes
are shown in sequence at 9.15pm
on Saturdays.

Musée de l'Ardenne
Open Tuesday to Saturday throughout the year, 10am-12noon, 2-6pm.

Musée Rimbaud
Hours as for Musée de l'Ardenne.

Parc Animalier de St Laurent
No charge.
Open April to September, 2-6pm
weekdays, 1.30-7pm weekends
and public holidays; October to
March 1.30pm-5.30pm daily.
Closed Thursdays all year round.

Pont-à-Bar

Ardennes Nautisme
(boats from 2 – 10 berths for hire).
Information on:
www.ardennes-nautisme.com
or ☎ 03.24.27.05.15

Revin

**Maison Espagnole –
Musée du Vieux Revin**
Open May to September – Monday
to Friday 1.30-6.30pm; weekends
and public holidays 2-7pm.

Fumay

Musée de l'Ardoise
Open April to September 10am-
12noon, 2-6pm; October to March
1.30-5.30pm.

Chooz

**Nuclear Power Station – Centre
d'Information du Public**
Open Monday to Friday 8.30-
12noon, 1.30-5pm; Saturdays and
Sundays 2-6pm.

Vireux-Molhain

Collégiale Saint-Ermel
Guided visits May to August,
10am-12noon, 2-6pm.

Givet

Fort de Charlemont
Open every day in July and August
10am-12noon, 2-6pm.

**Centre Européen des Métiers
d'Art**
Open every day 10am-12noon,
2.30-6pm. Closed Sunday and
Monday mornings.

Fromelennes

Grottes de Nichet
Open June to August 10-11.30am,
1.30-6pm; April, May and
September 2-5.30pm.

Renwez

Musée de la Forêt
Open July and August
9am-7pm; rest of year 9am-12noon,
2-5 (or 6) pm.

Rimogne

Maison de l'Ardoise
Open 10am-12noon, 1-6pm every
day except Mondays all year round
and Sundays also from October to
March.

Rocroi

Musée de la Bataille de Rocroy
Open May to mid-October 10am-
12noon, 2-6pm; mid-October to
April 10am-12noon, 2-5pm.

Sedan

Musée du Château Fort de Sedan
Open July and August 10am-6pm;
weekends, public holidays and
French school holidays, 10am-
12noon, 1.30-5pm; September to
June 1.30-4.30pm every day
except Monday.

Point de Sedan
Open every day except Sunday
8am-12noon, 2-6pm. No charge.

LOCAL HIGHLIGHTS

Best Walks

There is no shortage of magnificent walks, but note that between October
and January, there will be hunting in the forest every Sunday and on
certain other days. Sections being used for *la chasse* are always marked
on the roadside, but even so, all footpaths are said to be dangerous on
these days.

- The energetic *Boucle des Sept Roches* encircling the Meuse between
  Monthermé and Bogny. Either Tourist Office can supply you with a good
  map (on the leaflet *Sentiers de Labeur et Légends – Bogny-sur-Meuse*),
  and the paths are very well waymarked (white on red bars) all the way
  round. The total distance is 6.2miles (10km) – but allow 4 hours.

- The hike along the Dames de Meuse from Laifour to Anchamps. This will
  take around 3 hours on waymarked paths with an easy return by train.
  An excellent walk, but beware – the initial ascent from Laifour is one of
  the steepest around (and that is saying something here!). OT again can
  offer maps.

- The much less demanding circuit in the valley of the Semoy between
  Tournavaux and Haulmé can be found in the free publication *Promenades
  et Randonnées en Vallée de Semoy* (ask at OT Monthermé or Bogny).

- And there are many, many more routes, all well signed. Serious walkers
  should get hold of the Topoguide *Les Ardennes à Pied* – it is in French,
  but the maps and routes are first-class. Just watch the contour-crossing!

For cyclists

Mountain bikers are very well catered for in the Ardennes – but note that
the circuits are only officially open from 1 April to 30 September, on
account of *la chasse*.

- The Valleys of the Meuse and Semoy offer 22 circuits of varying difficulty,
  with many connecting links – over 250 miles (400km) of trails in all. The
  routes are very well waymarked, with signposts at all track junctions.

Free maps are available at all Offices de Tourisme, who will also have details of bike hire.

- There is a designated cycle and roller-blade track alongside the Meuse between Charleville-Mézières and Nouzonville.

- The 'Six Themed Itineraries' of the Ardennes are said to be suitable for both cars and bikes. But treat this with caution – certainly the one that covers the Meuse valley uses the main road, which bears heavy traffic.

Watersports

- The best centre is the Lac des Vieilles Forges, south-west of Revin. This vast lake sports a supervised swimming beach, a sailing centre and an excellent campsite.

- River cruises start from Givet, Monthermé, and Charleville-Mézières. Canoes etc. can be hired at Haybes, Charleville-Mézières, Haulmé and the Lac des Vieilles Forges.

- From mid-June to early September, electric river boats (complete with canopy) can be hired at Haybes, Fumay, Vireux-Wallerand and Givet.

For the Palate

- Jambon sec des Ardennes is traditionally prepared ham from 'free-range' pigs – and it is different!

- Every charcuterie exhibits a slippery spiralling pyramid of Boudin Blanc – a white sausage of pork with no additives (although just occasionally you may find it with onion). A lot better than it looks!

- And for desert you must have Tarte au Sucre, a pastry case with a very sweet filling of eggs and sugar and a caramelised topping.

And the most memorable

- Standing at the Roc de la Tour early on a sunny autumn morning – the beech trees were glowing amber, and the winding valley below was filled with puffy white mist.

- Asking to take a photograph of *boudin blanc* and finding that somehow we were being proudly served with a whole kilogram. It seemed churlish to stop the transaction.

- Walking down to the Calvaire des Manises on 11 November, a damp cheerless morning. Being a public holiday, *la chasse* was in progress, and streetwise wild boar are said to seek sanctuary round the graves. There were none. But in the background the shots rang out – and that forest holds its memories well.

7· Two parks and a city – the heart of Lorraine

Not many people would think of going on holiday to Lorraine. In our minds it belongs to a rather anonymous and uninteresting corner of northern France, a borderland ravaged by countless conflicts and saddened by memories of its role in that 'war to end all wars' less than a century ago. We know of no great wines from that part of the world and maybe we assume, on the strength of its several large cities, that its commercial importance must be industrial rather than agricultural. Nothing could be farther from the truth!

The French have dubbed Lorraine the *poumon vert* – the green lung. There are miles of open space here, rolling farmland, fruit-growing plains, forests and more water in the form of rivers, canals and lakes than in almost any comparable area of France. The cities of Nancy, Metz, Toul and Épinal are especially rich in architecture and heritage. And as for the wine – well, there is plenty, but it will not be easy to find outside this area, so coming here is an opportunity to try something different. The excellent Côtes de Toul has recently been given AOC status, but there are also the vineyards of the Côtes de Moselle and the much tinier Côtes de Meuse. The *gris* wines from the Côtes de Toul and from the area around Vic-sur-Seille are extra-special and yet almost unknown.

The other myth that needs to be dispelled is that Lorraine can readily be combined with Alsace. The two are kept apart by the high peaks of the Vosges, and although their names are often spoken together, their cultures are as different as their geography.

Lorraine is by far the bigger region – and, of course, it is much too large to be taken in on one single visit. But Lorraine has a – literally – golden heart, the city of Nancy. A medieval fortified town, it was later lavishly embellished and gilded by a one-time king of Poland and after all that, in the 19th century it became the birthplace of the Art Nouveau movement who liberally endowed its ancient streets with the most bizarre of buildings. Nancy is a strange and fascinating mixture, a wonderful place to saunter and browse, with new curiosities around every corner. And think – it is only 310 miles (500km) from Calais, just a four and a half hour drive and well within reach for a 'long-weekend'.

If you have more time to spend, things get even better. Nancy can absorb as much time as you would like, but when you feel in need of some fresh country air, it is right there on the doorstep. On either side of the city, huge swathes of the countryside have been accorded the status of Natural Regional Park, thus ensuring the preservation of the traditions and heritage of old Lorraine in these areas. There are eco-museums dealing with rural life, salt extraction and fish-farming in the 'lake-district', with plenty of discovery walks around lakes and salt-marshes. Old villages like Hattonchâtel in the west and Marsal in the east are well worth a wander – and there are surprises like the well off-the-beaten-track little village of Vic-sur-Seille, birthplace of the painter Georges de la Tour, where the main street now sports a first-class art gallery.

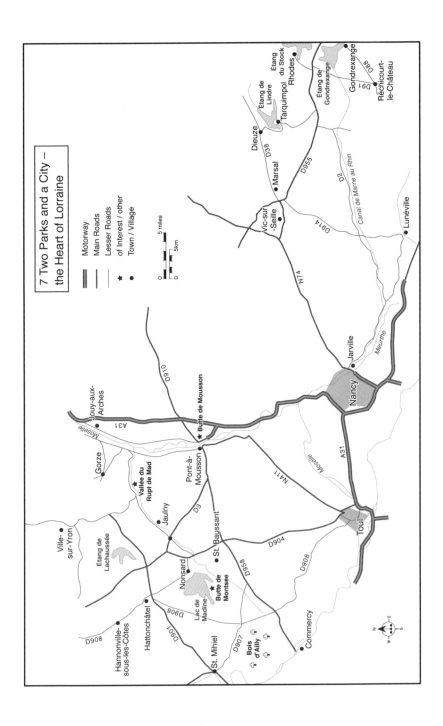

7 Two Parks and a City –
the Heart of Lorraine

Motorway
Main Roads
Lesser Roads
★ of Interest / other
● Town / Village

If war history is your interest, Lorraine, sandwiched between France and Germany, has seen it all as it passed from hand to acquisitive hand. In the Franco-Prussian war it was fought over and finally partitioned, the western part going to Germany. But the most evident scars are those of World War I, long winding trenches preserved because too much blood was spilled here for it ever to be forgotten, and woodland has kindly grown to cover the wounds. There are some excellent walks in the very lovely forests near St Mihiel, and yet it is a place of sadness.

NANCY

But let us now get back to a city that is far from sad, Nancy. Everything here exudes enthusiasm and good-living – and most of that is down to its time in the hands of Stanislas, ex-king of Poland. However we will begin the story at the beginning. Nancy grew up as a settlement at a crossing place on the River Meurthe and in the 11th century, one Gérard d'Alsace built his fortress here, so becoming the first Duke of Lorraine. The town received new fortifications in the 14th century, but of these only the distinctive Porte de la Craffe remains today. In the 15th century, Charles the Bold, Duke of Burgundy, held territory on either side of Lorraine (Burgundy and Flanders) and thought it might be convenient if that too came into his hands. Charles walked into Lorraine, but René II, Duke at that time, rapidly returned to muster forces in Nancy. Charles laid siege, but was killed in the ensuing battle. Lorraine remained a Duchy and its capital was Nancy. An interesting point is that René's emblem in battle was the double-barred Cross of

Lorraine, which in 1940 was adopted as the emblem of the Free French Forces.

In the 16th century Nancy prospered and Duke Charles III built a new town south of the old. Nancy became a religious centre at this time, with many monasteries being built. Lorraine survived as an independent Duchy until the aftermath of the Polish Wars of Succession when in 1738 Duke Francois III exchanged his territory for the Duchy of Tuscany. Louis XV of France suddenly found himself in possession of a very unstable Lorraine – and sealed Nancy's future fame for good when he decided to invite his father-in-law Stanislas, the ex-king of Poland, to take over the reins of the Duchy during his lifetime (after which it was to revert to France).

Stanislas certainly left his mark on Nancy, and at the end of the 19th century another group of people did the same. At that time new industry had been attracted to the city, and with it a group of tradesmen and intellectuals who were seeking new art forms based on nature and oriental themes. Under the leadership of Emile Gallé, an artisan well known for his ceramics, glassware and furniture, they formed the *Alliance Provinciale des Industries d'Art* – and thus was born the École de Nancy and the movement known as Art Nouveau. Scattered throughout Nancy are striking examples of its architecture – shops, banks, cafés, commercial establishments and the houses of its protagonists, all of them bizarre to 21st century eyes.

Seeking out the Art Nouveau in Nancy is time-consuming and very great fun, but let us start this exploration of the city at the heart of things (follow signs to the *Coeur de la Ville*) with the **Place Stanislas**. The square itself is now a pedestrian area, but there are plenty of well-signed car parks nearby. Place Stanislas is in fact a rectangle, flanked on all sides by matching elegant buildings in pale-coloured stone – the Hôtel de Ville, the Opera House, the Grand Hotel, the Fine Arts museum. All are three-tiered except for those on the north side, which were once taverns and now are shops and restaurants. Wrought ironwork is everywhere, garnished with lanterns dangling from the beaks of golden cockerels and further embellished with gilded crowns, leaves and fleurs-de-lys. Ornate fountains representing Neptune and his wife Amphritite play in the corners of the square – once wine, not water ran in their depths, and Amphritite apparently very closely resembles Madame de Boufflers, a favourite of Stanislas. All is presided over by the rather rotund figure of Stanislas himself, on a central plinth – a spot which, before the revolution, was occupied by a statue of Louis XV.

Before going any farther you would do well to pop into the Office de Tourisme at the south-west corner of the square to collect their leaflet, in English, entitled *Discovery Nancy*, because you are going to need it very soon (ask for the *Museums* leaflet and the *Art Nouveau* leaflet at the same time – they probably will not be on display). From the Tourist Office you might first head right, past the Opera House, to take a look at the formal tree-shaded **Place d'Alliance**. Its central fountain is modelled on Bernini's 'Fountain of the Rivers' in Rome. The houses around the square are as elegant inside as they are out with spiralling stone staircases and wrought iron balustrades by Jean Lamour. To catch a glimpse of one, look through the windows of No. 8 (do not worry – it is suggested by the Tourist Board), which was once the residence of Emmanuel Héré.

Back to Place Stanislas now and north through the grandiose Arc de Triomphe, again modelled on a Roman version (the Septimus Severus arch), and crowned with an assortment of gods and just a little more gold. Beyond the Arc de Triomphe

Stanislas, ex-King of Poland

Stanislas was already in his 60s when appointed to rule the Duchy of Lorraine, a committed gourmet, very much on the portly side and renowned for his love of the high-life – Louis XV could hardly have expected the long-term arrangement that this turned out to be. Stanislas ruled over Lorraine until his 90th year (when unfortunately his dressing gown caught fire).

During all that time, though he mostly lived in Lunéville, a large proportion of his creative energy was devoted to Nancy. Stanislas employed the finest artisans of the day, the architect Emmanuel Héré and the wrought-ironworker Jean Lamour to create a grand central square that is almost eastern-European in character and stunning even to this day. The magnificent Place Stanislas (originally known as the Place Royale) and the nearby Place de la Carrière and Place d'Alliance are together recognised by UNESCO as a World Heritage site.

and through well-gilded gates sits the **Place de la Carrière**. Quiet and imposing, the Palais du Gouverneur stands at its far end. Backing all this on the right hand side are the gardens of the Parc de la Pepinière, again a creation of Stanislas, but by turning left instead here, you can pass through another arch into the old town.

On the left is now the Church of St Epvre, built in the 1860s with contributions from all over Europe (most notably from the Austrian Emperor), while on the right, the Grande Rue takes you past the severe walls of the ancient but restored **Palais Ducal**, topped by gargoyles and enlivened by the elaborate equestrian statue of Duke Antoine over the main doorway. The Palais Ducal now houses the Musée de Lorraine, so extensive that it spills over into the one-time Convent des Cordeliers farther up the street. Beyond it all is the fine 14th century Porte de la Craffe.

At this point you can head straight back for lunch (Place Stanislas and surrounding streets offer some surprisingly good deals) or decide to do a little exploring with the aid of the leaflet you picked up earlier. Down the Rue du Haut Bourgeois you will find the Hôtel Ferraris and beyond, the Hôtel des Loups, both classic examples of Old Town architecture, but the real gem is the Hôtel d'Haussonville (carved stone balconies, wrought-ironwork, fountain and sculptured doorway) which is well-concealed in the Rue Trouillet – if you can find your way to the Place de l'Arsenal, you are almost there.

All that was just a whistle-stop tour of old town and Royal Nancy, but on the way you passed two truly excellent museums, each of which is worthy of a return. On the west side of Place Stanislas, the **Musée des Beaux Arts** was originally the old medical school. It now houses a fine collection of paintings from the 14th century right up to the present day. Rubens, Delacroix, Monet, Dufy, Picasso and more are here and there are some interesting paintings by local artists such as Emile Friant, whose human faces have an almost photographic quality. Scattered around are many sculptures, some of which bear names as famous as Rodin and Maillol. Do not make the mistake of leaving without going into the basement, whose entrance is separate. Remnants of the old town's 15th century fortifications have been uncovered here, and beyond them is the magnificent Daum collection of glassware and crystal. A video shows how this local firm became the producer of some of the most prized examples of Art Nouveau.

The other unforgettable museum is the **Musée Historique Lorrain**, housed in the Palais Ducal. This one is something of a mixture – everything, just everything relating to the region from the dawn of time to 21st century is here and not always presented in chronological order. There is little English text (although a translation is offered), and after a while you become dazed with the different themes as room succeeds room. The second part of the museum in the Convent des Cordeliers is more straightforward, basically recreating peasant homes in different parts of Lorraine over the centuries.

At last it is time to get to grips with the Art Nouveau, for which you will need to put in a little legwork and refer to the discovery leaflet again. At the Porte de la Craffe, you were quite near the **Maison Weissenberger** (down the Rue de la Craffe, turn right and it is on the corner of Boulevard Charles V) so that is a good place to begin. Weissenberger was one of the architects of the Nancy School and this is the house he built for himself. It is not one of the most outlandish, but it has a distinctive heavily patterned door and several stained glass windows. From the Maison Weissenberger you can cross behind the memorial arch, walk down the Rue Désilles and turn right to reach the **Maison Huot** (it is wrongly positioned on the discovery map). Maison Huot is so strange it belongs to the darker side of fairy tales – if you came across it deep in a forest of fir trees you probably would not want to hang around very long. But there it sits, beside the railway line in Nancy. The heavy asymmetrical architecture seems vaguely menacing, the windows are all different shapes and the builder seems to have had a particular aversion to right angles.

From the Maison Huot it is a fairly long walk along the Quai Claude le Lorrain to the Rue Raymond Poincaré, one of the town's main thoroughfares – but you can take heart because there is a reward coming soon. Cross the latter road, turn left for a few yards, then right and left immediately and you have arrived at the **Brasserie Excelsior**, a classic example of Art Nouveau well preserved to this day. Through the windows you can see banks of shiny seating, floral lamp-shades, sculpted ceilings and dapper waiters in black and white gliding silently between the tables. Lunch here is not cheap, but neither is it as expensive as you might have expected and the experience has to be worth it. Well fortified, you can continue with the tour!

A little farther along the same road is the **Chambre de Commerce et d'Industrie** where the artists Gruber and Majorelle have combined to produce a galaxy of interesting windows and a door bristling with blue spikes of wrought-iron. From here it is a short stroll down the Rue Chanzy to take a look at the **BNP bank** on the corner. Its wrought-iron work, like that of the Chamber of Commerce, is the work of Louis Majorelle. Yet more remarkable is the bank of **Credit Lyonnais** (farther along the Rue St Jean), where business is transacted beneath a high-arched ceiling of Gruber's most splendid stained glass. A little farther along the same road you can leave the art nouveau and step back into the 18th century with the **Cathedral**. Its most notable feature is a much more conventional wrought-iron work, this time by Jean Lamour.

Now it must surely be time to visit the museum of the École de Nancy. There is no designated parking for cars and it is a fairly long walk, so before you set out, just check it is not a Monday or a Tuesday (when it is closed). On the way to the museum you could take a look at the Art Nouveau buildings in the Rue de la Commanderie (Maison Georges Biet, the chemist's shop opposite and others) and the parallel Avenue Foch – and do not omit the short diversion to the **Villa Majorelle**, which surprisingly is well signed (the others are not). This, the one-time home of the wrought-iron-worker, was actually designed by Henri Sauvage, an architect from Paris. He seems to have gone out of his way to add touches of the bizarre with chimney pots like flowers and a strange Japanese-style balcony hanging off one side. Sadly the place, now privately owned, is in need of some repair.

The **Musée de l'École de Nancy** is outstanding, amazing from the moment you step in the door. One of the highlights must be the dining room created by the cabinet-maker Eugène Vallin for Charles Masson – leather-panelled walls, heavy curving furniture, bronze-and-glass light and painted ceiling. Another is surely the 'Dawn and Dusk' bed, with its overtones of human mortality, by Emile Gallé. Then there is the surreal 'Hand with seaweed and shells', the ceramic bathroom, lots of stained glass and even an example of everyman's, mass-produced, Art Nouveau furniture. All this work is now utterly priceless, as you will gather from the number of watchful attendants. Outside in the attractive garden, the building known as the aquarium has no fish but was built for meditation – and you may want to do that!

There are many other fine examples of Art Nouveau in Nancy. One you should drive to is the **Maison Bergeret**, situated in the district of the university and now used for their offices. Another rich hunting ground is the suburb of Saurupt (you could catch the tram to this one). Designed in 1901, the **Parc de Saurupt** was intended to contain more than 80 houses in Art Nouveau style. Only a few were ever built, but they are still there today. And if you want to go on, the *Circuits Art Nouveau* leaflet from the Tourist Office suggests 67 sites scattered across the city that are worth visiting.

Aside from all that, what other interest is offered in Nancy? Well, there are other museums – a Telephone museum, an Iron History museum in the suburb of Jarville and a first-class Aquarium (far more remarkable for its wealth of marine life than its stuffed animals upstairs). To the east of Place Stanislas, the **Port St Catherine** is a long waterfront on the Canal de la Marne au Rhin, with both pleasure and commercial basins, and a trip boat that offers cruises. Recent additions are the Japanese-style water-gardens alongside – a tribute to Nancy's twinning arrangement with the town of Kanazawa.

In the suburbs to the south of Nancy, the mainly 16th century **Château de Fléville** was once owned by the Dukes of Lorraine and among other rooms you can visit the sumptuous bedroom where Stanislas once laid his head. And for more outdoor activities, to the west of the town there is the **Parc de la Haye**, where, on what was clearly once a military base, there are now picnic areas, forest walks, children's playgrounds, an arboreal adventure park, VTT trails with cycle hire and the necessary eating facilities to provide for the visitors.

There is one other gem in Nancy (on the outskirts really, but accessible by tram) – the **Jardin Botanique du Montet**. Not merely gardens but also a research and conservation project belonging to the university, the splendid collections (roses, medicinal plants, alpine plants, arboreteum etc.) are spread across the slopes of a pleasant valley. All is free, but for a small consideration you also have access to five huge greenhouses housing plants from every continent.

NORTH OF NANCY

Nancy is surely one of Europe's greatest cities, but sooner or later you are going to want to get out to the surrounding countryside. The best place to start is at **Pont-à-Mousson**, about 18.5 miles (30km) north of Nancy and on the Moselle rather than the Meurthe (the Meurthe actually joins the Moselle just beyond

Nancy). Pont-à-Mousson is centred on the Place Duroc, a huge cobbled square surrounded by arcaded buildings dating from the 16th century. One of these is the *Maison des Sept Péchés Capitaux* – the House of the Seven Deadly Sins – and these are graphically depicted in the carvings on its façade. Pont-à-Mousson is the headquarters of the Natural Regional Park and the well-stocked Office de Tourisme in the cobbled Place Duroc can offer all the information you might want on the area.

For a brief look at the town itself, you could begin by taking the Rue St Laurent (across the square from the Tourist Office) to the Église St Laurent. Inside the church there is a very fine 16th century polychrome triptych portraying a number of Biblical scenes and on the opposite side, a statue of Christ carrying his cross by the local sculptor Ligier Richier.

Ligier Richier

Lorraine is very proud of Ligier Richier, born around 1500, and there is a story-cum-legend of him being 'spotted' in his youth by Michaelangelo. That one almost certainly is not true, but there is no doubt that he went to Rome for a number of years to learn his craft. His works are to be found in many churches and cathedrals all over Lorraine and a 'Ligier Richier Route' is offered for those wanting to track down the best of it.

From the Église St Laurent it is only a short stride to the riverside where there is a fine view of the grey Abbaye des Prémontrés on the opposite bank. This vast building is now used as a cultural centre but can be visited to get an idea of the impressive cloisters (now glassed in) and fine architecture including three elegant staircases (spiral, square and oval). Before returning you might also call in at the Église St Martin at the end of the bridge, where the sculpture of the Entombment is said to be the inspiration for Ligier Richier's later work on the same subject (now in St Mihiel). Pont-à-Mousson was once a university town, and its museum (behind the Office de Tourisme) reflects its scholarly roots – along with a curious collection of objects in papier maché.

For a splendid view over Pont-à-Mousson, the Moselle Valley and beyond, leave Pont-à-Mousson on the D910 (direction Saarbrücken) and, a couple of kilometres out of town, take a left, then right turn. The road leads up to the village of Mousson, above which the grassy **Butte de Mousson** is topped by the remains of a medieval château and a very modern chapel.

Back in the valley again now, and it is time to take a look at the western part of the Parc Naturel Régional de Lorraine. From Pont-à-Mousson, let us set out on the N57, heading north along the right bank of the Moselle. The first surprise comes at Jouey-aux-Arches, where enormous stone arches span the road, dwarfing everything around. They are the impressive remains of a Roman aqueduct, built to carry water from springs near the village of Gorze to the town of Metz, some 22 km. away. If you cross the river bridge here, more of the aqueduct can be seen on the other side –

less well preserved, its ivy-clad bulk breaks off abruptly in mid-air.

Gorze itself (take the D6 on the right) is a rather curious and fascinating place. In 749 the Bishop of Metz founded a Benedictine abbey here, an abbey that, under his direction, became instrumental in the development of Gregorian Chant, and grew throughout Europe to become the centre of an independent domain known as the *Terre de Gorze*. Nothing remains of this abbey today, but the 12th century St Etienne's church in the middle of the village is said to be the largest Gothic building in Lorraine. Nearby, fine Baroque architecture can be seen in the Abbey Palace built by Philippe Eberhardt de Loewenstein around 1700 – go through the archway to admire the staircase, fountain and chapel. The story of Gorze, its Roman aqueduct, Abbey and Gregorian Chant, is told in the little Musée de Gorze near the church. Its video (French only), shown in a stone cellar, may have added interest on a hot summer's day! Gorze is the starting point for several walks in the surrounding forest, which has its fair share of legends.

From Gorze you could return to the riverside road and then turn right on the D952, which runs through the **Valley of the Rupt de Mad** – a pleasant drive and one where you can admire the strange fortifications of the village churches in these parts. At Arnaville, Bayonville, Vandelainville, Onville and Waville, the church towers are solid structures, sometimes with evident machicolations from which weapons could be fired. In medieval times the whole village would have been fortified, with houses grouped in a horseshoe around the church and only one narrow point of access. From Waville the valley road continues past Jaulny, an ancient village with a hilltop château and large *abreuvoir* (water trough) in the village square. Beyond lies Thiaucourt-Regniéville, with its memories of war – huge American and German cemeteries and an army uniform museum. The valley continues through the farming community of Buillonville to Essey, a village also on the D904. Here you could turn north and then west through the village of Nonsard. It sits on the shores of the **Lac de Madine**, a large lake created in the 1970s as a water supply for Metz, and now boasting a huge leisure complex with sandy swimming beach, watersports and campsites. An entrance fee is charged for all this and unfortunately there are no views of the lake from the road otherwise.

For the moment, continue north to **Hattonchâtel**, a village that certainly is not short of a panorama or two of its own. Hattonchâtel sits atop a ridge sloping down to the Moselle valley across the vineyards of the Côtes de Meuse. It owes its present day existence to the benevolence of an American multi-millionaire by the name of Miss Bell Skinner, who, seeing it in its post-Great-War state of devastation, nevertheless became quite taken with the place and decided to rebuild it. The château she retained for herself – and it must be every would-be-château-owners dream, a symphony of patterned stonework, archways, turrets and red-tiled roofs, all set on the edge of a village green and with views to the distant blue horizon.

In addition to the château, Bell Skinner also provided the village with a water supply and restored several buildings in the main street, including the Mairie and the 13th century Église St Maur. The chapel beside the latter contains a polychrome stone altarpiece dating from 1523, said to be the work of Ligier Richier, while the Mairie itself now houses a museum devoted to the work of Louise Cottin, a celebrated artist of last century who gave a hundred or so of her works (oil on canvas) to this village. There are also frequent exhibitions of modern works here.

North and east of Hattonchâtel, the land descends to the flat, humid, fruit-growing Plain of Woëvre (the woëvre is a local legend, a mythical aquatic serpent). A few kilometres to the north on these plains is **Hannonville-sous-les-Côtes**, very much a working village, where one of the old terraced cottages has been restored as the Maison des Arts et Traditions Rurales. This one-time winegrower's home had but two downstairs rooms, a living room and a bedroom. Both have been imaginatively reconstructed, as have the outbuildings (with the addition of a resident pig) and cottage garden with medicinal plants. The upstairs houses changing exhibitions. This is a decidedly off-the-beaten-track museum with not even the facility of its own parking space, but its high quality cries out for more custom.

At this point you are a long way from Nancy and perhaps enough is enough, but if you enjoyed the eco-museum, you might also want to take in the eco-village of **Ville-sur-Yron** (around 12.5 miles (20km) away to the north-east, near Mars-la-Tour). Between this village and neighbouring Ville-les-Près, a short circular walk has been endowed with a dozen information panels pointing out features from the past still visible today – church, mill, *lavoir*, bridge, workers houses and the rest.

WEST OF NANCY

And that should be quite sufficient for one day! Yet another could be spent exploring the area to the west, which during the First World War was part of the *Saillant de St Mihiel*, an important bulge in the front line of fighting. Head first for the Lac de Madine and the hill known as the **Butte de Montsec** on its southern shores. Here the Americans have erected a memorial to commemorate the events of September 1918, when they eventually managed to break through the St Mihiel bulge with the taking of many prisoners. The memorial is a rather grand white circular colonnade with a relief map of the combat area at its centre – and a splendid view across the Lac de Madine to the plains of Woëvre beyond.

To both east and west of the Butte de Montsec there are remains of wartime trenches. The 'undiscovered' scene is to the east, near the village of **St Baussant**, where a map by the church shows a short route that can be followed. On tracks deep in the forest, rather weary information panels tell the story, and through the undergrowth you can scramble in and out of trenches belonging to both sides – surprisingly close to each other. There is a haunting quality about this lonely little-visited site.

In the opposite direction, the D907 takes you along the northern edge of the **Bois d'Ailly** in the Forest of Apremont. Here the relics of conflict are well preserved – German brick-lined trenches and the French ones, once lined by wood, now caving in; a German hospital, a French command post (take a torch for this one), an underground shelter. A series of car parks give access to the sites, but an even better insight is gained from embarking on an 11 mile (18km) waymarked trail (details from the Tourist Office at St Mihiel). It includes the village of Marbotte where the church was once used as a chapel of rest and the high altar, pietà and stained glass windows are dedicated to the 30,000 who fell near this place. A small museum here displays collections of arms, equipment, documents and anything else relating to those terrible days.

Having come so far west, it would be a pity not to call into **St Mihiel** itself. The town owes its existence to the establishment of a Benedictine abbey here in the 9th century. Totally rebuilt at the end of the 17th century, the graceful abbey buildings and abbey church of St Michel still dominate the centre of the town. The abbey library, added in the 18th century, today exhibits a collection of ancient manuscripts and books so rare that they may only be viewed through a large window. Visitors are consoled for this with exhibitions on specific themes – and the lavishly decorated hall in which they are held is worth a visit in itself. A museum of Religious Art in Lorraine is contained within the same building.

St Mihiel is renowned as the birthplace of Ligier Richier and the abbey church contains one of his works entitled *La Pâmoison de la Vierge* (translated as the *Virgin Swooning*). An even finer example is to be found in the church of St Etienne (driving from the library, turn left at the traffic lights, left immediately on Rue des Abasseaux and left again after the cemetery). *Le Sépulcre* (*The Entombment*) consists of 13 life-size pale stone figures and seems strangely ill at ease in a church with modern stained glass windows and plastic seating.

TO THE EAST OF NANCY

Your final excursion from Nancy must be to the eastern sector of the Natural Regional Park, where interest centres on the valley of the River Seille with its salt marshes and on the 'lake district' beyond. Leaving Nancy on the D74 (signed to Saarbrücken) you are very soon in pleasant undulating agricultural countryside that feels miles from anywhere. After 12.5 miles (20km) or so, keep right for Sarrebourg and take the first on the left – and by rights you should be in the middle of nowhere. But in fact you are in **Vic-sur-Seille**, and its ancient village street immediately greets you with the name of its most famous son, the artist Georges de la Tour.

Georges de la Tour

The son of a baker, he was born in Vic-sur-Seille in 1593 and somehow nurturing his talents, rose to a position at the court of Louis XIII. In 2003 la Tour was honoured is his home town with the opening of a very stylish modern art gallery. Its most prized possession is his darkly realistic painting of John the Baptist in the Desert.

The art gallery at Vic-sur-Seille really should not be missed, but there is more to the village. Its early prosperity came from the finding of salt in the river bed – and (with the aid of a leaflet picked up in the art gallery) you can explore an unexpected collection of fine old buildings including the Hôtel de Monnaie (1456) and the

17th-century Carmelite Convent. On the outskirts of town stands a gateway flanked by two towers, all that remains of the 15th-century palace of the Bishops of Metz. But with all this, Vic's greatest claim to fame is still its vineyard, which has seen recent regeneration, with the production of delicious *gris* wine.

Vic-sur-Seille is a fascinating place and not far away to the east is another. **Marsal** likewise owes its existence to the salt of the Seille valley, and was a major centre of production well before a turn of fate transformed it to a military fortress. These early fortifications were restored and renewed by Vauban in the 17th century. Today the *Porte de France* gateway to the village houses an exhibition of the old saltworkings and you can walk out on a raised footpath into the marshes to see the thriving colony of salt-loving plants. The village map identifies some of the old military buildings and there is a pleasant path around the now worn-down ramparts looking out over the boggy landscape.

On now to the lake country. Most lakes in France are formed from dammed rivers and very few are natural, but the lakes here fall somewhere between the two. In fact they were dug out in the Middle Ages to drain the very marshy terrain and then stocked with fish by Cistercian monks who were forbidden to eat meat. Today they are still important producers of carp, pike and perch. South of Dieuze (again a salt town) you reach the first lake, the **Étang de Lindre**. A path runs around its shores from Lindre Basse to the little village of **Tarquimpol**, where there is an eco-

museum telling the story of the area and offering high-powered binoculars for distant views of the wildlife on the water.

Beyond the Étang de Lindre there are others. The Étang du Stock is large enough to boast a trip boat starting from the harbour at **Rhodes**, from where pedalos may also be hired. Just down the road from here, the **Parc Animalier de Ste Croix** is home to more than 50 European species, roaming in semi-freedom in the forest beside the lakes.

The last place on this lakeland tour is **Gondrexange**, south of Rhodes (get there via Réchicourt–le-Château – you cannot turn off the N4) and situated on a lake of its own. Gondrexange also sees the meeting of two canals, the Canal de la Marne au Rhin and the Canal des Houillères de la Sarre, and it is very pleasant on a summer's evening to walk out on the track between the lake and the Marne/Rhine Canal to reach the meeting point – water, water everywhere! Naturally Gondrexange has its own little beach and a pleasant campsite alongside.

The return to Nancy can be made via **Lunéville** – but sadly the château that was once Stanislas' home suffered a terrible fire at the beginning of 2003, and at present there are no plans for its re-opening. The parkland though is still accessible to everyone and there are other attractions in Lunéville, including a bike-cum-motor-cycle museum with some unusual exhibits. Off-the-beaten-track devotees will quite possibly prefer to return along the D2, a lovely rural road crossing and re-crossing the Canal de la Marne au Rhin, with plenty of nautical activity in view all the way.

OFFICES DE TOURISME

Nancy
Place Stanislas BP 810
54011 NANCY Cedex
☎ 03.83.35.22.41

Pont-à-Mousson
52, Place Duroc
54700 PONT- À -MOUSSON
☎ 03.83.81.06.90

Dieuze
Place de l'Hôtel de Ville
57260 DIEUZE
☎ 03.87.86.06.07

**Parc Naturel Régional de
Lorraine (Park HQ)**
Logis Abbatiale
Rue du Quai BP35
54702 PONT- À -MOUSSON
☎ 03.83.81.67.67

PLACES OF INTEREST

Nancy

Musée des Beaux Arts
Open every day throughout the
year with the exception of
Tuesdays, 10am-6pm.

Musée de Lorraine
Open daily except Tuesdays,
10am-12noon, 2-6pm.

Musée de l'École de Nancy
Open every day except Monday
and Tuesday, 10.30am-6pm.

Boat trips on the canal
April to September – 1 hour cruises
around the city at 3, 4.30 and
5.45pm, dinner cruises at 8pm.
Lunch cruises at 11.15am (all year
round).

Château de Fléville
Open 2-7pm every day in July and
August; weekends and Bank Holidays from April to June and September to mid November.

Jardin Botanique du Montet
Open Monday to Friday, 10am-
12noon, 2-5pm; weekends and

Bank Holidays 2-5pm (Sundays and
Bank Holidays 6pm in summer).
Greenhouses are open in the
afternoons only.

Pont- à -Mousson

Abbaye des Prémontrés
Open every day 9am-6pm.

Gorze

Musée de la Terre de Gorze
Open from 2-6pm every day from
June to September, weekends and
Bank Holidays in April, May and
October.

Lac de Madine

Points of entry at both Heudicourt
and Nonsard although the latter is
the main centre. Swimming beach
supervised and all facilities open in
July and August.

Hattonchâtel

Musée Louise Cottin
Open 11am-1pm, 3-7pm every
day except Tuesday in July and
August; weekends and Bank
Holidays April – June and
September.

Hannonville-sous-les-Côtes

Maison des Arts et Traditions Rurales
Open July and August every day 10am-12noon, 2-6pm; rest of year 10am-12noon, 2-5pm, but closed Monday and Tuesday. Closed Sat and Sun mornings throughout year.

St Mihiel

The Benedictine Library and the Museum of Religious Art
(same hours) Open 2-6pm every day except Tuesday in July and August; week-ends and Bank Holidays from April to June, September and October.

Vic-sur-Seille

Musée Départemental Georges de la Tour
Open 9.30am-12noon, 2-7pm April to September, 9.30am-12noon, 2-6pm October to March. Closed on Mondays.

Marsal

Maison du Sel
Open 10am-12noon, 2-6pm, Thursdays to Sundays, mid-June to mid-September; afternoons only rest of year (closed Dec and Jan, except Dec weekends).

Tarquimpol

Maison du Pays des Étangs
Open 2-6pm Wednesdays, weekends and Bank Holidays, mid-February to mid-December.

Rhodes

Boat trips on the Étang du Stock
4-6 departures every day from April to October
Parc Animalier de Ste Croix
Open April to mid-Nov every day 10am-6pm (7pm in July and August, and on some Sundays).

LOCAL HIGHLIGHTS

Best Walks

- The 11 mile (18km) tour of the Saillant de St Mihiel. It is a lovely walk in itself, and the best way to get close to the events of 1914 here.

- Walks around the lakes. There is a pleasant walk along the waterside starting from Lindre Basse, but those more ambitious might like to follow the yellow-waymarked path circumnavigating the Lac de Madine. It is 11 miles (18km) in length – and of course it is no use looking for a short cut!

- The very watery walk at Gondrexange. From the village set out along the towpath of the Marne-Rhine Canal (beside the lake), turn right when you meet the Canal des Houillères, and then right on the far side of the lake (3 miles [5km] in all).

For Cyclists

- For circuits using minor roads, consult the free booklet *Goutez la Meuse à bicyclette*, obtainable from tourist offices in Meuse (basically in the area west of Nancy) and the similar booklet *Mille km à deux-roues* from the *département* of Meurthe-et-Moselle (around Nancy).
- Meurthe-et-Moselle also produces two leaflets detailing mountain-bike trails. The Parc de la Haye to the west of Nancy has a centre for VTT hire and there are 8 trails of varying difficulty in the accessible nearby forest.

Watersports

- The Lac de Madine is a huge well-managed playground offering watersports of all kinds – a swimming beach, a sailing school, boats and pedalos for hire, surfboarding. There are two campsites alongside.
- The little beach at Gondrexange is supervised for bathing in July and August. Other activities include sailing, wind-surfing, pedalos and cycle-hire.

For the Palate

- Obviously Quiche Lorraine. And if you are used to the British supermarket version, do not be put off. The real thing is quite different, made with cream.
- Nancy is particularly renowned for its macaroons and for the boiled sweets, Bergamotes. The latter are flavoured with essence of bergamot and are vaguely reminiscent of sweet Earl Grey tea.
- Mirabelles, yellow plums grown in profusion in Lorraine and found in tarts, bottled in syrup or transformed into a heavenly eau-de-vie.
- Then there are the wines and certain beers, chocolates, madeleines from Commercy and the Rum Baba (invented by Stanislas when he livened up a dry pudding by adding rum) – to mention only a few!

And the most memorable

- Place Stanislas. It was completely dug up when we arrived for this book, so that in itself was pretty memorable (we did not know in advance). But even diggers, drills, barriers and red and white tape could not detract from the magnificence of that architecture or the glints of sunlight on all that gilding. And all should be restored by April 2005, in time for the 250th anniversary of the square.
- Everything to do with the École de Nancy – with the prize perhaps shared between the furniture in the museum and the Daum collection.
- More simply now. The long evening light on the lake at Gondrexange with the coloured houses of the village reflected in the water.

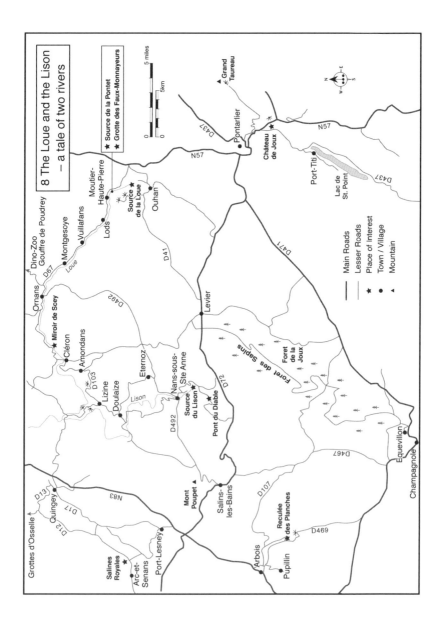

8 The Loue and the Lison
– a tale of two rivers

★ Source de la Pontet
★ Grotte des Faux-Monnayeurs

0   5km
0   5 miles

— Main Roads
— Lesser Roads
★ Place of Interest
● Town / Village
▲ Mountain

In 2003, four regions of France, feeling they were not getting their fair share of the nation's visitors, decided to market themselves together under the banner of 'Hidden France'. One of these regions was Franche-Comté – the others, Limousin, Auvergne and Lorraine are represented elsewhere in this book. But Franche-Comté is surely the most surprising. Here you are on the border with Switzerland in a land of high mountains, tumbling rivers, lakes, waterfalls, pine forests and alpine pastures, as picturesque a corner of France as any, and one that offers any number of opportunities for outdoor enthusiasts. Why should Franche-Comté not get the visitors? Well, in truth it does, but they are largely concentrated in the lake region of the south. To the north and east are the wild Jura mountains, less visited, but more than equally beautiful – and quite unique in character.

The Jura forms the watershed between the Rhine and the Rhône, a massive limestone block that descends in steps from the heights of the Swiss border to the plains of Burgundy. From the Swiss side, the mountains look a trifle austere; from the French, they are delightful, a series of ever-decreasing ridges, well-clothed in pine, alternating with green alpine meadows roamed by red and white *Montbéliard* cattle. Farm-steads here are attractive chalet-style buildings, with long sloping roofs covering both the farmhouse and the animals' quarters. This is the birthplace of some of France's most famous cheeses, Comté, Emmenthal and Mont d'Or to name but a few. The other renowned product of this region comes from the last and lowest of the slopes, where

the land falls to the valley of the Doubs – the Jura wines.

Not surprisingly, the Jura mountains are formed of Jurassic limestone (that is where the name came from) – and Jurassic limestone is highly permeable. Water circulates underground in these mountains, and rivers that appear entirely separate entities may well be connected by subterranean watercourses. This was shown dramatically by a famous incident in 1910, when a fire in the Pernod factory at Pontarlier on the Doubs resulted in the faraway River Loue becoming spiked with absinthe – locals say the trout jumped three times higher than usual! From time to time all this underground water bursts out at the surface, and of course the rivers that are so born may soon be swallowed up again. Heavy rains have a spectacular effect, causing waterfalls to surge from the hillsides and many an otherwise dry cave to pour water.

Such exhibitions of nature's caprices occur throughout the Jura, but nowhere do they have a more beautiful setting than at its very heart, in the valleys of the Loue and the Lison. Both these rivers emerge from huge caves in the rock, and their valleys include pools, waterfalls, gorges, pretty villages and innumerable viewpoints. This is a paradise for walkers, mountain bikers and canoeists – but even those who just come to look have plenty to feast their eyes on. And for those who stay here, when the river valleys themselves have been explored there are the one-time salt towns to the west, the vineyards (and home of Louis Pasteur) at Arbois, the forests of the south and the high mountains on the Swiss border.

Coming here, you will want to find a base centrally, as these winding roads do not make for fast travel. The pretty village of Nans-sous-Ste-Anne, close to the source of the Lison fits the bill very well – but Nans-sous-Ste-Anne has only one small hotel and a handful of gîtes to offer by way of accommodation, and not even a bread shop in the village. Levier on the plateau above has more in the way of facilities, including one of the best campsites in the area, but is not the most attractive of towns. To the north, in the valley of the Loue, picturesque Ornans has it all – but then it has the lion's share of the visitors, and hardly qualifies for 'undiscovered' status. Visit certainly, but maybe not stay!

SOURCE OF THE LISON

So let us return to the heart of things at **Nans-sous-Ste-Anne** to begin this exploration from there. The flower-decked little village sits beneath steep wooded slopes, at the point where the newly-born River Verneau joins the still very youthful Lison. If you turn off the main road here, a path immediately to the left leads up to the waterfall at the source of the Verneau – and to a popular Via Ferrata course on the cliffs above. From the minor road itself (D103), a lesser road soon leads down to a car park near the **Source of the Lison**. You are now in a blind valley and here, at its head, are some of the most awe-inspiring sights in the Jura. The Lison surges from a huge cave beneath the cliff-face to tumble into a wide blue-green pool – the more adventurous can climb up a dark, slippery passage through the rock on the left of the cave to a balcony above the emerging waters. A path leads steeply up above the source to a deep pool known as the **Creux Billard**, which is connected with the underground course of the Lison. Waterfalls plummet down the sheer rock face above and an inaccessible cave is said to bear evidence of habitation by prehistoric man. Just downstream of the source, a bridge over the river leads to another site of high drama, the **Grotte Sarrazine**. In the relative drought of a warm summer, this huge empty cave can be explored on foot – but after heavy rain, a powerful foaming torrent shoots from its mouth to crash its way down to the Lison below.

The Source of the Lison naturally attracts visitors, but if you want to leave them behind, walk downstream from the bridge following the lovely path on the left bank of the river. After about half an hour you arrive at the Taillanderie of Nans-sous-Ste-Anne (it can also be reached by car from the D492), a one-time 'edge-tool' factory. If that does not sound very exciting – wait and see. Until 1969 this rather run-down jumble of buildings produced billhooks, scissors, knives and cutting tools of all kinds. The machinery for this – turbine, hammers, and bellows for the forge – was activated by huge water-wheels driven by the nearby stream. All this is set in motion again during the visit, and whether you understand the French or not, you will be spell-bound by the antics of the guide who rushes around opening watercourses, hammering out scythes and generally leaping from one rocking, creaking bit of machinery to another, all alone in a factory that once employed dozens of men.

Having seen the source of the Lison, you will now want to head for the source of the Loue. The D103 from Nans-sous-Ste-Anne winds steeply uphill (with good views of the cliff above the Creux Billard) to come out at the village of Crouzet-Migette. A right turn here leads to the **Pont du Diable**, a narrow bridge that crosses high above the upper course of the Lison. The views from the bridge are breathtaking – but you can also descend steps (a lot of them) to the trickling stream below, its flow merely a fraction of that at the Lison's official source.

SOURCE OF THE LOUE

Back now to Crouzet-Migette and on to the main road, the D72. To the east is Levier, an undistinguished small town, most important as the northern portal of a splendid forest drive, the Route des Sapins. We will return to that one later – for the moment, the D41 now leads down to Ouhans, and beyond it, a turning on the left reaches the car park for the **Source of the Loue**. The little chalet restaurant here is stocked with maps as well as food and is 'open all hours' (and all days, with a roaring fire in winter). A wide downhill track (about 15 minutes on foot) leads to the source itself, another vast cave from which greenish water emerges to tumble past the remains of a former mill. Vegetation clings to the rock-face above, and although there is a hydro-electric station immediately downstream, the whole place has a peaceful air. From a platform on the opposite side of the river, Gustave Courbet, who was born locally, painted this spot 14 times.

Before rushing back to the restaurant (you will not anyway, because the path is steep) take a few minutes to stroll along the beautiful woodland path on the left bank of the river –

and if you enjoy a good walk, follow it downstream to Moutiers Haute-Pierre (you could return along the rim of the gorge – see Best Walks). On the way you can keep an eye open for the Vouivre, a serpent with wings (and a ruby on his head!) who hides in the caves by day and flies the length of the gorge by night. You will also pass the dramatic **Source of the Pontet**, and the **Grotte des Faux-Monnayeurs**, a cave reputedly used by money-forgers, and now accessed only by the stout-hearted who can climb an incredibly rickety ladder attached to an abrupt cliff-face. If you decide not to take the long walk from the source, the same two sites can be reached by a path descending from the D67 – which is where we will be going in a moment.

First though it is worth getting a look over the whole deep valley (in this upper part, known as the Gorges de Nouailles) from two magnificent viewpoints on its south rim. Return through Ouhans and up the D41 for about a kilometre, and then turn right on the D376. The first belvedere, that of **Renédale** is well-signed – simply follow the path from the village for about 5 minutes to a balcony above the deep wooded gorge with sheer rocky sides. The D67 road balances on a ledge opposite. After Renédale the road soon ends at the **Belvédère du Moine-de-la-Vallée**. There are picnic tables under the trees at this lofty perch, and a view along the length of the river from Moutier-Haute-Pierre at your feet to distant Ornans. The silver waters of the Syratu cascade 492ft (150m) down the far side of the gorge to join the Loue below, but you are way above it all.

FOLLOWING THE LOUE

Time now to return to Ouhans and take a picturesque drive down the valley of the Loue. The D67 is the spectacular road you might have expected from the *belvédère* sighting, a road which itself boasts two splendid viewpoints and a signed path descending to the Source du Pontet and Grotte des Faux-Monnayeurs. The pretty village of **Moutier-Haute-Pierre** is dominated by high rocks, the most notable of them all, the Haute-Pierre 2894ft (882m) directly above it. The lower slopes around the village are clothed in the cherry orchards for which this part of the Loue valley in famous. The next village downstream is **Lods**, and it was surely the view from the riverside – mill, white church and houses tumbling down the slopes – that earned it a place among the elite *plus beaux villages* de France. Lods no longer produces wine, but in its narrow streets can be found the stone houses of the *vignerons* who lived here in the 16th and 17th century.

Vuillafans, the next village in line, likewise bears witness to a former life. The *vignerons*' residences and those of other wealthy merchants are gathered around a delightful square on the left bank of the river, from which there is also a fine view of the restored mill. The village of **Montgesoye** then boasts a costume museum – dozens upon dozens of figures in traditional Comtois dress, gathered into an assortment of tableaux. From this point the river valley widens before the approach to Ornans.

Ornans is the biggest settlement in this part of the valley, and its reputation as the prettiest has resulted in a little overcrowding at times. Traffic battles through its narrow main street and squeezes with difficulty over the old bridge, overlooked by the tall building that was the birthplace of Gustave Courbet. The latter is now a museum devoted to his paintings, canvasses that show real landscapes and working people, as Courbet was one of the first to reject the romantic style of the 18th century. The bridge itself offers views of the mirror-like waters of the Loue reflecting perfectly the old balconied houses along its banks. At least that is how it is in theory – after heavy rains, such a scene can only be imagined, as the turbulent waters race past, seemingly threatening even the balconies' supports, and carrying away with them all semblance of tranquillity.

At Ornans a diversion presents itself, although it is one that really merits a day to itself. Just off the D492 to the north, the remote little village of Charbonnières-les-Sapins is the unlikely setting for a 'Dino-Zoo'.

Not for the faint-hearted

The Dino-Zoo is literally a Jurassic Park, a wooded valley from whose depths erupt the roars and howls of concealed life-size dinosaurs. Others lurk more obviously, surveying the grassy swards around the playground and restaurant. School-age children will love it – but beware taking timid toddlers, faint-hearted grandmothers etc.!

A few kilometres to the north of the Dino-Zoo (follow the signs), the **Gouffre de Poudrey** welcomes its visitors with a huge souvenir shop. Not an auspicious beginning, but the track behind the shop leads to an underground chasm of truly gigantic proportions, whose natural limestone formations are (questionably) enhanced by the 'music and light show' provided. Cave enthusiasts could continue to the **Grotte de la Glacière** (about 12.4 miles [20km] north-east), a cavern with an added dimension – ice in its depths all year round.

Back in Ornans again, the D101 now follows the river downstream. Shortly a chapel appears on the bank on the right hand side, while on the roadside itself stands a statue of Notre-Dame. The story goes that a young girl once had a vision of a statue of the Virgin engulfed by the gnarled trunk of an old oak tree. When the oak was opened up, a statue was indeed found, and that statue now reposes in the church, while the roadside Notre-Dame stands on the spot where the oak tree once grew.

The next scene on the descent is the **Mirroir du Scey**, another glassy stretch of looping river reflecting trees and even the hillside above, on which the scant ruins of the Châtel St Denis are outlined. Just downstream is the village of **Cléron**, and right beside the river bridge stands a turreted fairytale château. After capturing that one, you could give the camera a rest for a while and continue on the D9 (sign-posted Amancey) to reach the Hameau du Fromage on the outskirts of town.

On first sight, this *hameau* (hamlet) appears more like a Swiss chalet-restaurant – but persist. One side is indeed a cheese-orientated restaurant, but the other is largely devoted to the sale of regional produce, everything from enormous cow bells to the famous Jura *vin jaune*, not to mention the

cheeses again. It is worth holding off on all this for a while, because concealed behind the shop (you may need to ask for it – there is no obvious entrance) is an excellent museum that includes a gallery view of a cheese factory in action. After all that, the cheese tasting session with free glass of wine leaves you feeling pleasantly mellowed – and a little more informed to tackle the purchases.

After Cléron there is no longer a road closely following the river. Instead, you could return to the junction at the bottom of the hill and take the D103 that climbs behind the château. This soon reaches **Amondans**, a beautiful flower-clad hamlet of rural dwellings. From the end of the village street a château looks out across the valley – and you can get a similarly spectacular view by continuing on the D103 to the **Belvédère de Gouille Noire**, where way below you the Loue makes its way through a gorge with sides so steep it is said to have its own microclimate.

After turning right in the farming hamlet of Lizine, the road is running along a high ridge between the Loue and the Lison. Their confluence is but a few kilometres distant, a pretty spot, and on the way you pass two of the best balcony viewpoints in a region that is literally teeming with them. From the same pull-in beside the road you can look down on the green valley of the Lison from the **Belvédère du Moulin-Sapin** – and cross over to take a path through the woods (main track, then bear right – there are no signs) to the magnificent **Belvédère de la Piquette** overlooking the steeper gorge of the winding Loue. Back again in Lizine, you could return to Nans-sous-Ste-Anne through the village of Doulaize and then continue on the D15 to **Eternoz**, where there is a little ecomuseum devoted to the traditional occupations of the region (Musée des Métiers Ruraux). If instead you opt for the more direct route that crosses the river, the D139 through Alaise is a winding minor road that does its best to follow the Lison from the cliffs above and offers yet one more belvédère en route.

AREA OF THE SALT SPRINGS

Having explored the valleys of the Loue and the Lison, it is time to head west to an area that once prospered on the strength of its saline springs. The D492 heads west from Nans-sous-Ste-Anne to the town of Salins-les-Bains – and on the way you could stop off for a bird's eye view of the town from **Mont Poupet**. 5 miles (8km) west of Nans-sous-Ste-Anne, a winding road leads up this mountain, and it is a rocky outcrop on the side rather than the summit that you are seeking. From a small car park, just a ten-minute walk up a well-managed stepped ascent has you peering out over Salins and the sweeping Jura plain from a platform equipped with ceramic orientation table. This viewpoint is relatively high (just over 2625ft [800m]) and makes the claim so often made at viewpoints on this side of France – 'on a clear day you can see Mont Blanc'. It just never seems to be clear enough.

Down the snaking road into **Salins-les-Bains**, interest centres on the *salines*, the ancient salt mines. The Romans certainly knew about the salt seam here, but it was not until the 12th century that official salt-works were established, first belonging to the Counts of Burgundy and later to the King and then the State.

Precious salt

Salt was 'white gold', so desirable that employees of the salt-works needed to be searched before returning home each night. Smuggling salt was always a highly profitable business (it was taxed right up until 1945) and the closely-guarded enclave at Salins included a courtroom, stocks and prison to deal instantly with miscreants.

By the mid-1700s, it was becoming difficult to find enough local wood for the necessary evaporation process and a new saltworks was built some 12.4 miles (20km) away on the edge of the Forest of Chaux. The factory at Salins went into decline, but did not finally close its doors until 1962, by which time the salt water was used only to feed the town's thermal establishment. Today you can visit the underground machinery that pumped the salt water to a holding tank and go on to the huge room where it was heated and evaporated by furnaces beneath. The tour is conducted in French (with quite a lot of 'Question Time') but an excellent English translation is offered.

From Salins you will naturally want to go on to the replacement salt-works at **Arc-et-Senans**, to which the brine from Salins was originally transported by wooden pipeline – and that pipeline, too, had to be guarded throughout its length by customs officers. Today the path they patrolled (and that used by would-be salt thieves) has been made into a discovery trail with information panels – an excellent 17 mile (27km) cycle-ride or long walk, passing through the pretty riverside village of Port-Lesney.

At the end of the pipe-line, the Saline Royale at Arc-et-Senans makes a fascinating visit. The commission for its design was given to the architect Claude Nicholas Ledoux, who then came up with an 'ideal city', concentric circles of grey stone buildings that included accommodation and leisure facilities for the workers and their families. In practice, only half the first circle was ever finished. The imposing pillared building that was once the director's residence has in its time been struck by lightning and blown up by dynamite, but now renovated, contains an exhibition of other 'dream-cities' around the world. The only reference to salt comprises a few rooms in its basement – the original salt-extracting machinery here has all been destroyed.

A separate building houses the Ledoux museum, amazing scale models of the other grandiose edifices he designed throughout France, many of which were never built. Sadly his part in the construction of the ring of toll-houses around Paris put Ledoux firmly on the side of the aristocracy and he fell foul of the Revolution. Before leaving the Saline Royale, make sure to take a look behind the workers houses where the plots that were once their allotments are now fodder for the imaginative young minds at the local art school. And the intriguing contents of the gift shop, at the end of the tour, demand you reserve a little browsing time.

Arc-et-Senans is close to the Loue, and you could now follow this river all the way back to its confluence with the Lison. If you decide to do this, it is worth first heading south to Port-Lesney before going on to Quingey – at which point the speleologically-inclined could divert to the nearby **Grotte d'Osselle**, a cave that boasts easy access, and one with some of the finest geological formations in this part of the world (along with the skeleton of a cave-bear).

OF VINEYARDS AND VIEWS

From Arc-et-Senans, the alternative is to turn south to Arbois – although this lovely town, its surrounding vineyards and the impressive blind-ending valley known as the Reculée des Planches are worthy of at least a day's visit in themselves. **Arbois**, wine-growing town and one-time home of Louis Pasteur, is a town festooned with flowers. A fair proportion of these are piled on the roundabout in the central Place de la Liberté – which is best admired from a table under the arcades of *Hirsinger*, an establishment renowned for its high quality chocolates and ice-cream. More flowers adorn the façade of the Maison Pasteur, just down the street.

Louis Pasteur, born in nearby Dole in 1822, moved to Arbois at the age of seven, when his father purchased this house beside the River Cuissance in which to carry on his business as a tanner. Pasteur loved Arbois, and though he spent much of his later life in Paris, he returned to his family home every summer until the year he died. The house has been kept as it was in his time, with many family portraits adorning the walls of the living rooms downstairs, while on the top floor is the humble neat laboratory from which originated some of his huge legacy to mankind. Although the guides here speak only French, they will do so slowly and an English

Louis Pasteur

The third child and only son of tanner Jean Pasteur, Louis was born in Dole in 1822 and spent his childhood years in Arbois. At school he was no more than an average scholar, his particular talent being in the field of art (two of his drawings are displayed in the Maison Pasteur). Encouraged by his father, he obtained his baccalaureate, and then went on to the esteemed École Normale Supérieur in Paris to study science.

Soon he began his famous work on the processes of fermentation and 'pasteurisation'. Subsequently he studied silkworm diseases and anthrax – and the medical world was revolutionised by his discovery that most infectious diseases are caused by germs. But it is for his later work on rabies that Pasteur is most renowned. In 1885, a 9-year-old boy from Alsace was brought to Pasteur, having been severely mauled by a rabid dog. Pasteur had already developed a vaccine, but it had only been tried on animals. With the approval of two doctors, the young Joseph Meister was given the vaccine – and he did not contract rabies. A few months later, Jean-Baptiste Jupille, a shepherd from the Jura, was bitten while fighting with a mad dog who was attacking his friends. He too was successfully given the vaccine. A painting of Jupille repelling the attack hangs in the billiard room at the Maison Pasteur.

It was the triumph of this vaccine that paved the way for the foundation of the Pasteur Institute in Paris a few years later. Pasteur continued to work there until the end of his days, but, having bought the family house after his father's death in 1865, was always able to return to Arbois in the summertime

transcript is provided.

In spite of its many other attributes, Arbois is first-and-last the capital, the high-place of the Jura vineyard, the scene of the September wine festival known as the Fête de Biou. Many are the enterprises in town where you can sample the wines, but to get an idea of their production, take a short stroll to the Château Pécaud (from Place de la Liberté, turn down road beside *Hirsinger*, then second right), a turreted old building surrounded by vineyards that is now home to the Musée de la Vigne et du Vin. Here you can learn about the local wines – reds, whites and rosés that are light and fruity, the famous *vin jaune*, aged

in oak barrels and the unique sweet *vin de paille* (straw wine) for which the over-ripe grapes are dried on a bed of straw.

With all that knowledge under your belt, you will want to head for the local vineyards, of which the most famous is possibly **Pupillin**. Leave Arbois on the D469 in the direction of Champagnole and turn up the D246 where signed. The road winds uphill through rank upon rank of vineyards and at the entrance to the village you are greeted with a display of the different *cépages* (grape varieties). Farther on, amid an exuberance of roadside geraniums, there are many establishments to tempt you with *dégustation.* At the top of the hill, a wooden shelter looks out over the patchwork quilt of vineyards sweeping down to the valley below and picnic tables invite you to – well, perhaps open a bottle and hang around for a while.

At Pupillin, the **Reculée des Planches** and its cave are not far away. Descend to the D469 again, turn right, and in about two and a half miles (4km) look for a narrow road signed on the left, a road that drops directly into the blind end of this valley, where the little village of les Planches nestles at the foot of high cliffs. This whole scene is characteristic of a *reculée* (there are several more to the south) where resurgent springs gush from the base of the sheer limestone walls at the head of the valley. The springs here soon join to form the River Cuissance, whose main source is beside the cave known as the **Grotte des Planches.** To reach it you will need to cross the stone bridge and follow the river upstream – at the end of the road, a woodland path makes the final ascent to the cave mouth. Cave and underground watercourse are linked and the tour demonstrates some of the fantastic effects of erosion by water – but exactly what you see will again depend on recent rainfall.

Back at the river bridge in the village, the tiny road directly ahead (left from the Grotte) leads to the Petite Source of the Cuissance and the **Cascade des Tufs.** A path takes you uphill into the head of the valley. The spectacular spreading waters of the Cascade are soon reached, and the path then goes on to climb a wooded slope where silver streams can be seen trickling (or spurting) over moss-covered boulders. It is a fairytale scene, but trying to locate the source itself can be an unproductive occupation!

Having seen a *reculée* from the 'inside', you could now get a view from without. If you return to the D469 and follow it in the direction of Champagnole, you will pass through a cleft in the rock, and shortly afterwards, reach a roadside parking place opposite a café/restaurant. Behind the restaurant a short path leads to the **Belvédère du Cirque du Fer-à-Cheval,** a rocky perch suspended over the valley you have just left, with some added views of the distant mountains. If you cannot get enough of this sort of spectacle, you could bear left from here to the village of La Châtelaine, where a path beside the church leads to another belvedere with a slightly

---

The pine forest of la Joux

The **Route des Sapins**, suitable for both bikes and cars, comprises 26 miles (42km) of forest road, winding from Champagnole in the south (the Porte d'Equevillon is 2 miles (3km) east, off the D471) to Levier in the north. Along its length are 21 designated sites, each worthy of at least a pause – viewpoints, picnic sites, children's play areas, starting points of walks and cycle rides, discovery trails and an animal park. This is one of France's finest pine forests, and some of its trees reach the gigantic proportions only seen otherwise in the renowned forests of California. The biggest and best of all are voted 'Presidents' and along the drive you can see two of them garlanded with the *tricolor*!

different angle on the scene.

At this point you are some distance from Nans-sous-Ste-Anne, and if you do not want to retrace your steps, you could continue to Champagnole (not a remarkable town itself, but one with a top-class Office de Tourisme) and return on the delightful road through the great pine forest of la Joux. Even so, it must be said that this well-conceived woodland drive really deserves a lot more than a quick slot at the end of the day, so you might prefer to come back here at another time.

MOUNTAINS ON
THE BORDER

A final excursion in this part of the world must be to the mountains on the Swiss border. **Pontarlier**, the last big town on the plains, has little to detain you – although if you take the by-pass heading south, you will pass the premises (it cannot be called a museum) of Espera Sbarro, a huge showroom of futuristic brightly-coloured automobiles, the product of the eccentric mind of their Italian creator. This is hands-on stuff, and car-crazy youths will love it – but if you continue round the by-pass to the south of the town you can escape to the peace of the mountains instead.

The **Grand Taureau**, the solid hump that overlooks Pontarlier, is every-man's mountain – easy to climb and with stunning views from the summit. Its access road is signed to *Larmont*, and leads off the N57 immediately south of Pontarlier (if you reach the turning to the Lac de St Point you have gone too far), from where it winds and twists its way up the slopes, finally levelling to reach a car park one and a half miles (2.5km) from the top. In

July and August and at weekends, this is as far as your wheels can take you; at other times cars are permitted to continue the gentle ascent on tarmac to within a couple of hundred metres of the orientation table on the grassy flower-strewn summit. From here all the great names of the Alpes Bernoise are in view – the Jungfrau, the Eiger, the Wetterhorn, the Schreckhorn – all piled up on a distant jagged horizon.

From this point you could walk on over the summit and descend to a forest track that crosses into Switzerland. The border is marked by ancient stone posts, but no longer manned! Back at the car park (at the Chalet du Gounefay) a board shows you all the other possibilities for rambling and mountain-biking on this mountain, and there are plenty – including the 370 km Grande Traversée du Jura, a magnificent mountain biking trail that now has a hiking equivalent. Finer details for all these can be obtained from OT at Pontarlier, but for a short impromptu walk, look for the signs to the Belvédère du Joux as you descend the road from the summit. Following these (and the yellow on red bars), about 40 minutes of mostly forest walking brings you to a balcony looking directly at a massive castle perched on a huge rocky spike emerging from the valley below.

The **Château de Joux** dates from the 11th century, when it was built here to guard the great north-south trade route from Flanders to Italy. Since then its fortifications have been updated from time to time, and naturally Vauban was called in to secure the place after Franche-Comté was an-nexed by France in 1674. Unassailable as it looks, the château is surprisingly easily reached by road (off the N57), and visits here dwell heavily on its other life as a prison, in which it had several illustrious inmates. Mirambeau, General Toussaint Louverture and Berthe de Joux each have their sorry stories told as the visitors inspect their grim cells. Otherwise the greatest attraction behind these thick walls is the museum of 600 or so ancient arms-pieces, housed in five rooms of the keep.

You may or may not wish to call in at the château, but whatever you do, it is worth driving down the D437 (off the N57, behind the château) to the first shores of the **Lac de St Point**. This is another world – the landscape here is alpine and there is a beautiful view down the length of the lake from a lay-by at the side of the road. Across the water and backed by pine-woods is the curious settlement of Port-Titi, a collection of cheerfully painted wooden summerhouses with even more colourful boats drawn up

in front of them.

This uncharacteristic scene could be your last look at this part of the Jura but if you have time, the lakeside road will take you past Vézenay and the Source Bleue (said to be coloured by the tears of the unfortunate Berthe in the château) and on to Mouthe and the Source of the Doubs – which is rather commercialised and not as pretty as it might be. A more attractive proposition is the source of the Ain, across the wild country to the west, and nearby is the curious yellow-stoned medieval village of Nozeroy – from which you could again join the Route des Sapins to return. And at the end of all that wandering you will probably con-clude that there is nothing more lovely in all the Jura than the valleys of the Loue and the Lison.

OFFICES DE TOURISME

Ornans
7, Rue Pierre Vernier
25290 ORNANS
☎03.81.62.21.50

Salins-les-Bains
Place des Salines
39110 SALINS-LES-BAINS
☎ 03.84.73.01.34

Arbois
Rue de l'Hôtel de Ville
39600 ARBOIS
☎ 03.84.66.55.50

Pontarlier
14 bis Rue de la Gare
25300 PONTARLIER
☎ 03.81.46.48.33

Comité Régional du Tourisme de Franche-Comté
La City
4, Rue Gabriel Plançon
25044 BESANÇON cedex
☎ 03.81.25.08.08

PLACES OF INTEREST

Nans-sous-Ste-Anne

Taillanderie
Open every day July and August, 10am-7pm; May, June and September, 10am-12.30pm, 2-6.30pm; April and October 2-6pm; March and November, Sundays and school holidays only 2-6pm.

Ornans

Musée Courbet
Open July and August 10am-6pm, rest of year 10am-12noon, 2-6pm. Closed on Tuesdays in winter.

Dino-Zoo
Open July and August 10am-7pm; May and June 10am-6pm; April and September 11am-6pm; October 11am-5.30pm. Outside those months open only in school holidays.

Gouffre de Poudrey
Open July and August every day 9.30am-7pm; May, June and September every day 9.30am-12noon, 1.30-6pm (except Sept Wednesdays), April visits at 11am, 2,3, and 4pm (except Wed.). At other times only open on certain afternoons in school holidays.

Grotte de la Glacière
Open daily – June, July and August 9am-7pm; March to May 10am-12noon and 2-6pm; September (and October Sundays) 10am-12noon and 2-5pm; October, weekdays 2-4pm.

Cléron

Château de Cléron
Visits to the gardens and exterior possible during the summer months – no times given.

Le Hameau du Fromage
Open every day throughout the year 9am-7pm (last entry 6pm).

Eternoz

Musée des Métiers Ruraux
Open from June to September every day 10am-12noon, 2-6.30pm.

Salins-les-Bains

Les Salines
July and August, frequent visits between 10am and 5.30pm; Easter to June and first half of September, 6 visits daily; mid-Sept to Oct, Feb to Easter, winter weekends and school holidays, 3 visits daily.

Arc-et-Senans

Salines Royales
Open daily throughout year, July and August 9am-7pm; June, September 9am-6pm; April, May, Oct 9am-12noon, 2-6pm; rest of year 10am-12noon, 2-5pm.

Grotte d'Osselle

Open July and August 9am-7pm; June 9am-6pm; September (and October Sundays) 9am-12noon, 2-5pm; April, May 9am-12noon, 2-6pm; October 2.30-5pm.

Arbois

Maison Pasteur
Open every day from April to mid-October, with several tours each day.

Musée de la Vigne et du Vin
Open every day July and August
10am-12.30pm, 2-6pm; March to
June, September and October
10am-12noon, 2-6pm except
Tuesdays; November to February
2-6pm.

Grotte des Planches
Open every day from April to 2nd
November. 13 daily visits between
10am and 6pm in July and August,
otherwise 7 daily visits between
10am and 5pm.

Pontarlier

Espera Sbarro
Open every day throughout the
year 2-6pm.

Château du Joux
Open July and August 9am-6pm;
April to June, September, October
and school holidays 9.45-11.45am,
2-4.30pm; rest of year 10-
11.30am, 2-4pm.

LOCAL HIGHLIGHTS

Best walks

- If you can walk 9 miles (15km), you must take the walk from the source of the Loue to Moutiers-Haute-Pierre and back along the rim of the gorge – the so-called *Circuit des Belvédères*, no 10 in the folder *La Randonnée au Pays de Montbenoît – Haut- Vallée de la Loue* (obtainable from OT Ornans and from the café at the Source of the Loue). It is a 'best-ever' walk – and the only real difficulty comes in the last 5 minutes, with the steep(ish) descent to the car park.

- The *Chemin des Gabelous* (Customs Officers' Path) from Salins-les-Bains to Arc et Senans. Walkers on this 16.7 mile (27km) trail could ask the help of OT at either end in arranging a taxi for the return (or outgoing) journey.

- Walks on the Larmont massif (the slopes of the Grand Taureau). You probably saw the final information panel for the *Sentier Montagnard du Grand Taureau* at the top of the mountain – try following it from its start at the campsite in the valley below (8.7 miles [14km] – leaflet from OT Pontarlier).

- A footpath encircles the Lac de St Point and information panels point out some of its more notable features as you go. But – the trail is 14.3 miles (23km) in length, and being around a lake, there can be no short cuts!

For cyclists

This whole region is a paradise for mountain-bikers.

- Two shops in Ornans deal with VTT hire and five well-marked circuits of varying difficulty depart from the Office de Tourisme. Ask for the *Guide des Sentiers VTT* – and try one of the easier ones before committing yourself to the 27.3 mile (44km) 'black' *Moine de la Vallée* route!

- Seven circuits of varying difficulty are marked out on the slopes of the Massif du Larmont (whose summit is the Grand Taureau). Ask OT at Pontarlier for the map.

- Really ambitious mountain-bikers can tackle sections (or all) of the Grande Traversée du Jura. Maps and information (including accommodation) can be obtained from OT Pontarlier.

Watersports

- From May to October the canoe base at Ornans hires out canoes and kayaks for the hour, half-day or day, with several possibilities for trips down the Loue between Vuillafans and Cléron. There is another canoe base on the Loue at Quingey.

- Boats can be hired from Port Titi on the Lac de St Point in summertime.

For the palate

- The wines, of course! Arbois, Pupillin, Jura, and, if you can afford it, *vin jaune*. The nutty-flavoured latter is too 'strong' for most meals but is perfectly accompanied by –

- Jura cheeses. There are plenty of them, but if possible (it might not be, because it is only made in autumn and winter) try the ambrosial Mont d'Or – which, as a variation, can actually be cooked in the oven in the box it comes in (15 minutes at 200°C – and stand it in something to catch the seepage). And thinking of melted cheese, there's the local fondue.

- Fresh fish from the rivers and game from the forests. Of particular note is *truite au vin jaune*.

And the most memorable

- The scene at the Taillanderie where one young girl managed the whole show from selling the tickets to setting all that heavy machinery in motion and fashioning a scythe. It could not happen in the UK!

- It should be one of the sources, which are all spectacular – but let us go for our first sight of the Grotte Sarrazine, with water fairly hurtling from its gaping mouth to join the river below.

- Just the two of us (there was no-one else on the tour) standing quietly in Pasteur's laboratory in Arbois – and feeling the old man had just walked out for a while.

9. 'Nothing good comes from the Morvan'

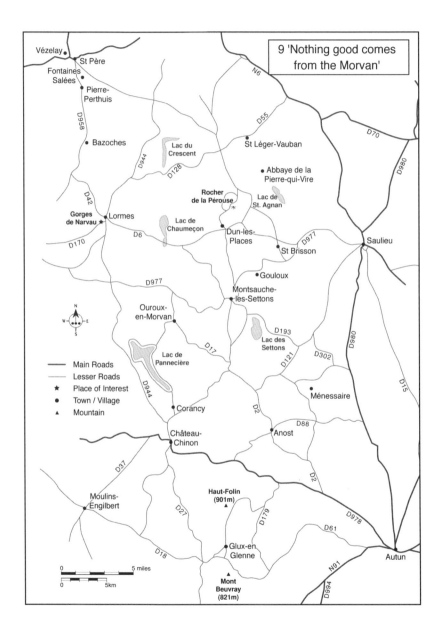

9 'Nothing good comes from the Morvan'

Vézelay
St Père
Fontaines Salées
Pierre-Perthuis

N6
D55
D70
D958
D980

Bazoches
Lac du Crescent
St Léger-Vauban

D944
D128

Abbaye de la Pierre-qui-Vire

D42
Rocher de la Pérouse
Lac de St. Agnan

Gorges de Narvau
Lormes
Lac de Chaumeçon
Dun-lès-Places

D170
D6
St Brisson
D977
Saulieu

D977
Gouloux
Montsauche-les-Settons

Ouroux-en-Morvan
D193
Lac des Settons

N
W   E
S
D17
D121
D302
D980

Main Roads
Lesser Roads
★ Place of Interest
● Town / Village
▲ Mountain

Lac de Pannecière
D944
Ménessaire
D15

Corancy
D2
Anost
D88

Château-Chinon

D37
Haut-Folin (901m)
D2

Moulins-Engilbert
D27
D179
D978
D61

0   5 miles
0   5km
D18
Glux-en-Glenne
N91
Autun
D994

Mont Beuvray (821m)

The rich soil of the rolling country-side of Burgundy produces a wealth of cereal crops and some of the finest wines in France. Burgundy is decidedly a fertile region, a place of abundance and affluence. That is, except for one small area at its very heart – the Morvan. In the Morvan the soil is thin, overlying a bed of hard granite and little grows well. Here the hills are more mountainous, the climate colder and the people, at least in previous times, poorer. Money was hard come by in the Morvan – with an economy originally based on poor cereals like rye, the men travelled to sell wood from the forests, and the women played their part by acting as wet-nurses for the wealthy of Paris. The more opulent Burgundians have been known to say 'Nothing good comes from the Morvan, neither good people nor a good wind'. But, despite all these negative comments, the Morvan is a truly beautiful area, without a doubt the most scenic part of Burgundy. With mountains, woods, streams, lakes and waterfalls, this is quite different terrain, and its merit was officially recognised in 1970 when it was accorded the status of Natural Regional Park.

The geological explanation for the Morvan's difference from the rest of Burgundy is that it is a last northern 'blip' of the Massif Central, aberrantly thrust by movements of the earth's crust into the calcareous soils of the Paris basin. So there are mountains here, and the rock of the Morvan is non-porous, leaving streams to cascade picturesquely down their slopes. In the valleys the streams have been dammed to give six large lakes, each of them blending well into the landscape. While crops fail in the Morvan, trees grow and 60% of the land is covered in ancient deciduous forest to which more recently conifers have been added. All this is a far cry from the ordered landscapes of vineyard Burgundy!

And now you are wondering what kind of holiday is possible in such a wild region. Of course the Morvan appeals primarily to lovers of the outdoors – watersports enthusiasts, anglers, hikers, mountain bikers and horse riders are all very well catered for. But the region is also completely unspoilt and the villages and small towns have changed little with time. The Romans were well acquainted with the Morvan and there are extensive remains of salt baths at Saint-Père and a superb amphitheatre at Autun, at the southern tip. The archaeological finds from the current excavations of the Gallo-Roman town on the summit of Mont Beuvray are unique in Europe.

For a rainy day, there is an unexpectedly plentiful supply of museums. Being a Natural Regional Park there are several devoted to aspects of rural life, but you can also learn about archaeology, art, prehistory, costume and the lives of Vauban and François Mitterrand, both of whom had strong associations with these parts. The Park headquarters at St Brisson will tell you all about the region's history, geography and geology, and has a special section devoted to the work of the wartime Resistance in the Morvan. Other interesting diversions are the town of Saulieu, famed for its gastronomy, St Honoré-les-Bains, a spa town and the pretty hilltop town of Uchon surrounded by huge boulders of bizarre shapes. And at either end of the region, the basilica at Vézelay and the cathedral at Autun are architectural masterpieces not to be missed.

In terms of its landscape and relief,

the Morvan can be divided into three regions whose margins are not too distinct. In the north, the *Morvan Ouvert* is the gentlest country of the three – rolling pasture grazed by Charolais is interspersed with tracts of woodland. Farther south in the *Haut Morvan des Collines*, the hills have become higher, and are now covered in forest. Swift-flowing rivers have carved out deep valleys and damming of the rivers has created the lakes much loved by the holiday-makers. The highest hills are in the *Montagne Morvandelle* of the south, rounded tree-clad summits of which the most lofty is Haut-Folin at 2956ft (901m). Between the hills, wide river valleys alternate with dramatic gorges, habitation here is less, and there are few pastures for grazing.

If you are planning a holiday in the Morvan you should probably aim to stay centrally. From north to south the Morvan stretches for about 62 miles (100km), and though the roads are better than you might expect, it will still take appreciable time to travel. The central section is in any case the land of the lakes, the region most geared to holidays and offering most accommodation. A suitable choice would be **Montsauche**, just 2 miles (3km) from the shores of the pretty Lac des Settons. Montsauche itself lacks old buildings – it was one of several villages razed to the ground in 1944 in reprisal for the activities of the Maquis. But although not particularly attractive, it does have a few shops, a petrol station and a bank, more facilities than are generally to be found in villages around here.

There are also a couple of hotels in Montsauche, but you may prefer to stay beside the **Lac des Settons** where there are at least two more in addition to three good quality camp sites, each with direct access to the shores. Other options are of course the many gîtes in this rural area. The Lac des Settons is the pride of the Morvan, the magnet that attracts the region's much needed holiday-makers (of whom virtually all are French) and has a setting as pretty as you could wish to find anywhere. Its banks offer swimming and the hire of pedalos or rowing boats, a trip boat plies the waters in summertime and the more energetic can walk or cycle the path that encircles its shores. Several restaurants cater for the visitors. So let us begin this exploration of the Morvan from Montsauche and the Lac des Settons, and first of all take a short trip that will set the scene for this area, a visit to the Headquarters of the Natural Regional Park near the village of St Brisson.

CENTRAL MORVAN

It is now more than 30 years since the Morvan became a Natural Regional Park, enough time for the region to get its act together very well. The **Maison du Parc** at **St Brisson** is a splendid example of what such a headquarters can offer. To reach it from Montsauche, take the D977 in the direction of Saulieu for about 6.2 miles (10km). On the way you will pass a small waterfall, the **Saut du Gouloux** (and if you have time, the nearby village of Gouloux boasts a clog-maker's shop). Just beyond the Saut du Gouloux, a left turn leads to the Maison du Parc, a lovely old farm complex, whose buildings house an Office de Tourisme, a shop selling regional produce, and two museums.

Of the museums, the Maison des Hommes tells the story of the hard life of the Morvan, how families struggled to make a living, and how for more than three centuries the main income came from the floating of wood down the rivers to Paris, where it was used for heating. When the wood trade became less profitable in the latter part of the 19th century the Charolais cattle were introduced – and you can pursue their story in a museum at Moulins-Engilbert, in the south-west.

The second museum is the Musée de la Résistance, and for this you can choose to equip yourself with headphones speaking in English. This area is very close to the one-time border with Vichy France and the remoteness of these hills offered shelter for several cells of Maquis. The Morvan is justly proud of them. Outside the museum, four themed itineraries are on offer taking you to important sites of Maquis activities – to pursue them you will need to read French, and sadly you realise that these men were sometimes far more brave than they were successful. Outside in the grounds of the Maison du Parc you will find donkeys and different breeds of cattle, an aviary, a children's playground, a small garden of medicinal plants, an arboretum (botanical names as well as French) and a half mile (1km) discovery trail (French only this time, but explanatory pictures) along the shores of the reedy Étang Taureau.

It would be quite easy to spend a whole lazy day at the Maison du Parc, but you might want to see some more of the locality before returning. Heading west on the D6 (note the deer enclosure on the right just after you set off), the road enters a deep valley where you can turn left to Dun-les-Places – the river bridge beside the auberge on the right was the scene of a Maquis encounter with the retreating occupation forces in September 1944. **Dun-les-Places** itself is a war-time martyr village, where in more reprisals, houses were set alight and 27 men were shot in front of the church door. A poignant memorial in white stone marks the spot. Beyond the church, a road on the opposite side is signed to le Vieux Dun and the **Rocher de la Pérouse**. The latter is a fine viewpoint, an orientation table perched on a rocky crest above the Cure valley, ringed by forested hills. The drive will take 20 minutes or so (on well-signed but narrow roads) and you have a steepish five-minute climb on foot at the end, but that panorama is worth it.

From the Rocher de la Pérouse, the road continues (it is one-way at this point) and eventually reaches the D10. A right turn here will return you to Dun-les-Places and Montsauche, but if the day is still young, why not turn left instead? At Quarré-les-Tombes (a village named from the 7th – 10th century limestone sarcophagi found here) you can turn off the main road to **St Léger-Vauban**. This little village is the birthplace of Louis XIV's prolific military architect Vauban – it was actually called St Léger-de-Foucheret at the time. At the top of the village a small museum offers three rooms of information, interesting in that it is mostly about his non-military life and the altruism that brought about his final decline from favour.

More of Vauban later – but now the road-signs are pointing to the **Abbaye de la Pierre-qui-Vire**, a living community of monks buried deep in the heart of the forest. Directions are impossible – just put your faith in those signs and go. The abbey is architecturally outstanding, an imaginatively conceived blend of old and new. Visit the megalithic stone (now 'Christianised') after which the site is named, look through the 'windows' to view the vast abbey complex, walk down to the church to appreciate the fine modern stained-glass, admire the carving of a monk on the main entrance and then go inside where the monks will welcome you. An excellent bookshop is accompanied by an artistic presentation of a monk's life, including a short video. If you continue along the road past the abbey, you will soon reach the abbey farm, where there is a shop selling home-produced cheeses. After that, get out of the forest whichever way you can, but if you follow signs to St Agnan, you will cross the tail end of the pretty **Lac de St Agnan**, the only one of the six lakes of the Morvan to be used for water supply.

MORVAN — THE NORTH

Back to Montsauche, now and another excursion. So far you have seen something of the central Morvan, the Morvan des Hauts Collines. Now we could head into the gentler country of the north and at the very northwest tip of the park area, visit **Vézelay**. As you approach you can under-stand the excitement of the pilgrims of the Middle Ages when they first caught sight of the abbey church on its hilltop (they called it 'Montjoie'). What you think of Vézelay may in part depend on the time of year. In high season, this simply is not 'off-the-beaten-track' and the car parks at the foot of the town may be full-to-bursting. At other times you may be able to drive right up to the basilica itself – not that you would want to, because the narrow Rue du Château that leads up to it is lined with some fascinating shops and exhibitions.

Vézelay was a major halt and meeting point of pilgrims on one of France's four great routes to the shrine of St James at Santiago de Compostela. Surprisingly the basilica contains no statues, cockleshell emblems or other references to the pilgrimage (just one latter-day wood carving), although the shops and Office de Tourisme are not going to let you forget about it, and an obviously recent addition is a metal cockle-shell let into the road outside. But the Basilique Sainte-Madeleine is nevertheless a magnificent edifice, deriving its name from relics of Mary Magdalene held in the crypt and south transept. Most of the building dates from the 12th century. It suffered horrendous damage in the Revolution and was on the point of collapse in the early 19th century when it was rescued by Prosper Merimée (the famed Inspector of Historical Monuments) and Viollet le-Duc (who master-minded its re-building).

To do justice to this basilica you would need a detailed guide book and plenty of time, but its most important features are undoubtedly the tympanum over the central doorway in the narthex (pre-nave), and the detailed carvings on the capitals. Both date from around 1200. The tympanum is a master work of innumerable scenes, figures and symbols, its overall message apparently God's welcome to those arriving here and his embracing of the whole world in his church. On the capitals, legends and biblical stories stand side by side – an English translation offered inside the doorway allows you to identify each one. Outside the basilica, there are fine views across the valley of the River Cure from the terrace on the south side.

Vézelay's basilica was built on the site of a former Benedictine community, and it was on the side of this hill in 1146 that St Bernard preached the Second Crusade. The site is marked with a large cross and nearby a small community of monks is centred on the Chapel of la Cordelle, which can be visited. The best way to do this is to walk down a track that starts on the north side of the basilica, passes through the medieval Porte St Croix and crosses the Promenade des Fosses to descend to the tiny stone chapel (although you can get to the same point by car on a very narrow road). The Promenade des Fosses is worth a return in itself – a broad tree-lined track that starts at the foot of the Rue du Château, it follows the town ramparts all the way, passing the old grey Porte-Neuve bearing the town coat of arms.

Leave Vézelay now and head down the hill to the pretty old village of St-Père – its position on the River Cure makes it an ideal base for outdoor activities including white water rafting and tree-walking. In the village, the road to Corbigny skirts an amazingly ornate Gothic church on which the hand of Viollet le-Duc has also been laid. Rose window, statues, gargoyles and multiple carvings can be seen on the outside, but park beside it for a few minutes (and watch those gargoyles if it is raining!) to discover an interior of greater simplicity with painted vaulting and interestingly carved faces on the corbels.

The former presbytery is home to the Musée Archéologique Régional with many finds from excavations of the nearby Roman salt baths, the Fontaines Salées – but before going in to the museum, you had better visit the site itself, a couple of kilometres away down the D958. These saline springs were known as far back as 2500BC. In the first century a Celtic

temple and thermal baths were built on the site, and the Romans deemed the waters to be beneficial for arthritic complaints. By the 14th century salt bore heavy taxation, and the monks of Vezelay, seeing the place as potential trouble, had the baths filled in. All has been revealed in the recent excavations, and the waters are again used in rheumatological treatments.

A further one and a half miles (2km) down the D958, the village of **Pierre Perthuis** sits high above the gorge of the River Cure and its tributary stream. Follow the signs to *les Ponts* for a scenic picnic site beside the mingling waters, where two old bridges, a footbridge and a high-arching new bridge can be seen crossing the various watercourses. For another scenic site, continue on the narrow road through the village (passing through a former château gateway) and then turn left to **la Roche-Percée**. Walk across the grassy plateau used as a car park to see the huge arch of rock (said to be composed of silicified granite), picturesquely set on the steep banks of the Cure. Upstream there are views of the village, its château and the new bridge spanning the gorge.

South on the D958 again now, and the countryside opens out as you go. Approaching the village of Bazoches, a brown-stoned château looks out from the hillside on the left. The 12th century **Château de Bazoches** once had a famous owner – Sébastian le Prestre, otherwise known as the Maréchal de Vauban.

Vauban's château

Vauban restored the château de Bazoches to his own designs and lived in it for more than 30 years until his death in 1707. The fine distant views of Vézelay from its windows must have inspired his work here, some of which is on display in rooms left unchanged since his time. Vauban himself is buried in the village church at Bazoches (in a chapel on the south side) – or at least most of him is, because his heart has been taken to Les Invalides in Paris.

Bazoches is on the fringes of the Natural Regional Park. Let us stay within its boundaries now and turn east off the D958 to the town of **Lormes**. It perches on a rocky spur above the River Narvau, and there is a viewpoint with orientation table on the right of the D42, just before entering the town. In the town, more fine prospects of the surrounding countryside are on offer at the top of the Rue du Panorama. Far below the Narvau crashes through a deep wooded gorge and a parking area on the D170 will give you access to marked paths leading to a waterfall, rocks, caves and viewpoints (273 yd [250m] back up the road, the flight of steps is an easier option). Leaving Lormes, the way back to Montsauche takes you past the end of the **Lac de Chaumeçon** – for the best views of the water, you will have to leave the D17 and head for Plainefas at the northern tip. But the largest lake of all, the Lac de Panneçière, lies to the south and will have to wait for another day.

SOUTH FROM MONTSAUCHE

Starting once again from Montsauche, you can reach the **Lac de Panneçière** via Ouroux-en-Morvan, and on this road there are some fine views of the water as you approach. Eventually you arrive at a highly impressive barrage, which seems to be supported by flying buttresses. Its prime purpose, like that of all the other lake dams (with the exception of St Agnan), is to control the flow of water into the Seine basin – the production of hydro-electric power is in this case a side-line. From the barrage you could follow the eastern shore as far as Chaumard (and perhaps beyond to the sad monument to the Maquis de Chaumard on the D505) or the western shore towards Corancy. Both are scenic drives. But whatever you do, the next port of call must be Château-Chinon.

Château Chinon with but 2500 inhabitants is the largest town in the Morvan. It was in this rather undistinguished place that François Mitterrand once became mayor and so began his political career. The town makes the most of that memory, with a 'François Mitterrand Walk' around its points of interest, offering one or two of his quotes along the way. Château-Chinon is set on the slopes of a small conical hill. At its windy summit are three bare crosses and a *table d'orientation* from which you can pick out Haut-Folin (it is the one with a telecommunications tower on top), Mont Preneley and Mont Beuvray – your first glimpse of the heights of the Montagne Morvandelle. Of course this viewpoint is on Mitterrand's trail, but when you descend again you can get a look at the later side of his life in the Musée du Septennat (the name refers to the seven year tenure of the presidency). This museum is simply a collection of all the state gifts the President received during his years in office. It makes a surprisingly entertaining browse for a rainy day – although this one is good enough to be taken in even when the sun is shining. What makes this miscellany of objects so fascinating? Possibly just the fact that they can all be identified with one single man.

A few metres down the road, the Musée du Costume has a good home in yet another fine 18th century building, but though the museum is well thought out, dress through the ages must play second fiddle to the diversity of the Septennat. Before you leave Château-Chinon there is one more sight to be seen (it is included in the Mitterrand Walk), the Monumental Fountain outside the *Mairie*. No piece of history this one – instead a strange collection of brightly coloured modern 'sculptures' gyrate gently as they shoot water from various orifices. It must mesmerise the town hall workforce.

On the outskirts of the park now, and with time to spare you could stray farther. To the south-west, the town of **Moulins-Engilbert** is a centre of cattle-rearing with a regular market. Charolais were imported to this region when the *flottage du bois* was failing about 100 years ago. Now the large white cattle graze every available pasture and the story of their lives, breeding and blood lines is told at another of the park's very well produced eco-museums, the Maison de l'élevage et du Charolais. A curious feature is its stained-glass windows!

There is not much more to detain you in Moulins-Engilbert (although the church also has fine stained-glass), and you could perhaps squeeze more into a long day by continuing to **St-Honoré-les-Bains**. Its warm sulphurous waters have been treating respiratory diseases since Roman times. The town boasts a classic thermal establishment, a casino, and a little tourist train – enough to market it as a holiday centre with easy access to the Morvan. And now it is a long drive back to Montsauche. To the east, the peaks you could see from Château-Chinon are very tempting – but they deserve a day to themselves.

THE MOUNTAINS OF THE MORVAN

Back in Montsauche again now and time at last to head for those mountains. If possible choose a fine day for the views, because heading south from Montsauche towards the heights you are going to pass through some of the loveliest scenery in the Morvan. Turn off the D37 before Planchez (another martyr village) and take the D17 in the direction of **Anost**. Wooded slopes, river valleys and isolated hamlets pass by your windows, and the pretty village of Anost perfectly fits the scene. Anost is a self-styled walking and mountain-biking centre, producing its own map of waymarked routes for both under the title *Anost Randonnées*.

At the centre of the village is one of the eco-museums of the Natural Regional Park, the Maison des Galvachers. In past centuries the Morvan was too poor for a living to be made within its confines. The *galvachers* took their merchandise (usually local timber, but also salt, wine, clogs and more) to distant parts in ox-drawn carts, each excursion lasting maybe several months. The museum pays tribute to the harshness of their lives. If you enjoy the visit, you could come back this way to take in another eco-museum, the Maison du Seigle at **Ménessaire** (north-east via Cussy-en-Morvan). Its theme is the ingenuity of the Morvan families in their use of rye (*seigle*), the only cereal crop to grow on the poor soil.

Time to leave Anost now and continue south on the D88. At the main road (D978) turn to the left, and then deep in the valley, take the first road on the right, which is signed to Mont Beuvray. Now in the Forest of Glenne, the road climbs steadily through the **Gorges of the Canche** – a pull-in allows you a glimpse of the rushing river far below. After about 3 miles (5km) a sign points right to Haut-Folin. Should you go there before Mont Beuvray? If you are going to see it at all, you probably should. It is best to reserve flexible time for the latter.

Haut-Folin is in many ways a disappointment – that is, to all except the Club Alpin Francais, who have cashed in on the colder climate of the Morvan and set up cross-country skiing routes around its lower slopes. But the mountain itself is covered in dense woodland and the only way to get a view would be to climb the telecommun-ications tower. So regard this as a pleasant forest drive that takes in the Morvan's highest point (2956ft [901m]) and continue the descent on the far side to the village of Glux-en-Glenne. From here it is but two and a half miles (4km) to Mont Beuvray and there is no difficulty in following the signs to the visitor centre beside the D18.

A visitor centre in such a wild place needs to be tasteful and this one is – a small Office de Tourisme beside a large but well-blended building that is both museum and conference centre. **Mont Beuvray** has an important story to tell – in the 1st century BC a town of some 10,000 inhabitants perched on its summit. The town was called **Bibracte** and it was the capital of a Gallic tribe, the Aedui (Edui to the French). Bibracte had its place in history. Here in 52BC Vercingetorix was proclaimed chief of the Gauls, and so began a revolt against the invading Roman armies. A little later Julius Caesar visited and completed the writing of his epic *De Bello Gallico* in the town.

The summit of Mont Beuvray is a lovely open grassy area known as la Chaume. A monument to M. Bulliot has been placed here and a *table*

The Aedui

The Aedui were a powerful Gaulish tribe occupying central France between the Saône and the Allier in the 2nd century BC. Apart from a brief period in 52BC they were important allies of Rome. Bibracte was not only their capital but also an economic centre, from where they traded with the Mediterranean regions and as far south as Italy – as can be seen from the coins retrieved from the site and the huge terracotta amphorae used to carry wine and oil long distances. The Aedui were also skilled craftsmen and in particular, metal-workers. Their workshops lined the street just inside the Porte du Rebout and many objects in iron have been recovered.

d'orientation looks east across the mountains to the distant but sometimes visible peak of Mont Blanc. Farther back, the 19th century Chapelle St-Martin stands on the site of a former Roman temple. To access all the sites it is possible to drive over the mountain – although it is probably preferable to walk. Returning downhill you can spend an hour or two in the excellent museum that very successfully brings everything you have seen to life with the aid of videos and reconstructions. And if you still have time and energy after all that, you can escape most of the other visitors by taking the 3 mile (5km) walk around the ancient ramparts, which is marked out with flashes of yellow. Much of the route is lined by *queules*, the gnarled twisted pollarded beech trees that are a feature of Bibracte.

It seems that the site of Bibracte was inhabited for about a hundred years only. After that time, the population began to move out to a new capital built for them at Autun. So now we will take another excursion from Montsauche to the town of Autun – and if you want to extend the day you could go first via the town of **Saulieu**, which has dubbed itself a centre of gastronomy. There is not a lot of immediate evidence for this (except for the cheese shop in the main street), but it certainly has a good endowment of restaurants for its size. Apart from this its most notable features stand together – the 12th century Basilique St-Andoche (its carved capitals are – almost – on a par with Vézelay) and the Musée Pompon.

Pompon, born in Saulieu, was a sculptor, and primarily a sculptor of animals. His most famous piece is the broad-footed 'Polar Bear', which won prizes at the Paris exhibition of 1920, but there are many others here, interspersed with odd snippets of information, such as how a sculpture in bronze is created. To reach the animals you pass first through a contrasting section on stone, with milestones and sarcophagi from the Roman period

Excavations at Bibracte

The discovery of Bibracte is a story in itself, and is due to the persistence of one Jacques-Gabriel Bulliot, from nearby Autun. At the time it was thought that the Roman town referred to as *Bibracte* was at Autun, yet Bulliot's researches led him to believe that it was at the top of Mont Beuvray. Eventually in 1867 he was given permission to dig – and a town of surprising complexity came to light, ringed by ramparts with clear entrance gates.

M. Bulliot spent all his time on the site (he built a cottage there), and when he grew old, the baton was passed to his nephew, an archaeologist himself. Then World War I intervened and excavations were brought to a halt – and resumed only in 1984. This time Bibracte was found to be surrounded by double ramparts and new areas were opened up. Recently the main entrance gate, the Porte du Rebout, has been reconstructed using Gallic techniques. Teams from universities all over Europe come to take part and for much of the year the excavation sites are open for public viewing.

and medieval statues, and the end is curiously enough a room full of menus from important banquets – maybe as an inducement to go out and sample the local gastronomy.

Twenty-five miles (40km) to the south of Saulieu, the town of **Autun** was built by the Emperor Augustus. His 'New Town' was intended to replace the Gaulish Bibracte and was to be the 'sister and rival of Rome'. Two of its old entrance gates still stand (the Porte St-André and the Porte d'Arroux – you would have arrived through the latter), along with part of a tower from the Temple of Janus. On the east of the town a theatre with a one-time capacity of 12,000 has been excavated. Today the ancient terraces must provide more than adequate seating for the football pitch alongside. Autun's splendour began to fade in the 3rd century AD and, with the withdrawal of the Roman legions, the town saw many invasions.

In the 12th century, a new cathedral replaced a church that had been destroyed some 400 years previously. At the highest point of the town, the Cathédral St-Lazare was built to house the relics of St Lazarus, carefully carried back from the south (relics were big business because they attracted pilgrims and so brought in revenue). Time and the Revolution took their toll on the cathedral and in the 19th century Viollet le-Duc was commissioned for restoration work. Today its greatest glories are much those of Vézelay – a magnificent tympanum on the central doorway, this time to be seen from outside the cathedral, and inside, a fine array of carvings on the capitals. More superb carvings have been preserved in the upstairs room of the Chapter House on the south side. Sadly the tomb of

Lazarus that once stood behind the high altar was a casualty of the Revolution. On the north side, the 16th-century fountain of Lazarus is always decked in flowers.

Just opposite the fountain, the Musée Rolin (named after a family that were instrumental in the revival of Autun in the Middle Ages) bears witness to Autun's eventful past life. Here are mosaics, statues and tombstones from the Roman era and a further stockpile of treasures unearthed at Bibracte, among them some of the large vessels used to transport wine. Other rooms house medieval sculptures, fragments of the missing tomb of St Lazarus and a large collection of paintings. The other museum to be visited in Autun is the Musée d'Histoire Naturel. If the stuffed animals lack appeal, a room upstairs displays the astonishing assortment of rocks to be found in the Morvan – and budding geologists can find a booklet describing two geological tours of the Morvan in the Office de Tourisme in the Champ de Mars. A whole day could easily be spent exploring Autun. If you want to see it all (ramparts, towers, a waterfall, other Roman remnants and a wealth of medieval buildings), OT can also supply you with their *Guide des Circuits Touristiques* offering three different walking routes around the town.

And finally, the Morvan has an outpost, the Beacon of **Uchon**. Fifteen and a half miles (25km) south of Autun, the hill is crowned with a delightful village, from which there are fine views of the Morvan. Easy walking paths from the village take you down the slopes to wander among a chaos of granite boulders. The whole unusual ensemble, though separated from the Morvan massif, has been included in the Natural Regional Park.

OFFICES DE TOURISME

Château-Chinon
Place Notre-Dame
58120 CHÂTEAU-CHINON
☎ 03.86.85.06.58

Saint-Brisson
Maison du Parc
38230 SAINT-BRISSON
☎ 03.86.78.79.57

Vézelay
Rue Saint-Pierre
89450 VÉZELAY
☎ 03.86.33.23.69

Autun
2, avenue Charles de Gaulle
71400 AUTUN
☎ 03.85.86.80.38

PLACES OF INTEREST

St. Brisson

Maison du Parc
Grounds open all year round.

La Maison des Hommes and Musée de la Résistance
Open May to September 10am-1pm, 2-6pm; April, October and 1st-11th November 10am-1pm, 2-5pm every day. Closed Tuesdays throughout the year except in July and August.

St. Léger-Vauban

Maison Vauban
Open 10.30am-1pm, 2.30-6pm (6.30pm in July and August) every day except Tuesday from May to September and weekends only in April and October.

Abbaye de la Pierre-qui-Vire
Exhibition rooms and shop open April to October 10.30am-12noon, 3-5.30pm every day except Sunday; February, November, December and all Sundays 11.15am-12.15pm,3-5.30pm. Visitors welcome at church services (daily Mass and Vespers).

Vézelay

Basilique Ste-Madeleine
Open daily throughout the year.

St-Père

Musée Archéologique Régional
Open April to October daily 9.30am-12.30pm, 1.30-6.30pm.

Fouilles des Fontaines Salées
Open as archaeological museum above.

Bazoches

The Château
Open every day from 25th March to 5th November 9.30am-12noon, 2.15-6pm (5pm after 1st October).

Château-Chinon

Musée du Septennat
Open July and August 10am-1pm, 2-7pm every day; May, June and September 10am-1pm, 2-6pm every day except Tuesday; mid-February to April and October to December 10am-12noon, 2-6pm every day except Tuesday.

Musée du Costume
Hours as Musée du Septennat.

Moulins-Engilbert

**Maison de l'élevage
et du Charolais**
Open 10am-12noon, 2.30-6pm
every day from May to mid
September, and weekends only
from Easter to end of April and
mid-September to 11th
November.

Anost

La Maison des Galvachers
July and August, open 2-6pm
every day except Tuesdays. June
and September, Saturdays and
Sundays only, 2-6pm.

Ménessaire

La Maison du Seigle
Open Monday (3-5pm) and
Thursday (2-5pm) all year round.

Mont Beuvray

Site of Bibracte
Free access throughout the year,
with the archaeological
excavations open from June to
October. Guided visits at 3pm
from mid-April to June and in
September; 2pm and 4pm in July
and August.

Museum of Celtic Civilisation
Open 10am-6pm (7pm in July and
August) every day from mid-
March to mid-November.

Saulieu

Musée Pompon
Open daily except Tuesday March
to October 10am-12.30pm, 2-
6pm (5.30pm March, October).
Rest of year weekends and public
holidays only, 10am-12.30pm, 2-
5pm.

Autun

Musée Rolin
Open every day except Tuesday
April to September 9.30am-
12noon, 1.30-6pm: October to
March 10am-12noon, 2 (2.30 on
Sun)-5pm.

Musée d'Histoire Naturel
Open 2-6pm except Monday and
Tuesday throughout the year. Also
open mornings (10am-12noon) in
June, July and August.

LOCAL HIGHLIGHTS

Best Walks

- The walk around the Roman ramparts of Bibracte on Mont Beuvray – a diversion to include the summit is possible (a map of the circuit is included in the booklet *Bibracte – Guide de Visite*).

- The path that encircles the shores of Lac des Settons. Nine miles (15km) in length, it will take you about 4 hours to complete and there are plenty of opportunities for refreshment and swimming en route.

- Other suggestions are a 2 mile (3km) route from Uchon exploring the curious boulders, or any of the walks in the lovely countryside around Anost. All can be found on free leaflets from local tourist offices.

- Serious walkers should get hold of the book *Le Morvan – Balades à pied*, published by Chamina (try Park HQ at St Brisson). There are 30 excellent walks in here, with first-class maps and good photographs. Anyone who reads French will enjoy the fascinating and informative text as well.

For Cyclists

- VTT circuits of varying difficulties are scattered the length and breadth of the Morvan – 137 of them at the last count. A topoguide of these, entitled *Le Morvan à VTT*, should be on sale at any Office de Tourisme in the region.

- Cyclists who prefer to keep tarmac under their wheels will find a map suggesting 34 circuits on minor roads for sale at the Maison du Parc in Saint-Brisson.

Watersports

- Rowing boats and canoes can be hired on both the Lac de Settons and the Lac de Panneçière.

- For those who like their water whipped up a little, kayaking and rafting are possible at several locations, in particular the Lac de Chaumeçon. Ask for details from any OT.

- The Base de Loisirs on the eastern shore of the Lac de Settons has a sailing centre and a swimming beach, supervised in summer. A trip boat makes regular tours of the lake in high season.

For the Palate

- In the Morvan, as you would expect, the cuisine is simple – but not lacking in flavour. Pork and ham are traditional favourites, and more recently a very fine sausage of both pork and ham marinated in white wine has been marketed.

- Other specialities include goat's cheese and fresh fish of all kinds from the local streams.

- And being at the heart of Burgundy, there is plenty of choice for wine to accompany the fare.

And the most memorable

- The peaceful view from the lovely grassy *Chaume* on the summit of Mont Beuvray – and just about everything else connected with the town of Bibracte.

- Walking around the Lac des Settons on a cloudless autumn day, with the water reflecting the bright blue of the sky and the golden beech trees providing perfect contrast.

- Who could fail to be impressed by the carvings on the tympanum at Vézelay?

10. Canal and river – the other Loire Valley

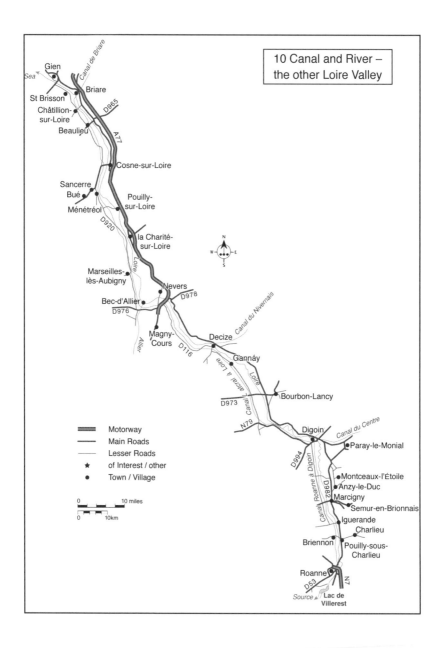

10 Canal and River – the other Loire Valley

Motorway
Main Roads
Lesser Roads
★ of Interest / other
● Town / Village

0 ———— 10 miles
0 ———— 10km

Sea
Gien
Canal de Briare
St Brisson
Briare
Châtillion-sur-Loire
D965
Beaulieu
A77
Cosne-sur-Loire
Sancerre
Bué
Pouilly-sur-Loire
Ménétréol
D920
la Charité-sur-Loire
N
W — E
S
Marseilles-lès-Aubigny
Loire
Nevers
Bec-d'Allier
D978
D976
Canal du Nivernais
Magny-Cours
Decize
Allier
D116
Gannáy
Lateral à la Loire
Loire
Bourbon-Lancy
D973
Canal
N79
Digoin
Canal du Centre
D994
Paray-le-Monial
Canal Roanne à Digoin
Montceaux-l'Étoile
D982
Anzy-le-Duc
Marcigny
Semur-en-Brionnais
Iguerande
Charlieu
Briennon
Pouilly-sous-Charlieu
Roanne
D53
N7
Source
Lac de Villerest

Most guide books regard the Loire Valley as simply that section of 'château-country' somewhere between Gien and Angers. But the mighty Loire is over 600 miles in length, and has already run well over half that distance before it even arrives at Gien. Surprisingly, very little is heard about its upper reaches.

The Loire is born dramatically enough, on the slopes of a scaly volcanic mountain high in the Cévennes – and its earliest days are described in Chapter 17. From these heights the Loire then descends through deep gorges before arriving at the plains of Forez, and thereafter its shallow valley cuts a south-north swathe through the heart of France. Around Gien the river suddenly seems to change its mind and head west – and in a way that is exactly what did happen, because when first formed in the Tertiary era, the Loire drained north into the Seine basin. Later movements and subsidence in the west caused it to turn and take its present almost right-angled course to the Atlantic.

It is the east-west section that now has most – but not all – of the châteaux (and the visitors), while the north-south section is particularly fascinating because every town and village on its banks bears witness to man's efforts to control and navigate the river in times past. By the 17th century the Loire was of great commercial importance – an importance that reduced dramatically when canals were built alongside the central section of the river all the way from Briare to Roanne. Even today commercial traffic as well as pleasure boats can be seen on the Canal Latéral à Loire and the Canal Roanne à Digoin.

The journey described here follows the fortunes of both river and canal for some 170 miles (274km), and it is genuinely possible to make most of the trip by boat as well as by car (for suggestions, see the information section). It will take you through the pottery town of Digoin and the island town of Décize, over the famous aqueduct at Briare and past some of France's finest vineyards (Sancerre, Pouilly, Giennois) – and if you can divert just a little there are bonuses like the Romanesque churches of the Brionnais, the *plus beau* village of Apremont-sur-Allier and the race-track of Nevers-Magny-Cours. And although there is a great deal of interest here, this voyage is quite off-the-beaten-track, in a part of France that is not on any holiday route and one that few stop to visit.

GIEN TO COSNE-SUR-LOIRE

This journey starts in **Gien**, the town where the Loire begins its bend to the west. The oldest building here is the château topping the town – the original was said to have been built by Charlemagne. Today's château houses a hunting museum (Musée International de la Chasse), where in addition to the expected rather grim weaponry and unfortunate stuffed victims, there are sections dealing with hunting-related fine art in the form of paintings, tapestries and ceramics. Below the château, the town sprawls rather attractively down to the riverside where shops and cafés tempt you to tarry awhile and enjoy views of the elegant 16th century bridge spanning the waters. Before you do though, it is worth a drive (or longish walk) to the north end of the waterfront and the Musée de la Faïencerie (Pottery Museum). Gien has been making glazed earthen-ware pottery for some 200 years and is particularly renowned for its deep blue glaze (*Bleu de Gien*) and the bright colours that decorate it. Dinner services are its most important output and you can purchase these, and other pieces, in the factory shop alongside the museum, as well as in many of the shops in town.

Beyond Gien the main road (D952) heads south for Briare and the canal, and as you go you can pick out the grey outlines of the **Château de St Brisson** above the trees on the opposite side of the river. Those with children might like to divert – the château has a fine display of bygone weaponry in its moat and on summer Sundays medieval catapults and battering rams are put through their paces. But on now to Briare and the first meeting of the canal heading south from Paris and the mighty Loire. It is an auspicious enough beginning, since the canal is carried high above the river on the longest aqueduct in Europe.

Travel guides do not make enough of **Briare**, but nevertheless it is hardly short of visitors. On the banks of the Royal River and with two canals rippling through its streets, it offers a wealth of waterside walks. The town trail suggested by the tourist office is rather long, and includes 14 bridges and seven locks, not to mention a very remarkable church and two museums. If you want to cut down on this, watery highlights are the peaceful green picnic area between the banks of the river and old canal, the quays of the Port de Plaisance linked by stylish green-arched bridges and, of course, the aqueduct itself, grandiosely flanked by four pillars bearing the coats of arms of Paris, Montargis, Nevers and Roanne.

The aqueduct is undoubtedly the town's biggest attraction. Opened in 1896, it is widely attributed to Eiffel (of tower fame), although it seems he was responsible only for the stonework, the design being that of a waterways engineer by the name of Léonce-Abel-Mazoyer. In the port alongside the aqueduct, an old barge sells souvenirs (and local wines), while a flotilla of trip boats offers visitors cruises to the other side and beyond, with or without sustenance en route. A boat hire base nearby buzzes with activity and a little tourist train stops here to take you round the rest of the town if you want to do things the easy way.

Leaving the water for the town itself, the church with its façade of glittering mosaics is immediately eye-catching. The story of these is told in the little Musée de Mosaïque et des Émaux (Museum of Mosaic and Enamel) at the top end of the town. Briare, like many other towns along the Loire, was once famous for its ceramic industry, but under one Joseph Bapterosse, the output here was largely buttons and fashion jewellery, earning the town the epithet 'City of Pearls'.

By the 1880s the production had turned to mosaics and a process of total vitrification created the enamels. Eminent artists of the day developed the designs. The little enamel museum has several fine exhibits, a replica of the angel on the church and a video showing how it is all done – a complicated procedure, unfortunately described in French only. But it is a place for picking up a mosaic souvenir or two, and the factory shop alongside has an interesting assortment of household tiles for sale. The museum may well inspire you to return to the church, commissioned by Joseph Bapterosse, where the interior is something of a mosaic exhibition.

The other museum at Briare is the **Musée des deux Marines** (Two Waterways), and this one is a must if

The Museum of two waterways

The 'Deux Marines' of this museum are river and canal navigations – Briare once thrived as a transhipment port between the two and you can still see its one-time quays beyond the Port de Plaisance. Packed with fascinating information, the museum is fortunately blessed with English-speaking staff who can explain it all. In its darkened rooms you will meet the flat-bottomed Loire boats (sapines) that once made the one-way trip down river, and were then broken up and sold for timber. Others, known as chalands, were fitted with a square sail to take them up river again – but this was only possible between Nantes and Briare, when the prevailing westerly wind was behind them.

The mid-17th century saw the beginning of the canals – the Briare canal was cut to connect the Seine basin with that of the Loire, and for the first time goods coming up or down river could be taken on to Paris. It was much later (1827 – 1838) that a canal was cut parallel to the Loire all the way down to Roanne, and the perils of river navigation were at an end. Well, almost! At one point canal and river had to cross and for many years (until the opening of the Pont-Aqueduct) this meant a dangerous traverse of the main flow for canal barges.

you are going to pursue the theme of watery navigation. All Briare's nautical past is explained, and there are working models of the Site de Mantelot, where canal barges once crossed the Loire itself.

Four miles (7km) upstream from Briare the **Site de Mantelot** is signed from the western end of the river bridge at Châtillon-sur-Loire. Now a preserved heritage site, its lock represents the end of the old Canal Lateral à Loire, and the tree-shaded rectangular pound behind it is the place where boats once queued to make the crossing of the river. Half a mile (1km) downstream on the opposite side was the lock at Combles, the start of the Briare Canal, and that short distance was the most dangerous part of any bargee's journey.

A long jetty was built out from the lock at Mantelot – you can see it today, extending as far as the bridge down-

stream, with a second less prominent jetty on the right. Boats worked their way between those jetties to get themselves two-thirds way over, then they were on their own. The passage upstream was most hazardous in time of flood, when the jetties were submerged and two anchors were needed. On average ten boats a year were lost on this crossing. After 1880, a tug and winch system reduced this loss of life, but it was nevertheless the perils of this stretch that prompted the building of the new canal and the Pont-Aqueduct.

If the river is not too high, it is possible to walk out on the main jetty, climb up the pillar of the road-bridge (a spiral path once used by draughthorses when their boats were crossing) and continue along the towpath of the old canal into Briare. The return to Mantelot can be made beside the new canal. Another worthwhile excursion from Mantelot starts by taking the path south along the riverside, which is well supplied with picnic-tables. It leads to the Gaston Nature Reserve – and if you do not manage to spot a beaver here, at least you are pretty sure to see the work of his teeth!

At this point it really should be time to get on with the journey, but it must be worth spending just a few minutes in **Châtillon-sur-Loire** itself. Its narrow streets lead up to the church at their summit, and here too the local industry is in evidence with fine mosaic Stations of the Cross. The houses in the square in front of the church are thought to date from the 15th century, and other remarkable buildings line the Rue Gelée opposite. At the bottom of the hill, the Tourist Office (surely one of the best stocked in France) will give you details of other streets worth exploring.

After Châtillon the road climbs to a plateau above the river. The first village is pretty **Beaulieu-sur-Loire**, and beyond it, the steaming towers of the Centre Nucléaire de Production d'Électricité dominate the scene. Standing on the banks of the Loire, the establishment was once open to visitors on production of a passport, but has been put out of bounds follow-ing the events of 11 September 2001. Across the road in the towers' shadow, the tiny Maison de Loire collects in-formation about the river and puts on a programme of changing exhibitions.

With the towers behind you, the next place on the horizon is the fairly busy town of **Cosne-sur-Loire**. Once again its centre (easily accessed from the river bridge) merits exploration – around the Place de la Résistance can be found an interesting Postal Museum and the Musée de la Loire Moyenne. Despite its name, the latter displays models and memorabilia relating to

this middle section of the Loire on its ground floor only, while reserving upstairs for works of art (including Utrillo, Vlaminck and others of note) and ceramics. Both museums are closed on Sunday mornings, but the compensation is a large and lively street market spilling through the heart of the town. The market is re-staged on a Wednesday, so that is the day to come if you want the best of all worlds!

SANCERRE AND THE WINE REGION

A few kilometres upstream and on the other side of the river, the village of **Sancerre** is a place of pilgrimage for wine-buffs, whether arriving by road or canal (the latter have their own taxi service). Crowning a little conical hill some 650ft (200m) above the river, the place once saw life as a Gallic oppi-dum. As a natural stronghold it was again important in the 15th century Wars of Religion, its inhabitants with-standing a siege of seven months, and for their stoicism finally being granted the right to practise their Protestant faith unhindered. Today it is the centre of an important wine growing region – but before seeking out the *caves* spend a few minutes exploring the jumble of narrow streets, ancient ram-parts and varied medieval buildings, of which one of the most notable is the 1508 *beffroi* (bell-tower) beside the Church of Notre-Dame.

The modern tourist office (conceal-ed half-underground in the central square) can offer a marked town trail to help you see the best of it all, in-cluding some superb distant views. From the Esplanade de la Porte César the vista extends east across the now-disused viaduct of St-Satur and the valley of the Loire to the blue distance where the first hills of the Morvan lift the horizon. In the opposite direction vineyards carpet the folded hills as far as the eye can see. The panorama takes on a more dizzying effect if you can climb the 200 or so steps up the grey Tour des Fiefs, all that remains of the 14th century Château of the Counts of Sancerre.

Time at last to sample the wine. The region produces mostly white from the Sauvignon grape and the somewhat unappealing term 'gunflint' is often used to describe its sharp dry quality. Reds and rosés from (the Pinot Noir) can also be found. Sancerre is not short of *caves* offering tastings, but consider just one short diversion – 5 km. to the south-west, off the D 955, is the pretty village of **Bué**, whose vineyards are said to be the 'King of Sancerre'. More than 40 wine-growers' establishments welcome visitors. Should it happen to be the first week in August, your *dégustation* will be accompanied by cavorting demons in the annual Witches Fair. But at any time of the year, the bonus in visiting Bué is that the return gives you the best possible views of hilltop Sancerre above its flowing patchwork skirt of vineyards – the scene pictured in many guide books and brochures.

Returning to the canal below Sancerre, the little village of **Ménétréol-sous-Sancerre** offers canal boaters pleasant moorings. From the waterside more *caves* can be reached – and signs direct you to a farm selling *crottins* (do not look in the dictionary) of goat's cheese, the local delicacy and the perfect accompaniment to the wine. Those venturing into the village will find other artisans' workshops to explore. Beyond Ménétréol the road follows the canal for a while, but you could – and should – branch left on the D59 to **Pouilly-sur-Loire**.

Pouilly is again famed for its AOC wines, producing both Pouilly-Fumé and Pouilly-sur-Loire (there is another wine with the name of Pouilly, Pouilly-Fuissé, but that fine wine is from the Maconnais region north of Lyon).

Once more the village abounds with *caves*, but having dealt with that side of the business, faithful followers of the river will want to head north along its banks to the state-of-the-art Pavillon du Milieu de Loire. It is a hands-on sort of place and children will have fun pressing the buttons, but the texts here are in French only. The roof terrace affords views up and down the river, where for 12 miles (19km) in each direction the banks are a designated nature reserve. Marked footpaths start from the Maison, and there is a picnic area and children's playground.

How long is the Loire?

Pouilly boasts that it is exactly at the mid-point of the Loire, and signs tell you that it is 496km to its source high in the Cévennes and 496km to its mouth on the Bay of Biscay, which does not quite fit in with the usual estimated length of 1020m.! It makes you realise what a small fraction of the whole is guidebook 'Loire Valley'.

Pouilly is on the right bank of the river and **la Charité-sur-Loire**, the next pause on your journey, is on the same side a few kilometres upstream. Nevertheless, it is worth going back across the river and entering la Charité from the west for two reasons – firstly because you get the classic view of the priory church and river bridge this way (the bridge is said to be one of the two oldest on the Loire) and secondly because you can park on the riverside with easy access to the part of the town that you probably want to see. Entering the narrow street at the end of the river bridge, you will straight away notice the excess of bookshops. La Charité is one of France's four or five book towns, a place where untold literary treasures lie for the most part concealed in fusty inner rooms, although possibly they may see light of day at one of the regular street markets.

The priory of la Charité is a treasure itself. Built in the 11th century as a daughter of the Benedictine establishment at Cluny, the renowned generosity of its early inhabitants brought the needy from all around to its gates – and earned the town its present name. As you approach from the river bridge, the tower ahead was one of two originals, latterly topped by a grey spire, and the courtyard beyond was once part of the vast abbey nave. The houses on the left of the courtyard (one of which now hosts the Office de Tourisme) have been built in the north aisle. What survives of the church is vast enough – the remainder of the nave, the transept and the chancel, with just a glimpse of the cloisters on the north side. The whole forms one of the most out-standing examples of Romanesque architecture in Burgundy – for all the finer details, a leaflet is on offer at the

Tourist Office. Some of the artefacts uncovered in the excavation of the priory site are exhibited in the town museum nearby (along with modern artwork, glassware and ceramics). And before you leave la Charité, you might just like to climb up to the ramparts behind for an overview of the whole priory site that includes the river and its elegant bridge.

LA CHARITÉ TO NEVERS

From la Charité it is only a short hop along the N7 to Nevers. The scenic route (D45) beside the canal will take rather longer – and there are a couple of stops to make on the way. The first of these is **Marseilles-lès-Aubigny**, a classic canal village and port, developed at the point where the Canal Lateral à Loire was once joined by the Canal du Berry. All that can now be seen of the latter waterway is a wooden lift bridge, curiously stranded on a tiny traffic island, but the port is attractive and still very functional, with commercial and pleasure boats moored. Alongside the port, the Quai Auguste Mahaut is named after the 19th century waterways pioneer who fought for the construction of this lateral canal in preference to the alternative plan of canalising the Loire itself. Immediately below the village flows the Loire, and long before the canal era, there was a port here, too, used mainly for the transhipment of iron ore. The riverside toll booth where monks once exacted revenue for each load passing has now become a restaurant of some repute, the Auberge du Poids de Fer – and the building looks to have changed little over the centuries.

A few kilometres to the south (still on the D45) is **Apremont sur Allier**, one of the *plus beaux villages de France* that are always worth a detour, even though some of them are rather over-subscribed. That criticism does not apply to Apremont though – the village sleeps quietly enough, its neat buildings in blended brown and beige contrasting with their bright flowered gardens, all strung out along the banks of the Allier. There was a port here once, and centuries before that the grey château was built on its bluff above the river. Its grounds are now the Parc Floral, the only attraction open to visitors, and they are lovely. Lawns, lakes and cascading water are graced with a Chinese bridge, a Turkish pavilion and a belvedere decorated with interesting ceramics.

Time now to return to the Loire and the city of Nevers. After reaching the D976, the aqueduct that carries the Canal Lateral à Loire across the Allier can be seen on the right – it is a 'single-track' stretch for boats, with traffic lights controlling either end. The first roundabout carries signs to the **Bec d'Allier**, the confluence of two wild sandy-banked rivers, the Loire and the Allier. You can drive north in a couple of minutes to view the site, but far more interesting is the well-marked walk to the confluence (a path known as the Sentier du Passeur) that starts from the nearby village of Gimouille.

Farther on down the D976, a left turn will take you across the river into the bustle of **Nevers** – and if you do not want to attempt its one-way systems, there is at least a little parking at the north end of the bridge. From here it is just a short walk up the narrow streets to the Cathedral and Palais Ducal. The latter dates from the 15th century and was once the residence of the Dukes of Nièvre.

Today it houses what seems a very scantily stocked Office de Tourisme for such a large city. Nevertheless, those who want to see the sights are offered a leaflet of two town trails, negotiated by simply following the blue lines painted on the pavements. It should be easy – but unless you want to do it all (2 hours +) just make sure you get the right line going in the right direction!

At least you cannot miss the impressively large Cathedral of St Cyr and Ste Julitte standing opposite. A hotch-potch of architectural styles, it was unfortunately hit by a stray RAF bomb in 1944 and has been rebuilt with some fine modern stained glass replacing the original. Its other unusual feature is the presence of two choirs, one at each end of the nave. Following the blue lines from the cathedral entrance (right, not left), you will also be led through the pottery quarter, around some very pleasant ramparts, and past the Frédéric Blandin Museum, which contains priceless ceramics and glassware. Other places of interest in Nevers are the Renaissance church of St Etienne (on the other blue line route) and the Convent of St Gildard, an ancient place of pilgrimage that now houses the shrine of St Bernadette.

If before leaving Nevers you would like to escape the urban scene and take a riverside stroll, there is an excellent path following the riverbank for about 2 miles (3km) downstream. It is an undemanding ramble, the sort that families take on a Sunday morning, and has been provided with display boards with information about the river flora and fauna – given by a parrot.

The parrot of Nevers

'Ver-Vert' is an integral part of Nevers folk-lore. The subject of a poem by one Gerret in 1733, he was the treasured and voluble pet of the nuns of the Visitandine Convent in Nevers. They proudly sent him downstream to show off his linguistic talents to the Sisters in Nantes – and predictably he learned an entire new vocabulary from the bargees en route. Ver-Vert was swiftly dispatched home and put into solitary confinement until the new words were forgotten – after which time the good nuns were so pleased to get him back that they gave him too many tit-bits and he promptly died from over-eating. A sad story!

At this point motor racing enthusiasts will want to take a detour to the Grand Prix track of **Nevers-Magny-Cours**, which sprawls over a vast area about 6 miles (10km) to the south, just off the N7. The museum near the entrance is devoted to Formula 1 racing, and to the Ligier team in particular. It is also possible to take a turn on the go-karting track or to get a driving lesson in a Formula 3 car on the Grand Prix circuit. Most days the air is roaring with all the wanabe Prosts enjoying their birthday treats at the wheel, and you can stand on the empty terraces to take in the scene.

AND ON TO ROANNE

Back to the river again now – or to the canal, which is more easily accessed from Nevers-Magny-Cours. A pleasant minor road follows the latter all the way to Décize. **Décize** itself is a fairly unimpressive place – a few remnants of ramparts and a central bell-tower are its most remarkable features. But the town has location, with so many waterfronts that you are never quite sure what you are looking at. Effectively, it is on an island between the 'old' and new courses of the Loire. To the north of Décize, the Vieille Loire is joined by the River Aron and the Canal du Nivernais, arriving from the heart of Burgundy. To the south passes the Canal Lateral à Loire and boats travelling from one canal to the other must use a short section of the Loire itself. Since all this takes place within the confines of the town there is always plenty of action, and the best point to view it all is at the tip of the island, reached via the lime-tree-shaded Promenade des Halles (from beside the Tourist Office).

On south again now. Canal followers (on the D116) can call in at **Gannay-sur-Loire** – the village has a tiny port, but more fascinating is the reverence given to a stump of a tree beside the Mairie in the long main street. Said to have been planted in 1597 by Sully, a minister of Henry IV, this much venerated specimen wears a little roof to keep out the rain and no longer seems to be quite alive!

A few kilometres east of Gannay on the other side of the Loire, the hilltop town of **Bourbon-Lancy** makes a welcome diversion from the rather flat landscape of the river valley. On the summit is the older part of the town – under the archway of the *beffroi* you can admire architecture surviving from the Middle Ages (note the 16th century half-timbered Maison du Bois and look upwards at the quaint little 'Beurdin' who rings out the hours). A very short stroll takes you around the old quarter, including ramparts and the pretty Jardin de la Collégiale. At the foot of the hill, Bourbon-Lancy is a very different place – a stylish, belle-époque spa town with an impressive thermal establishment. Alongside is an extensive lakeside park in which one corner has been reserved for a pleasant campsite.

South of Bourbon-Lancy, the first place of note (except that guidebooks rarely give it a mention) is Digoin. Briare and Décize may be watery places, but wettest of all must be **Digoin**. Four rivers join the Loire in Digoin and the town also boasts the junction of three canals – the Canal Lateral à Loire, the Canal Roanne à Digoin and the Canal du Centre. The latter is carried across the Loire on an aqueduct built much earlier (1834– 38) than that at Briare. At the town end of the aqueduct stands the new ObservaLoire, an imaginative museum encompassing all aspects of the river. On the ground floor, with walls of deep blue, you are under the water (fish and other inhabitants), upstairs has the navigation story again. A viewing arena with seats and binoculars invites you to survey the riverside wildlife (and, curiously, a storks' nest in summer – Digoin has a pair that return each year). The town's other distinction is again its pottery. Digoin has been an important production centre since Gallo-Roman times and examples spanning 2000 years are on display in the 14 or so rooms of the Musée de la Céramique beside the Office de Tourisme in the centre of town.

Beyond Digoin, the canal (now the Canal Roanne à Digoin) and river follow each other fairly closely all the way to Roanne. A tiny road sticks by the canal, while east of the river, the D982 speeds more urgent traffic south. But do not be tempted to hurry – this is interesting country! South of Digoin, the area to the east of the Loire is known as the **Brionnais** – a rolling countryside with field after field of Charollais cattle (the eponymous Charolles to the north-east is the breed centre), and dotted with ancient villages whose building stone is a distinctive pale blonde or yellow in colour. The Brionnais is a veritable exhibition of Romanesque architecture and it seems that every town or village has a church of some note.

If you have time for a big diversion, start first at **Paray-le-Monial** – its impressive 11th century basilica beside the calmly flowing Bourbince was directly inspired by Cluny. Inside, the sweeping plain high-arched interior has recently been restored, but you may have doubts about the wash that has been applied to the stone, presumably to recreate the original colour.

Today Paray-le-Monial is a great centre of pilgrimage, in France second only to Lourdes. In the late 17th century, a nun, one Marguerite-Marie Alacoque, received here visions of the Sacred Heart of Jesus – events that later led to worship of the Sacred Heart, the building of the Sacré-Coeur in Montmartre, and huge annual pilgrimages to Paray-le-Monial. The Chapel of the Visitation where these revelations were made can be visited – and if you get that far, it is worth going on to the Hôtel de Ville with its remarkably carved Renaissance façade, and the 16th century Tour St-Nicholas opposite. The Office de

Tourisme (beside the basilica) can give you a map.

Other churches in the Brionnais that merit attention are legion. Do not miss the carvings above and around the doorway of lovely yellow-stoned **Montceaux l'Étoile** and then go on (via the D174) to **Anzy-le-Duc** with its classical octagonal belfry. The carvings on the tympanum are fine here too – like those at Montceaux l'Etoile, they depict the ascension. If you continue south from here to **Semur-en-Brionnais** you can enjoy another fine Cluniac-style church, the Collegiale Saint-Hilaire, and this one is most notable for its unique interior 'hanging gallery' above the west door. Semur-en-Brionnais is yet another flower-garlanded village that has the distinction of belonging to the 144 *plus beaux* of France. The Chapter House beside the church houses a library and exhibition of Romanesque art, and you can also visit the ruined 9th century Château St-Hugues.

From Semur-en-Brionnais the direct road back to river and canal passes through **Marcigny**. Not too remarkable a place in itself, it does have a few buildings dating back a thousand years, and the 15th century Tour du Moulin, now a many-faceted museum, is interesting. Present day excitement is offered by the extensive street markets, held twice a week – and, since Marcigny is the home of the famous Emile Henry cookware, a large factory shop where you can pick up discounted items (in the Zone Industrielle, just off the D982).

South from Marcigny you are soon leaving the Brionnais, but there is just one more treat in store – the Romanesque church at **Iguerande**. Rather squat and heavy, and with little carving exteriorly, it is the warmth of the stone, the interior capitals and the glorious hilltop setting that make Iguerande memorable. Opposite the church, a tiny eco-museum (Reflet …Brionnais) paints a delightful picture of local life in past times. The main village of Iguerande stretches along the D482 at the foot of the hill. Crossing over this road, you can briefly renew your acquaintance with both the Loire and the canal before heading south again.

Reaching the cross-roads in the town of Pouilly-sous-Charlieu, there is a decision to be made. If you have not already overdosed on sacred art, the town of **Charlieu**, 4 miles (6km) to the east, has much more to offer. The old abbey here was said to have been 'the most decorative of the daughters of Cluny'. Ravaged by the Revolution, little of it remains, but it is still possible to take a guided tour – or simply to stand outside and admire the tympanum of the great doorway, where, fashioned in caramel stone, Christ in Majesty is attended by the four Evangelists. Charlieu itself is a fine town with some ancient houses gathered around the Place St Philibert. In the Ancien Hôtel-Dieu are two museums of note, one devoted to the local art of silk-weaving, the other a recreation of the hospital existing in this building a century or so ago. Just outside the town, the 13th century Couvent des Cordeliers has retained its cloisters, which offer yet another magnificent display of carvings in honey-coloured stone.

Turning west rather than east at Pouilly will bring you to quite a different scene – the canal-side village of **Briennon**. Once a thriving port that dealt largely with the loading of locally made tiles, Briennon today offers pleasure boaters smart moorings along its one-time wharves, where landscaped gardens have now been laid. At one end, the unique Parc des Canaux offers youngsters the opportunity to take radio-controlled boats through miniature canals and negotiate changes of level with locks, boat lifts and even an inclined plane. An old canal barge moored alongside gives visitors a glimpse of working life on the canal.

On at last to **Roanne**. A large, busy city thriving on its textile industry, it is probably not one in which visitors will want to linger for too long. Nevertheless, it has for a long time been an important inland waterways town. Coal from around St Etienne was loaded into the flat-bottomed Loire boats here long before the arrival of the canal and with it, the huge transhipment basin. Today that basin is full of pleasure boats of all kinds, some of them seemingly far too large to ever leave it for the narrow canal. At one end of the basin a lock links the canal with the Loire, and that surely is where you are headed – the southerly limit of canal navigation, the union of canal and river, a suitable journey's end. To find it, simply follow signs left to the Port as you arrive in Roanne on the D482 from the north. There is plenty of parking around the basin, and it makes a pleasant place to take your leave of the canal you have followed for so long.

The river, of course, goes on. It is at least another 187 miles (300km) to its source in the Cévennes, and a splendidly scenic journey all the way, culminating in the 'undiscovered' region described in Chapter 17. But if you just want to look around locally, the Tourist Office near the station should be able to help (the *Trois Gros*, one of France's top restaurants is here too if you are feeling a bit peckish!). For a day's excursion outside town, head south to the attractive Lac de Villerest (created by damming the river) and look in at the old combined village of St Jean-St Maurice on its western bank. To the west of here are the vineyards of the Côte Roannaise and above them, the wild and deserted Monts de la Madeleine with fine scenery and many viewpoints. If you get as far as the Rocher de Rochefort (beside the D51 above Arcon), try picking out the river bridge at Roanne in the far, far distance – a final view of the mighty Loire.

Offices de Tourisme

Gien
Place Jean Jaurès BP 13
45501GIEN
☎ 02.38.67.25.28

Briare-le-Canal
1, Place Charles de Gaulle
45250 BRIARE-LE-CANAL
☎ 02.38.31.24.51

La Charité-sur-Loire
5, Place Ste. Croix
58400 LA-CHARITÉ-SUR-LOIRE
☎ 03.86.70.15.06

Nevers
Palais Ducal
4, Rue Sabatier BP 818
58008 NEVERS
☎ 03.86.68.46.00

Digoin
8, Rue Guilleminot
71160 DIGOIN
☎ 03.85.53.00.81

Roanne
1, Cours de la République
42300 ROANNE
☎ 04.77.71.51.77

PLACES OF INTEREST

The following companies operate **hire cruisers** on the Canal Lateral à Loire and the Canal Roanne à Digoin:

Crown Blue Line
Bases at Briare, Décize.
☎ 03.86.25.46.64

Charmes Nautiques
Base at Briare.
☎ 02.38.31.28.73

Les Canalous
Bases at Briare and Digoin.
☎ 03.85.53.76.74

Connoisseur
Base at Gannay.
☎ 03.84.64.95.20

For more names and further details, try the website:
www.europeafloat.com/frln.htm

Gien

Musée International de la Chasse
Open January to May and October to December 9am-12noon, 2-6pm; June to September 9am-6pm.

Musée de la Faïencerie
Open throughout the year 9am-12noon and 2-6pm. No morning opening in January or February. No lunchtime closure weekdays in July and August.

Château de St Brisson

Château open April to mid-November, every day except Wednesday, 10am-12noon, 2-6pm Medieval weaponry displays on 'Summer Sundays' at 3.30 and 4.30pm.

Briare

Musée de la Mosaïque et des Émaux
Open June to September 10am-6.30pm; rest of year, 2-6pm. Closed January.

Musée des Deux Marines
Open June to September 10am-12.30pm, 2-6.30pm; March, April, May and October to 15th November 2-6pm.

Cosne-sur Loire

Musée de la Loire Moyenne
Open every day except Tuesday 10am-12noon, 2.30-6.30pm. Closed in January.

Musée de la Poste (Post Office & Postman's Museum)
Open every day except Monday morning and Sunday, 10am-12noon, 3-6pm.

Sancerre

Tour des Fiefs
Open only on bank holiday and
weekend afternoons. No charge.

Pouilly-sur-Loire

Pavillon du Milieu de la Loire
Open July and August every day
10am-12noon, 2-7pm; May, June,
September, October and school
holidays every day except
Tuesdays 10am-12noon, 2-7pm;
November to March (except
January) weekends only 2-6pm.

La Charité-sur-Loire

Church of Notre-Dame
Open daily from 9am-5pm
throughout the year.

Municipal Museum
Open July and August every day
except Tuesday, 10am-12noon, 2-
7pm; April to June and September
to November every day except
Monday and Tuesday, 10am-
12noon, 2-6pm; December to
March weekends only, 10am-
12noon, 2-6pm.

Apremont-sur-Allier

Parc Floral
Open : April to September every
day (but closed September
Tuesdays) 10.30am-12.30pm,
2.30-6.30pm.

Nevers

Musée Frédéric Blandin
Open daily except Tuesdays
throughout the year. May to
September 10am-6.30pm;
October to April 1-5.30pm
(Sundays 10am-12noon, 2-
5.30pm).

Nevers-Magny-Cours racetrack
Rides in race cars, track
experiences, go-karting and 4x4
track – contact Technopole, 58470
NEVERS-MAGNY-COURS,
☎ 03.86.21.80.00 for details

Digoin

ObservaLoire
Open July and August every day
10am-6pm (7.30pm Wed); May,
June, September and October 2-
6pm every day except Tuesday.

Musée de la Céramique
Guided visits June to October
10.30am, 2 and 5pm; April and
May 10.30am, 3 and 4.30pm;
November to March 3 and
4.30pm. Closed on Sundays
except Sunday afternoons mid-
June to mid-September.

Iguerande

Musée Reflet...Brionnais
Open April to 1st November
2.30-6pm.

Charlieu

Abbaye Bénédictine
Open Feb., March, Nov.,
Dec.10am-12.30pm,2-5.30pm;
April, May, June, Sept., Oct.
10am-12.30pm, 2-6.30pm; July
and August 10am-12noon, 1-7pm.

**Musée de la Soierie
(Silk Museum)**
Open February – mid-June and
mid-September to December 2-
6pm. Closed Mondays. Mid-June to
mid-September, open every day
10am-7pm.

Musée Hospitalier
Opening times as for the Silk
Museum.

Couvent des Cordeliers
Open Feb., March, Nov. 2-5pm and April, May, June, Sept., Oct 10am-12.30pm, 2-6pm. Closed Mondays in these months. July and August open every day 10am-1pm, 2-7pm.

Briennon

Parc des Canaux
Open April, May, Sept., Oct. 1.30-7pm. June, July, August 10am-12noon, 1.30-7pm.

LOCAL HIGHLIGHTS

Best Walks

- Walks from the Site de Mantelot. The distance along jetty and canal to Briare is about 4 miles (6km) – double it for the whole circuit. The yellow-flashed riverside path and *Sentier du Gaston* through the nature reserve forms a circuit of about 5 miles (8km).

- The Office de Tourisme in Nevers has leaflets on two excellent walks. The first of these is the two and a half mile (4km) *Sentier du Passeur* (Ferryman's Path), the walk from Gimouille to the Bec d'Allier, provided with information boards (in English too) and an observation hide at the confluence. The second is the 2 mile (3.5km) *Sentier du Ver-Vert* along the riverside in Nevers. A pleasant and easy ramble.

- Off piste now. If you have time at the end of the trip there is some splendid walking in the vicinity of Roanne. Seasoned walkers will enjoy the well-signed paths in the Monts de la Madeleine to the west. Easier walking is to be found in the region around the Lac de Villerest in the south – ask OT for the leaflet Val d'Aix et d'Isable.

Cycling

- The canalside towpaths are often fit for cycling and some have been replaced by quiet minor roads. The towpath along the Canal du Centre between Digoin and Paray-le-Monial is scheduled to open in 2004, and hopefully will be extended.

- OT at Nevers can offer a folder of routes along the 'loveliest back roads' of the *département* of Nièvre (*la Nièvre en Cyclotourisme* – 48 circuits).

- Mountain bikers get their best chance at the end of the trip with the Monts de la Madeleine. Ask OT at Nevers for routes.

Watersports

- The Zone de Loisirs at Chevenon (just south of Nevers) comprises a lake with supervised swimming beach, water-slide, pedalos, play equipment and picnic-tables.

- There are many bases offering canoe/kayak hire along the length of the Loire. For information on those in Nièvre, contact RANDONIÈVRE, 3, Rue du Sort, 58000 NEVERS, ☎ 03.86.36.92.98. Farther south, contact Camping de la Chevrette, 71000 DIGOIN, ☎ 03 85 53 11 49

For the palate

- This trip takes you through so many vineyards – Giennois, Sancerre, Pouilly, Côte Roannaise. You could lay down a cellar!

- The perfect accompaniment to the 'flinty' wines is the cheese Crottins de Chavignol.

- Look out for Brioche Pralinée – a pink-striped sweet bread typical of the Brionnais.

And the most memorable

- Walking along the Sentier de Ver-Vert in Nevers on a Sunday morning – cyclists, rollerskaters, joggers by the score and whole rambling families including dog and even horse were there. Around noon everyone suddenly disappeared – presumably someone had been left at home to rustle up a five-course lunch for them all.

- At the end of the trip, a balmy evening in the most attractive campsite at St Paul-de-Vézelin (Arpheuilles), overlooking the Lac de Villerest.

- Standing beneath a lime tree before the church at Montceaux-l'Etoile on a hot summer's day, and feeling completely dazzled by the colours of the stone. The carvings around the door are something special, too.

Following a river adds a theme, a sense of adventure to a holiday. This journey up the Creuse may not be quite in the same league as Burton and Speke's mammoth trek to the source of the Nile, but it may be, that like climbing a mountain, following a river to its source satisfies an instinct, and is something that has to be done simply 'because it is there'.

If you are thinking of a river-orientated holiday in France, it is more likely that giants like the Loire or the Seine will spring to mind. Both are rivers that empty themselves directly into the sea and are therefore referred to by the French as *fleuves* – the Creuse is only a humble *rivière*, ending its days by quietly mingling its waters with those of the River Vienne. But setting out to follow the Loire would mean a journey of more than 600 miles while trekkers up the Seine would need to negotiate the urban jungle of Paris. At merely 155 miles (250km) in length the Creuse is a holiday-sized river, and what is more, it spends its whole life in some of the loveliest and least-known countryside in France. As one Office de Tourisme put it, 'not even the French know the Creuse'. And that is exactly its charm – this is a quiet gentle river flowing through *la France profonde*, well away from the usual tourist trails. The bonus is that the Creuse is also a valley of artists – writers, poets, painters, sculptors, stone-masons and weavers have for centuries set up home along its banks and many are there today.

The Creuse has its origins on the edge of the Massif Central in a high land of lakes and forests known as the Plateau of Millevaches – literally,

this is the Plateau of a Thousand Cows, and no-one could miss the plump rich-brown Limousin cattle grazing every available pasture. But the journey described here starts from the other end, the final meeting with the Vienne, an event that takes place in somewhat unmemorable countryside to the south of Tours. Working upstream from this point you are very soon in Descartes (a self-styled town of philosophers), and from this moment on, in addition to some wonderful scenery, there is so much of interest all the way.

The spa town of la Roche Posay is followed by the Abbey of Fongombault, which invites visitors to its services in Gregorian chant. Farther on you reach the watery landscape of the Regional Park of the Brenne, and then the old town of Argenton, overlooked by the even older town of St Marcel with its Roman excavations. In the flower-decked village of Gargilesse, Georges Sand once had her home and while there you should not miss the well-preserved frescoes in the church crypt. Upstream again, the river has been dammed to create the attractive Lac de Chambon with the splendidly-sited ruins of the Château of Crozant at its southern tip and the little holiday villages of Chambon and Fougères on opposite banks. Here latter-day sculptors display their creations along waterside paths and, farther south, the sleepy village of Fresselines, where Monet once painted the river, is now home to a handful of present day artists and their studios. More craft work can be seen in the riverside towns of Aubusson and Felletin, both of which have been making Europe's finest tapestries for over 600 years. And the

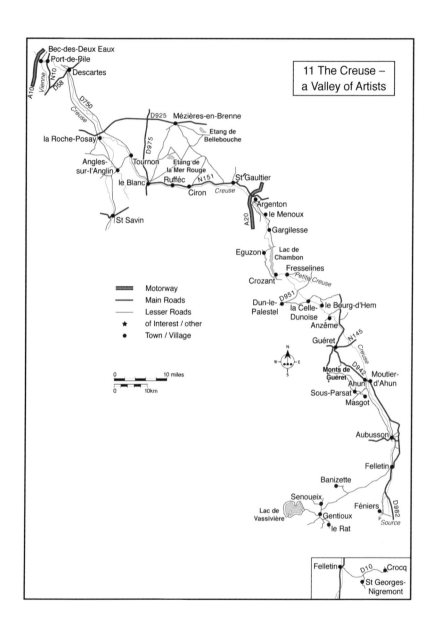

11 The Creuse –
a Valley of Artists

Motorway
Main Roads
Lesser Roads
★ of Interest / other
● Town / Village

0   10 miles
0   10km

Creuse is renowned for the skill of its stonemasons, many of who were involved in the building of Paris. Getting away from the artistic life, there is also plenty in this valley for outdoor enthusiasts or those with energetic children to be taken care of. Many villages have river (or lake) beaches for bathing and boating; outside Guéret the wooded hills are a paradise for mountain bikers (Europe's biggest permanent maze and a wolf sanctuary are also to be found here); and along the length of the river, there are innumerable waymarked hiking trails. At the end of the day, all wannabe explorers can seek out the sources of the river (they are signed and there is more than one) on the remote Plateau of Millevaches.

All this is only the bare bones of what is on offer in and around the valley of the Creuse – and there is more again to be seen if you are happy to do a little diverting. It would, of course, be perfectly possible to drive the whole length of the Creuse in a day, but you could equally well take a month over the route. Allow yourself as much time as you can afford, and you are guaranteed to return feeling you have explored the very heart of France. But it may be difficult to tell your friends where you have been, because few people have ever heard of the Creuse!

THE JOURNEY BEGINS

If you are going to play the game in following the river to its source you will certainly want to see its end before you set off. The **confluence of the Creuse and the Vienne** is about 12 miles (20km) south of Tours at a small place by the name of Bec des Deux Eaux – effectively, Mouth of

Two Waters. You can reach the spot by following the N10 south of St Maure-de-Touraine to the little village of Port-de-Piles and then turning west for a couple of kilometres. After crossing the bridge over the Vienne, a track on the right leads down to the riverside. This confluence seems almost a non-event, a quiet joining of the waters overlooked only by a handful of cows grazing peacefully in this unassuming flat countryside. Yet even so, someone has seen fit to provide a picnic table in a little clearing under the trees. A few metres farther on a couple of bar/restaurants stand beside the road and since this is such a small village, it seems there must be visitors who come just to see this confluence. When you have taken your fill of the scene, you are on your way.

Crossing directly over the N10, the road leads on to the town of **Descartes** a pleasant but unremarkable little town.

Named for a famous son

Descartes was born at Descartes, except that he was not really, because the place was named la Haye at the time. In 1967, the burghers of the town decided it was time to lift this quiet backwater from its anonymity and give it the status of a 'town of philosophy', renaming it in honour of its one great son, who was born here in 1590.

Its central square is dominated by a statue of the man himself, book in hand and globe at feet, looking down with possibly disapproving eye on the frivolous drinkers at the near-by bar.

A few metres away on the Rue Descartes you will find the Musée Descartes and by now you may well be thinking that there is nothing but Descartes in the whole place. Not so – the town council have been magnanimous enough to extend their street naming to all the other philosophers they could think of. Hence the square beside the Office de Tourisme is the Place Blaise Pascal – and it is here that you should think of parking the car if you want to visit the museum, which contains manuscripts and other memorabilia of the great man's life.

Leaving Descartes you can take the road south on either side of the river. The road to the east is slightly wider, but the one on the west is more scenic, winding lazily through old brownstone hamlets with snatched glimpses of the Creuse between its tree-lined banks. Each village seems to offer a picnic site beside the tranquil river. **La Roche Posay** is a town not earning even a mention in some of the standard travel guides, but is a delightful place for all that. The Romans were the first to record that the hot springs found here appeared beneficial to health and in particular were favourable for skin complaints. In the 16th century Henri IV's patronage established the town as an 'official' centre for dermatological treatment and on the strength of this la Roche Posay has flourished.

The town's centrepiece is a large square shaded by lime trees where fountains play and old men cast their boules from dawn to dusk and on into the night. From this square a road leads to the old town, passing one of the thermal establishments, the Hotel St Roch, on the way. A recently installed fountain and water trough enable everyone to take advantage of the healing waters and the addition of a tap allows the local population fill their bottles – and no doubt to never have a blemish on their bodies. Beyond an arched gateway is the old town where you can wander through the narrow streets to the 11th century church, walk out on the ramparts or descend to the bathing place beside the bridge over the river. The second thermal establishment in la Roche Posay is a rather more grand affair, built some 70 years ago alongside the road to Poitiers. On the slopes on the opposite side you can see its forerunner, the little Pavillon Rose, which itself was built on the site of a treatment centre founded by Napoleon for the benefit of his soldiers. Surrounding the pavilion are vast gardens and wide areas of green parkland that stretch to the campsite at the top of the hill.

DIVERSION TO A 'BEAU VILLAGE'

You have only just begun this journey up the Creuse and already it is time for a diversion. Seven and a half miles (12km) to the south is the tongue-twistingly named village of **Angles-sur-l'Anglin**, rejoicing in the prestigious title of *un des plus beaux villages de France*. An old château now in ruins sits on a bluff above the river (the Anglin) while the village itself spills down the cliff and across the bridge to the opposite side. Many stone houses garlanded with bright flowers and an old watermill on the riverside add to its photogenic qualities, but, perhaps unfortunately, at least at weekends and holiday times, Angles is not without its admirers.

An anticipated addition to the village attractions is a reproduction frieze of Magdalenian rock carvings (the original is in a cave nearby), but although there has been much publicity for this artefact, its ultimate siting has long been a matter of dispute. One of the more curious aspects of Angles-sur-l'Anglin is its drawn thread embroidery work known as the *Jours d'Angles* and produced uniquely by a handful of ladies in the village. This very fine craftsmanship is probably seen at its best in the little shop beside the Office de Tourisme (which appears to have remained unchanged over the last century), but anyone thinking of buying souvenirs in quantity will need to take a heavy purse.

If you have strayed this far from the Creuse, you will easily be persuaded to carry on south to **St Savin** where the Romanesque abbey church beside the river (now the Gartempe) is a UNESCO World Heritage site, and boasts what are said to be the most complete set of frescoes in all France. The most impressive of these are depictions of stories from the books of Genesis and Exodus to be found on the vaulting of the nave – and it is probably the subtlety of the tones rather than the artwork that will be most memorable. Apparently three colours only were used – red ochre, yellow ochre and green – and these were then mixed with white and black to produce this exquisite blend of shades. The figures themselves are very expressive, their long slender limbs giving the impression of life and movement. The best view of the whole length of this sizeable abbey church can be had by walking out over the river bridge, from which you can also admire the 14th century *vieux pont* still standing downstream on the opposite side.

ALONG THE RIVER TO LE BLANC

St. Savin is some distance west of the Creuse, and from this point you would do best to return to Angles sur l'Anglin and then head across to meet the river again at Tournon – although strict Creuse-followers would need to return to la Roche-Posay and take the riverside road from there. Whatever your choice, you now have a pleasant road all the way to Le Blanc, on the way passing **Fongombault Abbey**, a haven of peace tucked away in tall trees beside the river.

The abbey has as chequered a history as any, but in 1948 was restored to its original Benedictine order and is occupied by them to this day. It is not possible to visit the abbey itself, but you can go into the silent incense-laden church alongside where you are welcome to join in services held twice a day, and wallow in the timeless beauty of plainsong. Beyond the abbey is the village of Fongombault itself, its warm-stone houses typical of this part of the Creuse. At a little picnic site across the bridge you can pause to enjoy the calm river with its water-lilies and dipping willows.

Heading on south, cliffs soon appear on the opposite bank, their bald limestone faces demonstrating the bedrock in these parts. A few kilometres farther on you arrive at **Le Blanc**, a fair-sized town dominated by the Château Naillac on its perch above the river. Naillac is a château with two keeps, one of which one now houses the Ecomusée de la Brenne, a place full of fascinating information (sadly only in French although a rather quirky English translation is offered to help you round), making an excellent introduction to the area of lakeland you are about to enter.

The main part of the town lies downhill on the other side of the river and it is here you will find the church of St Génitour. St Génitour was a 4th century saint who, having just been decapitated for his faith, crossed the river with his severed head tucked underneath his arm and reached a chapel on the opposite bank. Putting his fingers through a hole in the door he alerted the blind guardian whose sight he promptly restored. St Génitour was subsequently buried in the chapel. There is still a hole in the door today and it is said that slipping a finger in this will heal all eye complaints – and for some reason, will also increase fertility.

NATURAL REGIONAL PARK OF THE BRENNE

Diversions, diversions! At this point the Creuse is running through the **Natural Regional Park of the Brenne** and it would be a pity to go on without just a glance at this interesting area where the natural landscape and ecology are sensitively managed while at the same time encouraging visitors. The Brenne is a relatively low-lying land of many lakes, its flatness broken only by a scattering of hillocks of heather-covered red sandstone – the *boutons*. The story goes that these out-of-character 'buttons' were lumps of mud shaken from the boots of the giant Gargantua as he strode across the boggy terrain. The lakes of the Brenne are in fact artificial and have been created by the building of dykes on each of which you will see a *bonde* – a sort of plug. When this is raised the lake will drain, a procedure sometimes carried out in the winter months to the excitement of the local pop-

ulation who come to catch the fish.

If you head north from le Blanc to the village of Douadic, the D17 to le Bouchet will then take you alongside the most extensive of the lakes, the Étang de la Mer Rouge. A small parking area gives access to a footpath beside the water. A few minutes down the road, the medieval Château du Bouchet has a long history dating back to its occupation by the English in the Hundred Years War. Visits are possible on certain days and there are fine views from its terrace across the Étang de la Mer Rouge.

Just around the corner from the château is the Maison du Parc, a stylish new building offering local produce of every kind – an excellent place to find presents to take home. The centre also sports a restaurant with a regional menu, offers a wealth of information about the Brenne (try the back room for its videos in English) and sells a range of maps for walking and cycling in the area. The two and a half mile (4km) waymarked walk starting from the Maison itself would give you an excellent feel for the landscape here – it is a case of simply following the blue flashes along the paths, but anyone wanting a map can get one at the desk.

If you can afford more time to explore this area, do not miss out on the Réserve de la Cherine, a few kilometres north of le Bouchet. The Brenne is remarkable for its population of European Pond Tortoises (*Cistudes d'Europe*) – fairly rare amphibians that are only found in waters south of the Loire. There are not that many in total, but around a hundred of them inhabit the Étang Ricot. A pull-in beside the D17 to Mézières (half a mile (1km) after its intersection with the D44) gives access to a hide overlooking this lake, from which you may be lucky enough to see one or two sunbathing on rocks beside the water.

A few metres down the road the recently built Maison de la Nature houses temporary exhibitions and renders views over another lake, this time the Étang de la Cistude. Still heading north and away from the Creuse, the little town of **Mézières-en-Brenne** is the regional centre offering its own campsite, hotel accommodation, a first-class Office de Tourisme and, behind the latter, a Maison de la Pisciculture that will tell you more than you need to know about fish and fishing.

If you would like to spend more time in this region, or would like to include some holiday atmosphere, head east from Mézières to the **Étang de Bellebouche**, the only one of the lakes in this region to offer swimming and boating facilities. The campsite here really springs to life in July and August as does the restaurant beside the pine-shaded sandy beach. Out of season you can still enjoy pleasant walks around the lake and other rambles farther afield for which the camp-site reception has details.

BESIDE THE CREUSE TO LE MENOUX

Time to return to the Creuse now, and pick up the N151 along its north bank towards St Gaultier. It is a fairly busy road but you can look forward to a couple of brief escapes. The first of these is the pretty village of **Ruffec**, lying just south of the road, 5 miles (8km) from le Blanc. Here an old honey-stoned priory stands peacefully beside the river bridge (it can be visited at certain times if you keep the monks' vow of silence) and upstream

there are views of a watermill with its broken paddles still in place. On an island amid the flow, a tiny tree-shaded campsite looks attractive.

The second respite from the main road is offered by the village of **Ciron**. Taking the first road signed on the right into the village, you will soon pass the tall grey column of the Lanterne des Morts, dating from the 12th century. Normally found in cemeteries (this one seems to have gone astray – although there is a church down the road), these lanterns were once lit at night to watch over the dead or sometimes after someone in the village had just died. You may consider continuing for a few minutes down the road beyond the *lanterne* – after crossing the metal river bridge, the imposing Château of Romefort stands on the left hand side. The square keep here is 12th century while the main building dates from the 14th, but all is private and unfortunately cannot be visited. A different view of the château can be had by taking a track before the river bridge, leading down to the opposite bank of the river – and naturally the view-point is supplied with picnic tables.

At **St Gaultier** it is worth once more leaving the road and heading into the town, where the white-stone 12th century priory church is under restoration. Beside this a steep track leads to a grassy path along the riverside. Follow it as far as you will – under the bridge and beyond. It offers a peaceful corner, and some lovely views of the Creuse.

Continuing upstream from St Gaultier in the direction of Argenton you will soon notice signs for the historic site of Argentomagus – and you could not do better than follow them. The medieval town of **St Marcel** now occupies the hilltop where the fine

Roman town of **Argentomagus** once stood. A car park gives visitors access to some of the Roman excavations and a museum – and if you have a few moments to spare (perhaps waiting for the latter to open) you can see the most interesting buildings of St Marcel itself by going through the old town gateway and following the red or blue arrows.

On the grassy plateau outside the town walls, excavations of the Roman site have being going on for over half a century and it is now possible to wander around the foundations of temples, the house of a wealthy citizen and the beautifully preserved site of a sunken fountain that must once have been a meeting place and the pride of the town. To preserve the best of the finds the museum has actually been built on top of a long section of walling where a crypt and a rare domestic altar remain in their original positions. The modest entry fee for this excellent museum is more than worthwhile. The path leads you down from prehistoric times to that of Argentomagus and local finds from all ages are displayed along the way. Video films offer some of the things you have always wanted to know – exactly how to rub two sticks together to get fire is a revelation!

Other remains from Roman times are to be found below the hilltop on the outskirts of modern-day Argenton and of these the vast semi-circular theatre is most worthy of a visit. For this you need to descend the hill, continue a very short distance along the road to Argenton and turn right immediately before the railway. There are no signs to guide you (do they not want people to know?), but at the end of this road a steep track leads uphill to the theatre. The whole area is enclosed by high railings and the access gate may or may not be open, but whatever the case, there is a good view.

Continuing towards Argenton, you could pursue the Roman theme by parking near the church on the outskirts (the Quartier Saint-Etienne) and walking down to the riverside where the bases of two pillars from the Roman bridge are still to be seen. The church itself must have been built from whatever local stone was available, and one of the blocks to the left of the main door reveals its earlier life by bearing part of a Latin inscription.

On now into the centre of **Argenton-sur-Creuse**. The town is busy with traffic, but you might like to leave your car and take a stroll. Two bridges cross the river in Argenton, the old and the new. Beside the latter the town pays homage to its main industry over the past century and a half with a museum devoted entirely to shirtmaking. The grandly-titled Musée de la Chemiserie et de l'Élégance Masculine clearly displays the French ability to produce an interesting museum from the most unlikely of topics and, though its texts are only in French, it will happily entertain you for a rainy hour or so with shirts old, new, virtual and famous and other sartorial accompaniments.

From the museum it is only a couple of minutes walk to the old bridge with its photogenic views. Both up and downstream from here medieval houses line the banks, their sagging wooden balconies leaning out over the dark river. High on the hill above, a huge gilt statue of Our Lady perches on top of the Chapelle Notre Dame-des-Bancs – the climb to reach it is rewarded by a splendid view over town and river, while from the rear, the distant Roman theatre can be seen sprawling down the hillside. Inside the chapel itself the small statue above the high altar is known as the *Bonne Dame d'Argenton*, and it is said to be she who kept the town free from plague in the Middle Ages. Ex-votos on the back wall give thanks for more recent acts of deliverance.

It is time to leave now, and follow the D48 along the east bank of the river. In 3 miles (5km), do not miss the turn to the village of **le Menoux**. When you arrive, you will think it a pretty ordinary-looking sort of place, and its church seems about equally undistinguished. Nothing prepares you for the shock on opening the door – the vaulting and upper walls are completely covered in swirls of vivid colour, bright near the west door, becoming more subtle as you approach the altar. All this is the work of the Bolivian painter Carasco, who took up residence in the village more than 30 years ago and can certainly be said to have made his mark there. If you want to see more, just follow the signs to his house (its fencing is unmistakeable!)

IN THE LAND OF
THE ARTISTS

Up to this point the Creuse has been gentle, calm and wide – now for the first time it is seen to be more turbulent as it flows through a deep gorge. At a viewpoint you can pull in, cross the road and admire the **Boucle du Pin**, a hairpin loop of river way below you, with the church at Ceaulmont sharing the view from the slopes on the opposite side. A display board explains that the river's change of character is related to geology – you are now leaving the sedimentary Paris Basin and approaching the Massif Central, a region of crystalline rocks like granite.

The road descends into the gorge as you head south, and soon there are glimpses of the village of **Gargilesse** (or to give it its full title, Gargilesse-Dampierre), a cluster of pink-tiled old houses and a church, all gathered on to a rocky ridge, deep in the gorge, but still high above the river.

Georges Sand

Gargilesse has long been a haunt of artists and musicians, and was once home to Georges Sand who based several of her novels on the village. At the far end of the narrow main street, her one-time residence is built over a stream and appears rather dark, damp and uninspiring. Internally it has been restored by her granddaughter and contains many memorabilia of the writer's life. Devotees of Sand's work may think it worthwhile to stray a little farther to visit her family home, the Château de Nohant (about 30 miles [50km] away to the east, just north of le Châtre), which has been preserved as it was in her time with many of her possessions.

Aside from its connections with Georges Sand, the crowning glory of Gargilesse is its 12th century church, built on a hillock above the village and encircled, along with the Office de Tourisme, by the vestiges of walls from a long-gone château. The walls and vaults of the old church crypt bear a fine collection of frescoes dating from the 13th to the 15th century. Guided tours of these are always possible but sometimes, out of season, you are allowed the privilege of the key to explore for yourself. Before leaving, spare a few minutes more for the church above – seemingly neglected and green with damp, its capitals display some of the most detailed and varied carvings to be seen in this part of the world. And for some modern day art, pop into the 'new' (18th century) château alongside, where there are always exhibitions.

South of Gargilesse the D40 leaves the riverside for a while – and then announces its return with a sign to the Barrage d'Eguzon. These huge dams built by the EDF (Électricité de France) are always less attractive than imposing, and this one is not improved by having its generating station adjacent to the viewpoint. Nevertheless, it is this dam that creates behind it the wide curving **Lac de Chambon** (sometimes called the Lac d'Eguzon), which must be one of the most scenic features of the whole Creuse valley.

Turning off towards the lakeside on the narrow D40a, you will first pass the road to the Plage de Bonnu, a very pretty but tiny beach area with limited parking (note the splendid private château just after the turn). Farther on you arrive at the hamlet of Fougères, a few houses and a long waterfront where you can swim, hire pedalos or simply sit in a beach-side café enjoying anything from multi-flavoured ice-cream to a full meal. A well-kept campsite enjoys exceptional views of the water, and from its far corner a marked path weaves its way amid gorse and heather all the way to Crozant at the southern tip of the lake. The first section of this path has been dotted with the curious creations of a local sculptor and you can see more of these by returning along the *parcours sportif* to the campsite.

The main resort of the Lac de Chambon is actually on the opposite side of the lake from Fougères, but is connected to it by passenger ferry in summertime. At other times it is necessary to take the D45 around the north end of the lake. The road takes you first to **Eguzon**, a pleasant little town with a museum of local life (Musée de la Vallée de la Creuse) open in summer. From here a lesser road descends to the village of **Chambon** with its wide sandy beach, harbour and facilities for boat hire, sailing and water-skiing.

On south again now to the tip of the Lac de Chambon, at which point you leave the *région* of Centre and enter that of Limousin and the *département* of Creuse itself. Here the River Sedelle meets the Creuse overlooked by the village of **Crozant**, and the ruins of its one-time ten-towered château cling to a high rocky spur above the mingling waters. The best views of the château are said to be from the road leading up from the river bridge and that may be true if you are sticking to your car but one of the finest panoramas in all the Creuse valley is revealed from les Fileuses, a rocky promontory bright with springtime broom or autumn heather, facing the ruins from the opposite bank.

To reach this idyllic spot, a *sentier de randonnée* (marked with bars of yellow on red) climbs the slope from the road near the end of the bridge – and you are distracted from its initial steepness by a scattering of intriguing sculptures tucked into the trees and heather beside the path. Sticking strictly to the waymarked paths (do not turn right to St Jallet), you should reach the little wooden seat at the viewpoint in around half an hour and it just has to be worth the effort.

This particular area of the Creuse has always attracted artists, and in the

19th century gave rise to its own impressionist school known as the École de Crozant. Crozant still has its artistic community but the focus seems to have moved upstream to the little village of **Fresselines**, where there are at least three artists' studios and now the new Centre Artistique des Peintres de la Vallée de la Creuse, explaining the story of the artists and offering exhibitions of contemporary work. Fresselines sits at the confluence of the Grande and Petite Creuse, a picturesque spot made famous by Monet who committed it to canvas more than 20 times during his stay here in 1889. The house where he lived bears its plaque and, following signs to the *Site de Monet*, you can walk through the woods beside the Petite Creuse to find the very place where he set up his easel.

An adventurous continuation to this walk involves crossing the river on stepping stones (while hanging on to a chain) and returning via the confluence itself. Back in the village, tear yourself away from the studios and spare a few moments for the church. Fresselines was for 20 years the home of the poet Maurice Rollinat. He died in 1903 and his monument is a bas-relief by Rodin entitled the Poet and his Muse, to be found outside the church on the east wall.

GUÉRET, AUBUSSON AND FELLETIN

At this point you are around half way through your journey – and the second part is as exciting as the first. Above Fresselines there is no road beside the Creuse, but make sure you return to the river at **la Celle-Dunoise**, just to enjoy the pretty picture of its bridge, church and houses climbing up the hill. A sandy bathing beach, a pleasant auberge and a well-kept little campsite may persuade you to stay around a while.

Beyond la Celle-Dunoise, this section of the Creuse has been dubbed the Pays des Trois Lacs – three dams in turn hold the river back, creating behind them wider 'lakes' where boating and bathing are possible. At **le Bourg d'Hem**, there is a memorial to the wartime 'Voice of the Free French' Pierre Maillaud (called 'Bourdan', as the village is pronounced) – and a fine viewpoint, with the river once more in a wooded gorge far below. The road from here leads towards Champsanglard and then crosses the bridge (the Pont du Diable) to climb to **Anzême**, a village perched on a cliff of frightening height above the swirling waters. The bridge has a classic story – it was apparently built by the devil in one night as a condition of his obtaining the hand of the miller's daughter in marriage. At the last moment she tricked him, shining her bright ring just as the dawn was about to break. With one stone still to set in place, the cock crowed – and the devil fled, leaving that one stone out of place, as you can still see today.

Anzême offers precipitous views from its church square and farther upstream, the riverside campsite and bathing beach at **Péchadoire** is popular with local holidaymakers. But now it is time to head south again, with perhaps only the village of Glénic warranting a diversion (for its Romanesque church and splendid view) before reaching Guéret, the administrative capital of the Creuse.

Guéret is actually set just a few kilometres west of the river – and, despite a scattering of fine houses by the stonemasons for which the Creuse is famous, you are unlikely to find much to detain you. The town's most notable building is an 18th century château housing the Musée d'Art et d'Archéologie de la Senatorerie, and surrounded by small but very attractively landscaped gardens. If your time budget is healthy, an hour or two could happily be passed browsing paintings, pottery, sculptures and Limousin enamelwork. Otherwise, pass it by and head off into the wooded Monts de Guéret, as 'undiscovered' an area as you could wish for, but still sporting a couple of tourist attractions – in addition to a first-class network of off-road cycle tracks.

If you do not fancy exploring these hills by mountain-bike, at least allow time for a drive to enjoy some of the lovely remote farmsteads and villages. Progress will necessarily be slow and it is impossible to recommend one particular route, but it is definitely worth making your way south-east to the village of **Sous-Parsat**. In the church here the artist Gabriel Chabrat has been given free-rein, and he has designed its stained glass windows and covered the entire walls and vaulting with biblical scenes painted in bright primary colours. The total effect is dazzling, and closer inspection invites you to trawl your memory to identify all these stories. On most days a board with the answers stands by the door. The village itself is delightful, a cluster of warm-stone houses decked with flowers and among them, a tiny tourist office packed with information on walks and cycle rides.

Before returning to the Creuse,

Attractions near Guéret

Leaving Guéret on the road to Bourganeuf (the D940), you will soon come across the first of the attractions under the title of le Labyrinthe de Guéret, said to be the world's largest permanent vegetation maze. Large it is certainly, but not too thick or too high. Do not be put off by this – finding the exit is not that simple and you will need to get help from the 'questions', thoughtfully provided in a variety of languages.

Just across the road from the maze the wolf park is signed, and it is now well worth following the long twisting road into the heart of the forest, as much to admire the style and imagination the French can bring to a project like this as to see the animals themselves. These creatures are effectively rescue wolves, unwanted animals brought in from zoos all over Europe, and given their own tract of forest in which to roam. You can roam too, and be surprised to find a dark shape slinking silently beside you – but do not worry, there will be a fence in between! Curiously enough, the wolf park is also the site of the Planetarium of the Monts de Guéret, with showings every afternoon.

Outside the entrance to the wolf park you can find a board showing all the mountain-bike circuits in these hills – two of them actually start from this point. The network of tracks and narrow winding lanes here offer 25 routes in all, ranging from the easiest courses for beginners to international trial circuits and two courses of descent. The best centre is possibly St Vaury (to the north-west), but information on all the routes can be obtained from any Office de Tourisme.

there is one other village that might claim your attention. **Masgot** (to the south-east of Sous-Parsat) is a curiosity. In the 19th century a certain François Michaud lived here and, being a sculptor, richly endowed his own village with his creations – figures of men and beasts sprout from walls, gates and gables. Latter-day sculptors have moved in on the scene, so you can also wander around their workroom and perhaps find a little (or large) something to take home.

At last it is time to find the river again – and by whichever road you reach it, do not even think of missing the village of **Moutier d'Ahun** (it is just north of Ahun and the D942). The village itself is a cluster of stone houses beside a picturesque old river bridge but it is the ruined ancient abbey that you must head for, and the stone sculptured west doorway to this is a treat in itself. Inside, the wood carvings by 17th century master-craftsman Simon Bauer are quite exceptional. In the old chancel hundreds of creatures in scenes both real and imaginary decorate the stalls, altar screen, lectern and more. When you have taken it all in, more spare moments could be spent back in the village, where the old mill now houses a collection of tools used by farmers and craftsmen of a bygone age.

South now, to the fascinating town of **Aubusson**, built on the flanks of deep valleys descending to join that of the Creuse. The main road takes you to the D990, to enter the town from the east, but you could instead look out for a turning that is signed only to Alleyrat. This is the old road, and it will bring you along the gorge of the Creuse and into Aubusson beside the river with its old houses and picturesque grey-granite bridge, the Pont de la Terrade.

The essence of Aubusson is contained in two streets, the Grande Rue and the narrow pedestrian Rue Vieille – both are almost entirely devoted to tapestry and lined with shops, galleries and workshops. On one side of the Grande Rue is the incongruous 30s-built Hôtel-de-Ville, where there are frequent tapestry exhibitions, while above it on the Rue Vieille, the Office de Tourisme can give you details of workshops that can be visited. It is housed within the Maison du Tapissier, a house such as might have been lived in by a weaver of previous times. In its basement workrooms, the *cartons* (templates) used for the designs and the fine blended colours of the skeins are most memorable. Upstairs the visit concludes (or begins) with a video of today's craftsmen at work. Out on the street again, you can escape the tapestries and climb the steep path to the bell-tower, offering breezy views across the old town to the ruined château on the hilltop opposite. To the right of the ruins stands the church of Ste Croix, which itself contains a tapestry dating from the 17th century.

Before leaving Aubusson one more visit is in order. Upstream from the town centre and opposite a car park beside the Creuse stands the Musée de la Tapisserie – a collection of some of the finest tapestries produced in Aubusson over the past 400 years. The intricacies of the 17th century tapestries are amazing, while latter-day works, in particular those of Jean Lurçat, are notable for their colour and striking design. Aubusson owes a huge debt to Lurçat who was responsible for the revival of this flagging industry some 50 years ago and has attracted many talented young artists to the town.

Leaving Aubusson to the south you

could take the little riverside road past the recreation area of the Barrage des Combes. A few kilometres farther on, the smaller town of **Felletin** makes less display of its tapestry connections, but it was nevertheless in this town rather than Aubusson that the migrant Flemish weavers of the 15th century first made their home. The premises of a handful of craftsmen are open for visits and the fine old château church houses a summertime exhibition. But for alternative entertainment you could climb the bell-tower of the Église du Moûtier in which 188 spiralling dark steps lead to a precarious platform with views over the town and surrounding countryside. And do not miss the picnic site with a lovely view of the Creuse and the old bridge as you leave the town to the south-west.

PLATEAU OF MILLEVACHES

Felletin calls itself the gateway to the **Plateau of Millevaches**, and so it is. Beyond the town the rolling countryside of woods, lakes and scattered pastures stretches endlessly to the horizon. Twelve miles (20km) to the south the first waters of the Creuse spring from the rough ground amid the trees and heather and that is your destination – but if you have the time, first take a look at the plateau itself. Limousin is the least densely populated region of France as a drive across Millevaches will soon confirm. This vast area has few farms and even fewer villages. But do not be discouraged by this – there are many places of interest worthy of a short drive and on the way you can enjoy the masses of colourful wild flowers and fields of lovely brown Limousin cattle.

Twelve miles (20km) east of Felletin you might take a look at **Crocq**, a hilltop town crowned by two towers, all that remains of its 12th century château. At the top of one of the towers, a very fine ceramic *table d'orientation* will introduce you to all the features of its magnificent view, including the far away ranges of the Auvergne capped by the Puy Sancy. Near the foot of the towers a little museum of local life has changing exhibitions, and you might also call in at the church to see its 16th century triptych depicting the life of St Eloi. Heading back towards Felletin, a few minutes pause at **St Georges Nigremont** is worthwhile – like Crocq, the village was once important in the defence of this region. Now an orientation table is pleasantly set in the square in front of the church and from it you can pick out the distant towers of Crocq backed by the Combraille hills where the River Cher has its source.

South-west from Felletin the country is wilder and yet more remote – it might be worth filling up with petrol before you go! Here the D990 leads to Gentioux – and on the way you could divert north to the Domaine de Banizette (a restored manor and museum of rural life) or, farther on, to see the tiny Roman bridge of Senoueix in its delightful setting. **Gentioux** itself has a dark 13th-century church decked with sculptures and scowling faces and a war memorial said to be the only pacifist war memorial in France. A child shakes his fist at the tall grey column on which the words *Maudite soit la guerre* (Cursed be the war) are inscribed.

Beyond Gentioux the D16a will take you to the **Site du Rat** – look out for a very inconspicuous sign on the right hand side of the road opposite a farm. The site itself is quite lovely, an old stone chapel tucked amid pines and broom where piled lichen-clad rocks look out over a wild valley. And finally, take the D8 from Gentioux to the **Lac de Vassivière**. Now you could well be in Scandinavia, with pines stretching down to the sandy shores of a blue lake dotted with islands. A road encircles the lake and there are at least five beaches on the way. Of these, Vauveix on the southern shore has its own campsite and it is surprising after driving through such a wilderness to find so many people here. But the place is unspoilt, offering families only the unsophisticated pleasures of boating, swimming, hiking and fishing in truly lovely surroundings.

Surprise on the lake

Vassivière has one very unexpected feature. From Pierrefitte on the southern shore, a causeway leads to an island that is a centre of contemporary art; its woods are scattered with modern sculptures (concrete 'Monopoly' houses and neon signs in the trees fall into this category) and a building said to be a ship with a lighthouse alongside presents some avant-garde exhibitions. The entrance to these is akin to walking the plank (see for yourselves) while taking the spiral staircase up the inside of the lighthouse is not for the faint-hearted. Families might prefer to take their pleasures on the island train or children's farm.

At last it is time to go in search of **the source** of the river. In fact at least two separate sources exist, the first being conspicuously signed but difficult to find, while the second is unobtrusively signed from the road but well-announced at the site with a map of the Creuse beside a very obvious spring. For the first, head south from Felletin on the D982 and then just a few metres to the west on the D8 towards Feniers. A sign points the general direction, but you will have to hunt for the source, a tiny oozing pool surrounded by bog and hidden in trees and bracken. For the second source, continue on the D8 and turn south on the D19/D36. Arrows will direct you to the site at the bottom of a track through the woods – and this time you just might like to take a bottle of something with you. After such a monumental journey, it is time to drink a toast to the river that has entertained you for so long – and perhaps add a few drops for good luck to the bubbling water as it sets off on its journey to the confluence near Descartes again.

185

OFFICES DE TOURISME

Le Blanc
Place de l'Hôtel de Ville
36300 LE BLANC
☎ 02.54.37.05.13

Argenton-sur-Creuse
13, Rue de la République
36200 ARGENTON-SUR-CREUSE
☎ 02.54.24.05.30

Guéret
1, Avenue Charles de Gaulle
23000 GUÉRET
☎ 05.55.52.14.29

Aubusson
BP 40 Rue Vieille
23200 AUBUSSON
☎ 05.55.66.32.12

PLACES OF INTEREST

Descartes

Musée Descartes
Open mid-February to mid- November daily (except. Tue) 2-6pm.

Angles-sur-l'Anglin

Château ruins
Open July and August every day except Tuesday 10.30am-12.30pm, 2.30-6.30pm; April to June and September, October Saturdays 2.30-6.30pm, Sundays and bank holidays as July and August.

St. Savin

Abbey of St Savin
Open July and August every day 9.30am-7pm; April to June and September 9.30am-12noon, 2-6pm (but closed Sunday mornings); rest of year 2-5.30pm every day.

Le Blanc

Ecomusée de la Brenne
Open July and August 9.30am-7pm every day; May, June and September 9.30am-12.30pm, 2-6pm every day except Monday; rest of year 10am-12noon, 2-5pm every day except Monday.

Le Bouchet

Château du Bouchet
One-hour guided tours during July and August and on some Sunday afternoons.

Maison de la Parc
Open July and August 9am-7pm; rest of year 9.30am-12.30pm, 1.30-6pm (5.30pm in January, November, December).

Mézières-en-Brenne

Maison de la Pisciculture
Open mid-March to mid-October every day except Tuesday 2-6pm.

St. Marcel

Musée archéologique d'Argentomagus
Open 9.30-12noon, 2-6pm daily (with the exception of Tuesdays) throughout the year.

Argenton-sur-Creuse

Musée de la Chemiserie et de l'Élégance Masculine
Open mid-February to end of year 9.30-12noon, 2-6pm every day except Mondays.

Gargilesse

La Maison de Georges Sand
Open April to September 9.30am-12.30pm, 2-7pm every day.

Église Notre-Dame
Church open all year round. Guided tours of the crypt during the summer months – ask at the Office de Tourisme nearby.

Eguzon

Musée de la Vallée de la Creuse
Open April to September every day except Tuesday 10am-12noon, 2-6pm (closed in morning Saturdays, Sundays and bank holidays); March, October, November weekends and bank holidays only, 2-6pm.

Crozant

Château ruins
Open daily Palm Sunday to mid-November 10am-12noon, 2-6pm (7pm July and August, weekends and bank holidays: no lunch break July and August).

Fresselines

Centre Artistique des Peintres de la Vallée de la Creuse
Open every day in July and August and at weekends only in June and September.

Guéret

Musée d'Art et d'Archéologie
Open every day mid-June to October 9am-12noon, 2-6pm, rest of year 2-6pm.

Le Labyrinthe de Guéret
Open from April to October 1.30-7.30pm (last entry 6.30pm) every day during school holidays; weekends and bank holidays only in term time.

Parc Animalier des Monts de Guéret 'Les Loups de Chabrières'
Open April to mid-September every day 10am-7pm (6pm April and May); mid-September to March, 1-5pm Wednesdays, Saturdays, Sundays, bank holidays only.

Sous-Parsat

The church is open every day throughout the year.

Moutier-d'Ahun

Église romane de Moutier
Open every day 10am-12noon, 2-6pm from mid-June to mid-September. Outside those months, open afternoons only with the exception of Mondays and Tuesdays.

Aubusson

Maison du Tapissier
Open 10am-12noon, 2-5.30pm (last admissions 45mins. before closing) every day throughout the year with the exception of Sundays and bank holidays between October and Easter. No lunch-break July and August.

Musée départemental de la Tapisserie
Open 9.30-12noon, 2-6pm every day except Tuesdays throughout the year (no lunch break in July and August and open Tuesday afternoons also).

Felletin

Église du Château
Open mornings and afternoons in July and August, afternoons only in June and September.

Plateau de Millevaches

Château towers at Crocq
Open every day July to September 9.30am-12.30pm, 2.30-7.30pm; May, June and October 10.30am-12noon, 2-6pm (5pm October).

Domaine de Banizette
Guided tours at 3, 4.15 and 5.30pm every day in July and August, last two weekends in June and first three weekends in September. Also Sundays at 3pm between 1st May and 16th November.

Vassivière – Centre d'Art Contemporain
Open daily throughout the year from 11am-7pm (6pm in winter). Free access to the sculpture park at any time.

LOCAL HIGHLIGHTS

Best walks

- The very beautiful footpath along the shores of the Lac de Chambon from Crozant to Fougères (and beyond). Follow yellow on red waymarks from the end of the bridge at Crozant. A lakeside circular walk of around 7.5 miles (12km) can be achieved using the ferry at Fougères – see the leaflet *Sentier de Pays du Val de Creuse* (from any OT) for this. The same leaflet offers you five excellent circular walks along the length of the Creuse valley between Argenton and Crozon.

- The wooded riverside path from which Monet painted the confluence of the Grande and Petite Creuses at Fresselines. In the village follow signs for the *Site de Monet*.

- Almost any of the paths around the shores of the lovely Lac de Vassivière – get the IGN map *Creuse Randonnée no. 5*.

For cyclists

- All the family will enjoy the Brenne Natural Regional Park. This is flat terrain and cycle routes are well-marked with coloured flashes. Where roads are used there is little traffic except at peak holiday periods. Suggested routes are on sale at the Maison de la Parc in le Bouchet and at OT in Mézières.

- The Monts de Guéret are marked out with routes suitable for mountain bikers of all standards. Could not be better! A topoguide with maps of all the routes is on sale at all local tourist offices.

- Many other towns and villages along the length of the Creuse (la Roche Posay, Angles sur l'Anglin, Crozant, etc.) offer bike hire and waymarked routes for both road bikes and VTTs. Just ask!

Watersports

- Riverside beaches where swimming is possible include la Roche Posay, la Celle Dunoise, Bourg d'Hem, Anzême, Jouillat and Péchadoire.

- Lake beaches offering opportunities for boating as well as swimming are to be found at Fougères, Bonnu and Chambon (on the Lac de Chambon), Guéret and all around the shores of the Lac de Vassivière. Possibly the best on this lake is at Vauveix on the south shore, where there is also an auberge and an excellent campsite.

For the Palate

- A particular delicacy of the Creuse is Potato pâté (*Pâté aux pommes de terre*) – basically creamy potato in a tart or *en croûte*. Another is the nutty-flavoured 'Creuse cake'.

- Products of the forest – chestnuts (often found in stuffing, but also in cakes, liqueurs, etc.) and a huge variety of edible fungi.

- *Clafoutis* is a speciality of the region of Limousin, an utterly delicious dessert of black cherries in batter. It can also be made with other fruit – but then it is not strictly a *clafoutis*!

And the most memorable

- The lovely view of the ruins of the Château de Crozant from across the river at les Fileuses.

- The amazing colours of the modern frescoes in the churches at both le Menoux and Sous-Parsat.

- Swathe upon swathe of bright yellow broom in springtime on the Plateau de Millevaches.

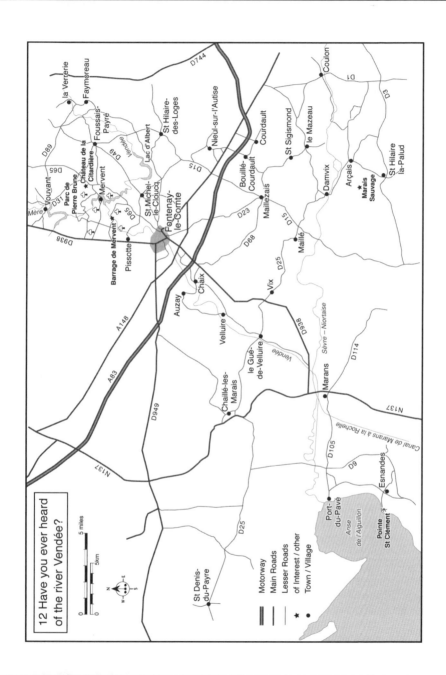

12 Have you ever heard of the river Vendée?

The coastline around the Bay of Biscay is hugely popular with British holidaymakers. By and large it provides the perfect ingredients for the annual family break – a particularly sunny climate, long safe sandy beaches, pine forest for shade, and easy accessibility from the Channel ports. The name Vendée seems to have become synonymous with the northern part of this much-loved coastline – and we forget that the Vendée is actually one of the 95 *départements* of France and that its territory also extends well inland. The present day *départements* of France were created after the Revolution and were for the most part (although you can soon think of a few exceptions) named after rivers.

So is there a River Vendée? Well, yes, there is, and it is well out of the public gaze, tucked away neatly in the southeast corner of the *département*. Its entire course is no more than 37 miles (60km) in length, but in that short space the River Vendée has passed from the high ground on the border with Deux-Sèvres, through gorges in the depths of the Mervent-Vouvant Forest, under the bridges of genteel Fontenay-le-Comte and across the western edge of the Poitevin marshes before mingling its waters with those of the Sèvre-Niortaise. In fact, that river sees some of the best of 'undiscovered' Vendée.

The whole area is fascinating, and other interest includes the *plus beau* village of Vouvant, the mines of Faymoreau, the abbeys of Nieul-sur-l'Autise and Maillezais and the Marais Poitevin itself – most particularly the atmospheric 'Wet Marsh' (*Marais Mouillé*) to the south of Fontenay. This low-lying region is a green labyrinth of duckweed-covered water channels, overhung with thick vegetation and peopled with croaking frogs, scurrying coypu and silent herons. It is best explored by the paddle boats that can be hired from the many tiny 'ports', but cycling and walking are popular here too – and even the car will take you to a whole host of fascinating corners.

But let us go back to the beginning. Even those seeking 'undiscovered' France occasionally need to use *autoroutes*, and curiously enough, the A83 (Nantes – Niort) is the very best place to start the exploration of this region. The service station known as the **Aire de la Vendée** (near St Hermine) is definitely more than just a pit stop on the way – in fact you could spend a couple of hours here. In seeking to divert the weary driver, imagination has run riot, and three buildings are now reached from board-walks above a marsh complete with frogs and marigolds.

The first of these buildings, *La Vendée en Images*, tells you all you could possibly want to know about the area in a room filled with multi-language computer screens. You could top up that knowledge with a short film in the *Théatre du Marais*, followed by a stroll on simulated water through the green depths of the *Vie des Marais Poitevins*. And back in the main building, a shop is stocked with all the traditional products of the Vendée – so if you want to get your take-home presents early, buy a tin of mogettes to eat with your supper, or even a little green angelica to nibble afterwards, this is the place to do it.

FONTENAY-LE-COMTE

With appetite whetted, it is time to get on to the real thing, and leave the *autoroute* for the town of **Fontenay-le-Comte** – it has to be the best place for a base, having the beautiful forest immediately to the north and the exciting swamps of the *marais* to the south. Fontenay is named from its *fontaine* – the Fontaine des Quatre Tias, couched in a 16th century façade, with a Latin inscription that translates as *The Fountain and Source of Fine Minds*. This grand title was given by Francois I (his salamander emblem is on the fountain), and certainly there were many fine minds in 16th century Fontenay. Rabelais, wordy satirist and creator of the giants Gargantua and Pantagruel, spent three years here studying Greek literature at the Franciscan monastery (1520-23) – he speedily defected to the Benedictines at Maillezais when Reformation literature was found in his possession. Another famous name of Fontenay-le-Comte was that of Francois Viète, who is often called the 'father of algebra'.

Father of Algebra

Francois Viète was born in Fonenay-le-Comte in 1540. Although he was not strictly speaking the first to have the concept of letters representing numbers, he was also well-versed in geometry and trigonometry. He established his position at the court of Henry IV by decoding messages meant for Henry's enemy Philip II of Spain, and finally by solving a problem posed by the greatly-esteemed Dutch mathematician Roomen, thus apparently upholding the honour of French mathematics.

Others of note in 16th century Fontenay were André Tiraqueau (friend of Rabelais, learned lawyer, father of 30 children, and perhaps not surprisingly, author of a treatise on matrimonial law) and the poet and magistrate, Nicholas Rapin, who lived in the magnificent Château de Terre Neuve on the edge of the town.

Fontenay had its heyday, and fortunately a few buildings from that time survived both the Wars of Religion, when the town was staunchly Protestant, and the Revolution. The Office de Tourisme can offer you a very comprehensive tour (aided by ceramic fountain logos let into the pavement) visiting these and every other point of note in the town. If you want to do things more simply, keep east of the river and head for one of the car parks signed off the busy main street, the Rue de la République. On the opposite side of these two car parks runs the town's former main thoroughfare, the narrow pedestrianised Rue des Loges. Although most of its houses are now shops, some have retained interesting façades – no 26 (wrought iron balconies) and no 84 (the Maison Millepertuis) are the most notable.

More recent additions to the scene are the loudspeakers supplying piped music and a couple of sculptures created from rusting metal parts!

The Rue des Loges ends at the river and the ancient Pont aux Sardines – so called because the quay alongside was where the fish was unloaded. If after crossing the bridge you turn left along the Rue de Commerce, and then first right, you will quickly arrive in one of the architectural gems of Fontenay, the Place Belliard. Fine arcaded Renaissance houses line one side of the square, but General Belliard on his central plinth determinedly looks the other way. He was born at no.11 and achieved fame by saving Napoleon's life at the Battle of Arcole. Leading from the Place Belliard, the narrow Rue des Pont-aux-Chèvres has the best display of Renaissance buildings in town – no.9 (on the right) has a fine balustraded staircase and was once the home of the Bishops of Maillezais; no.6 (on the left) has an imposing entrance gate topped by a rather time-worn statue of Laocoon; no.14 (the Hôtel de Rivaudeau) belonged to a one-time mayor of Fontenay and has a fine entrance porch, Doric columns and caryatids. The short street opens into the market square dominated by the slender crocketted spire of the 15th century Église Notre-Dame. Carvings of the Wise and Foolish Virgins around the door are worthy of attention, and it is sometimes possible to visit the 9th century crypt beneath.

At this point it is worth devoting a little time to the Musée Vendéen, which stands next door to the church. All the region's history is proudly displayed on its three floors – Gallo-Roman glassware recovered from a nearby sarcophagus, traditionally-carved furniture and a fine collection of paintings of local scenes by Vendéen artists (look out for the sardines being packed.) The historical model of the town with its commentary is interesting.

After the museum, there is only one place missing on this whistle-stop tour – the *fontaine* after which the town was named – or at least, partially named. The *Comte* in its title refers to the lord of the town who in its early days was the Count (*Comte*) of Poitou. Since after the revolution this was blatantly unacceptable, the town

enjoyed a short spell as Fontenay-le-Peuple (Fontenay-the-People). But back to that fountain – from the market square turn right (the raised tree-lined parking place on your left is the Place Viète), go right again on the Rue Gaston, and immediately left on the Rue Pierre Brissot. At its end, the Rue Goupilleau (slightly left) will bring you to the fountain in its Renaissance casing. When you have paid it sufficient homage (and found the salamander and the engraved names of the magistrates of Fontenay), the Rue Rochefoucault will quickly return you to the Pont-aux-Sardines – look out for the Hôtel de la Sénéchausée (1590) on the corner as you turn.

That may be enough of central Fontenay, but there is one place on its outskirts you should not miss – and once again it harks back to the 'fine minds'. The Château de Terre Neuve was built for the 16th century magistrate Nicholas Rapin by the architect Jean Morrison, who was also responsible for the houses on the Place Belliard. Although now a private home, the elegant L-shaped grey château, finished with pepper-pot turrets and fronted by statues of the Muses, opens its doors to the public in summertime. Highlights of the visit are the stone 'Alchemist's fireplace' in the richly decorated sitting room, and the carved chimney breast supported by two griffons in a dining room of similar elegance, but there are also the carved stone ceilings, period furniture, wood panelling from the Château de Chambord and a lot more. In latter years, the château was briefly (1940 – 43) home to the novelist Georges Simenon and it was here that he wrote *Maigret à peur* (Maigret Afraid), a tale of three killings set in the inevitably class-ridden society of Fontenay-le-Comte.

Just outside the gates of the Château de Terre Neuve, Fontenay has yet one more curiosity. The concrete octagonal Tour Rivalland was erected here in 1880 by a freemason determined that the spire of Notre-Dame should not rule alone on Fontenay's horizon. He cheated a little in taking advantage of the height of the land here, but was a good 10 years ahead of his time in using poured concrete for his chosen medium.

FOREST OF MERVENT — VOUVANT

After Fontenay, it is time at last to explore the forest to the north. The terrain is surprisingly hilly here and the dense covering of deciduous trees plunges over outcrops of granite into the winding gorge cut by the River Vendée. Near **Mervent** the river has been dammed, thus creating a snaking section of narrow lake, known as the Lac de Mervent. Leaving Fontenay on the D65 you will soon cross the upper end of this lake, after which the road climbs up to a crossroads near the Zoo de Mervent. You probably will not want to stop now (the attractive little animal park is worth at least a couple of hours of your time), but you could turn left here to return to the lake shore. The area known as *La Plage* (with restaurant of that name) offers pedalo hire and swimming in summertime. The village of Mervent looks down from its vantage point on the opposite flank and can be reached by another bridge a little farther along, this time crossing not the Vendée, but rather its similarly swollen tributary, the Mère.

Mervent is virtually perched on a rocky peninsula between the Vendée and the Mère and the best place for a view of the waters is the Parc du Vieux Château (which is now the garden of the Hôtel-de-Ville). The village has a central square surrounded by all the essentials – a couple of shops, a bar, a squat red-tiled Vendéen church (look for the weight-driven clock inside) and a little Tourist Office, which though it keeps some unusual hours, is nevertheless crammed with literature on every aspect of the forest, including its walking and cycling trails. A recent addition is the Adventure Park in the woodland behind the village (next to the camp site), where those with simian inclinations can test nerve and agility on five graded circuits through the branches. There are bouncy castles for the tiniest, while the craziest can take advantage of the 59ft (18m) bungee-jumping tower.

Back over the bridge across the Mère, a turn on to the D99 will soon have you in the depths of the **Mervent-Vouvant Forest**. At the Pont du Déluge, a high arched bridge over an entrant stream, you can walk down to the leafy glade beside the water's edge and perhaps be inspired by one of the walking trails that pass that way. If so, just wait a minute – the road soon crosses the route of the short *Sentier Sylvicole*, a nature trail marked by little blue arrows on sticks. You may not get much from the French text detailing the trees, but at least you will have a lovely forest walk.

Farther on signs point you up the valley to the **Parc de Pierre Brune**. It is surprising to find an amusement park in such an out-of-the-way spot as this and yet it blends quite well and offers mostly the unsophisticated attractions of a bygone age. Children will love its train, bumper-boats and enchanted valley of games – and the modest all-inclusive entry fee should not break the family bank.

Pilgrims' cave

In the steep cliffs up above the Parc de Pierre Brune is a cave known as the **Grotte de Père Montfort** – you can reach it by crossing the barrage and climbing the steep hill thereafter. From a parking area, steps descend to a hole in the cliffs that in 1715 offered shelter to a priest on a mission to convert the Protestant population to Catholicism. Louis-Marie Grignion de Montfort was later canonised and the cave became a place of pilgrimage.

On, on through the forest and signs are directing you left to the **Barrage de Mervent**. The dam is worth a look – white and gracefully curving, it is less forbidding than most – but note that this is a one-way road, you cannot simply turn round and come back. So maybe first you should continue out of the forest to the village of **Pisotte**, which is renowned for its Fief Vendéen wines, and lay in your supplies for the holiday. When you return across the Barrage of Mervent, the forest road takes you past interesting-looking clearings with picnic tables to arrive back on the D65 to Fontenay again.

That is enough of a forest excursion for one day, but at another time you should return on that same road (the D65, followed by the D31) to visit the delightful little village of Vouvant. On the way, at the hamlet of les Quillères, you might turn to take a brief look at the **Château de la Citardière**. Surrounded by its picturesque moat, this squat 16th century

château incongruously announces its present day function with a purple neon sign over the once-guarded drawbridge entrance – 'Crêperie'. And very popular it is too! Exhibitions and other cultural events are added attractions in summertime. Just up the road at La Jamonière, the **Maison des Amis de la Forêt** may be worth a pause, particularly if you have children on board. Forest flora and fauna are on display (some sadly stuffed) and there is a video of forest life.

VOUVANT

Vouvant is your ultimate destination, and it is one of the more appealing of the select *plus beaux villages* with a splendid hilltop situation above the looping River Mère. At the top of the village, the lonely building on the grassy swards is the Tour Mélusine, said to have been built (like many other edifices) by the fairy herself in a single night. It is always possible to climb the tower – if the door is not open you should be able get the key from the café opposite. On the turreted top, a symbolic Mélusine spins in the wind and you can share her view over village, river and forest.

In reality, the Château at Vouvant, which has now almost completely disappeared, is said to have been built by the Lusignan family in 1242 – but at this point fact and fairy tale become confused because the Lusignan family actually claim Mélusine and Raimondin among their number. At least one of their children, Geoffrey Longtooth, was real enough, a bloodthirsty character who plundered the Abbey of Maillezais in the 13th century. Be all that as it may, the place where the château once stood is now used for local events (and

The Fairy Mélusine

Mélusine has been adopted as the Vendee's very own fairy and today her symbol can be seen on many official signs and documents. The story goes that in her youth she murdered her father, and for this she was condemned to have the lower half of her body changed to that of a serpent every Saturday evening. When in due course she met Raimondin, the young nephew of the Count of Poitiers, she would naturally only agree to marriage on the condition that he never saw her on a Saturday evening. All went well for many years, the couple lived in the château at Vouvant (which Mélusine built in one night) and 10 children were born to them – although strangely, each child had a minor defect (a red eye, a small ear, a 'long tooth'…). Eventually curiosity overcame Raimondin and one Saturday evening he burst into his wife's room as she was taking a bath. While he recoiled in shock at the sight of her serpent's tail she flew out of the window, circled the castle three times and was never seen again.

She does however return to haunt Vouvant, and from time to time her cry can be heard over the village. Mélusine is accredited with the building of many castles and after her disappearance, each of these was said to crumble at the rate of a stone a year – hence, the châteaux of Pouzauges and Tiffauges are little more than ruins, all that currently remains of the stronghold at Vouvant is the watchtower, while at Mervent there is nothing at all.

for parking), and the Tourist Office alongside can offer yet more yarns of Mélusine in its basement rooms (the Maison de Mélusine).

Walking down from the château site, another place with a story is the attractive Cour des Miracles, just across the road. It is said that in the winter of 1715, Père de Montfort (of *Grotte* fame) was walking through this village when a dying child came out and asked him for cherries. The priest apparently told his grandmother to go and pick some – and the tree at the centre of this courtyard was found to be laden with fruit.

From the Cour des Miracles it is only a couple of minutes walk to the centre of Vouvant, where beautiful houses with brightly-coloured shutters ring the Romanesque church. Weird and wonderful creatures arch above the north portal of this church – monsters, cat's heads, birds and even Mélusine herself – or at least, a woman with a fish's tail. Beneath them Samson is seen wrestling with the lion, and again with Delilah cutting his hair. The Virgin Mary and John the Baptist have pride of place, with the Last Supper and the Ascension above them. The inside is less remarkable but it is worth going down into the restored 11th century crypt where various pieces of ancient sculpture found during excavation are kept. From the church, you must explore the ramparts – or at least what is left of them – including the postern gate. A pleasant path runs beneath with views over the river and the Vieux Pont (13th century).

NORTH OF FONTENAY

Pleasant though Vouvant is, it sees its share of visitors and hardly qualifies for 'undiscovered' status – to achieve that again you will need to travel just a few kilometres to the east (take the D31) to the village of **Foussais-Payré**. Here the doorway of the church displays even older carvings (11th century). Although some do look their age and one or two heads have been removed in religious conflicts over time they still form a remarkable ensemble in which Christ and the apostles appear above the door between graphic representations of temptations and other mystic figures. Side panels display the Passion and later appearance of Christ to the apostles.

Near the church are the 17th century market hall and the Auberge St Catherine, one-time home of Viète (although there is nothing to tell you so). Much more is made of a 16th century house standing on the opposite corner, and signs even direct you to the Fours à chaux (lime-kilns) a few kilometres out of the village, where you might wonder what the attraction is. Instead head on to **Faymoreau** and the Centre Minier (Mining Centre) at la Verrerie – on the way you will cross a little stream that is the infant Vendée.

This hilly area on the border with Dèux-Sevres once boasted several thriving coal mines. The one at la Verrerie was last worked in 1958. Now the village has a new lease of life with one of its buildings (actually a glassworkers' hostel) converted to a 'virtual' mine. The simulated descent of the mine shaft is the most exciting part of the visit, with some fairly uninspired tableaux in the tunnels beyond. The final room uses video and sound and light effects to tell the miners' story (French only, but an English translation is offered) after which you are free to browse the museum.

The village outside, being authentic, is at least as interesting as the mine. The houses are arranged in three long tiers around the hillside, with those for the lowest-grade workers at the top and those for the management at the bottom. Below them all, the rather grand Hôtel des Mines has been revived to serve meals to visitors, while on the far side, the chapel installed by the director's wife to cater for the workers' perceived spiritual needs has been given added appeal with a new set of windows. The work of Carmelo Zagari, these 19 works in richly-coloured glass have striking designs that link Christian themes with the work of the mines. A free brochure introduces and explains each window.

At Faymoreau you are in the upper part of the valley of the Vendée, and you could pursue the river north through St Hilaire-de-Voost to its inconspicuous beginning in the hills, but there is not a lot to see. If instead you turn tail and head down the valley on the D3, you will come alongside the river again at the **Lac d'Albert**, a particularly wide stretch formed by yet another dam on the river. Just past the village of Chassenon-le-Bourg, there is access to a beach complex with children's playground, canoes and supervised swimming.

This should really complete our exploration of the area north of Fontenay, but before leaving the forest for the marshes, you should not miss out on a fascinating place that seems to occupy a position half way between the two. To the east of Fontenay, **Nieul-sur-l'Autise** has its own stretch of *marais*, but it also has a most splendid abbey, a working water-mill, a botanical trail and a Neolithic site on the hillside above the town. The Abbaye Royale St Vincent must be your first port of call and it immediately impresses you with its state-of-the-art technology as you enter through a corridor of multi-lingual video screens describing the life of the monks. Farther on there is a display of medieval instruments, each of which magically bursts into song as you approach. But it is back to the 11th century when you enter the beautiful pale-stone Romanesque cloisters – where you can look for the sculpted funeral niche of Aénor of Châtellerault, mother of Eleanor of Aquitaine (next to the chapterhouse). Eleanor herself was born in Nieul-sur-l'Autise. Alongside the abbey, the Romanesque church again has a wealth of interesting carving around its portal.

On the opposite side of the main street from the abbey, the open grounds of le Vignaud host some unusual exhibitions, and on one side, sounds of trickling water lead you to the Maison de la Meunerie, the one-time home of the miller and his family. You can explore both their living quarters and the mill itself, which still grinds flour. On the nearby riverside, the trees bear their plaques at the start of the botanical trail. This is simply a pleasant riverside walk whose length can be adapted to match the time available – the entire 15 mile (24km) circuit would take a whole day, but just an hour would be enough to take you up to cross the river on the *barque-à-chaîne* (boat-on-a-chain) and return.

And when you finally leave Nieul-sur-l'Autise, it might be worth taking a few minutes to look at the neolithic site of Champ-Durand – it is signed off the road to Oulmes. There is open access to this exposed place where excavations have revealed three concentric rings of earth and stone defences dating from around 2500BC. French-readers can learn all about it at the hut on the site.

MARAIS POITEVIN

At last it is time to head south from Fontenay to take a look at the **Marais Poitevin**. with its two distinct parts – the Marais Desséché (Dry Marsh) to the west and the Marais Mouillé (Wet Marsh) farther inland, between Fontenay-le-Comte and Niort. The whole area enjoys protected status as an 'Interregional Park', and is very well-endowed with family-friendly cycle routes and walking trails.

History of the Marais Poitevin

It seems remarkable to think that as recently as Roman times this whole vast area was under the sea, and known as the Golfe des Pictons. On the western side, near Velluire and Chaillé, you can still see the former cliffs. Over the centuries the rivers brought down their alluvium and the sea brought in its silt to fashion between them a foul-smelling marsh, punctuated by rocky outcrops that had once been islands in the sea. The land was first drained by the monks of the Middle Ages and later completed by Dutch engineers brought in by Henry IV.

Taking the D23 from Fontenay the first village on the marsh is **Maillezais** – you can see it as you approach because Maillezais stands on one of the former islands, and the gaunt ruins of its abbey rear up above the flat landscape. The Abbaye St-Pierre has had an eventful a life as any, having been founded early in the 11th century and sacked by the notorious Geoffrey Longtooth 200 years later. Flourishing again in the 16th century, it played host to the reactionary Rabelais, and then went on to become a Protestant stronghold under the control of the writer Agrippa d'Aubigné, who had the place fortified. The whole story is told in a sort of primitive *son et lumière*, using the bare stone walls of the refectory as a screen. Other rooms in the same monastery building can be visited (including the kitchen and dormitories), but of the abbey church itself, little more than its evocative skeleton remains.

The Abbey of Maillezais has its own port on the marshes, a most attractive looking spot from where you can hire one of the traditional flat-bottomed boats and paddle off into the duck-weed-filled channels. There are little signs to direct you at every junction, but if you still fear getting lost (or just want an easier life), guided tours are available. Maillezais also has another tiny port outside the abbey and closer to the town. And now it is time to go deeper into the marsh, but before leaving Maillezais take a quick look at the church of St Nicholas in the centre of town – the doorway is ringed by a complete arch of acrobats and there are some other amusing sculptures.

It is just as easy to explore this flat land by bike as it is by car, and Maillezais is the starting point of a very well marked out cycle route of 47 miles (75km) leading through Chaillé to the coast at Aiguillon. But for the moment, let us stick with the car and head down the D15 to **Maillé**, from whose handsome port silent, electrically driven boats take visitors out into the *marais*. Just off the road to Vix, the Aqueduct of Maillé is a remarkable feat of engineering that shunts one canal under the other.

From Maillé you could continue to **Damvix**, which is one of the larger ports on the banks of the arterial river of the *marais*, the Sèvre-Niortaise. Cycle hire, too, is on offer at the quayside and you can pedal west along the riverbank or south into the thick greenery of the area known as the *marais sauvage*. To the east, the road follows the river up to **Arçais**, one of the prettiest ports with a 19th century château looking down on all the activity. Arçais can be busy in summertime, although again it is possible to escape to that remote *marais sauvage* (though preferably not by car). On the edge of this wild marsh, and signed from St Hilaire-la-Palud, **Les Oiseaux du Marais Poitevin** is an ornithological park where you can see some of the wildlife in its natural setting and take yourself off on footpaths into the swamps.

Back in the crowds of Arçais, you could venture yet farther on to the beaten track by continuing upriver to **Coulon**. This is surely the most popular spot on the whole Marais Poitevin and is preferably explored on weekdays out of season. Nevertheless, Coulon is attractive enough to warrant its inclusion in France's list of *plus beaux villages*. Traditional cottages line its wharves, and it was surely the density of water transport here that, along with the duckweed, abundant vegetation and maze of channels, earned this whole area the epithet of

Venise Verte – Green Venice.

As befits such a watery Mecca, Coulon's quayside is home to the eco-museum of the Wet Marshes, the Maison des Marais Mouillés. Here the development of the marshlands is told using a relief model, and you can also see how the eels are caught and the traditional boats (known as *batais*) made. You may well have noticed that these boats travel 'back to front' – the wide end goes first, while the rear, narrow and pointed, allows space for a skilled handler to propel the boat using either pole or paddle. Inexperienced do-it-yourself visitors are usually supplied with more than one paddle!

Coulon's other family attraction is the aquarium that is strangely housed in one of the rather touristy shops that surround the church. Fish include those found in the local canals along with more exotic species and the visit incorporates a slide show about the flora and fauna of the marshes.

After all that it is time to get off to the wilds again – you could head for **le Mazeau**, which has a pretty port far less frequented than those you have just visited. Over a bridge from the port, the narrow road continues along the waterside and makes a pleasant place from which to contemplate the marshland vista. Soon though it will be time to go home, and you must return through le Mazeau to **St Sigismond**, likewise with a small port. Just around the corner (on the road to Maillezais) is the Espace Marais, with more information on traditional life in the marshes.

From St Sigismond the road heads north through Liez to Bouillé-Courdault – where a right turn will take you to the interesting **Port of Courdault**. This is not a traditional port like those you have just seen – instead the long channel with its bulbous end was constructed in 1840 specifically to tranship goods from the plains on to the marshland waterways. Today the port is a most attractive quiet corner, with an inviting looking auberge/restaurant that might make a fitting end to your day.

The Marais Mouillé is surely a watery paradise, but we have been neglecting the river we set out to explore, which takes a line between wet and dry marshes through an area that is very much more 'undiscovered'. Leaving Fontenay, the Vendée turns west and takes its last look at the hills while passing under a rusting bridge between the villages of **Chaix** and **Auzay**, perched high on either bank. The bridge looks pretty insignificant, but nevertheless has the distinction of having been designed by Eiffel. The next place downstream is **Velluire**, and here the river is surely on the plains. To the north-west of the village, the flat grassland is communal grazing where local farmers turn out their marked animals at the end of the springtime floods, and bring them in again before the winter. South again, and just before **le Gué-de-Velluire** the D65 seems to be running along a clifftop. That is exactly what it is – or rather was – and an orientation table has been strategically placed to pick out all the features before you, most of which were once under the sea.

Le Gué-de-Velluire has a little port on the Vendée, and from there a narrow road hugs the riverbank all the way to l'Île d'Elle – but having had just a glimpse of the Dry Marsh, you might first want to divert west on the D25, which skirts the foot of the same cliff to **Chaillé-les-Marais**. Chaillé is the 'capital' of this area, and has a tiny eco-museum housed in a roadside farmhouse, just off the N137 (and should you be hunting for it, the Office de Tourisme is not far away). The Maison du Petit Poitou was once the home of the 'Keeper of the Dyke', who divided his time between farming the land and checking the water levels. One of the rooms offers a glimpse of the sort of life he might have enjoyed here a century ago. Next door the story of draining of the marshes is told, and a relief map allows you to highlight the various canals dug out by the monks and everyone else since. Other showcases display the wildlife of the Dry Marsh.

This diversion to the west could continue a lot farther (22 miles [35km]) to the superb ornithological reserve at St Denis-du-Payré – but we must return to the River Vendée. The little road from le Gué follows it faithfully to its confluence with the Sèvre-Niortaise – the latter can be seen across the road where you join the D938. This is an area of many waterways, and just across the river the town of **Marans** offers a variety of supervised and unaccompanied river trips. Farther along the quayside there is a marina filled with ocean-going craft. A straight broad canal connects Marans with la Rochelle, but the Sèvre-Niortaise wriggles its way across the flat plain to reach the mudflats of the Bay of Aiguillon, theoretically the 'sea'. The nearest you can get to the river's mouth is the tiny **Port du Pavé** (follow signs from Charron), which is no tourist attraction but rather a wide and very muddy slipway used by those tending the *bouchots* (stakes) of mussels in the bay.

The Anse de l'Aiguillon has been a centre of mussel farming since the 13th century and the eco-museum that tells you about it (the Maison de la Mytiliculture) has been given very smart new premises in the village of **Esnandes** to the south – coming from Charron, turn left at the entry to the town. This is one of the better eco-museums and gives a good insight into the seasonal toil of the mussel-farmer, as well as a few curious facts you could not pick up elsewhere. An English translation helps you understand all the detail and there is also a twenty-minute film-show about birdlife on the bay.

Right beside the museum and also under the care of its staff, the solid grey fortified church of Esnandes seems firmly planted in the flat terrain. Inside the church, model ships hang from the rafters, ex-votos given by mariners in thanks for their deliverance from some particular peril of the sea. Others who were similarly grateful but could not afford such extravagant offerings have simply scratched a picture of their boat in the stones of the church – look on the outside of the north wall for these, but if you cannot find them, someone from the museum will help. The museum too will give you access to the watchpath that encircles the church roof, from which the whole Bay of Aiguillon can be surveyed.

For more views of this grey *bouchot*-studded bay you could briefly take the road along the coast from Esnandes. When it finally rises above the salt-meadows you have reached the **Pointe St Clément** with parking, picnic tables and a *table d'orientation*. Here you can look out over the muddy waters that have somehow absorbed those of the Vendée and take a last look at this strange landscape that was so recently the bed of the sea, with the little mounds that were once islands just lifting the horizon. You have to admit that it is a very different view of the Vendée!

OFFICES DE TOURISME

Fontenay-le-Comte
8, rue de Grimouard
85200 FONTENAY-LE-COMTE
☎ 02.51.69.44.99

Mervent
13, Place du Héraut
85200 MERVENT
☎ 02.51.00.03.34

Maillezais
Rue du Docteur Daroux
85420 MAILLEZAIS
☎ 02.51.87.23.01

Chaillé-les-Marais
Le Nieul
60, bis rue de l'an VI
85450 CHAILLÉ-LES-MARAIS
☎ 02.51.56.71.17

PLACES OF INTEREST

Fontenay-le-Comte

Musée Vendéen
Open mid-June to mid-September 2-6pm every day except Monday; rest of year 2-6pm every day except Monday and Tuesday.

Château de Terre Neuve
Open every day from May to September 9am-12noon, 2-7pm for guided visits (but closed mornings in May).

Mervent

Zoo de Mervent
Open February to mid-November and Christmas holidays every day 10am-7pm; rest of year Sunday only 1-5pm.

Mervent Adventures
Open July and August 11am-7pm every day; mid-April to July, September and October Saturdays 2-6pm, Sundays and public holidays 11am-6pm.

Parc de Pierre Brune
Open July and August every day 10am-7.30pm; June every day 11am-7pm; certain days only in April, May and September – for details ☎ 02.51.00.20.18

Faymoreau

Centre Minier
Open July and August every day 10am-7pm; April to June and September to mid-November every day except Monday 2-7pm; rest of year Sundays only 2-6pm.

Nieul-sur-l'Autise

Abbaye de St Vincent
Open July and August 10am-7pm, rest of year 9.30am-12.30pm, 1.30-6pm.

La Maison de la Meunerie
Open June to September every day 10.30am-12.30pm, 2-7pm; May and some school holidays 2.30-6pm.

Maillezais

Abbaye de Maillezais
Open July and August every day 10am-7pm; rest of year 9.30am-6pm (but Sundays 10am-7pm).

St-Hilaire-la-Palud

Les Oiseaux du Marais Poitevin
Open Easter to mid-September 10am-7.30pm; end of March to Easter and mid-September to early November 2-7pm.

Coulon

Maison des Marais Mouillés
July and August every day 10am-8pm; rest of year every day 10am-12noon, 2-7pm (but closed Mondays outside school holiday periods). Closed throughout January.

St Sigismond

Espace Marais
Open May to September, 10am-7pm.

Chaillé-les-Marais

Maison du Petit Poitou
Open July to mid-September 10am-1pm, 2-7pm; April to June and latter half of September 2-6pm. Closed Sunday mornings.

Esnandes

Maison de la Mytiliculture
Open mid-June to mid-September every day 10.30am-12.30pm, 2-7pm; March to mid-June and mid-September to early November 2-6pm every day except Tuesday.

LOCAL HIGHLIGHTS

Best Walks

· The Office de Tourisme at Mervent has a free leaflet showing four waymarked circuits in the forest. The easiest of these is the two and a half mile (4km) *Sentier Sylvicole*. For those who want something more ambitious, the 4 mile (6.5km) *Sentier de Balingue* incorporates a little (safe) rock scrambling along the banks of the lake.

· The *Sentier Botanique de l'Autise* extends for 15 mile (24km) (divided into three distinct loops) through the villages along the banks of the river. A leaflet available from the Office de Tourisme at Maillezais (and elsewhere) gives a very clear map of the whole route. For a short fun stroll, take the one and a half mile (2.5km) circuit from Nieul, crossing the river on the not-so-easy to board *bateau-à-chaîne*.

· Every Tourist Office has a fund of leaflets describing walks in the *marais* along the banks of the canals. For maximum watery interest, the walks from Damvix score highly.

For cyclists

· For casual holiday cyclists the Marais Poitevin is very tempting – no hills, minimum use of roads and maximum interest in innumerable waterside villages. But beware – if you are not used to cycling at home, hard saddles combined with bumpy towpaths could have devastating results. Opt for a short circuit first time round!

· If you can manage longer distances there are many very well marked out circuits. Ask any Office de Tourisme for the map *Le Marais Poitevin à Bicyclette* and the brochure *Sud Vendée Tourisme – Loisirs et Randonnées*, which gives details of bike hire.

- It is now possible to cycle all the way from Maillezais to Aiguillon (50 miles [80km]) using designated waymarked tracks and minor roads. Check the route on the brochure *Vendée – Les Sentiers Cyclables*.

- Mountain-bikers will find ample scope in the Mervent-Vouvant Forest with 62 mile (100km) of waymarked tracks. Bikes can be hired from La Girouette at Vouvant (☎ 02.51.50.10.60)

Watersports

- Everyone coming to the Marais Mouillé is going to want to take to the water in one of those curious boats. For details of trips both with and without a guide, ask for the brochure *Des Promenades en Barque dans le Marais Poitevin*.

- The best place for swimming is probably the Lac d'Albert at Xanton-Chassenon, where there is supervision in high season. On the same site you can enjoy pedalos, wind-surfers and canoes. (Open every day in high season, weekends only in May and June).

- Non-supervised swimming is also possible from *La Plage* at Mervent, where there are also pedalos for hire. Almost next door, the *Base Nautique* offers windsurfers, canoes and kayaks for hire.

For the palate

- Mogettes – white haricot beans – are omnipresent. They are at their best when served with Vendéen ham. If you are self-catering, it is probably best to buy the beans tinned or bottled – dried ones need long soaking and simmering, and fresh ones are hard to come by (late summer only).

- The *marais* is renowned for its eels (*anguilles*). With apologies to the eel, the flavour is something between mackerel and chicken – and though not exactly a delicacy, it is a lot tastier than you might expect.

- Brioche Vendéen is a lovely light sweet bread, often flavoured with orange-water and maybe even something stronger. Other local specialities to look out for are derivatives of the wild marsh plant angelica (sweets, jams etc.), local goats' cheeses, Fief Vendéen wines and the liqueur Trouspinette (From blackthorn).

And the most memorable

- Staying on the beautifully kept little campsite at Maillezais and waking every morning to the silhouette of the abbey highlighted by the first rays of sunshine.

- Sunday morning on the quayside in Arçais, when an old man and his dog arrived by *batai* to collect the obligatory newspaper and baguette and punted off home again.

- The corridor of medieval instruments in the Abbey of Nieul-sur-l'Autise. Hi-tech by usual abbey standards, but absolutely fascinating.

In the long sweep of sun-baked golden sand that edges the Bay of Biscay there is one notable break, one deep slash into the hinterland – the estuary of the Gironde. And following that estuary inland, the crowds thin, the roads narrow and at times you might be a whole planet away from the hurly-burly of the resorts on the coast. Little lanes lead you to tiny fishing ports or through vineyards stretching to the water's edge. To be sure the pine fo-rests and the ocean, the larger inland towns and even Bordeaux are never far away, but this is a slice of rural France that is not on everyone's itine-rary. So here we are going to follow the estuary, first down its eastern shore and then up the west, a journey of around 93 miles (150km) and it is surprising how much of interest lies in this relatively quiet backwater.

The Gironde never exists as a river. The name is given only to the estuary formed from the confluence of the Garonne and the Dordogne, an estuary that is the largest of its kind in Europe, draining all south-west France from the Massif Central to the Pyrenees. Shallow and wide, with many sandy islets, its waters are like thick, brown chocolate, a 'muddy plug' being ever present where the down-flowing river meets the in-coming tide. On the eastern shore, the Gironde has some fairly impressive cliffs riddled with troglodyte dwellings, while further upstream are the vineyards producing Cognac, Pineau des Charentes and the wines of Blaye and Bourg. On the western side the low banks slope only gently to the water's edge. The narrow strip of land

here is protected by the pine forest along the ocean-shore, providing ideal conditions for the production of some of France's very finest wines. Here are the Médoc vineyards, surprisingly unvisited for all their fame, and you may briefly want to abandon the peace of the water's edge to investigate some of the big-name châteaux.

The banks on both shores of the estuary offer another kind of bounty – oysters, shrimps, lamprey and shad. So in making this journey you have a gastronomic treat in store, a potential nightly indulgence in the very best seafood and wine. But for anyone whose heart is not best accessed via the stomach, other attractions include some beautiful villages, the caves of Meschers, boat trips on the estuary, lighthouses that can be visited, the citadel of Blaye, the Romanesque churches of the Saintonge and, at the beginning and end of the journey, golden beaches backed by pine forest.

THE EASTERN SHORE — THE JOURNEY BEGINS

Looking at the map, the best place to start this journey would be Royan – it certainly faces the Pointe de Grave across the narrowest point at the entrance to the estuary. But Royan is one of the most popular holiday resorts on the west coast, and is far from 'undiscovered'! All summer long its roads, its restaurants, its beaches and its campsites are seething with holidaymakers. Visit it if you must – at least you will feel the contrast as you move upstream!

But let us for the moment ignore

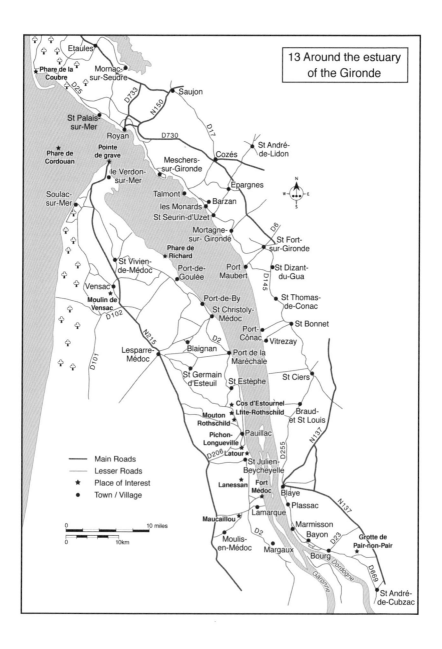

13 Around the estuary
of the Gironde

the popular stretch between Royan and La Palmyre and take a brief look to the north where the **Phare de la Coubre** is one of several lighthouses that herald the approach to the estuary. Climb the 300 steps here and you have a magnificent view not only of Royan, but of the wide sands of the Côte Sauvage to the north, backed by the extensive pine-woods of the Forêt de la Coubre. The vast beaches are pounded by Atlantic rollers, and are more suited to the needs of surfers than of swimmers, but at least they can easily accommodate the huge number of visitors. And the best way to reach those beaches is not by car, but by bike, along the many very pleasant cycle tracks that wind through the forest. Space at last!

From the Phare de la Coubre we first need to bypass Royan – and that gives an excellent excuse for visiting one of those *plus beaux villages* on the Seudre estuary just to the north. The Seudre estuary is famous for its oysters and tiny, pretty **Mornac-sur-Seudre** is one of the main centres. Narrow streets of blue-shuttered whitewashed houses with pink hollyhocks round their doors lead down to a picturesque harbour, where even the boats are blue and white! From here, signed trails lead you out between the beds where the oysters are reared, and you can buy some to take home or splash out in one of the restaurants on the quayside. Mornac has a 12th century Romanesque church, a narrow-gauge railway (it is on the line from la Tremblade to Saujon) and a handful of really top-quality craft shops with lots of browsing potential. You will not be alone here in high summer, but it is nevertheless a very welcome escape from Royan.

Back to the estuary now, and you could rejoin it south of Royan at the resort of **Meschers-sur-Gironde** – by which time the crowd will have thinned just a little.

The caves of Meschers

Meschers has cliffs of yellow limestone, the highest on the estuary, and those cliffs are tunnelled with caves that have been inhabited from time immemorial, mostly by those who were up to no good. Marauding Saracens, bloodthirsty Vikings, pirates, smugglers and wreckers – all came here. Then there were the more innocent – Protestants escaping religious persecution, fishermen angling for much sought after sturgeon and others who for one reason or another had lost their homes.

By the end of the 19th century, the caves had become centres of enter-tainment, with cafés and theatrical and musical performances. Finally there was a haut-cuisine restaurant serving caviar and local pineau (a blend of fruit juice and cognac). It closed in 1976.

Today many of Mescher's 50 or so caves are privately owned. Vying for your custom, two adjacent (and not dissimilar) complexes can be visited, the Grottes de Régulus (municipal) and the Grottes de Matata (private, including a hotel and crêperie). From the caves, the cliff road eventually drops down to Mescher's substantial port, a jumble of pleasure and fishing boats, and the departure point for a boat that takes passengers to view the caves and coastline from the water.

After Meschers the next place south is **Talmont-sur-Gironde** – and if it should be summertime, all thought of quiet banks and sleepy villages will leave your head at this point. In July and August the otherwise generous parking space outside the village becomes completely inadequate, and nearby fields are pressed into service, with their owners charging you for the privilege. Talmont is another of the elite *plus beaux villages*, again scoring highly on the white/blue/pink theme. But it is not the cottages you come to admire in Talmont, it is the 11th century church of Ste Radegonde that makes all that in-season hassle worthwhile. Balanced precariously on a rocky spur jutting into the sea, it is a much-photographed architectural gem, a geometrically satisfying blend of curves, arches and right-angles, all worked in pale stone under pink-tiled roofs. Pilgrims en route for Santiago de Compostela once came here to worship, and they must have taken the memory of this lovely church with them all the way to Spain.

And now at last you really are escaping. From Talmont, a road will take you out to Barzan and the Gallo-Roman site at the **Moulin du Fâ**. Guided visits take an hour and a half – a long time under the hot sun or pouring rain – and are in French only. But this extensive site is quite remarkable and is still undergoing enthusiastic excavation.

Back on the D145, **Les Monards** is a pretty port with lots of boats. Even prettier and totally unspoilt is **St Seurin-d'Uzet**, whose church stands alongside the harbour on a long inlet that fills and empties with the tide.

From here you can walk out on a path (past the excellent little camp-site) to the edge of the estuary where the sun magically sets into the sea. Beyond St Seurin, the scenic road leads on to Mortagne-sur-Gironde – a bigger place with more claim to fame, but still thankfully off-the-beaten track

Mortagne may be just down the road, but before going there you might like to take one longish diversion inland. Just to the east of you is cognac country and in the village of St André-de-Lidon (reached via Epargnes and the D129) is the **Domaine du Chaillaud**. The château here is set in beautiful botanical gardens where you can wander freely and even enjoy a picnic either before or after the visit – and there is no charge. Both gardens and distillery are the pride of the resident Deau family, who make you very welcome with a bilingual tour and easy-to-understand French film, all in an atmosphere laden with evaporating cognac (said to be the 'angels' share'). The tasting session at the end is, to say the least, generous. You will meet cognac and pineau again farther down the estuary (at St Dizant-de-Gua), but this visit to the Domaine de Chaillaud just has to be worth the diversion.

On at last to **Mortagne-sur-Gironde** – and there are lovely views as the road winds over hills before descending into the town. Mortagne itself is rather grey, but once you turn down to the port, all is life and colour. Along the coast road from the port is l'Hermitage, four bare rooms in the cliff face, once sheltering pilgrims who crossed the estuary here on their way to Santiago de Compostela. The fifth room is a rocky chapel dating from the 9th century, kept locked apart from the occasional tour in high season. A staircase cut through the cliff leads to its summit and views across the estuary.

SOUTH TO BLAYE

Below Mortagne the coast road goes on, with low marshes and flat fields of sunflowers and maize now separating you from the estuary. **Port Maubert** is another beautiful harbour, quiet even in high summer, with boats lined along pontoons on the wide channel and a pleasant little crêperie from which to watch the peaceful scene. The estuary itself is out of sight and accessible only on foot (10 minutes) or by bike. From Port Maubert you might like to head inland through the vineyards to **St Fort-sur-Gironde** to see one of the classic Romanesque churches of the Saintonge (the name given to the area around Saintes). This church dates from the latter half of the 12th century and has a rose window and a plethora of carvings both inside and out – the main doorway is curiously framed by horses' heads.

Just down the road now is St **Dizant-de-Gua**, another sleepy, pale-stoned village. In its main street, a glimpse of the gardens of the Château de Beaulon lures visitors to enter. Beyond the well-groomed lawns and bright floral borders the woodland conceals brilliant blue pools that are fed by underground fountains. The elegant château itself was once a palace belonging to the Bishops of Bordeaux. Today you can possibly enter just one room to sample the cognac and pineau produced in the distillery at nearby Lorignac.

South of St Dizant the D145 runs through farming country with good views over the marshes to the west and a windmill on the heights at Conac. At **St Thomas-de-Conac**, the prom-

inent church is another typical of the Saintonge – although the façade is 19th century, the interior is Romanesque, with some finely carved capitals. St Sorlin, St Bonnet and St Ciers have more views and from each, little roads lead out across the marsh to ports that are mere inlets on the side of the brown estuary. All of them are 'undiscovered' and all are worth a visit, but **Vitrezay** is perhaps more so than most, having a restaurant, waymarked footpaths and a *table d'orientation* looking out over the water.

South on the main road again, **Braud-et-St Louis** is a rather newer town, housing workers from its Nuclear Power Station on the waterside. France is ever keen to convince everyone of the benefits of nuclear power, and that station once housed a permanent exhibition and offered guided visits. Since the events of 9/11, all has been closed. Beyond Braud-et-St Louis the D255 crosses drained marshland as it heads for Blaye, and in summer time every ditch is bright with yellow spearwort.

Blaye is a fascinating place, centred on an enormous citadel built by Vauban in the 1680s. Part of a defensive network designed to keep the English out of Bordeaux, it was joined in this role by Fort Médoc on the opposite shore and a third fort on the Île de Paté. Today half of Blaye is still inside the defensive walls – houses, restaurants, museums and even the campsite. The citadel can be accessed by car on its eastern side through the Porte Royale, but there is no parking within the walls (other than on the campsite). Instead it is better to leave the car by the harbour at the foot of the ramparts – and while here, to pick up a leaflet on the citadel from the octagonal kiosk that is the Office de

Tourisme. Armed with this information, you can cross the grey arched footbridge spanning the moat to enter via the Porte Dauphine and explore the cobbled streets in whichever direction you like.

Do not miss the views of the estuary with its islands, (Île Nouvelle and smaller Île Paté) from Place des Armes and again from the Tour de l'Eguillette – and take a brief glance at the oldest enclosure of the citadel, the ruins of the 12th century triangular Château des Rudels. From one of its ancient towers, an orientation table points out the distant features of the landscape.

Not far away, the solid *Manutention* building once served as a prison, but now houses three excellent museums – an archaeological museum, a 'History of the Bakery Trade' museum and a permanent exhibition by the Conservatoire de l'Estuaire. An English translation is offered for each. The latter in particular is comprehensive and fascinating, all the story of estuary life, spread over several rooms. To do it justice, you would need to spend a couple of hours or more here.

Do not even think of leaving Blaye without tasting its wines! In summer time you will find the Cellier des Vignerons open (inside the citadel, near the Porte Dauphine); at other times head for the Maison du Vin in the Cours Vauban (the main road opposite the Porte Dauphine). Blaye wines are both red and white and are generally rather dry, although the different vintages vary somewhat. Special tasting sessions are on offer to help you choose between them – join in if you can, it is an excellent prelude to the rest of the estuary tour!

BEYOND BLAYE

From Blaye, a car ferry will take you across the estuary to Lamarque. Frequent, efficient and not expensive, these ferries are obviously preferable to the long drive round Bordeaux. But having tasted the wine of Blaye, you have to compare it with that of the next place to the south, Bourg. And there are one or two places worth looking at on the way. So let us first head south to Bourg (and perhaps beyond) before returning for the ferry.

Leaving Blaye to the south, the road first passes through the village of **Plassac**, where a remarkable site of three Roman villas has been excavated. Opposite the site is a museum displaying the finds, including some particularly fine wall-paintings. Beyond Plassac the road follows the river, and turning right at Thau, runs right along its banks. The sheer limestone cliffs in Marmisson house troglodyte dwellings with a view, reached only by steep footpaths, while in the estuary the silhouette of a World War II wreck looms darkly. The waterside road goes on as far as la Reuille, where you are obliged to turn inland and cross the vineyards to Bayon with its Romanesque church topped by a statue of the Virgin and Child. Returning to the estuary again, there is soon a roadside viewpoint looking over the Bec d'Ambès, where the Dordogne and the Garonne meet, although there is little appealing about this promontory now occupied by industrial sites. From here the road continues through the pretty hillside village of Pain de Sucre, graced by palm trees, to reach Bourg.

Like Blaye, **Bourg** has its fortifications – the ramparts top a steep cliff overlooking the gravy-like waters of the Dordogne. At one end of the cliff is the 17th century Château de la Citadelle, a stylish building set in pleasant parkland. Today it houses the Musée des Calèches (Carriage Museum). Having honed your taste-buds in Blaye you must now try the wines of Bourg – the Maison des Vins has a clifftop perch at the opposite end of town from the Château, and offers a wide selection of wines backed by details of their individual producers. Bourg wines are red only, and a thicker deeper colour than those of Blaye. From a much smaller appellation they are said to be more homogeneous in character.

If you have time to spare you could go on from Bourg. Three miles (5km) to the south (just off the D669) is the Grotte de Pair-non-Pair, with wall engravings of horses and ibex dating from some 30,000 years ago, while farther on at St André-de-Cubzac, the graceful 18th century Château du Bouilh is open to the public. But event-ually it must be time to leave and take that ferry to the west bank of the estuary, where for a while the story is that of wine, wine and more wine.

ACROSS THE ESTUARY AND ON TO PAUILLAC

As soon as the ferry creaks and shuffles sideways into the port of **Lamarque** you can see that the west bank is entirely different terrain. Leaving the port, the first landmark to greet you is the octagonal tower of the church in the village – and it looks out over a green sea of vine-yards stretching as far as the eye can see. In fact the vineyards of Blaye and Bourg occupy a slightly larger area than those of the Médoc, but it cert-ainly does not appear so to the visitor.

In the village of Lamarque you reach the D2, the main road along the west bank, and one lined all the way by the great wine-producing châteaux. To the south of you, the big name is that of Château Margaux – head that way if you like, but there are a lot more châteaux on your route north. Before meeting them, you might first want to see Blaye's counter-part on this bank, **Fort Médoc** (you passed the third fort, the one on the Île Paté, on the ferry) – turn north on the D2 at Lamarque and take the first signed turn to the right.

Fort Médoc is disappointing com-pared with the fine citadel at Blaye. The Porte Royale entrance is grand enough, bearing above it the smiling emblem of Louis XIV, the Sun-King, but inside there is only a very large grassy courtyard surrounded by re-mnants of assorted buildings and on the far side a sort of look-out platform commanding the estuary. It probably will not detain you long, and you can return up the road to the D2. Close to the fork (right for Cussac, left for Lamarque again) you will see a wine-growing establishment by the name of **Château Tour du Haut Moulin**.

Château Tour de Haut Moulin is not one of the biggest names (they pro-duce a *cru bourgeois supérieur* here), but like many similar establishments in this area, they are open to visitors and are happy to discuss the techni-ques of production and show you their *chais* (wine-stores) before offering free tasting. All this is managed very well in English at the Château Tour de Haut Moulin, and it is almost always open, so call in and enjoy your first taste of the magnificent wines of the Médoc.

Returning to the D2 again, you have a choice. A few minutes away, just west of Lamarque (on the D5) is the

Wines of the Médoc vineyard

The Médoc peninsula enjoys its own microclimate, protected from extremes of temperature by the proximity of so much water, and shielded from Atlantic breezes by the pine forests along the coast. The soil is actually poor and full of stones, thus causing the vines to root more deeply – and since the stones absorb the sun's heat by day and give it out again at night, they too help to keep temperatures consistent.

Four kinds of grapes are grown (Cabernet-Sauvignon, Cabernet-Franc, Merlot and Petit Verdot), with a predominance of the Sauvignon that contributes to Médoc's great quality of improving with age. Médoc wines are all classified – the finest is a *premier grand cru* (a distinction awarded to only five wines), followed by 2nd, 3rd, 4th and 5th *crus*, a *cru bourgeois* (about 50 per cent of all production), a *cru artisan* and finally the wines produced by many lesser growers who belong to cooperatives. To add confusion to this, the Médoc vineyard has eight different appellations determined by location – the best known of these are Médoc and Haut-Médoc, but there are also Pauillac, St Estèphe, Margaux, St Julien, Moulis and Listrac.

Château Maucaillou – again it offers a *cru bourgeois*, but they are keen to tell you that this one has won many prizes. It entices visitors with an added attraction, a wine museum where wine-making tools and equipment of previous times are on display, and you can test your 'nose' for wine with an assortment of puffed scents. A film shows the work of the château. A tour of the *chais* and wine tasting are naturally on offer, but this time it comes at a price (not included in entry to the museum).

Back north on the D2 once more, and a road on the left is signed to **Château Lannesson** – another château with an added inducement, in this case a horse and carriage museum. Divert or continue, whatever you do you will soon find yourself again on that wine road with châteaux and vineyards on every side. The next village is **St Julien Beychevelle**, and a road-sign at its entrance suggests that you

salute! The interpretation of this could be that such fine vineyards demand you pay your respects – but then it is probably a reference to the time when the Grand Admiral of France lived here, and ships passing on the Gironde were required to lower their sails to pay homage (Beychevelle = *baisse-voile*). Be that as it may, the wines of St Julien are much esteemed for their full body and delicate bouquet.

The **Château Beycheville** (right beside the road) offers tours and particularly attracts visitors with its pristine lawns and brilliant floral displays. If you turn right past its car parks, an avenue of plane trees will lead you down to the estuary and the peaceful little inlet of Port Beychevelle, from where the wine was once shipped, and there are more views of the lovely pale-coloured château as you return.

On the wine road again, and emerging from the sweeping vineyards on your right is the round tower of

Château Latour, one of the elite *premier grand cru* châteaux. Next to appear on this star-studded trail is a château seemingly lifted straight from a fairy tale, the pepper-pot-turretted **Pichon –Longueville.** There is even a pull-in from where you can take photographs opposite, but if you decide to cross the road, you can admire the room full of shining stainless steel vats while you consider whether or not to make a visit.

Beyond Pichon-Longueville is **Pauillac.** Obviously focussed on wine, the town is indisputably the 'capital' of the Médoc region. Forgetting the wine for a moment, Pauillac is an extremely pleasant town in its own right, with a long waterfront on the estuary. The port area with its yachts and fishing vessels offers a fine view of the town topped by the octagonal tower of St Martin's church. A visit to the church reveals a galleon-like boat hanging from the rafters, an ex-voto dating from 1836 that was clearly given in thanks for deliverance from some long-forgotten maritime peril. Back on the quayside (or almost) the curious little Musée des Automates is worth a visit. Two tiny back rooms are crammed with scenes of fanciful animal figures that spring to life at the press of a footswitch – and in the front room, some of the classic toys you may (or may not) remember from half a century ago are on sale. Pauillac has few visitors, lots of parking, an assortment of good hotels and a small municipal campsite that is seriously one of the smartest and best equipped in France – a great place to stay for exploring the Médoc.

You could start your visit to Pouillac at the Tourist Office – it is actually called the Maison du Tourisme et du Vin here, and for a small sum you can help yourself to a little tasting from the selection on tap while browsing through the literature. Wines and all things wine-related are on sale, a wine-growing video describes the yearly cycle and regular wine-tasting sessions are held in the basement room on summer evenings. All the châteaux offering guided visits have their leaflets here, so this is the place to make your choice and let the Office do the booking for you.

The wines of the Médoc are above all celebrated for their great quality of improving with age, and though this is true of all of them, it particularly applies to those of the appellation Pauillac. In this region are three of the five *premier grand cru* châteaux – Latour you have already glimpsed, but just to the north of the town are the best known of all, **Château Mouton-Rothschild** and Château Lafite-Rothschild. Both are just off the D2 and both offer visits, but Mouton-Rothschild definitely has the edge in including a Museum of Wine in Art and a magnificent collection of wine labels designed by famous artists. Both are attributable to Baron Philippe Rothschild who died in 1988 – the museum is his own private and priceless collection of wine-related tapestries, ceramics, jewellery and the rest, while the labels were the work of his friends including Picasso, Dali and Chagall, who were rewarded for their efforts with crates of wine. Touring the wine stores you learn a lot of fascinating detail and you are pretty sure to end up feeling confused about exactly what goes into which barrel when, but it is all an experience. Wine tasting is an optional and expectedly costly extra at the end of the tour (about £1 a teaspoonful is probably not too much of an exaggeration) but then this is the finest wine in the world!

After passing Château Mouton-

Rothschild the wine road has its finest hour with the elegant building of **Château Lafite-Rothschild** being quickly succeeded by the orientally-inspired **Château Cos d'Estournel** (the founder of the château, Louis – Gaspard d'Estournel, was rejoicing in his successful trade with India at the time). Vineyards surround the road, and since Lafite is *premier grand gru* and Cos d'Estournel *deuxième grand cru*, you would not want to casually pick a grape around here.

NORTH TO THE MOUTH OF THE GIRONDE

Cos d'Estournel, now purchased by the Mouton-Rothschild group, is actually in the vineyard of **St Estèphe**, which is a relatively small area, but one with the greatest density of growers. St Estèphe has its own Maison du Vin in the village square, where you can sample the classically deep-red wines from something like 60 different establishments. Opposite the Maison de Vin is a lovely mellow-stone church. Its brightly-coloured and gilded interior, automatically illuminated by chandeliers as you enter, comes as something of a surprise – it was created in the 18th century, by a priest who wanted to give his flock the finest possible place to worship

Descending from St Estèphe to its harbour on the estuary, you can look across the fields on the right to the imposing Château Phélan-Ségur (*cru bourgeois exceptionnel*). On the waterfront there are picnic tables under the trees and from here the road returning along the coast to Pauillac is very picturesque. Spindly-legged fishing platforms known as *pêcheries* line the shore all the way and some owners have even extended their domains to

the grassy banks, adding gardens, barbecues and picnic tables. But this journey continues north from the harbour of St Estèphe via St Seurin-de-Cadorne, where the 'added extra' of the **Château Vertus** is a museum of Médoc history.

At St Seurin, you could perhaps be persuaded to turn inland to visit the partially excavated Roman site of Brion at **St Germain d'Esteuil**. This latter is well off the beaten track and quite difficult to find (although there are signs), but you might do well to pick up a leaflet at the Maison du Patrimoine in the village first. And while at St Germain, you could continue north to **Blaignan**, where a widely-acclaimed nutty confection by the name of 'Noisettines du Médoc' is made by a local family. The visit here consists of someone donning a chef's hat and explaining both history and production in very rapid French, but includes a glass of wine and very generous sampling of the delicacies, which are irresistible.

Back to the coast again now – and little ports succeed each other all the way north. Just out of St Seurin, the **Port de la Marechale** is typical, a pretty little tidal inlet having much in common with those on the opposite bank. There seem to be no visitors here, even in high season, yet tubs spilling over with geraniums deck the quays, and a bench offers a restful spot from which to contemplate the rolling brown waters of the estuary.

Maybe it should be a case of 'if you've seen one you've seen them all', but those splendid little ports still keep luring you down to the water's edge as you travel north. Do not miss the larger-than-average port in the attractive village of St Christoly-Médoc, the tiny port of By, the double-channelled Port-de-Goulée, and the pretty Port de Richard, all strung out along the same road, still the D2, which by now is achieving some respite from the vineyards. Beyond the Port de Richard, a sign invites you to turn off across the flat marshes to the **Phare de Richard**. The cheerful little lighthouse has an interesting museum of all things estuarine on its ground floor and not too many spiral steps taking you to a platform with views across the estuary and up to the northern tip of the peninsula.

From the Phare de Richard all roads lead inland to **St Vivien-de-Médoc**, an unassuming small town that has its own tourist office and no tourists. Most curious is its church, where a very modern tower has been tacked on to the original Romanesque building. St Vivien is just east of the main road, the N215, and that road, running the length of the peninsula, seems to be a great barrier, keeping all the holiday-makers on its western side, while to the east there is seldom a soul to be seen. From St Vivien you can make your way down to the port, still well inland – and here you are

back in oyster country with boats loading and unloading the strange cylindrical 'collectors' on which the young oysters grow. Beyond the port are the fish farms, Eau Médoc and Petit Canaux. Shrimps and prawns are their speciality, and in particular the big juicy orange *gambas* that mature in the basins over the summer months. North of the fish farms, St Vivien has its own little beach on the estuary – where, being closer to the Atlantic, the water is now thankfully a shade more blue.

Stay off the beaten track if you will, but across that central road, the popular resort of **Soulac-sur-Mer** is at least worth a fleeting visit – and on the way, you could stop off at the **Moulin de Vensac** (just west of Vensac – follow signs from the village). Erected on this site in 1858, the windmill was last used commercially in 1939. It has now been restored by the last miller's descendants, and turns its sails into the wind to entertain and educate the visitors, who come in their droves in high season. After watching it in action, you can buy the various

Fishing in the estuary

For fishing on foot, the most popular and commonly used device is the *carrelet* – a huge square net supported from a wobbly-looking platform on stilts. The fisherman usually adds a cabin to this for his greater comfort. The nets are lowered at the appropriate tide and later winched in. Although they may look old, almost all the *carrelet* ensembles you see in the estuary today are new – la Tempête, the great storm that scoured France in the last days of 1999, destroyed more than 80 per cent of the originals.

Fishing boats are mostly of two kinds, yawls (or skiffs) and small trawlers. They are used to catch migratory fish that only visit the estuary at certain seasons – lamprey and shad in the spring, *mégreau* (Argyrosomus Regius) in early summer and young eels arriving from the Sargasso Sea as autumn begins are among the most profitable catches. Sturgeon (the source of caviar) were caught in the estuary up to 1982, when, near to extinction, they became a protected species.

flours it produces in the hut alongside. Soulac is a busy but rather different resort. In the belle époque it became popular with the rich and famous of Bordeaux who built their holiday retreats here – and favoured a particular design. Soulac has more than 500 'neo-colonial' villas, built of orange-red brick under white-painted eaves, all of which lend the place a more attractive air than it might otherwise have had. Strangely isolated among all these curious houses is the one really old and imposing building of Soulac, the Basilique Notre-Dame-de-la-fin-des-Terres. A Benedictine abbey dating from the 11th century, it slowly became covered in sand, from which fate it was rescued and restored in the 19th century. Today its cool dark interior is strangely peaceful amid the holiday bustle. Inside there are some beautifully carved capitals 900 years old, a polychrome statue of Our Lady of Land's End – and a statue of St James, recalling the time when British pilgrims landed near Soulac on their way to Santiago de Compostela.

Just up the road from the basilica is the seafront, long beaches of white sand facing the Atlantic, supervised for bathing in summertime. From here a little tourist train heads north through the pine forest to the Pointe de Grave, some 6 miles (10km) distant, and cycle tracks weave their way alongside. To the south of the town are more cycle tracks, and the beautiful and unique vegetation of the huge Dune d'Amélie, a nature reserve that backs the beach for more than two and a half miles (4km). A discovery trail starting from the D101E points out its interesting features.

Across the N215 again you are back in no man's land, on the vast estuarine marshes that were first drained around 400 years ago by Dutchmen accustomed to such feats of engineering. Cycle tracks cross the wilderness and lead to the shore. North from here, the cranes at the container port of le Verdon-sur-Mer stand out on the horizon and that is where you are heading – well, not exactly to the port area, but rather to the little town itself. Le Verdon, almost at the tip of the peninsula, is a pleasant small resort with first-class sandy beaches (one naturist) that is somehow almost entirely overlooked by the guidebooks.

Now you are almost at the end of the journey. Beyond le Verdon, the Pointe de Grave points a long rocky finger at Royan, half an hour away across the water. But do not rush to the boat – the Pointe de Grave is an interesting place. The lighthouse here is well worth a visit for its views (beware – the final ascent is via metal ladder) and for its museum, which relates to all the lighthouses of this area and particularly to the Phare de Cordouan, out to sea. Not far from the lighthouse is the departure point of the train that takes you through the pines to Soulac. Cycle tracks and footpaths head the same way. The Pointe de Grave was once a disembarkation point for pilgrims and the main coastal footpath south from here is now marked with a stylised scallop-shell, the emblem of St James.

And now your journey is at an end – almost. Every holiday should end on a high point and what could better fit the bill than – yet another lighthouse! But this one is unique. The Phare de Cordouan, guarding the entrance to the estuary from a rock 4.4 miles (7km) off shore, is reached by boats leaving both the Pointe de Grave and Royan. It is the oldest lighthouse in France, the ornate lower section (up to the second floor) having been constructed between 1584 and 1611, while the more austere upper part was added in 1789. The older part contains furniture dating from Napoleon III, the marble-floored royal apartments and even a chapel with fine stained-glass windows.

Audioguides (in English) tell you all about it, including the work of the resident wardens. Climbing the 311 steps to the lantern at its summit, you can take a last long look into the estuary of the Gironde – a suitable place from which to take your leave of this fascinating region.

OFFICES DE TOURISME

Royan
BP 102
17206 ROYAN
☎ 05.46.05.04.71

Blaye
Allées Marines
33390 BLAYE
☎ 05.57.42.12.09

Pauillac
La Verrerie
33250 PAUILLAC
☎ 05.56.59.03.08

Soulac-sur-Mer
68, Rue de la Plage
33780 SOULAC-SUR-MER
☎ 05.56.09.86.61

PLACES OF INTEREST

Phare de la Coubre
Open mid-June to mid-September
11am-1pm, 2-7.30pm.

Meschers-sur-Gironde

Grottes de Regulus
Guided visits in French every hour from 10.30am-5.30pm, mid-June to mid-September (much more frequently in July and August). April to mid-June and mid-Sept to October, afternoons only. English visitors are offered translated text for self-guided tours.

Grottes de Matata
Open February to November, 10am-7pm for tours lasting approx. 40 mins.

Barzan
Gallo-Roman site of Fâ (museum and guided tour)
Open July and August 10am-1pm, 2-5pm; June and September 2.30-6.30pm; April and May 2-6pm; October to March weekends and school holidays only 2-5pm (note last visit one hour before closure).

St. Dizant-de-Gua

Château de Beaulon
Open 9am-12noon, 2.30-6pm every day June to September and weekdays only October to April.

Blaye

Exhibition and museums at the Man-utention (common entrance ticket) Open every day 1.30-7pm, mid-April to October.

Cellier des Vignerons

Open 10am-12.30pm, 3.30-7pm, July and August only.

Plassac

Gallo-Roman Villa

Open April to October 9am-12noon, 2-7pm (6pm closing in April and October).

Grotte de Pair-non-Pair

Open every day except Monday (and certain holidays) throughout the year with several tours a day.

Château du Bouilh

Grounds always open. Tours of interior Thursdays, Saturdays and Sundays only mid-June to September (every day from 14 July to 15 August).

Fort Médoc

Open every day May to October 9am-8pm; March and April 10am-6.30pm (except Mon); November to February 10am-5.30pm (except Mon).

Château Tour du Haut-Moulin

Open all year round without appoint-ment. No hours stated.

Château Maucaillou

Open 10am-12noon, 2-6pm every day throughout the year (no lunch break mid-June to mid-Sept).

Pauillac

Le Petite Musée d'Automates

Open July and August, 10.30am-7pm; rest of year 10.30am-12.30pm, 2.30-7pm (but closed Sun and Mon in May, June and Sept; Sun, Mon, Tue and Wed rest of year).

Château Mouton-Rothschild

Guided tours every morning and afternoon from April to October, weekdays only outside those months. Advance booking is advised (particularly to get a tour in English) but even in high season, 48 hours notice is usually sufficient. OT at Pauillac will help, or ☎ 05.56.73.21.29 For visits to other **Château of the Médoc** region, contact OT at Pauillac. Almost all châteaux can be visited by appointment, some have definite opening hours in high season (part-icularly if there is an added museum), and some are unable to welcome visitors over the busy period of the grape harvest.

Blaignan

Noisettines du Médoc

Open July and August, 4 visits each afternoon except Sunday. Other times by appointment only.

Phare de Richard

Open July and August weekdays (not Tue) 11am-7pm, weekends 2.30-7pm; March to June and Sept, Oct every day (except Tue) 2.30-6.30pm.

Vensac

Moulin de Vensac

Guided visits (1/2 hour) 10am-12.30pm, 2.30-6.30pm : July and August every day, June and September weekends, April, May and October Sunday after-noons and bank holidays.

Soulac-sur-Mer

Train Touristique (train from Soulac to the Pointe de Grave)

Runs July and August, 5 times every day; April, May, June, September, weekends and holidays, 2 departures every afternoon.

Pointe de Grave

Phare de Grave
Open July and August 10am-
12noon, 2-6pm; April to June,
weekends and bank holidays 2.30-
5.30pm.

Phare de Cordouan
Boats leave the port at the Pointe de
Grave almost every day from July to
September. Times vary with tides.
Reservation necessary.
(☎ 05.56.09.62.93 or visit OT at
Pointe de Grave).

LOCAL HIGHLIGHTS

Best Walks

- From Mornac, follow one of the two routes through the oyster beds to the estuary of the Seudre and back. The Office de Tourisme on the quayside has maps with information (French only) but the waymarking is good and you will not get lost.

- Pauillac, St Laurent-Médoc and St Julien-Beychevelle all have waymarked circuits of different lengths. Most of these wind through the vineyards at some point – the best way to get a look at them without intruding. Ask at OT for maps and details (French text only, but maps and coloured waymarking are more than adequate to get you round).

- Walk through the forest on the pilgrim trail from the Pointe de Grave to Soulac, around 4.4 miles (7km). You could continue to Santiago (another 621 miles (1000km) or so) or get a train back.

For cyclists

- The Médoc peninsula is paradise for families who can cycle for mile after mile on specially designed tracks through the forest with no fear of traffic. The virtually total absence of hills is an added bonus! Free maps can be obtained from any OT and show routes for both on and off-road bikes. Cycles can be hired in Pauillac, le Verdon, Soulac and most towns.

- The cycle track network of the Gironde extends south to the Bassin d'Arcachon and even into the heart of Bordeaux. There is another short 7.5 mile (12km) section between Blaye and Etauliers. Ask for the leaflet *Les Pistes Cyclables de Gironde* for details of routes and places where bikes can be hired.

Watersports

- The estuary itself is only suitable for swimming north of Meschers on the east bank and at le Verdon-sur-Mer on the west.

- The pine-backed Atlantic coast is superb for surfing. Several resorts (St Palais, Soulac) have beaches where swimming is supervised in summertime, and several towns have open-air swimming pools (Blaye, Bourg, Pauillac, Souillac),

- Les Lacs du Moulin Blanc at St Christoly-Médoc are inland lakes where swimming is supervised in summer.

For the Palate

- Shrimps and prawns. Two sorts in particular are worth seeking out, – the enormous bright pink *gambas* and the tiny white *bichettes* (cooked in aniseed).

- Pauillac lamb – 60-day-old lamb fed only on it is mother's milk is a particular delicacy of the region. In summer you can visit a farm where these lambs are reared (book at OT) – but it may not enhance your enjoyment of the meat!

- Lamprey and shad are caught on both sides of the estuary in springtime. If you can, try *Lamproie à la Bordelaise* – lamprey in a sauce of Médoc wine. Shad (*alose*) may be cooked in sorrel (*oseille*).

- Look out for the delicious Canelés de Bordeaux, sweet cakes looking like miniature crème-caramels, even to the brown caramelised topping.

- And of course there is all that wine, not forgetting the Cognac and Pineau des Charentes (try the latter on melon!).

And the most memorable

- Standing on a lonely shore at St Seurin d'Uzet and watching a deep-red sun sinking into the sea.

- The collection of wine labels at Château Mouton-Rothschild. Fascinating.

- Entering the ancient basilica at Soulac and finding it packed to the doors with folk in beach attire (well, almost) singing their hearts out at morning Mass.

The present day *département* of Gers was once the heart of the pre-revolutionary province of Gascony – a swash-buckling full-blooded place, peopled with brave-hearted musketeers (according to Dumas anyway), and blessed with rich cuisine, thick red wine and golden brandy. The Gers is half-English by tradition, more French than France, and just a little Spanish as well. Few people holiday here because it is obviously on the way to somewhere else – another 60 miles (97km) and you can reach Lourdes and the Pyrenees (and crowds of visitors as well!). From the Gers you can see the high rocky peaks on the horizon, sirens luring you to continue south. Why should you stop? No-one has even heard of the Gers (the 's' is pronounced, by the way) and most guidebooks give it only a couple of minutes of their time, being consumed with the scenic virtues of what lies beyond. There are no mountains in the Gers, merely rolling hills – but you need no more than that to show off to advantage all the lovely honey-stoned *bastide* towns, relics of the Middle Ages, when England and France tussled over this land for 300 years.

There is no doubt the Gers has a colourful history. The bastides are the direct result of Henry Plantagenet's propitious marriage to Eleanor of Aquitaine, and his subsequent accession to the throne of England in 1154. England ruled this south-west corner of France, and the French kings did not like it. Skirmishes ensued, and both sides built their fortresses – surprisingly they were very similar, with streets laid out in a grid around a church and central market square. In the 15th century the English finally retreated, but the splendid bastides remain to this day, and nothing can be more pleasant on a hot afternoon than sipping a glass of local wine in the cool of a covered arcade beside a market square 800 years old.

Of course the Gers' history did not end there – or begin there either. The Romans were here (one of the most sumptuous villas in southern France has been excavated at Séviac), and they were followed by the Visigoths and Franks, and then by the Vascones who arrived from the Spanish side of the Pyrenees in the 7th century. This Spanish blood possibly explains the Gers fondness for bullfighting, which continues to this day with bullrings in several small towns.

The Middle Ages saw a different kind of invasion in Gascony. The mortal remains of St James had been found at Santiago de Compostela in the north-west corner of Spain and pilgrims from all over Europe were flocking to worship at his shrine. All the major routes across France passed through Gascony, with the southernmost two (those from le Puy and Arles) crossing the region that is now the Gers. At the height of its popularity, half a million pilgrims a year were arriving in Santiago – and a large proportion of them would have come through the Gers. Maybe there are few tourists today, but there certainly were many in the Middle Ages!

Along the pilgrim routes sprang monasteries and hospices offering shelter, and churches (often displaying relics of other saints) where they could worship as they passed. Today some

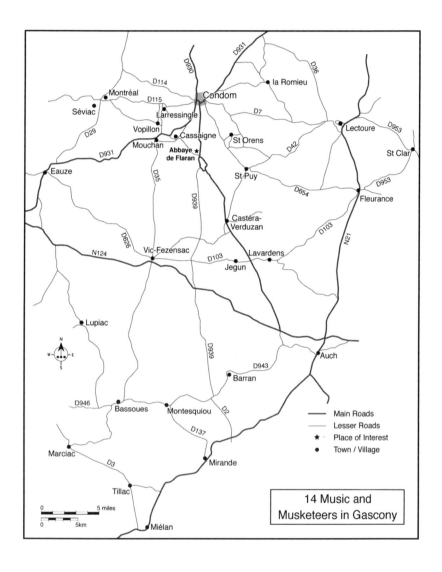

14 Music and
Musketeers in Gascony

of the finest religious buildings in all France are still to be found in the Gers – most notably, the imposing Cathedral Ste-Marie in Auch and the tiny Collegiale St Pierre in le Romieu with its delightful frescoes. And with the recent revival of interest in the *Chemins de St Jacques*, you can again see pilgrims on the highways and by-ways, each one recognisable by the scallop-shell of St James displayed on his ruck-sack or hat.

And what more can be said of the Gers? Undoubtedly they are fond of music here. The Spanish influence is again evident in the festival of Latin-American music, held annually in the little town of Vic-Fézensac – but then they also revel in bands of all kinds in Condom, in Country and Western music in Mirande and in jazz, glorious enthusiastic jazz, all the year round in Marciac. The Gers knows how to party and invites everyone to join in. And with the celebrations go the food and drink – the region prides itself on having the finest cuisine in France, including pigeon and duck, foie gras and rich fruit pastries, all of which are perfectly accompanied by the Côtes-de-Gascogne wines. And of course any meal should be rounded off with a drop of golden locally-produced Armagnac, swirled gently in a bulbous glass, warmed with the hands to increase the aroma, and sipped ever so slowly.

CONDOM

Let us start this exploration of the Gers in the north, where the landscape is at its most attractive, a pastoral scene of red earth, yellow sunflowers and sparse habitation, with hills that are just too steep to be called rolling, succeeding each other in waves as you

go. Across this terrain the pilgrims come, and it is one of the most pleasant sections of their long journey, with a new vista revealed from every crest. The largest town here is **Condom**, set in the valley of the River Baïse, with a cathedral that seems too big for it rising from its heart, and back streets that are dotted with elegant mansions (known as Hôtels) from its 18th century hey-day. The Gothic-style Cathedral of St Pierre dates from the early 16th century and is most notable for the arch of statues above its south door. Its interior was almost entirely renewed following the Wars of Religion – dark and cool, it offers brief respite from the Gascon sun for many a pilgrim on the trail.

North of the cathedral the vaulted cloisters have likewise been restored and offer a cut through from one side of the town to the other. Beyond them the former Bishops' Palace now houses administrative offices and around the corner, its rather grand stables shelter the Musée de l'Armagnac. Armagnac has been the *raison d'être* of this western side of the Gers for some 700 years, and this little museum is enough to give you a good insight into its history. The most impressive exhibit is an enormous 18-ton wine press, naturally on the ground floor, while upstairs, an excellent short video (with English version at the press of a button) describes the current methods of production. Armed with such knowledge you could take yourself off to one of the establishments in town that offer tasting – the visit to Ryst Dupeyron (in the Hôtel de Cugnac on the Rue Jean Jaurès) also includes a tour of the *chai* (barrel store where the brandy is ageing) and a few historical items and tableaux.

Condom has grown weary of Anglo-Saxon jokes about its name and on

Armagnac, Floc and the wines of the Côtes-de-Gascogne

The production of Armagnac begins with the distillation of white wine to give a liquid that is about 60 per cent alcohol. This clear liquid is then transferred into oak casks, which impart colour and reduce the alcohol content over years of maturation. After several years the brandy may be moved on to casks made of older wood to further improve its qualities. Finally, brandies of different ages and origins are blended at the discretion of the *Maître de chai*. Armagnac brandies are classified according to their age – the youngest is three-star, the next VSOP, VO or Réserve, and the oldest XO, Extra or Napoleon. And remember – half the pleasure of brandy is its aroma. It should be served in a glass that is wider at the bottom than the top and warmed with the hands before drinking.

Floc is simply a mixture of Armagnac and grape-juice, the regional equivalent of the Pineau des Charentes from farther north. Served cold, it makes an excellent aperitif – and goes well with fruit, especially melon.

The Côtes-de-Gascogne are widely popular fruity wines. Nine-tenths of the production is white wine, which can be drunk as a cool aperitif or as an accompaniment to fish dishes. Red Côtes-de-Gascogne, served at room temperature, goes perfectly with the local poultry dishes, while the rosé will fit just about any occasion.

the principle of 'if you can't beat 'em, join 'em' has installed a tiny Musée de la Préservatif (*Préservatif* being the French equivalent) in the back streets between the cathedral and river. The changing exhibitions here are intended purely as 'fun', although the museum is not advertised in the way others are. And Condom would like you to know that its name probably derives from the Latin *condominium*, meaning shared ownership.

FROM CONDOM
TO THE WEST

The area to the west of Condom is full of interest, and if you leave the town in this direction, you will cross the river beside the port. The quays here once saw the transhipment of brandy destined for Bordeaux and it

was for this reason that the Baïse was first canalised. Today the river is still navigable to its confluence with the Garonne in the north and a short distance upriver to the south. On the quayside a boat-hire base is busy in summertime and cruises of varying lengths are also on offer, of which the most popular is the day-long return trip to the Abbey of Flaran.

At last it is time to head out into the countryside, and taking the D15 west from Condom, a left turn in about 3 miles (5km) will take you past a field of medieval war machines to the fortified village of **Larressingle**. No doubt with an eye to its tourism potential, the village has been dubbed the 'Carcasonne of the Gers', which has to be overstating things a bit. Nevertheless, hilltop Larresssingle has a 16th century keep, an adjoining church and a ring of tiny houses, all encircled by intact ramparts. The village was once an official residence of the Bishops of Condom, and as such was entered by a fortified gateway, reached by a drawbridge over the moat.

Larressingle's inscription in the list of *plus beaux villages de France* probably accounts for most of its plentiful visitors today, while the others are the ever-present pilgrims who like to collect Larressingle's prestigious stamp for their passports. In their honour, a little museum by the name of la Halte du Pélerin has been set up in one of the houses, its few rooms crammed with extremely lifelike tableaux of medieval life both on the trail and at home. Out of season you may be offered a simple tape recorder with English tape to guide you round – it is excellent!

Leaving Larressingle it is worth taking the steepest downhill road (opposite the entrance), which leads to the **Pont d'Artigue** over the River Osse. This bridge with its curious irregular arches dates from the 12th century when it was in constant use by the pilgrims, for whom there was a hospital alongside. Today the bridge is included in UNESCO's World Heritage list. While here you might cross the river and turn left to the village of **Vopillon**, where the tiny church contains beautiful naïve frescoes dating from around the same time as the bridge.

On west again now, and the road is flanked by the extensive vineyards of Armagnac country. This region is technically the Ténarèze, producing a brandy that needs long ageing, and is not quite so refined as that from the region of Bas-Armagnac farther to the west. The next town is **Montréal-du-Gers**, a classic bastide with criss-crossing medieval streets surrounding its arcaded central square. Pass it by for the moment and turn south on the D29 instead, because first you must visit the **Gallo-Roman Villa of Séviac**, which is said to be the most remarkable of its kind in the south-west of France. You have to wonder who it was that could own such a sumptuous villa, with marble columns, under-floor heating and a huge detached bathing complex with hot and cold basins and a swimming pool. Most memorable are the beautiful colours and designs of the mosaic floors, of which about thirty sections remain on the site. When you have seen it all, you can return to Montréal where the museum at the Tourist Office under the arcades displays yet more mosaics, along with pottery, coins and jewellery found at Séviac.

North of Montréal, the D29 follows the valley of the Auzoue to the village of **Fourcès**. Fourcès is too-pretty-to-be-true, a uniquely circular bastide entered by a bridge over the river flanked by two grey castles.

Flower Festival

The central 'circle' of shady plane trees in Fourcès is surrounded by buildings you can only be amazed are still standing, including the half-timbered Mairie and, up an alleyway, an ancient bell-tower. Floral displays are everywhere, but Fourcès' finest hour comes on the last weekend of April every year, when the little village attracts visitors from far and wide with its Marché-aux-Fleurs.

From Fourcès, the D114 will return you directly to Condom, but if the day is still young, why not return to Montréal and continue to Eauze, where there is more treasure to be seen? On the way you could go for a really off-the-beaten-track diversion to find the **Église St Pierre-de-Genens**, a tumbled-down little church that still retains a 7th century block of marble sculpted with the chi-rho Christian symbol above its doorway. From Montréal, turn east on the D15 for about a kilometre, and then south on an unmarked road. After a further couple of kilometres, the church is tucked away down a track on the right hand side. Leaving the church, you could carry on down the road, bearing right at the next junction – after lots of wiggles across the hill, the one-track road delivers you to the D29 to Eauze.

Eauze (pronounced É-auze) is built on the site of the Roman town Elusa. Not a remarkable place in itself, it nevertheless has a brown-stone, high-vaulted church, with frescoes curiously replacing stained glass windows behind the altar. But Eauze's main claim to fame is its Treasure, kept securely guarded in the basement of the Musée Archéologique in the centre of town.

The treasure came to light in October 1985 when two men, working on excavations near the railway station, casually stuck a trowel into the ground before going home one night. When the trowel was withdrawn, two coins were stuck to its blade – and the men worked on frantically in the autumn dusk to get just a glimpse of what lay in a trench beneath. They hardly dared leave the site that night. Early next morning the mayor was called, the site was guarded and soon all France knew about the treasure –

fabulous jewellery and 265lb (120kg) of different gold and bronze coins. It was obvious that this was not just personal wealth but rather a coin collection, and it seems that when this corner of France was threatened with barbaric invasion in 261AD, the owner had carefully buried his family's most valuable possessions. The treasure was originally taken away to Paris, but was later returned to Eauze where it is proudly displayed to visitors along with other Roman artefacts.

Sitting between the Ténarèze and Bas-Armagnac, Eauze was officially proclaimed the capital of Armagnac by prefectorial decree in 1802. There are several establishments in the town where you can taste both Armagnac and its popular derivative Floc (made with the addition of fresh grape juice) but you might want to hang on a while because there are yet more such opportunities on the way home to Condom at the renowned Château de Cassaigne.

So let us now take the D931 and turn off in the village of **Mouchan**, where the stubby little church dates from the 10th century (the base of the belfry). Inside there are interestingly carved capitals and a lot more, but sadly, it is often kept locked.

Just to the east of Mouchan, the **Château de Cassaigne** was again a one-time residence of the Bishops of Condom. Today the beautiful pale-stoned château and its lands are totally dedicated to the production of fine Armagnac. The free visit includes the old château kitchen with bread oven and chimney, the *chais*, aromatic with fumes of maturing Armagnac, a short video (in English if that is what the majority want) and some very generous tasting.

TO THE EAST OF CONDOM

It is only 3 miles (5km) from Cassaigne to the well-preserved Cistercian Abbey of Flaran – but that could be visited on another day when you head south for Auch. For the moment, let us turn our attention to the lovely country to the east of Condom. A short drive over the switchback hills will take you to **la Romieu**, a beautifully timeless village grouped around a 12th century collegiate church. The church and accompanying palace here were built by one Arnaud d'Aux, a cardinal and cousin of the Pope of the time – his gravestone stands to the right of the altar today. On the opposite side is the sacristy, where frescoes of dark red angels, stars and other biblical elements are so precious that you may only look from a distance. A narrow spiral staircase leads up the octagonal tower, from where there is a good view of the little Cardinal's Tower (all that remains of Arnaud's palace) and behind it, the rolling landscape of the Gers. Downstairs again, you have the pleasure of strolling through beautifully decorated cloisters before you leave. Naturally such a church was on the medieval pilgrim trail and 21st century pilgrims often spend the night in la Romieu, taking advantage of the special meals offered by the restaurant in the arcaded street.

Sharp eyes in la Romieu will notice the abundance of stone cats lurking on walls and windowsills – and there is even a statue of a sort of cat/woman raised on a plinth. In answer to the many questions asked, the newsagent now sells leaflets giving the full explanation. The bare bones of the story are that the village was once saved from a plague of rats by the multitudinous pets of a cat-loving (and even cat-like) little girl by the name of Angeline.

Before leaving la Romieu, you might like to visit the interestingly laid out Jardins de Coursiana, just out of the village down a very minor road to the south (the direction the pilgrims come from). The main feature is the extensive arboretum with trees grouped according to their classification, but there is also a kitchen garden, an English garden and a garden of medicinal plants, all in a delightful setting. And if all that convinces you that la Romieu is a place where you could spend some time, *chambres d'hôtes* are plentiful in the vicinity (thus catering for the pilgrims) and there is a campsite of very high quality just outside the village.

The town of **Lectoure** is about 7.5 miles (12km) east of la Romieu – the most attractive way to get there is possibly via the village of Marsolan. Lectoure is the capital of this easterly, agricultural region of the Gers, which is known as the Lomagne. The town perches dramatically on an outcrop of chalk rock – a spot once occupied by a Gallic tribe called the Lactorii and later by the Romans, who thought such a quirk of the landscape an appropriate place to worship their gods.

Lectoure has seen a few skirmishes over the years and wears a rather faded air. At the top of the main street, the bulky cathedral with its ornate tower was rebuilt for the third time after it was demolished by Louis XI's troops in 1472. Today the elaborately carved choir stalls are probably its best feature. Beside the cathedral a rather steep street leads down to the Gothic Fontaine de Diane, but the half-timbered houses lining the street have more appeal than the fountain, whose waters look black and uninviting even though fish swim there.

The most interesting place to visit in Lectoure is the Musée Archéologique, which has found sympathetic lodging in the cellars of the Bishops' Palace. A guide unlocks the gate for you to descend to rooms filled with Roman artefacts – a remarkable collection of altars once used in 'bull worship', a few decorated coffins, lots of pottery and coins, and some mosaics, among them the superb 'Head of Oceanus' brought here from Séviac. A lighter side of Lectoure is represented by the Lac des Trois Vallées, a huge watersports complex on the eastern side of the town (signed from the N21 – do not try the back lanes!). Swimming pools, lakes, pedalos and giant waterslides offer fun for all the family – including dogs, who have their own swimming lake!

Lectoure is said to be the melon capital of the fertile Lomagne, while to the east, St Clar prides itself on the quality of its white garlic (*ail blanc*). Every Thursday in summer and autumn, the town stages its pungent garlic market and surpasses itself with an imaginative garlic festival on the second Thursday in August. If you are not here at those times, St Clar is still worth a visit. It is a sort of double bastide (English and French sides) with two arcaded squares, one of which contains la Halle, a 13th century wooden-pillared market hall. Beside the Vieille Église (not the big main church) alleyways lead into Vieux St Clar, a few streets that genuinely belong to another age.

From St Clar, the D953 takes you to **Fleurance**, another bastide town, set in the valley of the River Gers. Fleurance's particular pride is its arcaded market hall, at each corner of which a statue represents one of the seasons. The nearby Église St Laurent boasts three windows by master craftsman Arnaud de Moles, a foretaste of the magnificent collection of his works in the cathedral at Auch.

From Fleurance you can amble home along the D654. At **St Puy** you have another opportunity to sample the products of the local vineyards at the Château de Montluc at the top of the town. Montluc is particularly renowned as the originator of an ambrosial fruity liqueur by the name of Pousse-Rapière, which is most often drunk in a cocktail with locally-produced sparkling dry wine. A short history of the château and a tour of the *chais* precede the anticipated delectable *dégustation*, which takes place on a terrace with a view.

Soon after le Puy, a turn on the right is signed to **St Orens-Pouy-Petit**. The village perches on a hill, and comprises a jumble of medieval dwellings cut through by one straight-and-narrow street and a tangle of alleyways, all well garlanded with flowers. Church and 16th century château are incorporated into this typically Gascon ensemble. Recently a couple of local artists have set up their studios here, and you cannot help feeling that it will not be long before the place will be risking its soul as one of the *plus beaux villages de France*. Visit it now!

CONDOM TO AUCH

Back again at Condom now, and it is time to move our base to the capital of the Gers, Auch. Travelling south on the D930, the first distraction is the **Abbaye de Flaran**, signed on the right hand side. The abbey was founded here beside the River Baïse in 1151, and although the Wars of Religion and the Revolution have taken their toll, it is the best-preserved example of a Cistercian abbey in the Gers today. You enter through the cloisters (only one side of which is original 14th century) and go on to the kitchen, refectory, beautifully-pillared chapter-house and high-vaulted light church. Stairs lead up to the 17th century dormitories, clearly untouched since the last monks (and their visitors) laid their heads here. The abbey has in recent years been in the possession of the *département* of Gers. Restoration work is continuing and one room houses a permanent exhibition on the Chemins de St Jacques (pilgrim trails) through the Gers, while another suite is given over to temporary exhibitions of art work.

South of Flaran, the D930 skirts the hilltop bastide of Valence-sur-Baïse and continues up the valley of the Auloue to the spa town of **Castéra-Verduzan**. Water seems to be what the town is all about, and you can head for the refined setting of the thermal baths or have some family fun on the extensive beaches and lakes of the *base de loisirs*, just to the north.

South of Castéra-Verduzan the D103 crosses your road. To the west here is the bastide of Jégun, followed by **Vic-Fezensac**, well-known for both its bull-fights and its festival of Latin-American music, held at the end of July. If instead you turn east on the D103, you soon arrive at **Lavardens**, a superb example of a *castelnau*, a fortified and usually elevated village surrounding a château. In this case the forbidding-looking château overhangs the cliff on the western side, its severe lines much tempered by the handsome church belfry at the opposite end of the village. Narrow streets range in tiers down the south-ern flank and conceal a couple of restaurants and high-quality craft shops that make for interesting browsing. The

château itself was never finished, but you can visit it to admire the attractive ochre and brick patterned floors, take in the current display in the exhibition room and be staggered by the distant views of the Pyrenees from its top windows.

The château is not the only place from which to enjoy those mountain views – the road east to Roquelaure climbs quickly and soon gives not only a magnificent prospect of the Pyrenees but also, looking backwards, one of the most appealing views of Lavardens. This narrow road winds through lovely agricultural countryside and leaves you in no doubt that you are entering the territory of *foie gras* as it approaches Auch.

AUCH

Auch is a fitting capital for the Gers – like the countryside, there is nothing ostentatious about it. Perched on a hilltop above the River Gers, the centrepiece and pride of Auch is its cathedral and at first glance you may well wonder why, because it is certainly not the solid twin-towered exterior that takes the breath away. But step inside and you have it immediately. The richly-coloured windows by 16th century master-glazier Arnaud de Moles depict lifelike figures whose remarkable faces verge on being caricatures. Look out for long-nosed Abraham beside craggy-featured Melchisedek in deep scarlet robes, and the expressions on the faces of Noah, Ezekial, St Peter and the Sybil of Eritrea in the next window. A booklet (in English) from the cathedral shop will guide you round.

And when you have surveyed all 18 windows, turn your attention to the centre of the cathedral – the choir stalls are yet more outstanding. Carved in dark oak that had been hardened by 50 years in water, there are said to be 1,500 characters here. The number does not matter – you will never have time to examine them all in detail. But Old and New Testament characters, prophets and sybils are ranged under the high canopies, stories of Christ's life are told between the stalls and a wealth of different characters (animals, children, mythological beasts, angels, men at work, monsters and more) are scattered on the stalls and misericords. A small fee is charged for entry to the choir stalls, for which you will receive a sheet identifying every intricate figure. And if the great organ built by Jean de Joyeuse (1694) should be playing at the same time, your cup will be running over!

Out in the open air again, the tower behind the cathedral is the Tour D'Armagnac, built as a prison in the 14th century. Beside it a wide staircase known as the *Escalier Monumental* descends to the river. No doubt inspired by the fluctuation of river levels below, the first landing of this staircase bears a Latin inscription describing the Great Flood. Farther down, a bronze statue of charismatic musketeer D'Artagnan stands haughtily surveying the land that gave him birth (which is actually behind him – you will be going there soon). It is a long way down to the bottom (234 steps) and 'that which goes down must come up again'. But a different route will divert you from the arduousness of the climb, and on the way you can see something of the narrow alley-ways termed *pousterles,* by which residents in medieval time descended to the river for their water.

From the foot of the Escalier Monumental turn right, and then right again up the Rue Arexy. This leads up to the steep Pousterle de l'Est, at the top of which the gate in the ramparts on the right is the Porte d'Arton. Here you could continue on the Rue de la Convention with other pousterles leading steeply down on the left. A right turn now will take you on to the Rue Espagne, with the Maison Henry IV on your left – Henry apparently stayed here with Catherine de Medici in 1578. A fine stone staircase with wood panelling is visible from its courtyard. The Rue Espagne leads back to the Place de la Republique, the main square in front of the cathedral, thus completing this mini-tour of Auch. The Office de Tourisme (housed in a fine half-timbered 15th century building near the west end of the cathedral) can offer two much more comprehensive itineraries.

Before leaving Auch you must make time to visit its rather different museum. South American art before the time of Columbus is its most important exhibit and it seems strange to see pottery and artwork from Aztec civilisations displayed here. The most treasured piece is a 16th century mosaic of feathers entitled the Mass of St Gregory. The museum does exhibit more conventional fare in the form of Roman relics and traditional Gascon costumes.

THE COUNTRYSIDE WEST OF AUCH

And now it is time to leave Auch for the countryside and many bastides to the west – take care if you find yourself approaching the roundabout on the Place de la Libération (in front of the cathedral) where *priorité à droite* definitely still exists! From Auch the busy N21 will speed you quickly south-west to **Mirande**, a bastide with a large arcaded square and streets crossing each other with orderly mathematical precision. There is nothing orderly about the church though, which seems to have thrown a long arm across the road to support itself. The arm contains an outer porch attached to the belfry – and whatever its original purpose, today it certainly provides photogenic attraction for Mirande's not-too-many tourists. Not-too-many that is, until the second week in July, when the whole town goes wild with American country music and fans of everything else transatlantic come to join in the scene. If you are here at a quieter time, the Musée des Beaux Arts (next to the Tourist office and opposite the church) has some interesting paintings and a display of fine ceramics from all over France.

On down that busy road again, and **Miélan** is another bastide with ancient half-timbered houses grouped around its central arcaded building now housing the Mairie. You are well off-the-beaten track in Miélan, and heading for those Pyrenees to the south – there's a fine viewpoint about 3 miles (5km) out of town beside the N21. Have a look or turn your back, the next stop on this itinerary is **Tillac** (reached via the D3) to the north – and it is not strictly a bastide but a castelnau like Lavardens, although the land here is flat. Nothing now remains of the once-important château, but the main street retains a magnificent display of half-timbered buildings, their upper floors supported on irregular wooden pillars. At one end of the street is an archway and fortified tower; at the other is a 14th century church. Tillac is on the pilgrim route from Arles and the church boasts a wooden statue of a pilgrim and a gilded St James on the altar.

Beyond Tillac, the D3 continues down the valley of the Boues to the town of **Marciac**. Marciac itself is a fine bastide, but think Marciac, think jazz – everything else pales into insignificance. Marciac has been holding its festival of jazz for more than 25 years now, and has seen the biggest names (Herbie Hancock, Ray Charles, Dizzy Gillespie, Dee Dee Bridgewater) on its programme. For 10 days or so in August the town stages one huge extravaganza with outdoor and indoor performances – but not content with that, there are also frequent concerts throughout the year. All visitors must call into the jazz museum, where the names of the great are signed on the bricks of the walls as you enter. After that, it is headphones on to swing your way through Dixieland, New Orleans, Be Bop and the rest and it is all very enjoyable, for the uninitiated as well as for seasoned enthusiasts. Marciac also boasts a very fine watersports complex whose facilities for swimming and canoeing can be enjoyed by visitors throughout the summer.

If you have given Marciac the attention it deserves, it may be time to return to Auch now. If that is the case, you will absolutely have to come back this way, because north of Marciac (some 15.5 miles [25km], but it is a very scenic drive) is the village of **Lupiac**, the birthplace of the redoubtable D'Artagnan. The Centre D'Artagnan does its best to tell the story, mingling fact and fiction. There is not a lot in this museum, but at least you can hear the story told in English through headphones (more than once!) and the film is enjoyable. After the visit, natural curiosity will spur you to seek out the family seat of Castelmore – drive north on the D102 for about 2.5 miles (4km), but note that the château is private property, and you can do no more than glance through the gates.

D'Artagnan – the man and the myth

The rôle-model for the chief character in Dumas' popular novel *The Three Musketeers* was apparently one Charles de Batz-Castelmore, who was born at the Château of Castelmore, just north of Lupiac, in 1611. One of a large family, he set out to seek his fortune in Paris at the age of 19, enrolling in the King's Guards. The name D'Artagnan belonged to his mother's side of the family and was adopted by him for its aristocratic ring. As D'Artagnan, he entered the regiment of musketeers, and in time became a friend of Louis XIV's first minister, Cardinal Mazarin, and then of the king himself. The Musketeers were a turbulent, noisy crew, but essentially daring, brave and extremely loyal to each other. Flamboyant D'Artagnan fitted into the scene perfectly and it seems that three of his close friends were the models for Athos, Porthos and Aramis. D'Artagnan rose to the position of Captain-Lieutenant, taking part in many campaigns before dying a hero's death at the siege of Maastricht in 1673, with a musket shot in the neck

And now it is finally time to go back to Auch at the end of this journey. The best road is the D943, heading west through **Bassoues** with its remarkable 14th century dungeon in the main street. Farther on the village of **Montesquiou** is yet one more picturesque castelnau – the gateway and half-timbered houses at the lower end of the main street are all that remains of its former life. And finally there is **Barran**, a last and most attractive bastide, distinguished by its twisted church spire and handsome entrance gate with pond outside. By now you know there is more to Gascony than music and musketeers – there is brandy and bastides, cathedrals and castelnaux, and pâté and pilgrims, for a start...

OFFICES DE TOURISME

Auch
1, Rue Dessoles BP 174
32000 AUCH
☎ 05.62.05.22.89

Condom
Place Bossuet
32100 CONDOM
☎ 05.62.28.00.80

Mirande
13, Rue de l'Evêche
32300 MIRANDE
☎ 05.62.66.68.10

Lectoure
Place de l'Hôtel de Ville
32700 LECTOURE
☎ 05.62.68.76.98

Aignan
Place Colonel Parissot
32290 AIGNAN
☎ 05.62.09.22.57

PLACES OF INTEREST

Condom

Musée de l'Armagnac
Open April to October every day
except Tuesday 10am-12noon, 3-
6pm; rest of year 2-5pm every day
except Monday and Tuesday.

Larressingle

La Halte du Pélerin
Open May to September every day
10.30am-12.30pm, 2-7pm; April
and October every day except
Monday 2.30-6.30pm.

Montréal-du-Gers

**Villa Gallo-Romaine de Séviac
(ticket also admits to the Musée
des Fouilles)**
Open every day July and August
10am-7pm; March to June and
September to November 10am-
12.30pm, 2-6pm.

Musée des Fouilles de Séviac
Open May to September 10am-
12noon, 2-6pm (Sundays and
public holidays 3-6pm); February to
April weekdays only 10am-
12noon, 3-6pm; October to
December weekdays only 10am-
12noon, 3-5pm. Closed Mondays.

Eauze

Musée Archéologique
Open June to September 10am-
12.30pm, 2-6pm; February to May
and October to December 2-5pm.
Closed Tuesdays and Bank holidays
throughout the year. Also closed
January and first weekend in July.

Château de Cassaigne

Open July and August every day
10am-7pm; rest of year 9am-
12noon, 2-6pm. Closed Mondays
from mid-September to mid-June.

La Romieu

Collégiale
Open May to September 10am-
7pm; October to April 10am-
12noon, 2-6pm.

Les Jardins de Coursiana
Open every day from Easter to 1st
November 10am-8pm. Closed
Wednesdays (except in school
holidays) and Sunday mornings.

Lectoure

Musée Archéologique
Open all year round 10am-12noon,
2-6pm (but closed Tuesdays from
October to February and all public
holidays).

St Puy

Château de Montluc
Open Monday to Saturday 10am-
12noon, 3-7pm; Sunday and public
holidays 3-7pm. Closed in January
and on Sundays and Mondays from
October to May.

Abbaye de Flaran
Open July and August 9.30am-7pm;
February to June and September to
December 9.30am-12.30pm, 2-6pm.

Lavardens

The Château
Open July and August every day
10am-7pm; rest of year 10.30am-
12.30pm, 2-6pm (5pm November
to March). Closed mid-January to
mid February.

Auch

Musée d'Auch
Open May to September every day
10am-12noon, 2-6pm; October to
April every day except Monday,
10am-12noon, 2-5pm.

Mirande

Musée des Beaux Arts
Open every day except Sunday
and public holidays 10am-12noon,
2-6pm.

Marciac

Territoires du Jazz
Open April to September every
day 9.30am-12.30pm, 2.30-
6.30pm; October to March
Monday to Friday 9.30am-
12.30pm, 2-6pm,Sundays 11am-
1pm. Last entry half an hour before
closing.

Lupiac

Centre D'Artagnan
Open July and August every day
10.30am-7pm; September to June
every day except Monday 2-6pm.
Last entry one hour before closing.

Bassoues

Donjon de Bassoues
Open 20th July-20th August 10am-
7pm; April to June, September and
October 10am-12noon, 2-6pm;
rest of year Wednesdays and weekends only 10am-12noon, 2-5pm.

LOCAL HIGHLIGHTS

Best Walks

· The best marked and most used routes are surely the pilgrim trails – the GR65 from le Puy-en-Velay (from Lectoure to Eauze and beyond) and the GR653 from Arles (from Auch to Marciac and beyond). The company Transbagages (☎ 0820.04.54.71 office open between 4 and 8pm) offers transport for both pilgrims and/or their baggage on the le Puy route. If you want to join in for a day (or more) you could give them a ring and see what is possible.

· Every Office de Tourisme should have its own folder of circular walks to offer. The countryside around la Romieu is particularly attractive – ask for the collection of 21 routes under the title *Randonnées en Lomagne Gersoise* and you should have plenty to choose from.

· A couple of interesting, short (but contour-crossing) routes start from the hilltop village of Lavardens. There is a map on a board near the church, but you could collect the same from OT at Auch – or really go wild, and invest in the topoguide *La Gers à Pied,* an excellent publication that more than justifies the expense. In addition to the circuits at Lavardens, it offers 28 more across the region and should set you up for the holiday!

For cyclists

- 14 cycle routes of lengths between 36 and 76 miles (58 and 122km) have been marked out across the Gers. Each has a different theme and there is possibility for lodging on each. For more information contact the Comité Départemental du Cyclotourisme de Gers, As Quees, 32120 MAUVEZIN, ☎ 05.62.06.91.47.

- The area around Lectoure is particularly well-endowed with VTT circuits – 15 in all are marked out, and a map for each is available on a pocket-sized laminated card that can be carried with you. Circuits start from Lectoure, Fleurance and la Romieu – ask the appropriate OT for more details.

Watersports

- The Gers is particularly well-blessed with large lakes offering sandy beaches, safe bathing and facilities for family boating. The Lac de Montréal, the Lac de St Clar, the Lac des Trois Vallées at Lectoure, the watersports centre at Castéra-Verduzan and the Lac de Lupiac near Aignan are all excellent spots to cool the family down on a hot afternoon, with perhaps the prize going to the Lac des Trois Vallées for its waterchutes and bubble-pool.

- Mirande and Marciac also have large lakes for boating and fishing (there are electric boats at Marciac) but not bathing – instead there is a swimming pool on each site.

- Boats may be hired for the day or the week from the quayside at Condom and river cruises with refreshment on board will take you as far as the Abbey of Flaran.

- Canoeing on the rivers is possible from Auch, Condom and Mirande – ask the appropriate OT for details.

For the palate

- Multitudinous flocks of ducks and geese attest to the popularity of the controversially produced *foie gras*. In addition to being served as a cold pâté, it can also be fried or served in pastry (pâté en croûte).

- Popular meats are pigeon and duck, put into a casserole or roasted. The ideal accompaniment is red Côtes-de-Gascogne – or you could look out for the excellent fruity Madiran wines from the south-east of the Gers.

- And finally the Armagnac. Produced around Condom over 700 years, it comes in forms too many to list, is incorporated into the aperitifs Floc and Pousse-Rapière, and even finds its way into a cake under the name of Germanac (otherwise composed of sponge, almonds and raisins). Take some home for Christmas!

And the most memorable

- Coming over the hill to Lavardens on a bright spring morning and suddenly seeing the huge jagged snow-covered peaks of the Pyrenees spanning the horizon to the south.

- The choirstalls in the cathedral at Auch. They are incredible.

- Walking around the superb tableaux of the Halte du Pélerin in Larressingle with a heavy old-fashioned tape-recorder in our hands. Even Larressingle is off the beaten track in April, and there were no other visitors to be disturbed by the very clearly delivered English commentary.

- And my husband would not let me omit his personal glimpse of heaven in the form of the 40-year-old Armagnac he was offered in the Château de Cassaigne!

15. Prehistory in the Pyrenees

Think prehistoric man and cave-art and you will pretty certainly think Dordogne. It is probably true that there is nothing in the rest of France to compare with the cave paintings of the Vézère valley, which has been dubbed the 'cradle of prehistory', but the Dordogne is one of the most popular tourist areas in France and there you may have to share 'open' cave trips with many others, or find yourself needing to book a tour a week in advance. Those seeking 'undiscovered' France have an alternative to all this in the region known as Ariège. Maybe the caves here are not so numerous and the artwork not quite so colourful, but there is still an enormous wealth of drawngs, paintings, engravings and other artefacts to be seen – and, as can sometimes happen out of season, there is a certain excitement in finding yourself, lamp in hand, on your own personal guided tour of a cave.

So where and what is Ariège? Ariège is a *département* of the region of Midi-Pyrénées, and, like most *départements* in France, it is named after its principal river. The River Ariège tumbles from the high peaks at the eastern end of the Pyrenees near the Andorran border and heads north through the Plantaurel Hills (effectively the foothills of the Pyrenees) to end its journey crossing the plains to join the Garonne. The many caves are particularly concentrated in the centre of this region, and most of those that can be visited are grouped around the cheerful little town of Tarascon, sitting astride the hurrying river. A couple of kilometres to the south, high on the sides of the Vicdessos valley, the Grotte de Niaux is considered to be a 'major'

cave along with Lascaux in the Dordogne and Altamira in Spain. Its famous *Salon Noir* reveals some first class prehistoric artwork from the Magdalenian era – bison, ibex and reindeer, with good perspective and impressive facial expressions. A couple of lesser caves nearby contain more drawings and some fine engravings, while the vast cave of Lombrives is renowned for its monumental stalactite formations.

A recent arrival on the Tarascon scene is the Prehistory Park, where, in addition to state-of-the-art technology talking you through a recreation of the Niaux cave, children are catered for with the opportunity to try a few prehistoric skills for themselves. Farther to the north of Tarascon there are two more spectacular caves – Labouïche involves a journey by boat through its subterranean chasms and le Mas d'Azil was the source of some remarkable finds including many prized carvings and engravings that are displayed in the nearby village museum.

Ariège can offer you a cave for every day of the week, but if spending that much time underground is a little more than you had bargained for, there are plenty of alternatives here. In the south, the Pyrenean scenery itself is magnificent, and as this area is outside the National Park of the Pyrenees, it attracts fewer visitors. Above Tarascon the road to Andorra runs alongside the Ariège and first reaches the spa town of Ax-les-Thermes. Beyond it is the Nature Reserve of the Orlu Valley with its population of isards (Pyrenean chamois) and marmots. The wild flowers of this mountainous area are

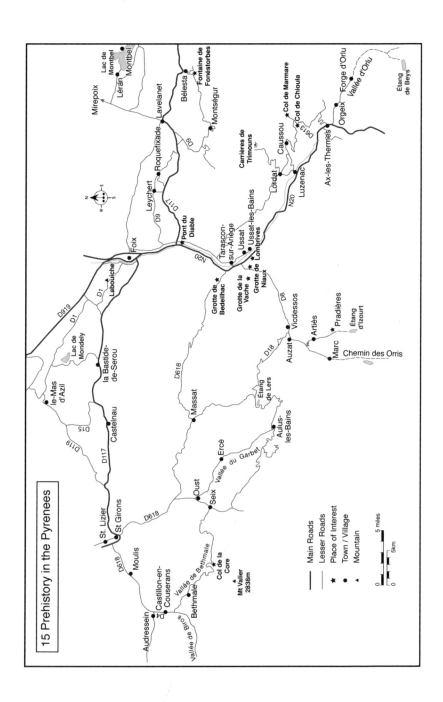

15 Prehistory in the Pyrenees

especially fine in springtime, while in summer the slopes are carpeted in bright pink alpenrose. Tarascon itself is situated at the meeting point of several valleys and each of these offers splendid mountain drives with high viewpoints and a network of well-marked hiking trails. At the highest levels, blue alpine lakes nestle in rocky cirques ringed by peaks that are snow-covered till mid-summer.

The east of the region is entirely different in scenery and here the lower Plantaurel Hills bear witness to the tribulations of the dissenting Cathars of the 13th century. Of their strongholds in Ariège, the tragic ruins of the château of Montségur springing from their rocky perch are perhaps the most poignant, but crumbling Roquefixade is a natural rockery of wild flowers, an idyllic spot for a picnic with a view. And finally, those who seek the 'undiscovered' cannot fail to be delighted with the west of Ariège, where the green valleys of the area known as the Couserans seem to have remained unchanged over the centuries and many traditional craftsmen have their workshops. The valley of Bethmale has its own peculiar rural history and, entering civilization again, you can find out about it in all its fascinating detail in the museum of the Bishop's Palace at St Lizier.

TARASCON-SUR-ARIÈGE

If caves are your prime objective on this holiday you will probably want to base yourself at Tarascon – or **Tarascon-sur-Ariège** to give it its full title. Although only a small town of around 3000 inhabitants, it caters for its visitors with a handful of hotels and a particularly well-equipped all-year-round campsite beside the river

on the outskirts of the town. The setting is splendid. The hills rise steeply all around, but everything in Tarascon is under the watchful eye of the 13th century Tour de Castella, a circular clock tower perched high on rock above the racing waters of the Ariège. The tower is the remains of a fortress destroyed on the orders of Richelieu in 1632 – a time when Tarascon was already thriving on account of the abundant iron-ore in the area. Beneath the clock tower the few narrow streets of the Medieval town offer an interesting stroll, while the newer town spills across the bridge to the other side of the river.

Everyone coming to this area will want to visit the **Grotte de Niaux**, and since numbers here are limited, it will be necessary to telephone first or call at the Office de Tourisme to book your place. Depending on the season, you probably will not have to wait more than 48 hours. Situated just to the south of Tarascon, the cave is reached from the D8 road to Vicdessos – and it must be said that the access road is the sort on which you would prefer not to meet anyone coming the other way. This little hazard negotiated, the cave mouth itself provides parking for a couple of dozen vehicles, including buses (and do not even think about them on the way up!).

Niaux is a fascinating place. No evidence of human habitation has been found in the cave and it is thought that the men who produced the fine drawings of the Salon Noir were cave dwellers in the valley below who came up here just for that purpose. Those drawings are not graffiti, scrawled on the walls by anyone with a few moments to spare but rather carefully executed works of art adorning a cavern that was a sanctuary, a sacred place. Along with drawings of bison, ibex, reindeer and horse are symbols that are not fully understood – dots of different colours, dashes, circles, 'claviforms' and arrows, all of which must have had special meaning. It seems that these paintings were not all produced at the same time but rather over a period as long as a thousand years. The Salon Noir has many secrets but just for the few minutes you are there it inspires you to imagine early man alone in this cavern, producing these superb paintings by the light only of a flaming torch or burning wick of oil.

There is of course much more to Niaux than the Salon Noir, but this is the only section open to the public, a distance of about 765yd (700m) from the cave entrance. In the vast underground network beyond there have been many other finds, including a celebrated 'Dune of Footprints', where the prints of three young children of some 12,000 years ago are preserved for all time. To see a recreation of these, you will need to visit the **Parc de la Préhistoire** on the outskirts of Tarascon, where the Salon Noir is also reproduced in more-than-accurate detail – the drawings have actually been enhanced to their original state by the same artist that recreated the caves of Lascaux. All is revealed to you by means of infra-red sensitive head-phones while walking through an atmospheric, darkened space to the background sound of dripping water. Outside in the sunshine again, the park is now geared to children, who can throw prehistoric spears at mock-up prehistoric bison, build a prehistoric camp of animal skins or try their own hand at painting a prehistoric wall – life-skills for Magdalenian youngsters but entertainment for those of today.

Many other nearby caves contain wall paintings, but the only one of these that is accessible to the public is the **Grotte de Bédeilhac** on the D618 to Massat. Here visits are less formal than at Niaux, being arranged at regular intervals throughout the day and catering for as many people as turn up. Here (or indeed at any of the caves) you may be fortunate enough to be taken round by the diminutive and energetic Réné Gailli, a local speleologist and author of several books on the caves of Ariège. M. Gailli speaks only a little English, but his enthusiasm overcomes all language difficulties! From the enormous vaulted entrance (large enough to have landed an aeroplane and presently housing a huge gas balloon for scientific research), a little scrambling by torchlight will bring you to more

Magdalenian Man

The artwork in the caves of Ariège dates from the Magdalenian era, between 11,500 and 10,500 years ago. At this time even the south of France was cold – cold enough for the reindeer that now thrive only in arctic climes to be living in these valleys. Men lived in caves to protect themselves from the cold and were 'hunter-gatherers'. In fact it is likely that predominantly the men were the hunters and the women the gatherers – and that she had more chance of finding supper than he had! Hunting was carried out with spears and harpoons, usually made from the antlers or bones of reindeer.

cave art, engravings and relief carvings.

Tarascon has yet two more caves worth visiting in its vicinity. The cave of **la Vache** is opposite that of Niaux, and is only reached on foot after a hike of 15 minutes or so. The few wall drawings here date from the Bronze Age rather than the Magdalenian, are more stylised, and are to be found near the entrance rather than the interior of the cave. There is not a great deal to see now in the depths of la Vache, but finds here included much evidence of habitation, piles of animal bones (the vestiges of paleolithic feasting) and a collection of both tools and weapons with many elaborate carvings. Some of the finest of these works are now displayed inside the cave.

Off the N20 to the south of Tarascon, the fourth cave, **Lombrives**, has less to do with prehistoric art than with geological formation, but has the distinction of appearing in the Guinness Book of Records as the largest cave in Europe. You will not get to visit it all, but by booking ahead you can upgrade the regular hour and a half visit to one of three or four hours. Highlights include the gigantic 'mammoth' stalactite formation and an underground lake – and the violin and flute concerts held in the cave on summer evenings.

THE VALLEY OF THE ARIÈGE

If you have managed to visit all those caves (Labouïche and le Mas d'Azil are much farther north and we will come to them later), it is high time to get some fresh air. Tarascon sits at the hub of a number of radiating valleys, so opportunities for exploration are fairly well defined. Let us begin

with the main valley, that of the Ariège, which can be followed south to the Andorran border. The N20 accompanies the river all the way and can be busy, but you can avoid the traffic for at least the first few miles by taking the very much lesser road on the opposite bank instead. On this route you will first pass the village of Ussat and then arrive at **Ussat-les-Bains** with its classically 19th century spa town architecture. The arches of the old thermal establishment are fronted by fountains and flowers, but behind all that Ussat has modernised itself and now includes the present-day affliction of 'stress' high on its list of treatments. Since the road ends at Ussat-les-Bains you will need to cross the river and join the main road to continue up the valley – but you will not have to stay on it for long before another diversion presents itself.

About ten and a half miles (17km) from Tarascon (or about seven and a half miles [12km] from Ussat-les-Bains), the village of Luzenac sits on the opposite bank of the river. From here you can follow the D2 in the direction of Caussou – and not for nothing is this road called the Route des Corniches! A left turn before Caussou will continue the scenic drive and take you on to Lordat where a ruined château sits spectacularly on an outcrop of rock above the valley. This elevated site hosts regular demonstrations of birds of prey in flight. Beyond Lordat the road has just one destination – the talc quarries, the **Carrières de Trimouns**. Situated at an altitude of 5906ft (1800m), there is no higher point attainable by road in this area. From the parking area a bus will take you to a viewpoint from where you can see not only the white steps of the workface but all the summits of the upper valley of the

Ariège – and it might be worth-while to take a pair of binoculars along with you.

Time to return to the valley now, but those who cannot get enough of this high level scenery can opt instead to go on to Caussou and continue on the D2, which now snakes its way through the mountains to reach the Col de Marmare. Turning right here on the D613, you soon arrive at the Col de Chioula where you can leave the car and take a half hour climb to the summit (4944ft [1507m]) with its fine views of the surrounding peaks. The D613 then descends with not a few hairpins of its own to reach the spa town of **Ax-les-Thermes**. The alternative to that long mountain drive is of course to keep on the N20 – Ax is a mere ten minutes or so up the road from Luzenac.

Whatever you do, allow yourself a little time to spend in Ax because you are going to want to take your socks and shoes off! At 78°C, the thermal springs of Ax are the hottest in the Pyrenees. Steaming water runs down the gutters of the main street and at its upper end a large square pool of it, known as the Basin des Ladres, is available for all to cure their afflictions. You can bathe here or, like most of the visitors, simply sit on the steps and dangle your feet in. Today the waters are said to be particularly effective in rheumatic and respiratory disorders, but the pool was originally built in the 13th century to heal those who had contracted leprosy while on the Crusades. Behind the pool, the Hôpital St Louis is a 19th century version of one that undertook their cures. Hot water spouts from a fountain alongside the pool offering the opportunity to take some home, but heavily pungent and sulphurous as it is, this is not water you will want to drink.

ORLU NATURE RESERVE

If you have spent the day in the mountains it will be time to go home now – but beyond Ax there is one more treat for which you should return. Leaving the town on the D22, the road now follows the Oriège River through the Vallée d'Orlu. Some 20 years ago this valley became a national nature reserve, and well it might be. The Orlu Nature Reserve offers some stunning mountain scenery, a huge variety of wild flowers and the chance to spot some of its abundant wildlife population – in particular, the herds of Pyreneen chamois (known as isards) and the shy, furry, long-toothed marmots. The D22 will take you past the village of Orgeix and on to the hamlet of Forges d'Orlu, where the brand new Observatoire de la Montagne is a high quality museum of mountain life that should not be missed. Sadly the texts and dialogue here are in French only but the presentations are outstanding.

Children (and their parents) will enjoy the nearby Maison des Loups, where you can walk through the woods and see the wolves in something like a natural setting – and (well out of their reach) a few lambs, goats, donkeys, ducks and the rest. Beyond Forges d'Orlu, the road leads on into the mountains and the heart of the Reserve. A further 15 minutes or so uphill driving will bring you to a large parking area beside the river, the end of the road. From here you proceed on foot, across the river, through the woods and on beside the Oriège. The track is heading for the little alpine lake of En Beys and, beyond it, the high mountains, but well before all that (after maybe three quarters an hour's walking) you reach territory likely to be frequented by isards. The valley here is quite open with grassy slopes backed by forest, ideal for grazing herds. Although they can move very quickly, they are not shy and will probably stay around long enough for you to get a good look.

Farther on the track continues its gentle climb until, perhaps an hour and a half from the start, you reach a wooden bridge across the river in a beautiful setting. Up to this point the walk has been quite easy, but now the track narrows and the climb becomes fairly steep, although not particularly difficult otherwise. The route is always well waymarked (bars of white on red) and it takes you through woods and across rock-strewn slopes where the marmots hide until at last (around three hours from the start) you come to the top of a rise and can look down on the blue waters of the Étang d'en Beys with the little grey stone refuge hut beside it. And, unlikely as it may seem, that hut is a restaurant and coffee shop – at least for the summer months – and you can get yourself some refreshment before the return. The climb to the Étang d'en Beys is undoubtedly a full day's hike and a certain fitness is needed to undertake it, but it makes a superb introduction to the mountains.

THE VALLEY OF RUISSEAU DE VICDESSOS

Back to Tarascon now, and the next valley, moving in a clockwise direction, is that of the Ruisseau de Vicdessos. At the lower end of this valley the caves of Niaux and la Vache face each other on opposite flanks and the little

village of Niaux boasts an excellent museum (Musée Pyrénéen de Niaux) devoted to the pastoral lives of the people of this region over past centuries. The valley is steep-sided with the occasional remote village perched on its slopes.

After driving for about 20 minutes or so you reach **Vicdessos** and its neighbouring village of **Auzat**. Mountain streams thread their way through the streets of both, creating some picturesque scenes. This area is very popular with hikers and the Office de Tourisme at Auzat has a wealth of literature on the many paths and a lot of personal knowledge and advice they are happy to share. The mountains around here are particularly rich in *orrys* (sometimes spelt orris), drystone circular huts roofed with turves of grass, in which shepherds once lived while tending their flocks in their summer pastures. The very best way to see these is to walk the **Chemin des Orris** from the parking area at Carla (above the village of Marc), but the access road to this is rough. If you want to go, it might be best to discuss it with the Office de Tourisme in Auzat first.

A site more easily reached is the parking area at the electricity station of Pradières, above Artiès. From here the trail (the GR10) climbs fairly steeply to the Étang d'Izourt and on the way passes a beautiful grassy slope ringed with alpenroses, where several orrys are sheltered by over-hangs of rock. It is an idyllic spot, but when you reach it, just imagine spending four or five months alone up here, sleeping on a bed of straw and vegetation.

Auzat and Vicdessos are by no means the end of the road – although you cannot imagine how it could possibly continue looking at the ranges all around. In fact the D18 continues from Vicdessos up the valley of the Ruisseau de Suc, and a couple of hairpins near the start are all it needs to get it on its way. The big hairpins come later as the road makes its final ascent to the summit at **Port de Lers** – but by then you will have decided the drive is well worth while on account of the spectacular waterfalls hurtling down the rock faces on your right and disappearing into the valley below. At the Port de Lers the views open up to the west and the scenery is that of wide open alpine meadows. A little farther along the road sweeps downhill again and far below you can see the lonely Étang de Lers in its green glacial valley. Many tortuous kilometres beyond the lake, the road reaches Aulus-les-Bains at the head of the Garbet valley, but that is in the area known as the Couserans, and we will return there later.

TARASCON TO FOIX

The next obvious excursion from Tarascon is along the road on which you probably arrived here – the N20, following the River Ariège downstream towards Foix, the administrative capital of this region. About 6 miles (10km) north of Tarascon, it is worth making a detour to follow the signs to the **Pont du Diable** – one of the hundreds of bridges in France purported to have been built by the devil! As usual he was tricked by the local population here, and achieved only the soul of a cat for his pains. Be that as it may, this original stone 13th century bridge makes a picturesque sight, spanning the Ariège in the depths of a green gorge.

A few kilometres farther on at Montgailhard, a further digression from the main road is offered by the **Forges de Pyrène**, a museum of crafts and tools spread over a landscaped park of 12.4 acres (5 hectares) and equipped with a restaurant and picnic areas. There is plenty for all the family here, so if you include this in your itinerary, you won't be doing much more that day.

Beyond Montgailhard, your arrival at **Foix** is announced with a first glimpse of its distinctive three-towered château, sitting on a huge rock apparently emerging from the centre of town.

Brief history of Foix

Foix has been here a long time – caves in that rock show evidence of occupation in prehistoric times. Later on the Romans built a fort here, while the forerunner of the present château was erected around a thousand years ago. Later a medieval town grew up around the base of the rock and today you can wander through its narrow streets before making the climb to the château.

Inside the château, the Musée Départemental de l'Ariège retains something of the château's military history (it boasts the usual catalogue of assaults and sieges) along with exhibits of archaeological finds from the many caves of the area. Climbing to the top of the round tower is hard work, but the reward is a fine view over the town and the valley of the Ariège.

BEYOND FOIX

To the north-west of Foix, the limestone Montagnes de Plantaurel offer more opportunities for underground escapades. A journey of 3.7 miles (6km) along the D1 will bring you to the **Grotte de Labouïche** – the parking area is opposite the cave entrance and is provided with a café where you book tickets and wait your turn. France is always very keen on its records – the highest, oldest, largest, etc. – and Labouïche claims the distinction of having the 'longest navigable underground river in Europe open to the public'. The journey by boats (there is more than one) is to say the least spectacular, with the highlight being the tumbling waters of the Cascade Salette.

Beyond Labouïche, the D1 continues north-west for about 15.5 miles (25km) to the village of le Mas d'Azil, and on the way it passes just to the north of the pleasant Lac de Mondely, where summertime bathing, boating and fishing are on the agenda. **Le Mas d'Azil** is home to a museum where you will undoubtedly be returning later, but for the moment, turn left on the D119 to find the cave itself – not that you can miss it, as the road runs right through it. The vast vaults of le Mas d'Azil were once home to prehistoric man, and the importance of the finds here have resulted in the naming of an Azilian era, a period between the Magdalenian and the Bronze Age, approximately 9000 and 4000BC.

More recently the cave has given shelter to those escaping religious persecution – the Cathars of the 13th century and the Protestants in the Wars of Religion, some 400 years later. The latter were pursued by Cardinal Richelieu, who in his attempts to capture them destroyed a whole floor of the cave. Today the cave still houses a few of its treasures, among them the famous *galets peints* (painted pebbles) and some carvings on bone. The animations in one huge gallery include a Magdalenian family sitting around the cooking pot while an impressively large Pyrenean Bear (there really are very few of these around now) looks on from across the floor. A film of the cave's history projected on the rocky ceiling is largely lost on non-French speakers.

Although the cave itself lacks some of its original merit, its treasures housed in the village museum are truly exceptional. Tools, needles, weapons and exquisitely fine carvings are here, the most prized of all being the renowned *faon aux oiseaux* (fawn with birds), the head of a *baton propulseur*. If you cannot work out how this projectile works, just ask whoever is at the desk of the museum – the village of Mas d'Azil has staged its very own prehistoric weapon competitions, and everyone here is an expert at this particular form of stick throwing!

CATHAR COUNTRY

Back to base now, and the next excursion is to the east of Ariège and the land of the Cathars. Their strongholds actually extended north and east of here, including Carcassonne, Toulouse, Albi and Béziers as well as Foix and the north of Ariège. To see something of their fortresses in this area, first head north towards Foix and then turn east on the D117 in the direction of Lavelanet. Now you are in the Plantaurel Hills following the valley of the River Baure and after maybe 6 miles (10km) driving you can see some grey, crumbling ruins camped rather precariously on a rocky outcrop on the northern side. These are the ruins of the Cathar stronghold of **Roquefixade**, quite obviously a spot with a commanding view of the whole valley.

Beneath the towering rockface, the pretty village of Roquefixade is the starting point of a rather steep path up to the ruins, but for anyone with a little more time to spare there is a splendid and overall less arduous alternative. The Cathar strongholds are connected by footpaths, possibly trails once used by the Cathars themselves, and the whole route, stretching from Foix to the Mediterranean, goes under the name of the *Le Sentier Cathare*. To sample just a short stretch of it you could start in the village of Leychert to the west (the path can be joined near the church – peep in at their magnificent altarpiece while you are there), and follow the waymarked trail for an hour or so to reach Roquefixade. It is as scenic a route as you could imagine and decked with wild flowers all the way. The château itself is only partly accessible but the view and the setting are more than worth any effort you may have to make to get there.

Having passed the Château of Roquefixade, look out for a turning on the right, the D9 taking you to **Montségur**, the most famous of all the Cathar fortresses. The road climbs towards the château seemingly clamped to its rocky 'Pog' and then takes you round to the south side from where the access is easiest. Even so, you can look forward to half an hour of stiff climbing to reach the summit with its square solid château. In the village of Montségur just down the hill, an archaeological museum displays finds from the early days of the encampment on the rock and tells some of the Cathars' story.

In the summer of 1243 the château was first besieged by troops after Cathars had attempted to kill members of the Catholic Inquisition. Ten hard months later the Cathars surrendered. They were given two weeks in which to recant, but even so most chose not to do so, and more than 200 of them walked down the hill and on to a funeral pyre. The path up to the château crosses the site of their martyrdom and in 1960 a monument was placed there in commemoration. The fall of Montségur

The Cathars

The Cathars were a 12th century sect whose beliefs had some similarities to eastern religions. The ideals of Catharism had probably been brought to this south-west corner of France by merchant travellers from the orient. The Cathars held a 'dualist' view of the world – a belief that God created the good in it and Satan created the evil, and that the two were for ever in competition. Their ideals of poverty, chastity and humility were in conflict with the rather more loose values of the established Roman Catholic Church and their direct rejection of many of its tenets led to their persecution and finally to their complete obliteration after the fall of Montségur in 1244.

marked the end of the Cathar religion in France. The present Château of Montségur is not the original that fell that day, but one built half a century later to replace it.

Beyond Montségur the road soon enters the valley of the River Hers – and reaches the site of a very curious phenomenon, the 'intermittent fountain' of **Fontesorbes**. Here water that has filtered through the limestone plateau of Sault emerges in a vault under the rocks. In the dry season of the year (July to November approximately), this resurgence follows a regular cycle of 35 minutes in every hour. When the fountain is not in spate, visitors can walk to the back of the cave.

North of Fontesorbes and the town of Bélesta, anyone with children will be interested in the lovely **Lac de Montbel** – it possibly merits a day's visit on its own account. The western shore at Léran boasts a picnic site, beach and sailing club, while the eastern shore at Montbel has a bathing beach. A walking trail 9 miles (15km) in length encompasses the whole lake, and is marked by yellow flashes. Beyond Montbel the road to the north soon arrives at **Mirepoix**, another one-time Cathar settlement, where the centrepiece is a town square surrounded by carved wooden arcades dating from the 14th century.

THE GREEN VALLEYS OF THE COUSERANS

Finally it is time to head for the **Couserans**, the green valleys in the west of Ariège. Head north to Foix again and then west on the D117 to St Girons. Horse-lovers will want to pause at **le Bastide-de-Sérou**, where there is a regional centre for the breeding of Mérens horses. The Mérens is a breed local to Ariège – short, black, bearded, docile and extremely hardy, there are plenty to be seen in this area. A perhaps humbler contrast is the nearby donkey farm just off the main road at Castelnau. Their chief product is donkey milk soap, and if you arrive at the right time you can watch the milking.

St Girons is the administrative town of the Couserans, while its twin, **St Lizier**, boasts some historic buildings. The 17th century red-roofed Bishop's Palace stretching across the hillside can be seen for miles around, and is worth visiting for its views alone, including its *table d'orientation* that names no fewer than 69 of the Pyrenean peaks before you. Inside the building you will find a museum of this area, with a particular section relating to the valley of Bethmale collected by one Jacques Bégouden. Born into a local wealthy family at the turn of the century, he was given a Bethmalaise wet-nurse – and, as he says, it may have been through her milk or the appealing colours of her traditional costume, that he became inspired to a lifelong interest in the valley. Would it be better to visit the valley of Bethmale before coming to the museum? Maybe. But whichever way round you do things, while you are in St Lizier, spend a few minutes in the Cathedral (just below the Bishop's Palace) and take a walk around the elegant two-storey cloisters where the pillars have some finely carved capitals.

From St Girons, the 18 valleys that comprise the Couserans spread out like a fan to the high peaks on the border. With so much wild country before you, which way should you go? If the museum at St Lizier has whetted your appetite for Bethmale, head west on the D618 – and first consider a pause at a roadside barn near the village of Moulis. There are many craftsmen at work in the Couserans, and the one you will meet here is a maker of *pyrenousts* (the regional equivalent of the *santons* of Provence). His tiny moulded and painted figures represent a wealth of traditional occupations and crafts, not to mention animals, pilgrims, figures from the nativity and others. Jean-Marie Mathon is more than happy to tell you about his creations.

Just down the road at **Audressein** another craftsman is at work – Jusot the clog-maker. At his shop off the village street you can watch his efforts and marvel at some of the designs, particularly the high-curved and pointed traditional clogs of Bethmale. While in Audressein, call in at the old riverside church, which once welcomed pilgrims on the route to Santiago de Compostela – the vault of its porch is decorated with 15th century murals.

Leaving Audressein, turn south on the D4 to the pretty village of Castillon-en-Couserans and continue to les Bordes with its ancient bridge over the River Lez. Here is a junction – ahead now the road continues up the valley of Biros to the old village of Sentein and beyond, while the road climbing to the left heads for the valley of Bethmale. If you decide to explore **Biros** first, glance up the first valley on your left (that of the Riberot), which is backed by the huge bulk of Mont Vallier, at 9311ft (2838m) the highest peak in the region.

The road up the **Vallée de Bethmale** climbs quite steeply. This valley is rich in tradition and it is not that many years since its inhabitants all wore ethnic-style costumes with long skirts and woven waistcoats. The village of Bethmale itself is unannounced and

sits below the road on the right. Beyond it the road climbs to the tiny Lac de Bethmale, surrounded by beech trees and crouching below a peak of over 6562ft (2000m) From here the road ascends again over the Col de la Core and, traversing some wild country, drops to Seix in the valley of Salat. North of Seix, the village of Oust gives access to the **Vallée du Garbet** – but spend a few moments first in the church at Vic d'Oust, not far from the junction. Its painted walls and vaulting are typical of this area.

The valley of the Garbet is more open than that of Bethmale and is scattered with barns and farms with stepped gables. At the head of the valley, **Aulus-les-Bains** is something of a surprise, a spa village with tourist facilities and a thermal establishment welcoming visitors to its swimming pool. Above the village (at a hairpin on the D8) a broad track leads up to the **Cascade d'Arse**, a spectacular and photogenic waterfall. It is not too severe a climb, but the board at the foot of the track tells you how many calories you will be burning off en route – all courtesy of the spa! The D8 from here leads over the Col de Lers to Vicdessos and Tarascon.

The Couserans has one extra delight in store for anyone who should happen to be here in early June. Several of its villages stage a Fête of the Transhumance, celebrating the moving of flocks of sheep (and even Mérens horses) to their summer quarters in the mountains. Anyone can join in and follow the animals on their trek with much music, partying and feasting along the way. These celebrations surely characterise Ariège – from low hills to high mountains with a people steeped in tradition; and, of course, a history going back many thousands of years.

OFFICES DE TOURISME

Tarascon-sur-Ariège
Centre Multimédia
09400 TARASCON-SUR-ARIÈGE

Luzenac
6, rue de la Mairie
09250 LUZENAC

Foix
29, rue T. Delcasse BP 20
09001 FOIX

St. Girons
Place Alphonse Sentein
09200 SAINT-GIRONS

PLACES OF INTEREST

Tarascon-sur-Ariège

Grotte de Niaux
Guided tours virtually every day of
the year, more frequent (every 45
minutes) in July, August and
September (9.15am-5.30pm).
Strong footwear recommended.
☎ 05. 61.05.10.10 for booking or
call at the Office de Tourisme in
Tarascon.

Parc de la Préhistoire
Open July and August every day
10am-8pm; April to June,
September and October 10am-
6pm (7pm at weekends) except
Mondays. Last tickets at least half
an hour before closing.

Grotte de Bédeilhac
Open July and August 10am-6pm
every day; April to June,
September, October and other
holiday periods 2.30-4.15pm
(Sunday visit 3pm only).

Grotte de la Vache
Opening arrangements and hours
the same as at Bédeilhac.

Grotte de Lombrives
July and August visits every 20
minutes from 10am-7pm; June and
September 4 visits daily; May 3
visits daily; outside those months,
4 visits daily weekends and bank
holidays only between Palm
Sunday and 11th Nov. Shortest
tour lasts one and a half hours –
longer tours by appointment.

Lordat

**Les Aigles du Château de Lordat
(Birds of Prey)**
Open April to October every day
10.30am-12.30pm, 2-6pm (last
entry 1 hour before closing).
Displays at 11.30am, 2.30 and
4.30pm. Closed Tuesdays outside
school holiday periods.

Carrières de Trimouns
Open from May to Mid-October.
Guided tours of 1 hour depart at 4
p.m. every afternoon except
Sunday, with more (5 daily) during
the months of July and August.
Closed at weekends. Contact the
Office de Tourisme at Luzenac
before setting off as visits will be
cancelled if mountain visibility is
poor.

Ax-les-Thermes – Orlu

Observatoire de la Montagne
Open every day 10am-7pm in
'summer'; every day except
Tuesdays 10am-6pm in 'spring';
every day except Tuesdays and
Wednesdays 10am-6pm in
'autumn'; holiday times only in
winter (except Tuesdays).

La Maison des Loups
Open April to August every day
10am-5.30pm (7pm July and
August); September and October
every day except Monday and
Tuesday 11am-5pm.

Refuge d'en Beys
Open for snacks, drinks, meals etc.
every day during June, July and
September and on weekends in
May and October.

Niaux

Musée Pyrenéen de Niaux
Open every day, July and August
9am-8pm; rest of year 10am-
12noon, 2-6pm.

Foix

Les Forges de Pyrène
Open July and August every day
10am-7pm; June and September
every day 10am-6pm; April and
October every day except Monday
1.30-6pm. Closed January.

Château de Foix
Open every day July and August
9.45am-6.30pm; May, June and
September 9.45am-12.30pm,
1.30-6pm; rest of year 10.30am-
12noon, 2-5.30pm except
Mondays and Tuesdays between
November and March. Closed
January.

Grotte de Labouïche
Open July and August 9.30am-
6pm; June and September 10am-
12noon, 2-6pm; April and May 2-
6pm (10am-12noon Sundays also);
1st October to 11th November
Sundays only 10am-12noon, 2-
6pm (note last departure
45minutes before closing). Visits
last 1 hour 15minutes.

Le Mas d'Azil

Cave and museum (same hours)
Open July and August 10am-6pm;
June and September 10am-
12noon, 2-6pm; April and May 2-
6pm (Sundays 10am-12noon also);
March, October and November 2-
6pm Sundays only.

Montségur

Château of Montségur
Open every day throughout the
year 9.30am-6pm approx. (earlier
closing in winter, later in summer).
Guided visits every day in July and
August and at weekends in May,
June and September. Closed in
January.

Archaeological museum
Open May to August 10am-
12.30pm, 2-7.30pm; September
10.30am-12noon, 2-6pm, rest of
year afternoons only (closed for
month of January).

St. Lizier

Bishop's Palace
Open July and August every day
10am-6.30pm; rest of year every
day except Monday 8.30am-
12noon, 2-5.30pm (but closed at
weekends from September to
March).

LOCAL HIGHLIGHTS

Best Walks

• The magnificent climb to the Lac d'en Beys in the Orlu Nature Reserve above Ax-les-Thermes. 3 hours each way.

• The *Sentier Cathare* between Leychert and Roquefixade – just a tiny section of the long-distance path, waymarked with bars of yellow on red. Starts approx. 200yd (200m) along the road from the church. 1 hour each way.

• The climb to the beautiful Cascade de l'Arse from Aulus-les-Bains. One and a half hours each way.

The IGN map Haute-Ariège no.7 covers all these three routes. For a good collection of very easy walks throughout Ariège (the sort you could take the children on), look out for the book *Les sentiers d'Emilie* (Rando Editions) – the text is in French only, but maps and routes are first-class.

For cyclists

• Road cycling in the mountains is fine if you are training for the Tour de France, but a bit hard going for the average family. Take your bikes down to a lower level – the area around the Lac de Montbel for example.

• Most Offices de Tourisme can offer routes for off-road bikes and Ax-les-Thermes even transports them to its ski-stations in the mountains for a downhill run – ask at the Office de Tourisme.

Watersports

• The Lac de Montbel near Mirepoix and the Lac de Mondely near le Bastide-de-Sérou both have swimming beaches supervised in summertime. Montbel, the largest lake in the south-west, also offers pedalos, canoes, electric boats and a sailing school.

• Foix has both outdoor and indoor swimming pools.

• Descents of the Ariège by canoe are possible between Ornolac (Ussat-les-Bains) and Mercus. Contact Ariège-Évasion on ☎ 05.61.05.11.11. Details of other canoeing possibilities from Comité Départemental de Canoë Kayak de l'Ariège, 09000 FOIX (☎ 05.61.65.20.65). Ercé in the Couserans offers other watersports including rafting (☎ 05.61.66.88.90).

For the palate

• Croustades – fruit tarts with lovely flaky pastry. A speciality of St Girons, every patisserie is full of them.

- Hypocras – an aperitif with a herby, reputedly 2000-year-old recipe (it was apparently a favourite of Hypocrates).

- Cheeses from the Couserans – look out for the mild cows' milk cheeses Bethmale and, from Seix, Rogallais (which is also slightly fruity).

And the most memorable

This should be the artwork of the Grotte de Niaux, but let us not go for the obvious. Instead –

- Hearing the whistles of hidden marmots on the climb to the Étang de Beys – and catching the odd glimpse of a furry bottom scuttling over the rocks.

- Just three of us walking by torchlight through the caverns of Bédeilhac, completely mesmerised by the exuberant ramblings of M. Gailli.

- A picnic with a view amid the springtime flowers at Roquefixade – and the arrival of a pair of hungry wild goats!

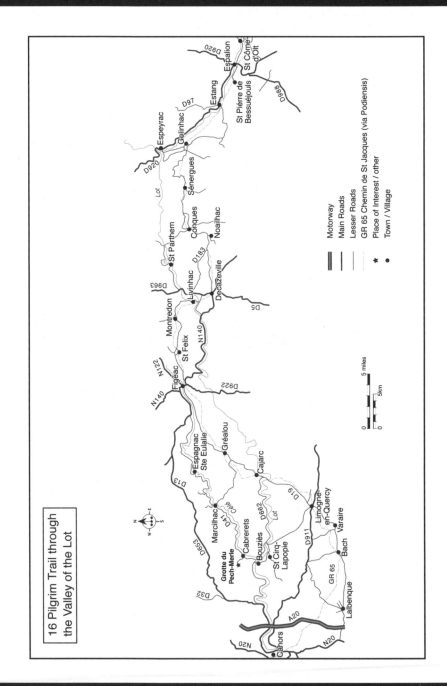

16 Pilgrim Trail through the Valley of the Lot

Motorway
Main Roads
Lesser Roads
GR 65 Chemin de St Jacques (via Podiensis)
★ Place of Interest / other
● Town / Village

St Côme d'Olt
Espalion
D920
D988
Estang
St Piérre de Bessuéjouls
D97
Golinhac
Espeyrac
D920
Sénergues
Lot
Conques
Noailhac
St Parthem
D183
Decazeville
Livinhac
D5
D963
Montredon
St Felix
N140
N122
Figeac
N140
D922
Espagnac
Ste Eulalie
Gréalou
Cajarc
D13
Marcilhac
D41
Célé
D662
Lot
D19
Cabrerets
Bouziès
St Cirq-Lapopie
Limogne-en-Quercy
Grotte du Pech-Merle
D911
Varaire
Bach
GR 65
D653
D32
Laibenque
A20
N20
Cahors
N20

5 miles
5km

253

This story begins after the Crucifixion, when the apostles scattered themselves to spread the gospel as widely as possible. It is said that James the Great went to Spain, and that when he later returned to the Holy Land he was beheaded for his faith on the orders of King Herod Agrippa. His body was taken to the coast, and (at this point we enter the realms of legend, fantasy, miracle or whatever) put into a boat made of stone, which was then carried by wind, currents and angels to arrive just one week later at the place now known as Padrón, on the north-west coast of Spain. There in Galicia the mortal remains of St James were buried in 44AD.

Some 800 years later, a local hermit had a vision of a bright star ringed by many lesser ones shining above a particular point in the hills. On investigation of the spot, the bones of three men were uncovered, and were declared to be those of St James and two of his followers. Alfonso II, King of the Asturias, ordered a church to be built on the site and the flow of pilgrims to the town that became Santiago de Compostela began (campus stellae = field of the star). By the 11th century more than half a million a year were arriving, and Santiago had become a major venue for pilgrimages, outclassed only by Jerusalem and Rome.

Across France four main routes developed (starting from Paris, Vézelay, le Puy and Arles), routes that eventually joined together to cross the plains of northern Spain. Along these *Chemins de St Jacques* hostels, chapels, monasteries and hospitals were built to offer shelter to the pilgrims, way-

St James

St James is referred to as James the Great to distinguish him from two other apostles, James the Less and James the Just. He and his brother John were the sons of Zebedee, and according to the Gospels, they were fishermen on the Sea of Galilee at the time they were called by Jesus. With Peter and John, James was clearly one of Jesus' closest friends and he is mentioned as being present at many of the important events in Jesus' life – the healing of Jairus' daughter, the Transfiguration, the Garden of Gethsemane (where the three are called apart from the others), the post-resurrection appearance on the lake shore of Tiberias.

Although Acts 12 tells us that James was slain by Herod Agrippa, there is unfortunately no hard evidence that he ever carried out an evangelistic mission in Spain, let alone that the remains found in Galicia were his. Nevertheless, St James has been venerated in Spain since the earliest days of Christianity and it is said that he miraculously appeared to fight for the Christians against the Moors at the Battle of Clavijo in the *Reconquista*. Because of this, he is often depicted as *St James Matamoros* (St James the Moor-slayer), in addition to his many appearances as a pilgrim. In 1884, a Papal Bull officially declared the relics at Santiago to be authentic. Most interestingly, 20th-century excavations under the cathedral at Santiago revealed a Roman stone, inscribed with the names Athanasius and Theodore – known to be those of James' own disciples.

side crosses sprang up and churches brought in relics of other saints so that pilgrims would stop to worship as they passed and so bring business to the communities. Around 1150 a book entitled the *Codex Calixtinus* was produced, and included what was effectively a first-ever travel guide that detailed the best paths, safe river crossings, pure water sources, places of lodging and any other information useful to the traveller.

Of the four French routes, the one from le Puy (the *Via Podiensis*) has the distinction of being the route taken by the very first official pilgrim, Godescalc, Bishop of le Puy in 950. It subsequently became the most popular route, entailing a journey of 932 miles (1500km) to Santiago, which a pilgrim might hope to complete in around two months. Against him would be all the hazards of the road, including wolves and brigands, foul weather, swollen rivers, and high mountains. Clad traditionally in a cloak and broad-brimmed hat, with sandals on his feet, a staff in his hand and little or no money in his wallet (he was meant to rely on charity), there was no certainty that a pilgrim would make it to Santiago alive – and if he did, he had yet to make his way home again.

Over the centuries the popularity of pilgrimages declined, until at the beginning of the 20th century only a handful of pilgrims a year were arriving in Santiago to claim their Compostela (a certificate saying they had completed their journey). In the 1980s the tide turned, and suddenly there were pilgrims of a new kind taking to the road. Although now dressed in gore-tex and hiking boots, today's pilgrims, like their predecessors, still carry the pilgrims' symbolic scallop-shell (the *coquille St* *Jacques*). In the Middle Ages these shells were to be found only on the coasts of Galicia and so had become the emblem of St James.

New pilgrims have new motives for their journey. A recent French survey showed that *spirituelle* is still the reason most frequently given – although that spirituality might now have a wider implication such as a desire to find themselves, or come to terms with a problem. Others simply go for the adventure, or for the cultural interest, since UNESCO declared these ancient pilgrim routes to be a World Heritage site in 1998. Curiously enough, only a small proportion of those undertaking this journey are regular ramblers at home – somehow the Chemins de St Jacques remain something more than straightforward long-distance trails.

Presently around 90,000 pilgrims a year present themselves at Santiago for their Compostela, although on a Holy Year (a year when St James' day, 25th July, falls on a Sunday) the numbers may be two or three times as great. Of course there are several other routes to Santiago, but this section of the Lot valley forms part of the popular Via Podiensis, and you are pretty sure to meet some pilgrims – and to recognise them by the heavy packs on their backs, usually surmounted by a scallop-shell. We shall keep them company from their first encounter with the River Lot until they finally leave it at Cahors, a distance of some 124 miles (200km).

St Côme d'Olt to Espalion

The journey for us begins in St Côme d'Olt, a lovely little town of medieval streets where a pilgrim following the Via Podiensis first meets the river. To

255

get here from le Puy he has travelled only 90 miles (145km) but has crossed some of the most inhospitable terrain on the route, the high plateau of the Aubrac. Covered in alpine grassland, it is bare and windswept, a land used traditionally only for the summer grazing of cattle, an empty wilderness with long distances between possible places for rest. If you can arrive in St Côme d'Olt via the D987 from Aubrac you will get a feel for this landscape – and how pleased pilgrims are to leave it behind for the green shelter of the Lot valley!

St Côme d'Olt itself is a delightful place. Included among the prestigious *plus beaux villages de France*, it has remained an unspoilt working village, and has not become a show-piece or been taken over by craftsmen as have so many of the others in this list. Instead its centre-piece is a lovely cobbled square from where the church of St Côme and St Damien thrusts its twisted grey spire high into the sky and the 13th century Hôtel de Ville stands quietly remembering its former days as the château of the Lords of Caumont and Castelnau. Through this tiny shaded square the pilgrims come and go, maybe pausing to eat their lunch on the steps of the church – where at their feet you can make out the shape of a scallop-shell among the cobbles.

Narrow medieval alleyways lead out of the square in all directions. The route the pilgrims take bears the white on red markings of a Grande Randonnée – in modern day parlance, this trail is officially the GR65. From here it heads down to the river, but before you go that way, it may be worth following the waymarks 'backwards' for a few minutes to take a look at a building the pilgrims passed on their way into St Côme. The 10th century chapel of la Bouysse, a seat of the Penitents Blancs, belongs to the early days of pilgrimage and once had a pilgrim hospital standing alongside. No longer in use, it still stands looking out to the Aubrac from where the pilgrims come.

At last it is time to go in the right direction and head downhill between the leaning houses to cross the lovely Gothic bridge over the Lot (*Lot* is simply a French corruption of the Occitan name *Olt*). The ancient stone cross at the centre of the bridge is adorned, like many others you will meet, with pebbles placed by passing pilgrims. From this bridge their journey today continues on the narrow road along the riverside to Espalion, but things were very different in the Middle Ages! Although valleys offered shelter they also brought the problems of flooding, lurking brigands and hungry wild animals, and pilgrims were unwilling to remain long in their confines. Instead they reached Espalion by a track climbing the slopes on the left bank – you can take it today and be rewarded by fine views along the length of the valley, most especially from a high rocky peak where now stands the statue of the Vierge de Vermus. If you want to enter into the spirit of this journey from the start, you could do no better than take a circular walk combining the old and new routes, thus walking in the footsteps of the pilgrims. Beware though – even a short distance of this trail is addictive, and you may soon find yourself making plans for the next few hundred miles to Santiago.

Espalion is a lovely old town whose highlight for the pilgrims is the pink-stoned Église de Perse at the foot of the hill beneath the Vierge de Vermus. The church was built on the site where St Hilarian was beheaded by Saracens in the 8th century, and above its Romanesque portal the rather alarming carvings representing the Apocalypse are tempered by a calmer depiction of Pentecost. Tucked into a corner above, naïve but expressive figures of the Three Kings greet the Virgin and Child. The cool, bare interior is reached by a push-button door you can only trust will let you out again, but the risk seems worthwhile for a glimpse of the one-time bright frescoes adorning the vaults of the transept and some interesting carved capitals. A modern altar completes the scene.

Down in the town, more prized buildings of Espalion include an 11th century bridge built by the medieval monks who specialised in such things (the *Frères Pontiff*), and alongside it, the 16th century Vieux Palais that was once the residence of the governors of Espalion. From the bridge itself you can admire the old tanner's houses lining the riverside.

A latter-day invention

Espalion's recent addition to the scene on the riverside is the shadowy figure of a heavily-clad diver emerging from the water! The town is honouring the work of three of its residents who in the late 1800s invented a compressed air regulator to aid trapped workers in the nearby mines at Decazeville, and then went on to develop its potential as the first aqualung.

Just up the road, the large Église St Jean houses a museum (Musée du Scaphandre) displaying a colourful array of historic diving suits and accompanying miscellaneous equipment – while another museum in the same building (Musée Joseph-Vaylet) offers more conventional fare in the form of ancient pottery, furniture and other household effects. Espalion's third museum, the Musée de la Rouergue is located in the old prison, and concerns itself with customs, traditions, costumes and other details of local life.

From Espalion the Chemin de St Jacques continues down the river valley – and it is an alluring prospect as this whole section between St Côme and Estaing has been specially cited by UNESCO for its natural beauty as well as its heritage value. Nevertheless, there are a couple of places, quite unrelated to the pilgrim trail, which you might like to visit before moving on. The hillside above St Côme (reached by the D206 from the end of the bridge) bears a curious natural phenomenon known as the *coulée de lave* – the lava flow. The 'lava' is actually basalt broken up into small pieces during the Ice Age, and the wide rocky 'river' crossing the road and descending the hill makes an impressive sight.

Not far away is the tiny unspoilt village of **Roquelaure** with its dark turreted château perched dramatically on the rim of the gorge and beside it, a little chapel containing a fine presentation of the entombment. Back in Espalion again, the Château de Calmont d'Olt, crowning a conical hill to the south of the town, cries out for exploration. In practice it is a youngster's paradise with medieval catapult machines demonstrating their capabilities, and knights in appropriate costume firing everything from a cannon to a longbow. More senior members of the family could content themselves with the extensive view ranging from the valley below to the heights of the Aubrac.

And finally, the road that leads to Calmont d'Olt (the D988 to Rodez) goes on to **Bozouls**, a small town with a 'hole in its heart'. This *Trou de Bozouls* is actually the abrupt gorge of the looping River Dourdou, and although you are tempted to think that some catastrophic event must have inflicted such a crater on the town, clearly things were the other way round, and all those houses clutching the edge were deliberately built there for whatever reason. There are various viewpoints and the road snaking into the depths connecting both halves of the town makes an interesting drive.

ON TO CONQUES AND FIGÉAC

But back to the pilgrims and their onward journey from Espalion. Again they soon leave the riverside, climbing through a lush green valley that shelters the village of **St Pierre de Bessuéjouls** – you can reach it by car by turning off the D556 where signed. The beautiful pink sandstone church here is essentially Romanesque and has some finely carved capitals, but its most remarkable feature is the belfry. Retained from the original 11th century building, it has a chapel built into its first floor reached by dark narrow staircases from the nave. The stone altar here dates from the 9th century, making it one of the oldest on the whole route. Just up the road, the few houses of the village are picturesquely grouped around a bridge over the stream and a back garden shelter has been pressed into service as a bar for thirsty travellers. Five miles (8km) more of scenically

winding path lead the pilgrim from here to his next place of rest, the village of Estaing.

Estaing is yet another village to have found inclusion among the *plus beaux* of France. Its dark château dominates the riverside scene and has a hint of the oppressive rather than the beautiful about it, but there is still a fine Gothic bridge, and the village itself comprises a pleasant medley of medieval streets and alleyways that, like those of St Côme, have escaped commercial exploitation. Estaing's only concession in this direction appears to be the abundance of Laguiole knives for sale – crafted in the nearby town of that name, they are the finest on the market (but you will need to dig deep into the pocket to become a proud owner). Pilgrims arriving in Estaing are directed to visit the church of St Fleuret at its heart, where a Gothic cross outside the main doorway bears on its shaft a tiny pilgrim with hat and scallop-shell, kneeling before the crucified Christ. A side chapel on the north aisle houses a gilded statue of St James himself.

The Way between St Côme and Estaing has been easy for the pilgrims, but now they are faced with a long steep climb through the woods as they once more abandon the valley to reach the plateau above. You could follow them immediately (by taking the road towards Villecomtal and then turning on the D20) – but to see a little more of the Lot, you might first want to continue on the road alongside it to **Entraygues**. This little town built at the confluence of the Lot and the Truyère surprisingly is something of a holiday centre, offering canoeing excursions on the Lot among its attractions. The town itself is again blessed with well-preserved medieval streets and a 13th century bridge over

St Roch

St Roch was born around 1295 and was the son of the governor of Montpellier. In youth he gave away his worldly wealth and set out on pilgrimage to Rome where he encountered many communities stricken with the plague. Subsequently devoting his life to caring for plague victims, he was said to have achieved some miraculous cures. When St Roch himself contracted the plague (represented by an infected sore on his leg), he went to live in isolation in the forest, accompanied only by his dog, who fetched his daily food. Thus he is generally depicted pulling back his coat from his afflicted left thigh, with the dog at his side carrying bread in its mouth.

At the time the plague was at its height, many churches on the le Puy route changed their dedication from St James to St Roch, trusting that he would protect their communities. This link between the saints probably explains the frequent appearance of the 'pilgrim version' of St Roch, complete with wide-brimmed hat, staff and scallop-shells.

the Truyère.

From Entraygues a narrow road hugs the north bank of the Lot, mimicking every twist and turn all the way to Decazeville. But we are committed to the pilgrim's path, a trail crossing the high plateau – and there are many gems along the route before it descends again to the river. A narrow road climbing from the end of the bridge at Entraygues will pick up the *Chemin* again at **Golinhac**, a village not short of views from its lofty perch on the rim of the valley and one well-geared to the needs of the pilgrims. The municipal campsite here is accompanied by a pilgrim hostel with more mod cons than most – and the menu at the stylish restaurant opposite the church makes you think a 21st century pilgrim's lot is not so bad after all.

Do not leave Golinhac without a peep in the church, where a statue of St Roch as a pilgrim, scattered with scallop-shells, stands to the right of the altar. St Roch is someone you will

to meet again and again on this part of the trail and churches in the next two villages, **Espeyrac** and **Sénergues**, likewise boast his effigy. Both villages are worth a look – Espeyrac is simply pretty, while Sénergues has a grey 15th century château (with even older tower) in its main street, and splendid modern stained glass windows in the church alongside.

From Sénergues the pilgrims head west to one of the high spots of their journey, the village of Conques, still some 6 miles (10km) away – motorists can share their route for a while as it passes through **St Marcel**, where the window above the church door bears three scallop-shells. **Conques** is the third *plus beaux village* on this star-studded trail, and for all its prestige, the first impression for the pilgrims who scramble down the rough path from the empty landscapes above might be that of shock at finding themselves in a popular tourist venue. But the pilgrims are soon won over. Conques is beautiful

Saint Foy

Saint Foy was born in Agen at the end of the 3rd century and adopted the Christian faith. Little is known of her life other than that when she refused to make a sacrifice to pagan gods, the occupying Roman authorities appallingly had her grilled on a brazier and then beheaded. She was just 13 years old at the time.

Two centuries later her mortal remains were transferred to a basilica built specially to house them, and they apparently worked miracles, healing the blind and securing the release of prisoners. Clearly these were precious relics, and in the 9th century, a monk from Conques set out to acquire them for his community. He spent 10 whole years living with the monks of Agen and earning a position of trust before finally making off with the relics and taking them home to Conques. Saint Foy herself was evidently unperturbed by this medieval covetousness, because it is said that in subsequent years her output of miracles was doubled!

– in the steep-sided gorge of the Ouche, an 11th century twin-towered abbey church sits amid well-conserved medieval buildings decked in blended shades of brown.

The story of the village revolves around that of St Foy (Saint Faith in the English version), who was an early Christian martyr. The abbey church at the centre of the village is dedicated to her, and if you see nothing else here, at least take time to admire the tympanum over its west door. Crafted in local limestone with touches of medieval paintwork still showing, there could be no better portrayal of the contrasting glories of heaven and torments of hell than in this tympanum. Passing pilgrims must have received a very clear message! In the centre sits Christ in Majesty, while below his feet the souls of men are weighed in the balance. To the left is heaven, inhabited by Mary, Saint Peter, Charlemagne and Abraham among others, and between them all St Foy in a faded blue dress prostrates herself

before a welcoming hand. In hell on the right every mortal sin is graphically punished in medieval fashion and otherwise respected figures such as kings and monks are not spared. The predominant colour is red. Appropriate Latin texts divide the different themes, and the tiny characters that peer down on it all from the arch just above the tympanum apparently have more mathematical, mystical and theological significance than the casual observer could possibly guess. The whole affair is fascinating, and if you feel moved to ponder it further, it is worth getting an explanatory booklet (in English) from one of the nearby bookshops.

The interior of the abbey church has rather less to offer than the tympanum, but it is certainly impressive on account of its great height. There are beautiful carved capitals and a modern wooden statue of St James. The recently-installed windows by the artist Pierre Soulages appear insignificant at first glance, but they are designed to fill the church with light and enhance the simple architecture of the interior. The sacristy bears traces of frescoes depicting the martyrdom of St Foy and her relics were once kept securely behind an iron grill in the chancel where pilgrims, passing at a suitable distance in the ambulatory, could pay them homage. Today those relics, encased in a gold reliquary studded with jewels, take pride of place among the collection known as the Treasure of Conques. More ornate reliquaries, portable altars and statues are presented alongside, and you feel disconcerted that a religious institution should own such great riches. Treasures of different sorts, from Romanesque capitals to Aubusson tapestries, are displayed in the building that houses the Office de Tourisme.

Aside from its other glories, Conques boasts a network of medieval streets weaving their way between its different levels. Near the church there are craftshops in plenty; walk farther out and you can escape the throng to enjoy some splendid old half-timbered buildings and views over the grey-stone roofs of the village. The cobbled Rue Charlemagne (on the right facing the church) is the route by which pilgrims leave for their onward journey. It descends rapidly and a walk of 10 minutes or so will take you to the perched Chapelle St Roch, from which there is an excellent view of Conques.

After climbing out of the deep valley below Conques, pilgrims are offered a choice of route over the next few kilometres. Today most take the easier option that follows minor roads to the pretty village of **Noailhac**. On the summit above this village is yet another chapel dedicated to St Roch, with a fine figure of the saint in pilgrim attire above the door and another in his non-pilgrim role inside. Beyond Noailhac the *Chemin* descends to the Lot valley again past the mining town of **Decazeville**. It does not have a lot to interest the pilgrims – although the church does house a priceless set of paintings depicting the Way of the Cross, by the 19th century Symbolist painter, Gustave Moreau. Motorists might want to make a detour to see something quite different – la Découverte, the largest open cast mine in France. The Office de Tourisme offers a map giving directions to a viewpoint over the mine, and guided visits are possible in high season.

From Decazeville it would be easy to follow the Lot all the way to Figéac, but that is not the way for the pilgrims. Instead they again climb, past Livinhac-le-Haut (not really 'haut' at all, but on a low mound above the looping river) and on to Montredon. Before you follow them, you might just want to divert east along the valley of the Lot for a few kilometres to the village of St Parthem, where the Maison de la Rivière Olt devotes itself to the river in its every imaginable aspect. This recently-opened museum includes video projections and an arboretum along the banks of the Lot.

Back again to the pilgrims, who by now have reached the crossroads below **Montredon**, where the tiny restored Chapelle Notre-Dame with its inside gallery is worth a pause. By this point you will have realised that almost all the churches along the *Chemin* are open, and that many of them provide picnic tables and even water points outside for the pilgrims. This little chapel is no exception, and while here you might like to walk up to the church of St Michel at the centre of the village, which had a former life under the Hospitaliers de St Jean.

'*Ultreia*' – Onward – is the pilgrims' greeting, and from Montredon you can follow them onward to one of the route's lesser-known gems, the diminutive **Chapelle de Guirande**, standing beside the D2. Behind the altar are fine 15th century frescoes depicting Christ in Majesty, attended by Saint Matthew, Saint John, Saint Madeleine and Saint Namphaise.

The next village on the route is **St Felix** (again the D2 will get you there), and here the beautiful 11th century tympanum clearly shows Adam and Eve, the tree and the serpent. Inside there is a modern stained glass window of St James. From St Felix the route heads as directly as it can to Figéac, and you must do the same – but no-one could miss seeing the prominent church of **St Jean-Mirabel** on its hilltop nearby, and you might like to divert to admire yet another Romanesque portal before calling it a day.

Figéac actually stands not on the Lot, but rather on its tributary, the Célé – although the Lot itself is only 3 miles (5km) to the south at this point. The town developed on the site of a monastery, built here in the 9th century. Over the years the visiting pilgrims were the tourists who brought the town its prosperity, yet strangely in the Wars of Religion it became a stronghold of the Calvinists. Fortunately it escaped destruction, and Old Figéac retains a maze of winding streets and hidden corners, with many buildings dating from the 15th century and earlier. This quarter is best navigated with the aid of a town trail (in English), obtainable from the Tourist Office – which itself is housed in the 13th century town mint (the Hôtel de la Monnaie). Before leaving that building, you might consider popping upstairs to the Musée de Vieux Figéac,

a couple of rooms housing a jumble of antique household items, furniture, tools, coins, clocks, tapestries and plenty more.

The most surprising of all Figéac's nooks and crannies on this trail is without doubt a little courtyard known as the Place des Écritures. Surrounded by honey-stoned medieval buildings, its floor is a block of shiny black granite in which strange hieroglyphics are engraved. This huge work of art (by the American artist Joseph Kosuth) is a copy of the Egyptian Rosetta Stone, a memorial to the brilliant academic Jean-François Champollion, who was ultimately responsible for its translation – although he did have some help with this from the earlier attempts of Englishman Thomas Young. Champollion was born in Figéac in 1790, and his nearby home is now the Musée Champollion, invested with information about the hieroglyphics and a wealth of sometimes macabre artefacts from ancient Egypt, naturally including a mummy.

After Figéac, most pilgrim guides offer a choice – the scenic route along the valley of the Célé or the historic route that crosses the high *causse* (limestone plateau) to reach the Lot at Cajarc. Almost all opt for the latter – a pilgrim wants to stay true to tradition. But you, with a car, can choose either, or even both, so first let us take a quick look at the very beautiful valley of the Célé. A minor road follows the river all the way to its confluence with the Lot near the village of St Cirq-Lapopie

THE VALLEY OF THE CÉLÉ

There may be few pilgrims heading this way, but the first village along the valley, **Espeyrac Ste Eulalie**, nevertheless boasts a pilgrim hostel and welcome centre in the buildings of a one-time priory. A modern wooden sculpture of St James stands outside. Surprisingly the church in this very picturesque village is kept locked and is only accessible on guided visits. Inside are remnants of the 13th century church that was once attached to the priory.

Beyond Espeyrac Ste Eulalie, the valley is particularly attractive, with white limestone bluffs along its flanks – downstream those cliffs are always present but their colour tends to grey and even pink. At **St Sulpice**, troglodyte houses seem pressed into the rock-face. The next village in this peaceful valley is **Marcilhac**, whose 10th-century abbey is currently being restored. Its history includes a long and unseemly monastic quarrel over the ownership of Rocamadour (valued for its wealth) and subsequent virtual destruction by the English at the time of the Hundred Years War. There nevertheless remain a sculpted tympanum from the abbey's earliest days, finely-wrought capitals in the chapter-house and some interesting frescoes in a side chapel. The village itself includes a quiet square shaded by plane trees beside the river. A couple of kilometres directly above Marcilhac (or so it seems from its steep access road) the Grotte de Bellevue displays some truly exquisite limestone formations.

Equally impressive configurations in limestone are to be found in another cave towards the end of the valley – but that cave, the renowned Pech Merle, is also blessed with an abundance of prehistoric artwork. Visits here are regulated, so this is the time to 'phone for a reservation before making your way slowly, and enjoying every turn of this scenic route beside the river.

The first diversion to detain you is the Open Air Museum at Cuzals, signed off the road after the pretty village of Sauliac. Scattered over a wide area, it represents about twenty little museums and workshops demonstrating crafts, agricultural tools and machinery from a bygone age. Bread is baked, clogs are made, the mill grinds corn and cattle draw the carts – it is a day's entertainment for all the family.

Farther on, no-one could pass the proffered glimpses of the Musée de l'Insolite (Museum of the Unusual) in the cliffs before Cabrerets without feeling curious, so perhaps that, too will occasion a pause. And while in Cabrerets, it is worth just crossing the river for the best view of its two châteaux. Clinging to the clifftop, the ruined Château du Diable was an English stronghold in the Hundred Years War while to the left the later (15th century) Château Gontaut-Biron grimly surveys the valley.

And now it is time at last to take the road ascending to **Pech-Merle**. This surely is the cave that has it all. In its depths, the several chambers are decorated with line drawings of bison, mammoth and ibex, negative hand prints, coloured dots of unknown meaning, a realistic engraving of a bear's head and the well-known painting of two spotted horses (one strangely with the outline of a fish on its back). In a muddy bank are footprints left here some 20,000 years ago, and the limestone formations surrounding all these are quite splendid in themselves, including unusual phenomena like 'discs' and 'cave pearls'.

That this magnificent cave is on show today is thanks to the disobedience of two teenage boys back in 1922 – their priest, a speleologist who was interested in prehistory himself, had earlier been lost in the cave for several hours, and had forbidden them ever to go near it! They went all the same, and were rewarded with the first glimpse of its treasures. All the finds that were subsequently made are now explained in the museum dedicated to the priest (Musée Abbé-Lemozi), close to the entrance. English visitors are offered headphone translation for the film in the museum, and in the cave itself, an English translation of the commentary in large bold print (legible in the dark!).

Returning again to Cabrerets, the confluence of the Lot and the Célé is just two and a half miles (4km) to the south at **Bouziès**. The roads following each river likewise meet here, and just a kilometre or so west of the junction, rock arching above the D653 houses a complex of fortified caves dating back to the Hundred Years War (the Défile des Anglais). Nearby, a narrow bridge (with almost impossible turn) carries light vehicles across the Lot into the village itself.

Pleasure boat cruises up and down river start from Bouziès but its main attraction is the riverside towpath (*Chemin de Halage*). From the car park, the white on red waymarks of the GR36 lead you upriver (approx. 550 yd [500m]) to where a deep groove cut into the rockface forms the long platform from which loaded barges were once towed. A walk of around half an hour or so will take you along the length of this towpath to a lock bypassing a weir on the river – and at this far end, the 'wall' of the towpath has been embellished with bas-relief sculptures. From this point you can continue on foot to reach the fourth and final *plus beaux village* on this tour, that of St Cirq-Lapopie.

Car-bound travellers can get to the same place by returning over the Lot, or by taking the D40 from the car park at Bouziès. The latter road climbs, wriggles and ducks its way through the various outcrops of rock (high and wide vehicles beware!) to reward the intrepid traveller with what is probably the very finest view of **St Cirq Lapopie** and the Lot valley. Continuing downhill, you can park the car and explore the village on foot. Despite its lovely cobbled streets, fortified church, ancient château and magnificent viewpoint on the rock, you will realise that you have strayed well into 'discovered' territory again and it is time to get back to the pilgrims – most of whom were left at Figéac.

FIGÉAC TO CAHORS

From Figéac the pilgrim route rejects both river valleys in favour of the *causse*, the high limestone plateau that lies between. This limestone plateau in fact extends very much farther afield and has recently been granted recognition as the Natural Regional Park of the Causse de Quercy. Pilgrim guides sometimes describe this area as boring, and perhaps it is if you have to spend three whole days walking across it. But it is also very beautiful, with a scattering of colourful limestone-grassland flowers amid junipers and stunted oak trees. With much loose stone readily available, there are drystone walls, an abundance of no-longer-used drystone huts (here known as or *gariottes* or *cazelles*), and many, many prehistoric dolmens.

From Figéac the route heads southwest to Cajarc, and one of the pleasantest spots on the journey is just beyond **Gréalou** where an ancient dolmen stands boldly beside the track, and on the opposite side, one of the oldest stone crosses on the route is piled high with pilgrim stones. You can find it by following the way-marked trail north from its crossing of the D82 a couple of kilometres from Gréalou.

At **Cajarc** the pilgrims are again in the Lot valley, which is akin to an oasis in this arid country. A knot of medieval streets surrounds the town's open central square – where the church again houses a statue of St Roch. Georges Pompidou was once a councillor in Cajarc and his donation has provided the town's Centre d'Art Contemporain (on the Figéac road), a modern art gallery that houses exhibitions. Other interest in Cajarc lies in its riverside port area and in its large *Plan d'eau*, an open-air water-sports complex which, being unique in these parts, is signposted for miles around.

From Cajarc the pilgrims are again up on the *causse* and heading next for **Limogne-en-Quercy**. This pleasant little town has a tiny museum of rural life in the rooms above its Tourist Office, and a large *lavoir* to the south (on the D24) that is typical of the *causse* in this area. Dolmens in profusion are to be found in the vicinity of Limogne – the Office de Tourisme will direct you to the four best of these, which have been classified as Historic Monuments.

The next village on the trail, **Varaire**, has a *lavoir* that once served as the village fishpond and still seems well stocked today – although presumably the locals are no longer encouraged to dangle a line as some of those fish seem very golden. Farther along, the village of **Bach** was named after an 18th century German immigrant family, and they were surely prolific

as the name occurs frequently in the area today. Near Bach, those pilgrims who chose the Célé valley route rejoin their more traditionally-inclined colleagues, having trekked due south across the plateau from St Cirq-Lapopie.

After Bach the trail continues across the *causse* on an old Roman road known as the *Cami Ferrat*, and for pilgrims this straight track flanked by low stone walls really does offer little of interest. Its very loneliness made it a place of danger for pilgrims in the past, and alternative trails were developed, passing along the route of the present-day road to **Lalbenque**. This small town is now particularly famous for its truffle markets, held every Tuesday between November and March. With bandits out of the frame, the route today is again more direct and a pilgrim's only thought is to hurry west-wards – this is one of the longest stages of the journey, with virtually no over-night accommodation on the 20 miles (32km) between Varaire and Cahors. When the pilgrims finally descend from the heights of the Mont St Georges, the spread of Cahors below them is a more than welcome sight.

Surprisingly, the trail does not go into **Cahors** at all – although almost all pilgrims do. Instead it turns left under the cliffs along the riverside, passing the Fontaine de Chartreux that since Roman times has supplied all the city's water, and finally reaching the Pont Valentré. Recently pilgrims have been encouraged to cross the Lot and continue along its right bank to arrive at the same point – and this is also the way for car travellers who are provided with adequate parking near the bridge itself.

The **Pont Valentré** is a feature more attractive in reality even than its photo-graphs might suggest. The original

14th century bridge here had six arches but no machicolated towers, which were added later to enforce the defences. The whole was eventually restored in 1879 with some minor modifications – and what was created as a military structure appears today as the most beautiful of bridges, elegantly spanning the dark wide river. Don't miss the tiny impish 'devil' clinging to the stonework near the top of the centre tower. He was put here by the 19th century restorers of the bridge to commemorate the first structure here, for whose build-ing the devil's help was apparently enlisted – and as usual he was tricked and received no soul for his pains! Here on the river bank we must take leave of the pilgrims. They, like you, will probably want to go into Cahors – the cathedral of St Etienne and the streets of the old town are full of interest. But soon they will be back on the trail, climbing the steep cliff from the end of the Pont Valentré, passing the sign that tells them that there are only another 1184km to go to Santiago de Compostela! Are you tempted to follow them?

Offices de Tourisme

Espalion
BP52-2, rue Saint Antoine
12500 ESPALION
☎ 05.65.44.10.63

Entraygues
30 Tour de Ville
12140 ENTRAYGUES-sur-TRUYÈRE
☎ 05.65.44.56.10

Conques
Place de l'Abbatiale
12320 CONQUES
☎ 0820 820 803

Figéac
Hôtel de la Monnaie
Place Vival BP 60
46100 FIGÉAC
☎ 05.65.34.06.25

Limogne
Grand Place
46260 LIMOGNE-en-QUERCY
☎ 05.65.24.34.28

St Cirq-Lapopie
Place du Sombral
46330 SAINT-CIRQ-LAPOPIE
☎ 05.65.31.29.06

Places of Interest

Espalion

Musée du Scaphandre
Open July, August and school holidays. Hours from the Office de Tourisme.

Musée Joseph-Vaylet
As the Musee du Scaphandre.

Musée du Rouergue
Open July and August every day (except Saturday morning) 10am-12.30pm, 2-7pm.

Château de Calmont d'Olt
Open July and August every day, 9am-7pm; May, June, September and school holiday periods, every day except Thursday and Friday, 10am-12noon, 2-6pm.

Conques

Treasure of St Foy
Open July and August 9am-12.30pm, 1.30-7pm; April to June and September 9am-12.30pm, 2-6.30pm; rest of year 10am-12noon, 2-6pm.

Musée Joseph-Fau
Same hours as the Treasure.

St Parthem

La Maison de la Rivière Olt
Open July and August every day except Friday 11am-1pm, 2-6pm; May, June and September Wednesdays, Sundays and Bank Holidays 2-5pm.

Figéac

Musée de Vieux Figéac
Open July and August every day 10am-7.30pm; rest of year every day except Sunday 10am-12noon, 2.30-6pm (open Sunday mornings May, June and September).

Musée Champollion
Open March to October 10am-12noon, 2.30-6.30pm except Mondays (but open Mondays in July and August); rest of year 2-6pm except Mondays.

Marcilhac-sur-Célé

Abbaye de Marcilhac
Guided visits.
Open July and August 10am-12.30pm, 2.30-6.30pm; June and September 10am-12noon, 2-6pm; April, May and October 10am-12noon, 2-5pm. Closed Sundays and Mondays.

Cuzals

Musée de Plein Air du Quercy
Open July and August 10am-7pm; June 9.30am-6.30pm; April, May and September 2-6pm. Closed Saturdays.

Cabrerets

Musée de l'Insolite
Open April to September 9am-1pm, 2-8pm.

Grottes du Pech-Merle
(ticket includes entry to Musée Abbé-Lemozi).
Open every day from late March to October 9.30am-12noon, 1.30-5pm. No more than 700 visitors a day are allowed in the caves and you are advised to book 24 hours in advance (or even earlier in July and August).

Cajarc

Centre d'Art Contemporain Georges-Pompidou
Open all year round every day except Monday 10am-12noon, 2-6pm (3-7pm in summer). Closed Sunday mornings.

Limogne-en-Quercy

Musée d'Arts et Traditions Populaire. Free entry
Open July to September every day except Monday 10.30am-1pm, 4-6.30pm; rest of year, Saturday 10.30am-1pm, 3-5.30pm and Sunday !0.30am-1pm.

LOCAL HIGHLIGHTS

Best Walks

- The pilgrim routes between St Côme d'Olt and Espalion. Take the riverside road (past the campsite) from Espalion to St Côme – it makes a good place to pause for lunch (there are two restaurants). Return the same way as far as the first bridge over an entrant stream, and immediately after it take the track climbing uphill on the left. You soon pick up the white on red waymarks again and they lead you all the way back to Espalion, with a possible 30 minute diversion to the viewpoint at the Vierge de Vermus. Total distance is around 7.5 miles (12km).

- It is possible to create another 7.5 mile (12km) circuit on the route starting from Cajarc. Follow the GR65 north out of Cajarc as far as the hamlet of le Verdier and return by the alternative GR65A. The IGN Série Bleue map 2238O will help, but again the white on red waymarks will lead you. And encounters with pilgrims are virtually guaranteed!

- It should be possible to follow short sections of the trail with the help of a recently-arrived company called Transbagages, who are offering transport for both pilgrims and/or their baggage. ☎ 0820.04.54.71 during their office hours (4-8pm) to see what is possible, or visit their website www.transbagages.com

- Forget the pilgrims and take a walk along the dramatic towpath at Bouziès. It will take you the best part of half an hour to reach the lock, after which you could continue by following the white on red waymarks of the GR36 to St Cirq-Lapopie (about another hour). The Tourist Office at St Cirq-Lapopie offers a rather sketchy map of the route on a glossy leaflet.

For cyclists

- 10 well-signed VTT routes of varying challenge are included under the title of *Espace VTT Gorges Lot et Truyère*. Most start or pass through Entraygues or Golinhac. More details from OT at Entraygues.
- VTTs can be hired from the base at the Plan d'eau du Surgié, Figéac. They will offer advice on the marked circuits in the area, provide maps, and if needed, a guide to accompany you.
- VTT routes across the *causse* start from Limogne. VTTs can be hired from the base in the Place de l'Église every day except Sunday from April to September.

Watersports

- There are many, many canoeing and kayaking bases on both the Lot and the Célé. Cajarc, St Cirq-Lapopie, Bouziès, Cabrerets, Sauliac, Marcilhac, Entraygues and Figéac are just a few.

- Marcilhac has a small beach on the Célé and the Lac des Galens, off the Laguiole road from Espalion, offers supervised bathing in July and August. Otherwise there are swimming pools at Figéac (Domaine du Surgié), Cajarc and Espalion.

- The much-publicised *Plan d'eau* on the Lot at Cajarc provides facilities for water-skiing, fishing and boating – but not swimming!

For the palate

- Aligot is a dish from the Aubrac and mountains of Aveyron. It is simply a blend of seasoned mashed potato, cheese, and crème fraîche – which makes it very sticky to serve! It can be eaten alone as a starter, or as an accompaniment to a meat dish.

- Walnut trees are abundant in the Lot valley. The nuts can be eaten raw or incorporated into sauces, cakes, oil (for salad dressing) and even liqueurs.

- Products of Quercy worth seeking out include Agneau de Quercy (the meat of the rather lean-looking sheep reared on the limestone *causse*), ceps (edible brown fungi), pâté de fois gras and of course, truffles (for those who can afford them!).

And the most memorable

- Trolleys for transporting pilgrim luggage are a relatively new phenomenon and, sitting on the church steps at St Côme d'Olt, we were amazed to see the most undersized of pilgrims towing the most oversized of rucksacks balanced shakily on two wheels. Was it really going all the way to Santiago?

- The Chapelle de Guirande. Creeping in through the tiny door of this wayside chapel – and finding some very well-preserved frescos inside.

- Driving over the rather scary mountain road from Bouziès and suddenly emerging at the viewpoint above St Cirq-Lapopie and the Lot. Splendid.

Although present-day pilgrims come from all over Europe, and indeed from America, Canada, Japan and elsewhere, Britain is as yet fairly poorly represented. If you are interested in walking one of the routes to Santiago – or in just finding out more about them – you will find that a charity by the name of the Confraternity of St James is very helpful. Contact them at 27, Blackfriars Road, London SE1 8NY. Their website www.csj.org.uk offers lots of historical information and practical advice.

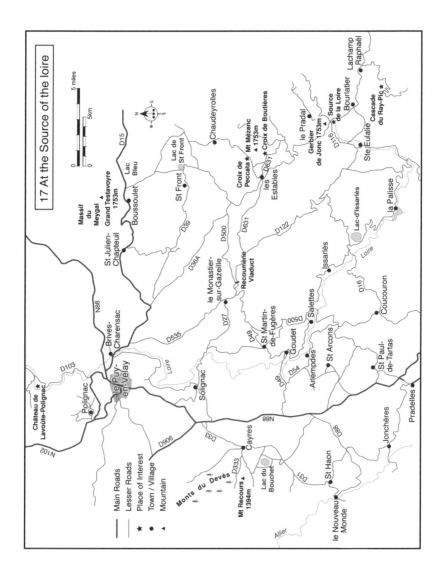

17 At the Source of the loire

Main Roads
Lesser Roads
Place of Interest
Town / Village
Mountain

Every French schoolchild learns that the source of the Loire, France's longest river, is in the Cévennes, on the slopes of a mountain known as the Gerbier de Jonc. It is a curious name (of mixed derivation, meaning 'rocky peak') and it is a curious mountain – a huge scaly hump, the most spectacular of the line of volcanic peaks that form the watershed between the Mediterranean and the Atlantic. These mountains are 'sucs', peaks formed when molten lava escaping from the earth's surface cooled very quickly in contact with the air. The result is an enormous mound of shale with water circulating freely between the volcanic plates and escaping to the surface at different points – the Loire has not one but many sources on the Gerbier de Jonc. Since the name is so well engraved on the French heart, the spot, although remote, is not without its visitors, its auberge and a few wayside stalls in summer, but it nevertheless makes a memorable setting for the birth of the 'Royal River'.

If you make the scramble to the top of the Gerbier de Jonc (and it is not as difficult as it looks) you will have a good view of another distinctive summit to the north-west – the flat-topped Mézenc. The view from the top of this one is said to encompass a quarter of France and is well worth the effort to get there. But the Mézenc has another remarkable display on offer – its unique flora are a botanist's dream. On the summit grows a type of groundsel found only on one other mountain in the Pyrenees, and you can also come across arnica, gentian and the insectivorous sundew. All that may require some botanical knowledge, but none at all is needed to be stunned by the carpet of wild daffodils and purple mountain pansies that covers these high pastures in springtime.

Most of the other attractions of this wild region are also natural ones – volcanic peaks and ridges, basalt flows, cascading waterfalls and clear lakes in the craters of one-time volcanoes. Villages are few and far between but often very attractive – two of them, Pradelles and Arlempdes, are included in the prestigious list of 144 *'plus beaux villages de France'*. The Loire itself takes a wide sweep south passing on its way the village of Ste Eulalie (the scene of a 'Violet Fair'), the lovely blue Lac d'Issarlès and the 'first château of the Loire' at Arlempdes before reaching brief civilisation in the form of le Puy-en-Velay.

Built in the crater of a volcano with two volcanic pyramids at its heart, le Puy makes a fascinating diversion for a day on-the-beaten-track again. But you will probably come to this region answering the call of the wild rather than that of the city, so it might be as well to find a base in a village not too far from the centre of things, the peaks of the Gerbier de Jonc and the Mézenc. Just to the west of the Mézenc, the old village of les Estables has metamorphosed to an all-year-round activity centre blessed with hotels, gîtes and other accommodation, while campers and caravanners could head for the little lakeside site at St Martial at the foot of the Gerbier de Jonc, or the very well appointed site at Goudet farther to the west. For these and other campsites in the mountains the season is short (usually from mid-June to mid-September). Earlier or later visitors will find the nearest site open at Brives-Charensac, just east of le-Puy-en-Velay.

THE GERBIER DE JONC

Wherever you stay, you are in this region to see the source of the Loire and your first visit must be to the **Gerbier de Jonc**. The mountain is signposted from les Estables, and the D36 offers a pleasant drive through lovely high country, on the way crossing the *départemental* border from Haute-Loire into Ardèche (which is also the regional border between Auvergne and Rhône-Alpes). Coming up to the mountain, you will first reach the Auberge du Gerbier de Jonc on the left hand side, with plenty of roadside parking. This is the place to stop. Farther along the road are the stalls selling regional produce, but if you get there, you have gone too far.

Beside the auberge, the shaly conical peak rises abruptly and the path to the summit is clearly signed. With such a stony ascent, it is not surprising that the path has recently been closed on account of erosion (summer '04), but hopefully it can be re-instated because the view from the top is magnificent. Volcanic peaks stretch in every direction – the Mézenc is obvious, while much closer and to the right of it is the dark pyramid of Suc de Sara. Below your feet the forest stretches deeply into the valley of the Pradal river and beyond it, the eastern horizon is the far distant Alpine chain. Another crop of conical *sucs* sits immediately to the west while in the south the bizarre summits continue into the distance.

Leaving the mountain itself, it is time to sort out the sources of the river.

The *Sentier des Sources de la Loire*, a footpath 2 miles (3km) in length defined by splashes of blue paint, starts off on the opposite side of the road from the auberge. The first source visited, the oozing marsh below the mountain, is maybe the least memorable (although in a dry summer it will possibly be the only one in water). Later on you reach the confusingly-named Véritable, Authentique and Geographique sources, the latter two being alongside the road where the stalls of regional produce flourish.

More experienced walkers can enjoy an excellent 7.5 mile (12km) discovery trail starting from the Gerbier de Jonc and winding through the forest to the little stone village of le Pradal, very deep in the valley below. It gets you well off-the-beaten-track where you have an opportunity to see some of the local wildlife (red squirrels and marmots in particular, and perhaps overhead the huge pale form of a Circaët Jean-Leblanc, the harrier eagle) – but beware the climb back up!

From the Gerbier de Jonc the road heads south into the wilderness. At a bleak road junction, the little eco-museum in the low grey Ferme Boulatier convinces you that this is one of the remotest places in France, and yet it has a beauty of its own. Beyond Boulatier it is worth going on to Lachamp-Raphaël and the **Cascade de Ray-Pic**. The most spectacular waterfall in the area (although just how spectacular depends on rainfall), Ray-Pic is reached by turning right after the village and then negotiating the many hairpin bends as the road descends into a wooded ravine. A further 20 minutes or so on foot will take you to the depths, where the waters of the Bourges hurtle over a precipice of volcanic basalt with impressive spray.

THE MÉZENC

Even if you have not scrambled to the summit of the Gerbier de Jonc, you must by now have had many views of the distinctive, table-topped **Mézenc**, which at 5751ft (1753m), is the highest peak in this area and the third highest in the Massif Central. **Les Estables** is actually sitting on the lower flanks of the mountain. The extremely well-stocked Tourist Office here (it has information on two departments and beyond, which is unusual in France) hands out simple maps of a circular route that includes the summit and will take about 3 hours. Otherwise the shortest climb is made from the Croix de Peccata (D631 from les Estables, then follow signs to the left) where there is plenty of space for car parking and a very obvious marked path heading gently upwards into the trees. It does get steeper, but is never too demanding – around 45 minutes should see even the most novice walker on the top.

The Mézenc in fact has two summits. To conserve energy, you could bypass the northern one, topped by a simple cross, and head directly for the southern summit, the higher by 13ft (4m), which has two of the most splendid orientation tables you are ever likely to meet. Each is a semi-circle of slate carved in relief, giving it a sort of 3-D effect and making it easy to distinguish the many distant ranges named. One of the tables looks to the Auvergne, the other to the Alps – where (as usual, on the clearest of days), it is just possible to see the pinnacle of Mont Blanc. And with all that distant splendour there is the equally impressive floral display at your feet. Local tourist offices offer a tempting (if rather costly) volume to aid with identification. A no-effort alternative to the mountain top is another *table d'orientation* on the D631 below the Croix de Boutières (car parking at the Croix). Although this one is not quite in the same league as those at the summit, it still offers a really magnificent alpine view.

NORTH OF THE MÉZENC

If, after all that climbing, you still want to go on, this is the time to explore the area to the north of the Mézenc. This particular region is very popular for Nordic skiing and the landscapes are wide and open. Through the village of Chaudeyrolles, surrounded by marshland, the road leads to the **Lac de St Front**, one of the volcanic crater lakes. On high and exposed ground, St Front often looks less than inviting, being whipped up by the wind that scours these high pastures and having no beach but rather open grassland surrounding it. Nevertheless a small area is marked out for swimming, and other watersports are possible in fine weather. Above the lake is the village of St **Front**, its solid granite buildings roofed by slabs of stone (*lauzes*). The 11th century Romanesque church, built of dark multi-coloured volcanic rock, is said to be the finest on the plateau with a *clocher à peigne* – literally a 'comb-steeple', a bell wall typical of this area.

North-west of St Front (via the pretty valley of the Aubepin) is **St Julien-Chapteuil**, one of the larger villages of the area. Its church in pale stone is enormous, a priory dating from the 11th century with obvious more recent additions – all surrounded by pathways of 'cinders'. Turning east from here on the busy D15, you soon reach the village of Boussoulet and beyond it, a little road that turns north and climbs into the forested **Massif du Meygal**. Cycling and walking routes cut through beautiful woodland and there is another sweeping view from the summit of the Grand Testavoyre, just a few minutes from roadside parking. Descending again to the D15, you are only a couple of minutes from the **Lac Bleu** – a small lake as azure as its name suggests. Beside it, a 'Discovery Park' (la Lauzière du Lac Bleu) displays tenth-scale miniatures of typical local buildings, faithfully recreated, with every stone cut by hand.

BESIDE THE INFANT LOIRE

Let us go right back to the Gerbier de Jonc now, and follow the Loire through its earliest stages. From the mountain, first head south down the D116 in the direction of **Ste Eulalie** with the Loire gathering strength at your side. About 2 miles (3km) down the road, after passing a stone cottage on your left, pull over and take a look

backwards – here the little tributaries are joining at your feet, while in the background the old scaly mountain looks down on the river to which it has given birth. It is a classic view. A little farther on, a first bridge crosses the Loire on your left. Ste Eulalie is just off the 'main' road but is pretty and worth a visit – just opposite its small Tourist Office is a typical Ardèchois farmhouse with roof of genêts (broom).

From Ste. Eulalie, the river continues south for a few kilometres until, coming face to face with the Suc de Bauzon, it turns tail and flows northeast. The little village on the bend is named Rieutord, meaning the river turns. The road follows all this faithfully, and then skirts the Lac de la Palisse, the curving lake produced by the first dam on the river. Beyond la Palisse, the road bends wildly to negotiate the valley of the Gage before running down to the shores of the picturesque **Lac d'Issarlès**.

Beyond the lake the road descends to a road junction in the valley. From here, the D16 heads west to Coucouron (another village with a popular watersports lake), but

Lac d'Issarlès

Issarlès is another crater lake, but what you see here will depend on the season. For much of the year, water is drawn off from the depths of Issarlès to feed a hydro-electric power station, and the lake may be less than full. In summer, levels are restored and Issarlès becomes the local sea-side – and a beautiful one at that.

The bright blue circle of water is backed by pine-woods and overlooked in the distance by the 'crouching lion' of the Mézenc. Colourful pedalos and canoes dot the water and from the wide sandy beach an area has been cordoned off for supervised swimming. A couple of hotels and a lake-side campsite offer accommodation and a handful of bars and restaurants provide the necessary fare for the visitors.

followers of the river will want to branch right almost immediately in the direction of the village of Issarlès. The road climbs and then follows the rim of the valley above the Loire itself. Reaching the D500, there is a wonderful drive past Salettes (note the bell-wall again) and along the gorge to Goudet – or you could turn left, cross the river and then follow the D54 to Arlempdes.

Goudet and Arlempdes are riverside villages that are both well-worth a visit, and being only a couple of kilometres apart, the average fish would have no difficulty getting between them. But the villages are on opposite sides of the river and this is wild country – for earth-bound mortals the distance is five or six times as great. But let us leave the villages for the moment. We have followed the Loire on its long loop south when in fact the shortest route to Goudet and Arlempdes from les Estables is via the D631 to the west – and that road passes through another village well worthy of attention, le **Monastier-sur-Gazeille.** (see feature box)

Out of town, le Monastier has another attraction – and if you arrived from les Estables, you will have passed right under it. The gracefully curving Recoumène Viaduct spans the valley of the Gazeille on eight arches, the tallest of them 217ft (66m) above the tiny river. The viaduct is the most spectacular of 12 on the Transcévenole railway, a route across the Cévennes that was designed by the engineer Paul Séjourné, who was considered to be something of a

Le Monastier and Robert Louis Stevenson

Le Monastier is a long village, strung out on a ridge above the valley of the Gazeille. Its main claim to fame could well be its Romanesque abbey church and associated buildings, or its museum-in-a-castle tucked away behind – all are beautifully built from what were clearly the colourful outpourings of a local volcano. Instead it is all down to a donkey.

In 1878 Robert Louis Stevenson came to le Monastier to retreat from an ill-fated love affair in more northern climes. Here it was that he paid extortionately for an obstinate animal he named Modestine and then set off south through the Cévennes – the result was his famous Travels with a Donkey. It took Stevenson 12 days to travel the 137 miles (220kms) to St Jean-du-Gard, and from the sound of it, it would have been quicker without the donkey.

Today the local tourist board has realised the potential of all this. The route is now well-waymarked and well-provided with accommodation while more and more farms are offering donkey-hire and one-way transport. The excellent and helpful Office de Tourisme in the main street has a section devoted entirely to the trail – and the cindery Musée Municipal has made over a room to everything it could find out about Stevenson, translated into English. The rest of the museum sports no translations, but its fees are modest, and it is worth visiting for its atmospheric room of archaeological exhibits alone.

genius in his field. But, economically speaking, the Transcévenole was built too late. By the time all those viaducts and tunnels were completed (1925) road transport had taken over, and the track itself was never laid. Now the section between Peyrard and Présailles makes an impressive walking and cycling route of 16 miles (26km) – and mad bungee-jumpers plunge from the heights of the Recoumène on summer weekends.

GOUDET, ARLEMPDES AND BEYOND

West of le Monastier, you can leave the D500 for the D49 and the village of St **Martin-de-Fougerès**, where the church has a *clocher à peigne* with four bells. The area around is particularly known for its green lentils (*Lentilles Verte du Puy*), and in July, fields of these can be seen shining blue in the distance. Blue? Well, the lentil plant does have tiny blue flowers, but it is the more florid *Bleuets des Champs* (Cornflowers), particularly flourishing in the lentil fields, that lend their colour.

Puy lentils

Green lentils have become increasingly popular in recent years, their virtues being sung by several eminent French chefs, and in 1996 they were accorded the distinction of an *appellation d'origine contrôlée* (AOC).

From St Martin the road makes a dramatic descent into **Goudet**, offering those who dare to look, fine views of the village below, the crumbling Château de Beaufort on the hill opposite and a curious lump of rock behind the village known as the Rocher du Pipet. With the road more horizontal again you can admire the brightly-patterned roof of the church tower, almost Burgundian in style. Goudet is a gem, a huddle of pink-roofed houses, their streets bisected by tributary streams hurrying to join the Loire. Houses and bridges are decked with flowers. The church beneath the shining roof stands on the site of a former abbey – and nearby, an old house serves as a base for Archéo-Logis, an organisation responsible for local excavations that offers visitors topical exhibitions of its finds. Tourism seems to have found little foothold in Goudet – despite a small hotel, two campsites and a donkey-friendly *ferme auberge* (Goudet is on the Stevenson Trail), there are no shops and the greatest attraction is the ruined hilltop château that has recently been taken over by a group of artisans.

From Goudet, **Arlempdes** is best reached via the D49 (west) and D54, a route not short of vistas. Arlempdes is one of the select *plus beaux villages* of France, yet like Goudet, it makes no concession to tourism. Its château was built by the Montlaur family a millennium ago. Today only a skeleton remains, and the château is most remarkable for its position, clinging to a bizarrely-shaped basalt outcrop high above the Loire. The most prominent feature is a little chapel of red volcanic rock. Guided tours of the château are offered in the summer months, while out of season you can have more fun conducting yourself around – the Hôtel du Manoir will give you the key. A fairly lengthy English text is on offer, but it is worth the entry fee just to enjoy the splendid views along the river valley. When you come down you can also admire the cobbled village street with its 11th century gateway, and the elaborate cross in front of the church.

If you have time or you can stay in this area, there is a lot more worth exploring. Just south of Arlempdes is the village of St Arcons with its shrine in a cave and beyond that the village of St Paul-de-Tartas (Romanesque church with *clocher à peigne* and viewpoint on Mont Tartas). A few minutes south again and you arrive at Pradelles – another esteemed *plus beaux village* but a very different proposition from Arlempdes. Just off the main road (the N 88), Pradelles welcomes plenty of visitors and seems almost a small town – although one of the conditions of a *plus beau village* is that it must have fewer than 2000 inhabitants. The Tourist Office in the main street offers a historic trail, including a 12th century convent, Penitents Chapel and old prison, but its most photographed buildings are definitely the arcaded edifices in the central Place de la Halle, where important commercial business was once transacted.

Today, Pradelles' biggest attraction is its 'living' museum of the Cheval-de-Trait (Draught Horse). For the purpose of entertaining visitors, different breeds of these spend the summer months living in the stables in the lower floor of the museum. Above them, all the carriages and harnesses that go with their job are exhibited – and then there is a model village, outdoor games, a children's farm and much more, all on a site with some splendid views.

Unusual form of transport

Beyond Pradelles (turn right where signed at the end of the village), you can see the same countryside from a different angle if you take to the Vélo-Rail, along the line of the former railway. A heavy iron platform pedalled by two, it offers fun for all the family – and some hard work when you meet one coming the other way (it needs to be lifted off the rails!).

West of Pradelles, the road soon meets the valley of the Allier and with it, a truly spectacular railway that threads its way through the rocky flanks of the valley in a series of alternating tunnels and viaducts. Day trips on this amazing rail are organised from Langogne (3.7 miles [6kms] south of Pradelles on the N 88) – the destination is almost 2 hours distant Langeac, and you can opt for a simple out-and-back or one with added extras at the other end. For just a sample of this railway, head north from Pradelles and then take the D88 to the west. The road soon follows beside the Allier to the village of le Nouveau Monde, built here in 1870 for the railway workers who were constructing the amazing quarter-of-a-circle Viaduct de Chapeauroux. Turning right for St Haon, the road climbs and you can stop, look back and wonder at such a feat of engineering. At the top of the slope the grey village of St Haon feels like the end of the world. Maybe it is, but it also has a fine old 12th century church with a Romanesque porch, polychrome chevet and one of the most splendid bell walls.

From St Haon the D31 heads north to very different terrain, the densely wooded **Monts du Devès** and, within them, the **Lac du Bouchet**. All this is the territory of the Nordic skiers again – their pistes double as walking routes in summer and are clearly marked through the forest. The Lac du Bouchet itself is a circle of water surrounded by pines. No streams feed the lake and none drain from it, yet the water is pure. There is an attractive tiny sandy beach for bathers and pedalo hire from the hotel on the opposite shore.

A discovery trail, the Sentier de Garou (3 mile [5km]) circumnavigates the lake and a 1.2 mile (2km) long Parcours de Santé (fitness trail) strikes off into the forest. There are other good walks starting from the wooden ski chalet at le Bouchet, but farther on in the forest (you can take your car via the D333 from Cayres) there is a pleasant trail up Mont Recours whose wide-viewed summit has been kitted out with two *tables d'orientation*.

POLIGNAC AND LE PUY

This has been a long diversion and it is time to return to the Loire. If you have been in the Monts du Devès it is worth pausing at **Cayres** (neo-gothic church with *clocher à peigne*) and then taking the D33 north-east and continuing to **Solignac**. Perched above the Loire, the village has some good views (and good walks) into the gorges below. From here the road scenically follows the river all the way into **Brives-Charensac**. This largish town suffered terrible flooding in 1980 and its riverside has since been rebuilt with pleasant gardens. Beside the main road bridge, two arches of

an ancient toll bridge still valiantly span the waters. Brives-Charensac is almost a suburb of le Puy-en-Velay, but the river bypasses le Puy – let us do the same for the moment and continue north of the town to the curious domain of the Polignacs.

The Polignac family have been land-owners in these parts since the Middle Ages and several of their members have risen to positions of national importance. Their first château was at the place now called **Polignac** (3 miles [5km] north of le Puy-en-Velay off the N102), and was perched on a huge block of volcanic basalt rising some 328ft (100m) above the plains below.

This strange place has an even stranger history. In Roman times it was the site of a Temple of Apollo – but his priests were rather worldly-wise! Those wishing to 'consult the oracle' were shown first to a room in the base of the rock where they spoke their requests out loud and presented gifts. A hidden tunnel in the rock carried their words to the priests in the temple above, where stood a huge stone mask of Apollo. By the time the visitor made it to the top of the hill, the priests were ready with their reply – which, with the aid of a megaphone, appeared to come directly from the mouth of Apollo.

Around a thousand years ago the Polignac family first came to this hill and built an impenetrable fortress where the Temple of Apollo once stood. From here they levied tolls on pilgrims en route to le Puy and thus fell foul of the bishops of that city. Over time their hilltop stronghold was altered and extended but today it is largely in ruins. The 14th century keep still stands – and houses an assortment of Roman relics including the mask of Apollo. From its summit there is a view of le Puy, the Mézenc and Meygal mountains and all the Velay.

The Polignacs forsook their bleakly-positioned residence some time in the 16th century and moved off downstream to a rather more sheltered site guarding the entrance to the gorges of the Loire. The **Château of Lavoûte-Polignac** (in the village of the same name, 6.2 miles [10km] north of le Puy) is all a medieval château should be, severe in aspect with thick walls and pepper-pot turrets, but is magnificently positioned beside the looping river. The elegance of the interior is in complete contrast to the façade – the Dukes of Polignac still live here and welcome visitors to their home.

Before leaving this part of France you must make one venture on to the beaten track again. In contrast to the surrounding countryside, **le Puy-en-Velay** is scarcely short of visitors. But it is quite unique – so just take a deep breath and go! Busy roads ring le Puy, but on the south side of the town is the Place du Breil and beside it, the Place Michelet, a huge parking area that is well signed. From here it takes just a couple of minutes to cross that busy road and find yourself immersed in cobbled back streets with a wealth of fascinating shops.

Heading away from the main road and turning left you are pretty sure to reach the Place du Martouret and beside it, the Place du Clouzal, where the Office de Tourisme has recently been sited. Here they will offer you a map of the town detailing two pedestrian circuits, two hours and three hours in length (English version available). Now taking a comprehensive tour of le Puy involves some pretty serious leg-work – there are 134 steps up to the cathedral alone, a further 262 up the Rocher Corneille, then

there is St Michel d'Aiguillhe (268 steps), let alone all the ups and downs in between. You may need to be selective. But the cathedral is on everyone's list, so from the Office de Tourisme, keep right and right again into the Rue Raphaël, where you will first meet le Puy's time-honoured industry of lace-making at the Centre d'Enseignement de la Dentelle au Fuseau (no.38-40-42). The centre offers demonstrations and courses by the hour, the day or the week – or even by correspondence.

Beyond the lace-making centre you soon reach the fountain at the foot of the famous Rue des Tables, a splendid cobbled hill lined by lace-makers plying their trade, completely dominated by the many-storied patterned façade of the Cathedral at its summit. Climbing up on a hot day, the dark interior of that building impresses with its instant coolness, but overall is less remarkable than the outside. Most notable is the lavishly dressed statue of the Black Virgin on the high altar (a copy of an original destroyed in the Revolution) and perhaps the huge fresco of St Michael in the gallery north of the chancel. On the other side stands a wooden statue of St James, not unusual in itself, but le Puy is the starting point of the most important of the Chemins de St Jacques, the medieval pilgrim routes to Santiago de Compostela in Spain where St James is said to be buried. The pilgrimage is again popular, and each morning at 7am the bishop blesses those setting out on the 1000-mile (1609km) trek at the feet of that statue.

Behind the chancel on the south side is the sacristy, where some of the cathedral's treasures are housed – and here too is kept the register signed by pilgrims leaving for Santiago. The other notable feature of the cathedral is the cloisters on the north side for which there is an entrance fee. Dating from the Romanesque period they have beautifully carved capitals and above them, a decorated cornice verging on the Islamic. Towering above all is the gleaming statue of Notre-Dame-de-France on the Rocher Corneille – she was created from the molten metal of 213 canons captured at Sebastopol. Further exertion will earn you a fine view of the town from the viewing platform at her feet, but the more intrepid can continue the ascent through the body of the statue to neck level.

After the cathedral, the other literal highlight of le Puy is the Chapelle de St Michel d'Aiguilhe, seemingly growing out of a pinnacle of rock in the north of the town. From the cathedral, the walk will take about 15 minutes – head down the steps (helpfully signed 'vers Compostelle'!) and at the top of the Rue des Tables turn right. Keep the same direction

(with a little wiggle or two) and you will see the curiosity right ahead. St Michel was built in the 10th century to celebrate Bishop Godescalc's return from Santiago (he was the very first pilgrim) and has clung to the rock ever since. After 268 short vertical paces you can admire the carvings and mosaics of its portal, its paintings, objects d'art and the rest more closely.

Le Puy has a lot more to offer – the Musée Crozatier with its history of lace-making, the many squares and houses of the old town, the Pannesac Tower, the Convent of St Claire – and, if you are up early in the morning, the trickle of pilgrims of different nationalities, each bearing his scallop shell, setting out on the journey of a lifetime to Santiago de Compostela. Just outside the town, the river, too, departs on a long journey. From le Puy, it is almost 1000km to its mouth at St Nazaire on the west coast. You cannot help wanting to follow it...

Offices de Tourisme

Les Estables
Le Bourg
43150 LES ESTABLES
☎ 04.71.08.31.08

Le Monastier-sur-Gazeille
32, Rue St Pierre
43150 LE-MONASTIER-SUR-GAZEILLE
☎ 04.71.08.37.76

Pradelles
Avenue du Puy
43420 PRADELLES
☎ 04.71.00.82.65

Le Puy-en-Velay
Place du Clauzel
43000 LE PUY-EN-VELAY
☎ 04.71.09.38.41

Places of Interest

Ferme Bourlatier
Open May, June, September 11am-
6pm, July and August 10am-7pm.

Champclause

La Lauzière du Lac Bleu
Open July and August 10am-7pm
(other times only by appointment).

Le Monastier-sur-Gazeille

Musée Municipal
Open June, October 2.30-5pm;
September 10.30am -12 noon,
2.30-5pm; July, August 10.30am-
12noon, 2-6pm. Closed Mondays.

Goudet

Archéo-Logis
Open July to September, daily,
11am-7pm.

Château de Beaufort
Open mid-July to end-August
10am-7pm.

Arlempdes

Château d'Arlempdes
Open March to October 9am-6pm.
Guided tours in July and August.

Pradelles

Musée Vivant du Cheval de Trait
Open April, May, June, Sept 2-6pm
(closed Mondays and weekends);
July and August 10am-7pm.

Vélo-Rail
Open April to June, September,
October 1-6pm; July and August
9am-7.30 pm – but as there are at
present only 11 'bikes', secure
reservation first –
☎ 04.71.00.87.46

Langogne

**Le Train Touristique des
Gorges de l'Allier**
Departs Langogne 11.15am daily.
Return by one of the regular service
trains in afternoon (and the trip can
be made in reverse). Reservations
from OT Langogne, ☎ 04.66.69.20.23

Polignac

Forteresse de Polignac
Open April to June, September to
mid-November 10am-6pm; July
and August 9am-7pm.

Château de Lavoûte-Polignac
Guided tours in afternoons June to
September, mornings also in July
and August.

Le Puy-en-Velay

**Centre d'Enseignement de la
Dentelle au Fuseau**
(lace-making centre)
Open July and August, Tuesday to
Friday 10am-12noon, 2-5pm;
Saturday 9.30am-4.30pm.

Cathedral cloisters
Open 9am-5pm daily (later in
summer) with 2 hour lunchbreak
outside July and August.

**Rocher Corneille and Statue of
Notre-Dame de France**
Open October-mid-March 10am-
5pm; mid-March-April 9am-6pm;
May, June, Sept. 9am-7pm; July
and August 9am-7.30pm.

Rock and Chapel of St Michel d'Aiguilhe
Open May-September 9am-6.30pm; Mid-March to April and Oct to mid-Nov 9.30am-12noon, 2-5.30pm; Feb. to mid-March 2-5pm.

Musée Crozatier
Open May to Sept. 10am-12noon, 2-6pm, closed Tuesdays; October to April 10am-12noon, 2-4pm, closed Tuesdays and Sunday mornings.

Distillery of Verveine du Velay (at Blavozy)
Guided tours and shop open Tuesday to Saturday 10am-12noon, 1.30-6.30pm throughout the year except January and February. Sunday and Monday opening also in July and August.

LOCAL HIGHLIGHTS

Best Walks

- Walks around the Gerbier de Jonc – the easy 2 mile (3km) route around the sources, and the much more demanding 8 mile (12km) Sentier de Découverte taking you into the valley below. Get routes from OT Les Estables.

- The fairly easy path up the Mézenc for those stunning views – no need for a map.

- Walks in the Monts du Devès – the Tour du Lac around the shores of the Lac du Bouchet is a mere 2 miles (3km), but you could upgrade to the Sentier de Garou or Mont Recours. Leaflet from Office National des Forêts or OT le Puy.

- The circuit of the Lac d'Issarlès is 3 miles (5km), but seven other routes are signed from the lakeside. Try OT Les Estables for routes, or OT Langogne.

- The Chemin de Stevenson – and you do not really need the donkey. The 137 mile (220km) trail from le Monastier-sur-Gazeille to St Jean-du-Gard can be covered in about eight days. A topoguide covers the route and OT at le Monastier can provide an up-to-date list of overnight accommodation.

For cyclists

- In the Monts des Devès there are two fairly severe (*sportif*) VTT courses and an easier 15.5 mile (25km) route. Ask at OT for the leaflet produced by the Office National des Forêts. Several other routes are also waymarked.

- The Transcévenole is perfect for family cycling – but you need a head for heights from time to time.

- VTT routes from 6 to35 miles (10 to 56km) in length in the region of the Mézenc are obtainable from OT at Les Estables.

Watersports

- The Lac d'Issarlès and the Lac du Bouchet are volcanic lakes offering good facilities for bathing – both have sandy beaches and summertime supervision. Pedalos are for hire at both and the Lac d'Issarlès also has canoes.

- The Lac de Coucouron (just west of the village) is an artificial *plan d'eau* with supervised swimming, pedalo hire and a snack bar on site.

- Brives-Charensac has a canoeing base on the Loire (beside the campsite).

For the palate

- Lentilles Vertes du Puy – they actually are tasty.

- *Fin Gras* du Mézenc. Meat from cattle fattened over winter on hay from the Mézenc pastures takes on a particular slightly herby flavour and is 'delicately infiltrated' with fat. Considered a great delicacy!

- Verveine du Velay – a herby liqueur containing *verveine* (verbena), cultivated on the hills of the Velay. Verveine du Velay comes in green, yellow and red varieties – all is explained at the distillery 3 miles (5km) east of le Puy (see Places of Interest).

And the most memorable

- Just about everything to do with the Mézenc – the gigantic view from the orientation tables and most especially the brilliant springtime carpet of purple mountain pansies.

- Seeing the huge form of a Circaëte Jean Leblanc rear up beside us and his massive shadow cross the road – must be terrifying if you are a mouse!

- Reading the names of so many pilgrims in the Sacristy at le Puy-en-Velay. Twenty-one had left for Santiago de Compostela on the last day we were there.

- The Bishop's early morning blessing in the cathedral at le Puy, where more than 50 pilgrims from all over the world carried rucksacks and scallop-shells. In September 2005, we, too, set out for Santiago de Compostela.

18. Heights and depths in the Diois

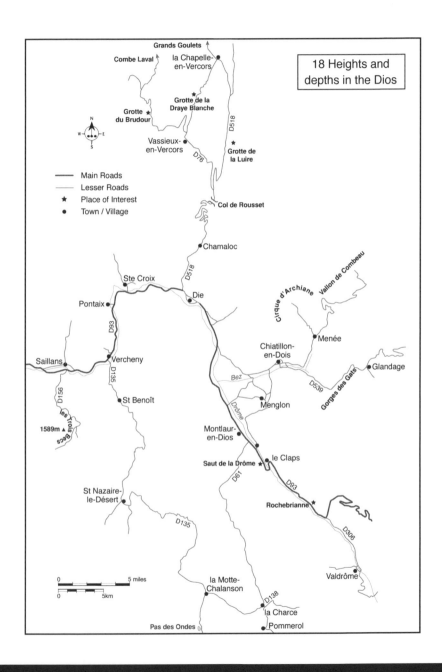

You may well be thinking where on earth is the Diois (pronounced dee-wa)? The answer to that is it is simply the area around the town of Die. And if that gets you no nearer, Die is on the River Drôme, in the *département* of the same name, immediately to the north of Provence. The latter probably explains why not so many people stop here – anyone coming this far south is going on to the Côte d'Azur or at least to the Luberon. But the Drôme valley is lovely, full of lavender, sunflowers, vineyards and walnut trees, a sort of Provence without the people, and with an added hint of alpine flavour from the north. The landscape has its drama too. Behind Die rises the sheer face of the Glandasse, the rocky edge of the Vercors plateau that magically turns from white to pink as the sun sets, and becomes grey and veil-like as night falls. And farther up the valley there is the Claps, a pile of gigantic boulders brought down when a mountain 'collapsed' some 700 years ago.

Die is naturally the centre of the area, a medieval town on a Roman site, with a lively twice-weekly market. Its particular claim to fame is its unique wine, Clairette de Die, as light and sparkling as its name would suggest. Die's backdrop may be the rather stark Glandasse, but the hills on the opposite side of the river are far less severe and the easily-climbed Croix de St Justin affords some excellent views over the town and up the valley.

Within easy reach of Die there is plenty to explore – the pretty villages of Luc-en-Diois and Châtillon-en-Diois, the impressive rocky Cirque d'Archiane, the Saut de la Drôme waterfall and the isolated abbey at Valcroissant for a start. If you do not mind travelling farther, an hour's drive will take you on to the green alpine plateau of the Vercors, marvellous for hiking, biking and just enjoying the outdoors, but also home of wartime France's most courageous Resistance heroes. The Vercors can never forget the events of the summer of 1944 and no-one could fail to be moved by the museum and memorial at Vassieux.

A similar distance to the south of Die is the region known as the Drôme Provençal, famed for all that Provence is famed for with a few added extras like limes and herbal tea. And back again to the Drôme valley – should you be here in the height of summer, the bonus is that the river itself becomes a perfect family playground, shallow enough for safe canoeing and with many bathing places along its course. It is not exactly 'undiscovered' at this time, of course, but for some reason British visitors are few and far between.

The obvious choice for a base in this area must be Die, but there are also a few hotels in Châtillon and Luc-en-Diois. Campers have it made here – the village of Menglon surprisingly boasts a top-of-the-range site, but there are many others of excellent quality all along the riverbank, each of them with its own stony beach with potential for swimming.

DIE

Since **Die** is indisputably the capital of the Diois, that would seem to be the best starting point. The centre of Die is no place for a car (it is a maze of narrow one-way streets) so you will need to head for one of the parking places signed off the peripheral main road. The largest of these, the Aire de Mayrosse, on the south-east side of the town, is also the site of the new Office de Tourisme – and from there you can get a leaflet (English version) describing a pretty all-inclusive town trail.

Essentially, Die's history goes back a long way. In Gallo-Roman times it was the capital of a people known as the Voconces, and when the Romans withdrew, the remaining residents built the thick ramparts to defend against the new wave of invaders. The first glimpse of Roman Die is just along the road from the Tourist Office – turn right facing the building, pass under the viaduct and look to the left. The old grey archway is the Porte Saint Marcel, dating from the 3rd century AD – on the town side, the keystone is the head of a bull. Ramparts stretch from here around the east side of the town, but leave them for the moment and walk uphill through the arch, turning left on the Rue de l'Armellerie. At its end, the Place de la République is dominated by the pale grey-stoned cathedral, topped by a wrought iron campanile. Its doorway belongs to the original 12th century building that was destroyed in the Revolution. Inside, take a look at the carved woodwork, especially the walnut pulpit.

On the south side of the cathedral doorway two roads head downhill and both arrive at the Place de l'Hôtel de Ville. On the lower side of the square is the former Bishop's Palace, not much to look at in itself, but within is the remarkable St Nicholas Chapel. Its floor is a beautiful 12th century mosaic representing the universe – a central Pole Star, the four rivers of earthly paradise and some added bulls' heads. The walls are hung with hand-painted wallpapers almost 300 years old. Unfortunately the chapel is a well-kept secret, and only two guided visits a week are on offer – in French. At other times you have to content yourself with the information panel outside.

Returning to the cathedral, you could now turn left into the Rue Émile Laurens, which eventually meets the main thoroughfare, the Rue Camille Buffardel. Just to the right at this point is the little archaeological museum, looking almost like a shop front. Its most important exhibits are Gallo-Roman artefacts, including altars on which bulls were sacrificed to the goddess Cybele (hence the prevalence of bulls in the town), but there are also Romanesque sculptures from the cathedral.

Just behind you, at the west end of the main street, a road on the right leads up to the ramparts. They can be followed (with some initial uphill effort) right back to the Office de Tourisme on the other side of town. On they way there are information panels pointing out where various bits of discarded Roman sculpture found their way into the walls, and where the old Roman aqueduct once ran.

Die's latter day importance rests on its wines – the first of these is the absolutely unique Clairette-de-Die and the second a Crémant, which is also produced in seven or eight other areas in France. The place to find out about them is the well-advertised Jaillance, whose *caves* are on the main road just west of the town centre. The tour at Jaillance takes you into the bowels of the earth where, to a background of operatic music, changing lights and flowing water, you learn that the precious Clairette is first cooled (the Romans dangled it in the river), thus retarding fermentation and producing a sweet sparkling wine of lowish alcohol content – or perhaps you may not learn, as the *son et lumière* is in French only, but there is always someone ready to translate afterwards. At the end of all the explanations and a tour of the stores, *dégustation* is offered, and on a hot day these cool wines are like nectar.

Grapes and wines

Clairette is produced from a blend of two grapes, the Clairette and the Muscat, while Crémant comes from the Clairette grape alone and is the result of double fermentation, tasting (to the uninitiated) just like champagne.

DOWN RIVER TO THE WEST OF DIE

To pursue the story of the wines, Vercheny on the D93 to the west of Die has an interesting vineyard trail – and if you are heading that way, there are a few other places worth exploring at the same time. The road west of Die follows closely beside the river and in summertime there is likely to be plenty of watery activity all the way.

The first place worth a pause is **Ste Croix**, just off the main road 5 miles (8km) from Die, where there is a monastery and botanical garden. Incredibly narrow streets lead up through the village to the peaceful hilltop setting (note the width restrictions, and maybe leave your car at the bottom). The monastery is currently in use for residential courses and offers only an exhibition from time to time, but there is free access to the 'botanical garden' – a long path winding downhill through very mixed woodland. The trees are given botanical names as well as French and you appreciate the different climatic influences here with familiar trees like hawthorn and sycamore standing side by side with umbrella pines, juniper and olive. Back beside the monastery there is a garden of herbs and medicinal plants.

Returning to the main road again, it is just a couple of kilometres farther to **Pontaix**, a beautiful riverside village of ancient houses in blended shades of grey overlooked by a 12th century keep. Narrow streets make parking almost impossible, but do not miss just a quick glance into the Protestant Temple, parts of which overhang the river (it is just to the left over the bridge). The frescos date from the 15th century and you are proudly shown a tiny fleur-de-lys, said to have been painted here by Louis XIV.

Farther down the valley, **Vercheny** declares its importance in the production of Clairette and Crémant with many roadside *caves* that can be visited. Carod Frères include a free visit to their Musée de Clairette, again explaining the unusual technique of its production. The *Sentier Viticole* (Vineyard Trail) is actually in Vercheny-le-Haut – turn north off the N93 and after passing through the village of Peyrache, park on the verge near the war memorial. From here the signed path takes you off into the vineyards where both Clairette and Muscat grapes are grown and a series of information panels describes the annual round of the *viticulteur*. Sadly this is 'French only' but the setting is superb, high on the flanks of the valley with the gaunt peaks of the Trois Becs dominating from the south-west – you could go for that alone. The more fluent can entertain themselves with proffered questions as demanding of mathematics as of French.

Having come this far down the Drôme you may as well go a little farther to **Saillans**. Its Office de Tourisme offers a 'town trail' with no fewer than 30 points of interest. The most important of these are a couple of Roman milestones, one in front of the Office itself, the other inside the town hall (which may or may not be open). After that you can just wander through the old streets to the riverside and watch the canoes, or maybe call in at the silkworm farm (west end of the village) where, with English headphone translation, you can meet the creatures themselves, hear about their life-cycles, and admire their shining cocoons. From Saillans you could drive up the D156 on the opposite side of the Drôme for a closer look at the **Trois Becs** range, the highest peak of which is a grand 5213ft (1589m). Hiking here is for the experienced, the main trail being the GR9, which does at least avoid the summits. Less daring adventurers can book accompanied excursions at the Office de Tourisme in Saillans and opt to trail chamois, watch the sun rise, or roam the mountains by night.

INTO THE MOUNTAINS

Back in Die again now, and having seen something of the river valley, it is time to make a few forays into the mountains. Just east of Die, the ancient **Abbey of Valcroissant** crouches in a verdant corner below the rocks of the Glandasse. Beside the abbey a footpath leads into the Vercors nature reserve – an information panel details the wildlife that thrives beyond and it all looks inviting.

The Abbey of Valcroissant

The abbey itself is a Cistercian establishment dating from 1188. Today it is a working farm and residential centre. Informal tours of the abbey are given every afternoon – they are in French only, but since most visitors are Dutch or Belgian, impromptu translations are welcomed. There are many interesting archaeological features, but what sticks in the memory is the sight of cows stabled under hallowed vaulted ceilings and hay stored in lofts where choirs once sang.

Farther to the east, one of the finest sights on the Glandasse is the **Cirque d'Archiane**, a high semi-circle of white rock closing off the valley of the Archiane stream. From Die it is reached via the D539 and **Châtillon-en-Diois**, the loveliest village in all this area, and more than worth a diversion from the main road that bypasses it all. Châtillon's ancient buildings cling to a slope beneath the scant remains of a 13th century château. Its flower-bedecked streets converge on a central bell-tower and fountain and the village claims to have '150 climbing plants'. That seems a conservative estimate when you explore the network of winding alleyways (known here as *viols*) where vegetation springs from every pot and crevice, thus creating an abundance of photogenic scenes. To make sure you see it all, the Tourist Office on the main road offers a village plan. Latter-day Châtillon flourishes along the riverside with attractive swimming pools, playground and campsite.

Beyond Châtillon you can soon leave the pleasant valley of the River Bez with its orchards and vineyards to follow the wilder narrow valley of the Archiane into the Cirque. The impressive curve of white limestone ahead is interrupted by a central promontory known as the Jardin du Roi. The story goes that the Dauphin Louis XI once gave this land to a shepherd, who had helped him out of trouble when he was out hunting here. The narrow road ends at the village of Archiane, tucked beneath the rock, where a farm and the Refuge d'Archiane both offer refreshment. The latter also puts on a *son et lumière* relating to the Vercors Nature Reserve on certain summer evenings.

Beyond the village you must continue on foot. A steep rocky path climbs to two waterfalls – or you can follow the more ambitious circuit by the name of *Les Carnets d'Archiane* that skirts the foot of the rockface itself. Good (French) information panels are provided for this one, but just do not believe the time estimates offered (maybe multiply by two). Nevertheless this is a lovely path with an abundance of wild flowers and butterflies; you get a good view of the rocks (which appear striped with deposits of coral and algae at close quarters), a good chance of spotting some of the ibex that were introduced to Archiane in 1989 – and maybe even a glimpse of the resident pair of golden eagles. Do not forget the binoculars!

Returning from Archiane, a left turn in the village of Menée could take you up the **Vallon de Combeau**, which is particularly known for its wild flower display. But this excursion into the wilderness really deserves a whole day to itself. Instead, you could perhaps end the day by turning left before Châtillon and following the D539

through the **Gorges des Gats** as far as Glandage. Spectacular but not oppressive, there are picnic spots in these slit-like gorges and even a bathing place on the river. But high-topped vehicles beware – there are many rocky overhangs and tunnels. It is passable, but not comfortable. Finally, west of Châtillon again, it is worth noting the bathing place and leisure centre known as the Lac Bleu, just off the road to Menglon. It may be a bit late in the day if you have done all that mountaineering, but you can always return.

Up the valley of the Drôme

Time now to take another excursion up the valley of the Drôme south of Die. Beyond the turning to Châtillon it is surprisingly open, with fields of cereal crops and sunflowers, often bordered by walnut trees. After the village of Montlaur, the D61 turns off to la Motte Chalanson. Reserve that one for another day and continue on the main road to **Luc-en-Diois**, a pleasant little town with some interesting back streets. The local favourite walk to the summit of La Cabanette (2395ft [730m]) has been transformed into a 'Witches Pathway', a sort of treasure hunt game for families – but sadly vandals have been at work. It still makes a good walk though (and maybe the witches will be reinstated) – OT has the route.

Just south of Luc-en-Diois, the impressive boulders of **le Claps** squeeze the main road to a narrow cutting. These assorted giants apparently split off from the Pic-de-Luc mountain quite spontaneously in 1442 – you just hope it cannot happen again. As the road bends right there is a parking area beside a deep blue pool in the river. On the bank opposite, picnic tables are sited under the trees and the sandy beach offers swimming in this most bizarre of locations. A few hundred metres farther on, the road again winds through boulders and beneath it the Drôme leaps into its own mini blue pool (the **Saut de la Drôme**).

From the Claps it is possible to pursue the Drôme all the way to Valdrôme, a ski-station village high in the mountains. On the way (about 6 miles [9 km] from the Claps) you will pass the hilltop ruined Château of Rochebrianne where you could pause to take in a *Sentier de Découverte*. One arm of this goes up to the ruins, the other is devoted to the Marais de Bouligons, a marsh at the foot of the mountains. To be honest, there is not a lot of information on this discovery trail, it is more an opportunity to take a walk – and do not think a marsh walk is flat! **Valdrôme** itself is an outdoor enthusiast's paradise, with walking routes, VTT circuits, orienteering course, fitness trail, discovery trail and the rest. Once again, this one merits a day of its own.

THE VERCORS

Staying in Die and looking at the sheer edge of the Glandasse every day, it does not take long before you are wondering what other world lies beyond it. The answer is, of course, the Vercors – a high limestone plateau cut through by several deep gorges, but in this undeveloped southern part, an expanse of scrubby grassland backed by dense forest.

The road from Die into the Vercors at first climbs gently, passing the pretty village of Chamaloc and its lavender fields. Further on the wild convolu-

tions begin as the road ascends the rocky cliff and the 'other world' effect is enhanced by the tunnel at the summit. Emerging from this you are in the ski station of the **Col de Rousset**, whose the most interesting feature is the chairlift surrounded by ranks of colourful broad-wheeled 'scooters' (*trottinherbes*) used for the local summer sport of Glisse d'Été. With or without the scooter, the chairlift transports you to the nearby summit where a whole family of orientation tables defines every point on the spectacular horizon. Tracks lead off across the alpine pastures at your feet and hollow cow bells ring in the distance. But if the sight of all that empty space has made you keen to walk round here, beware – the two local circuits offered by the Tourist Office at the Col de Rousset are both rated 'difficult' (which you may think an understatement).

Heading north from the Col de Rousset, keep left for **Vassieux-en-Vercors**. The road leaves the forest and crosses a wide belt of sparse grazing land before reaching the village. The German troops landed on this plateau one terrible day in July 1944 and pieces of their gliders have been left in memory. From here they set out to annihilate Vassieux and its people – today the buildings of the village are all new.

At the centre is the Musée de la Résistance, a collection of memorabilia, documents and personal accounts of the tragic events in the Vercors, all assembled by a Vercors Maquisard by the name of Joseph la Picirella. Among the photographs displayed are some of the most shocking you will ever see. The museum extends over two floors, is free of charge and all the more moving for its simplicity – allow plenty of time to work out the French texts. Outside the museum there is another glider skeleton and a memorial graveyard with tombstones of glass. The rebuilt church nearby has a light interior with colourful stained-glass windows. The names of the 74 Civilians of Vassieux who lost their lives are engraved near the door, and again on a memorial in front of the town hall.

Vassieux is a village that must always live with the past, but it does have another side. Situated on the walking and cycling route known as the *Grande Traversée du Vercors*, it offers good opportunities for both activities. And just out of the village to the south (on the D 615) is a different and very lively museum, devoted to the region's much more distant past. The Musée de la Préhistoire du Vercors is located on the site of a flint-cutting workshop, operational some 4,500 years ago. Prehistoric cutting techniques are demonstrated in the visit, and you can also learn how to start a fire with sticks or cook a Neolithic pancake.

Back again to Vassieux, and its third museum (north on the D198, turn left at the National Cemetery of the Resistance) is again devoted to the Resistance. The Memorial of the Resistance is as sombre in content as the Museum, but a much more state-of-the-art-affair, a modern building following the contours of the hillside above Vassieux. This time the dreadful story can be heard in English with the aid of headphones. Beyond a dark room describing the death of a child you escape into the light and a fine view over the lovely valley where it all happened.

Vassieux was of course not the only place on the Vercors to suffer in the

The Vercors and the Résistance

The limestone Vercors plateau is a natural fortress, a high table of land ringed by peaks from which sheer cliffs fall to the valleys below. As such it became a natural focus for Resistance groups, who were established in the Vercors as early as 1942. A 'Plan Montagnards' was conceived in which, at the moment the allies should effect a landing on the south coast, airborne troops would be landed in the Vercors to attack from the rear. The plan was approved by de Gaulle and the allies, and an airfield was built in readiness. But somehow the plan was lost in the bureaucratic corridors of London.

With the Normandy landings on 6 June 1944, Resistance members began to pour into the Vercors, very quickly numbering around 4,000. On the 3 July the Vercors proclaimed itself to be a free republic and flew the Tricolor. The Nazis could ignore this no longer and a series of savage attacks began. The people of the Vercors appealed to the allies for help and on the 21 July gliders were seen landing on the airfield. Briefly it seemed that their pleas had been answered. It was very soon realised that the gliders were those of the enemy, and on that day 15,000 troops including an SS division poured into the Vercors. In a week of brutality more than 600 Resistance members and 200 civilians lost their lives and more were deported. The Vercors was in ruins.

summer of 1944. Other villages (notably St Nizier-du-Moucherotte, Malleval and la Chapelle-en-Vercors) were set on fire and all over the plateau there were scenes of confrontation, bravery and brutality. At present, 10 main sites are identified with a memorial, while others have a more simple marking – in fields, forests or on roadsides in the Vercors you may come across a humble yew tree bearing a plaque.

Leaving the Memorial you have a choice – return to the valley and continue to la Chapelle-en-Vercors or continue on the D76 into the forest and the mountains. After a long wiggly 6 miles (10km) or so on the latter you reach the Grotte du Brudour with its underground watercourse and as far again and a bit more brings you into the breathtaking gorges of the Combe Laval, on nearly the most terrifying road in the Vercors (see below!). But it all takes time. If instead you prefer to continue to La Chapelle-en-Vercors, the road heads north through rather gentler scenery. After a few kilometres you pass the **Grotte de la Draye Blanche** – a cave with some interesting stalactite formations in the vicinity of which fragments of animal bone and other remains dating from 45,000 years ago have been found. The visit has been made more family-friendly with the addition of a small animal park alongside.

La Chapelle-en-Vercors is another rebuilt village, again a centre for outdoor activities in the surrounding mountains. The central Office de Tourisme offers a good selection of walking and cycling routes. Nazi reprisals in this village consisted of taking 16 young men as hostage, and shooting them as the place was set on fire. Their memorial is the farmyard where it took place (in the main street) and beside it a darkened barn where you are asked to meditate for a moment.

North of La Chapelle-en-Vercors the road continues into the **Grands Goulets**, a succession of tunnels cut into the sheer cliffs of the deep gorge of the Vernaison – complementing these with some dramatic overhangs, this route must take the prize for the Vercors most spine-chilling ride. Note that this is no place for high vehicles! But if you do manage to negotiate the Goulets you arrive eventually at Pont-en-Royans (11 miles [18km] from la Chapelle, but allow an hour), where the Parc Naturel Regional du Vercors has a headquarters with lots more information.

At this point you are a very long way from Die and it is time to return – you can easily see that the Vercors merits more than a day of anyone's time. So let us now pick up the D518 heading south from La Chapelle-en-Vercors towards the Col de Rousset. After St Agnan-en-Vercors the road passes the **Grotte de la Luire** on the left hand side. If you stop here, take heed of the notices – this cave is seriously cold. Start by putting on all the warm clothes you have with you and then do not spurn the blankets offered at the entrance. The cave is of both geological and historical interest, and the guided tour is conducted in French only but you are given an English translation.

In July 1944 the entrance chamber to this cave was briefly used as a field hospital for those wounded in the assault on the Vercors. The German troops subsequently executed both patients and staff and the walls bear memorial plaques. The cave itself is of enormous depth. Exploration so far has achieved 1476ft (450m) downwards and 19 miles (30km) inwards, and somewhere way down there flows the River Vernaison, which can reveal itself dramatically after heavy rainfall. The visit ends looking down into the great abyss – and you cannot wait to get out into the warm sunshine again.

SOUTH TOWARDS PROVENCE

The Col de Rousset marks the boundary between northern and southern vegetation, and to the south of Die the landscapes soon have a lot in common with Provence. A final outing could be to the Provençal market at la Motte-Chalancon or the attractive bathing lake at the Pas des Ondes, at the southern limit of the territory considered to be the Diois. Taking again the valley road to Luc-en-Diois, a right turn on the D61 soon has you up in the mountains where Provençal vegetation clothes the slopes. Jonchères with its pink-tiled roofs is an attractive perched village and down in the valley again, tiny Bellegarde-en-Diois is pretty in a different way.

At la Charce you reach the valley of the Oule and one of its tributaries has cut some very dramatic gorges. Turning left to **Pommerol**, you are soon dwarfed by towering walls with fantastic shapes and pillars created by erosion. The road is narrow but has passing places – any traffic you meet is likely to be coming from an improbably but very beautifully sited campsite at the end of the gorge. At Pommerol, it is as well to retrace your steps (the going gets even harder from here) to **la Charce**, where you could take a couple of minutes to admire the two-towered Renaissance château on the corner before turning back on the D61. Take note of the many lime trees lining the road – from here south to Buis-les-Baronnies, this is the land

of lime-tea.

A few minutes farther along the road, **la Motte Chalancon** is a medieval village with narrow cobbled streets (here called *calades*) climbing to two ancient towers at their summit. There is a 12th century church and an abundance of *fontaines* and *lavoirs*. The Monday market here is very popular and very Provençal – bright patterned cottons, olives and spices, a feast for the senses. A waymarked footpath along the left bank of the Oule links La Motte Chalancon with the **Plan d'Eau du Pas des Ondes** – if you take it, you have a chance of spotting one of the beavers that frequent these clean waters.

Otherwise continue on the D61 for a further 1.5 miles (2.5km), from where you have a fine view of the turquoise waters of the Plan d'Eau overlooked by the hilltop ruins of the Château de Cornillon. This is the limit of the Diois, 31 miles (50km) south of its capital, and a very pleasant spot for a family outing, with safe swimming and refreshment facilities alongside. For the brave, there is indeed an alternative route back to Die. The D135, narrow and tortuous, was constructed at the end of the 19th century over a period of 40 years. From la Motte-Chalanson it climbs to its summit at the Col des Roustans (3379ft [1030m]) and descends between high peaks into the valley of the Roanne at the remote village of St Nazaire-le-Désert (*Désert* signifies a place that was once a hermitage or retreat). Much farther downstream you can admire the 'perched village' of St Benoît-en-Diois as you return to Vercheny and the main D93 again. This is not a route to choose if you are in a hurry – but it will complete your exploration of this most unusual area.

Offices de Tourisme

Die
Rue des Jardins
26150 DIE
☎ 04.75.22.03.03

La Chapelle-en-Vercors
Place Pietri BP 5
26420 LA CHAPELLE-EN-VERCORS
☎ 04.75.48.22.54

Saillans
Montée de la Soubeyranne
26340 SAILLANS
☎ 04.75.21.51.05

Places of Interest

Die

Musée d'histoire et d'archéologie de Die
Open July, August 3.30-6.30pm every day except Sunday; May, June and September Thursday and Saturday only 3.30-6.30pm.

La Cave de Die Jaillance
Easter to 1st Nov., tours at 10.15, 11.15 am, 2.15, 3.15, 4.15 and 5.15 pm every day.
Winter tours at 11am, 2.15, 3.15 and 4.15 pm every day.

Ste.-Croix

Jardin-Botanique de Ste Croix
Free admission all year round.

Vercheny

Carod Frères
Musée de la Clairette
Said to be open every day, but no times stated.

Saillans

La Magnanerie de Saillans (Silkworm Farm)
Guided visits May to September 10am – 6.15pm.

Abbaye de Valcroissant
Guided visits at 5pm. May – Fridays; June and September – Wednesdays; July and August – Mondays, Wednesdays, Thursdays and Fridays.

Archiane

Son et Lumière
Wednesdays and Fridays at 6pm, mid-June to mid-September.

Vassieux-en-Vercors

Musée de la Résistance
Open every day from April to September 10am-12noon, 2-6pm.

Musée de la Préhistoire du Vercors
Open July, August every day 10am-6pm; April to September every day 10am-12.30pm, 2-6pm; October to March weekends 10am-12.30pm, 2-5pm. Different prehistoric skills may be demonstrated on different days. For more information and reservation, ☎ 04.75.48.27.81

Mémorial de la Résistance
Open April to September every
day 10am-6pm; October to
December every day and January to
March every day except Mondays
and Tuesdays 10am-5pm.

Grotte de la Draye Blanche
Open July and August 9am-
6.30pm; May, June and September
9.30am-6pm; April and October
10am-5pm; rest of year school
holidays only 10am-4pm. Guided
visits every hour.

Grotte de la Luire
Open from April to October,
9.30am-6.30pm (5.30pm April and
October) with lunchbreak taken
outside July and August.

Plan d'Eau du Pas des Ondes
Supervised bathing in July and
August, 11am-7pm.

LOCAL HIGHLIGHTS

Best Walks

- Routes around Die. Ask OT for the English version of the folder 10 *Randonnées pour tout la Famille* (ignore the title, these walks would do credit to the average British rambling group). Among the descriptions is that of the climb to the Croix de St Justin from Die – a 5.5 mile (9km) circular route with an ascent of 2133ft (650m), well worthwhile for the view. Anyone needing to upgrade after that can move on to *10 Randonnées en montagne autour de Die.*

- The Carnets d'Archiane trail at the Cirque. Whatever the signs on the route say, expect to take about 3 hours unless you are particularly fit. The route is included in the folder *Autour de Châtillon-en-Diois*, but you will not have any difficulty following it without. A good path, but some steep descents near the end.

- Routes on the Vercors plateau. A series of leaflets in French (*18 itineraires commentés en Vercors drômois*) is fortunately accompanied by a really good map. No waymarking, but signposts at all path junctions. Difficulty levels are indicated (*Cotation*).

For cyclists

- The key to all cycle routes in the area is the IGN map *La Drôme a Vélo* in the *Plein Air* series.

- VTT enthusiasts have plenty of scope here. Valdrôme is the Mecca, but Die and Saillans are well-supplied with marked circuits – ask at OT.

- A 81 mile (130km) marked cycle route follows the Drôme all the way from its source to its confluence with the Rhône. The drawback is that the route includes three sections (Valdrôme – Luc-en-Diois, Ste. Croix – Pontaix, Pont d'Espenel – Canal de Saillans) on the busy and not too wide D93.

Watersports

· Swimming without supervision is possible in the Gorges des Gats, at the Claps de Luc and at various other riverside sites (many of which are attached to campsites). Bathing is supervised at the Lac Bleu near Châtillon-en-Diois and the Plan d'Eau du Pas des Ondes.

· Die, Pontaix, Vercheny and Saillans are main starting points for canoe-kayak excursions on the Drôme – but there are many other places and many organisations. Ask any OT for details.

For the Palate

· Obviously the Clairette and Crémant wines. They should both be served cool and are perfect for a hot day.

· Guinea-fowl (*Pintadeau*). Guinea-fowl from the Drôme has actually been given an AOC label.

· Walnuts – and in particular walnut oil. Discover its uses at the Ferme Monge at Arnayon, about 4 miles (7km) north-west from the Pas des Ondes. Limes and other fruits are here too. Open 7am-8pm for sales.

And the most memorable

· Swimming in the cool blue waters of the Drôme at the end of a very, very hot day.

· The magnificent view of all the Vercors summits from the orientation tables at the Col de Rousset.

· Watching the Glandasse change from white to pink to grey every evening as the sun went down.

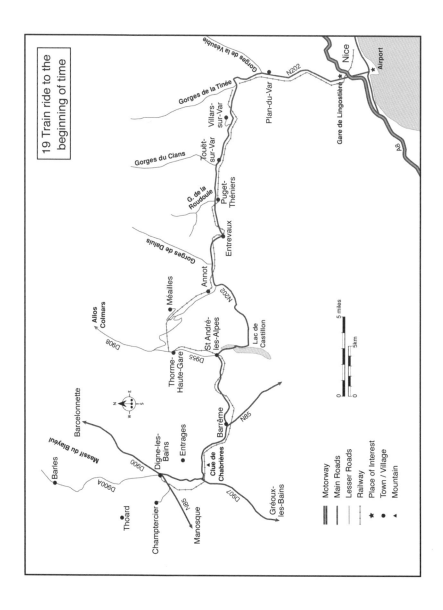

19 Train ride to the beginning of time

Motorway
Main Roads
Lesser Roads
Railway
★ Place of Interest
● Town / Village
▲ Mountain

5 miles
5km
0
0

Nice
Airport
Gare de Lingostière
A8
N202
Plan-du-Var
Gorges de la Vésubie
Villars-sur-Var
Gorges de la Tinée
Touët-sur-Var
Gorges du Cians
Puget-Théniers
G. de la Roudoule
Entrevaux
Gorges de Daluis
Annot
N202
Méailles
Allos
Colmars
D908
St André-les-Alpes
Lac de Castillon
Thorme-Haute-Gare
D955
Barcelonnette
Massif du Blayeul
Barles
D900A
D900
Digne-les-Bains
Entrages
Barrême
N85
Thoard
Champtercier
N85
Clue de Chabrières
D907
Manosque
Gréoux-les-Bains

297

There is not much about Provence and the Côte d'Azur that is away from the tourist trail – and in taking a train ride you are hardly going off the beaten track! But this train ride is special, a journey through some of Provence's finest scenery, and its end point is a fascinating area that is not too well known to British visitors. The romantically named *Train des Pignes* ('Pine-Cone Train' – on account of the fuel it used during the First World War) sets out from the chic heart of Nice four times a day to head through the valley of the Var into the mountainous landscapes surrounding the town of Digne-les-Bains. Digne, a spa town amid the lavender fields, is also the centre of a designated geological reserve. This is a splendid ride to a splendid region, and the bonus is that it is so readily accessible. Think – the Gare de Lingostière, the first stop on the train's journey, is just a 10-minute taxi ride from Nice airport. Here is a possibility for a long-weekend excursion.

The narrow-gauge railway from Nice to Digne was begun in 1890 and, being such a complicated feat of engineering, took over 20 years to complete. Other mountain tracks were built at the same time, but this is the sole survivor – a 93-mile (150-km) stretch that incorporates more than 50 bridges, viaducts and tunnels, while climbing through a height of 3281ft (1000m) from the sea to the mountains. The original locomotives on this route were of course powered by steam – and summer Sundays still see one nostalgic puffer heaving its way along a 12-mile (19km) section in the centre. But the regular trains are smart little diesels, having just one or two carriages according to demand. Deferring to the view, they are equipped with wide panoramic windows and even sport a little map of the route on the drinks trays beneath each one.

Along the way you can catch glimpses of the gorges of the Vésubie, the Tinée, the Cians and the Daluis, look out over the blue expanse of the Lac de Castillon and admire the churning milky waters of the River Asse as they race beside you through the rocky Clue de Chabrières. And to break the journey, you could visit the lovely little town of Annot, set amid gigantic grit-stone boulders or climb to the citadel on its rocky perch at Vauban-fashioned Entrevaux. The more energetic might even hike to the vast unexploited cave at Méailles or go for a swim in the lake (and try a bit of paragliding) at St André-les-Alpes.

Tickets for this train allow you to stop off for hours or even days (they simply write on the ticket), but whatever you do, it is worth reserving a generous helping of time for Digne-les-Bains at the end of the line. The old town has re-invented itself with a heavy sprinkling of modern sculptures and a museum with some thought-provoking material. Added to that, there is 'Samten-Dzong', the home of a remarkable Tibetan explorer – and of course the superbly presented Geological Museum.

After all that, you could hire a car to venture farther and see some of the unique imprints of prehistoric life in the mountains around Digne – fossils of shells and undersea creatures, the skeleton of an ichthyosaurus, footprints of birds on a 20-million year old beach, and marks of water courses long gone. The landscape itself is a geologist's paradise with enormous banks of black marl clay (*robines*), deeply slashed rocky gorges (*clues*) and most awe-inspiring of all, the rocky twists and curves of the 'Vélodrome'.

Most of the protected sites of the 'Geological Reserve' are within easy reach of the town of Digne, and the tourist office and geological museum can offer plenty of literature to guide you to them.

Of course it is perfectly possible to follow almost this same route by car – roads accompany the rail through the river valleys and you would need to divert only at Méailles, where a tunnel takes the train under the heights of the watershed. If you travel by car, you have the advantage of being able to do some exploring on the side as you go. But there is nothing to compare with the excitement of that rattling, scuttling little train – and it is a pleasure to be able to enjoy this truly spectacular scenery without the stress of driving. So let us get started on the journey right away.

THE VALLEY OF THE VAR

If you are already in Nice, the voyage begins at the terminus on the Rue Alfred Binet, which is about 15 minutes' walk from the sea-front; if you are starting from the airport, a quick taxi ride will deliver you to the Gare de Lingostière, the train's first stop, just to the west of the town. You will have to be a little patient for the excitement to begin, because for the early part of its journey the Train des Pignes doubles as a commuter train, stopping first in the suburbs and then in the outlying villages of Colomars, St Martin-du-Var and Pont Charles-Albert.

All this time the wide valley of the River Var is to your left and the busy N202 to your right, but suddenly things change – the road splits and the rail track is between the two lanes of traffic heading north and south.

After Plan-du-Var, the valley sides close in dramatically and a glance right when crossing the metal viaduct reveals the steep sides of the Vésubie Gorge. Suddenly both carriageways, rail and river are rushing together through the rocky Défile du Chaudon, whose end is marked by a view of the Gorges of the Tinée backed by high mountains. On hurtles the train, stopping briefly at Malaussène before reaching the village of **Villars-sur-Var**. To be accurate, the station is in the separated lower part of the village – Villars itself is on the cliff above, and is remarkable for the wealth of fine paintings in its church. With a car, it is worth a drive up the snaking road; on foot it is a long hard climb, so it is probably better to sit this one out on the train – besides, there is a lot more to come.

Beyond Villars the train next arrives at **Touët-sur-Var**, a really delightful village and one that may be worth a few hours pause in the journey. The old village clings to a sheer rock face and is probably best reached via an earth track that ascends from the road just before the school – reserving the steep cobbled path for the descent! This village is beautifully preserved, its ancient houses decked with flowers and painted in Provençal colours. At the top of the hill, the pastel-shaded church is built over a tumbling mountain stream – if its door is open you can lift a cover in the nave to see the waters below. Beside the church a tree-shaded square gives a magnificent view of the village and valley below (including the railway) and a little auberge can offer resuscitation.

Back again at the station, there is more food on offer at the 'Bar Chez Antoine'. By now you have probably noticed the stations, all of which look as if they have been lifted directly from a World War II film set. Most are family homes, and as there are only eight trains passing each day, there is plenty of time for family life. You may well see washing hanging from the windows, children playing on the platform and chickens scrabbling on the line. When a bell signals the approach of a train, *maman* shuffles out in carpet-slippers to make an adjustment to the points and may even have to issue a ticket or two. Touët-sur-Var is no exception, and the little bar-restaurant represents added business.

But it is back on the train again now, and almost immediately after Touët, time to look out for the impressive Cians Gorges on the right. Those with a car might like to take a detour – the limestone of the lower gorge gives way to red schist higher up and if you make it up the contorted road to the village of Lieuche, there are splendid views from the church terrace. Train travellers continue to **Puget-Théniers**, not a remarkable town in itself, but one that is home to an original steam train that is taken out on occasional trips up the line to Annot.

Beware the roads!

In Puget-Théniers, signs urge car travellers to explore the Roudoule gorges to visit an eco-museum and a mine, but beware – those gorges are more austere than most, and the access roads some of the 'hairiest' you are likely to encounter.

Just eight minutes up the line from Puget-Théniers, **Entrevaux** is definitely a place not to be missed. It certainly is not 'undiscovered' (in summer there are coachloads of visitors), but it is

such a curiosity that it would be a pity to pass it by. Built on a loop in the Var, its strategic position involved it in numerous conflicts, but the fortifications you see today are the work of that ubiquitous military architect Vauban, after Louis XIV, threatened by neighbouring Savoy, finally ordered the place to be made impregnable. The town was given ramparts, entrance gates, ditches and drawbridges, while the château on its rocky pinnacle became a fortified citadel. Not surprisingly, Entrevaux subsequently withheld all attacks.

Today summer-time tourists throng its narrow streets, calling in at purpose-built attractions like the motor-museum and the bread oven. At the bottom of the town the richly decorated cathedral is always open – and the Tourist Office in the gateway can tell you how to access the ramparts. The crowd thins a little if you take the zig-zag path to the hilltop citadel – no doubt on account of both the entrance fee and the effort required in climbing that relentlessly-inclined cobbled track under the blazing sun. The building at the top is sadly neglected and although you can explore quite extensively (look-outs, dungeons, and more) it is the sort of place where you will need to keep a very ware eye on the children. Outside the town walls again (and across the car park and bridge), you might like to visit the 15th-century oil and flour mills, still operational today. But do not get back on the train before you have sampled Entrevaux's own culinary speciality, a thin-sliced dried beef known as Secca. If you are not eating in the town, tuck a few slices in your pocket for supper (and see the 'Palate' section below).

ENTREVAUX TO ANNOT

After Entrevaux the train soon leaves the valley of the Var for that of the Coulomp, and then that of the Vaïre. The next stop is **Annot** (the final letter is pronounced, as is often the case in Provence) – and if you leave the train nowhere else, it is worth doing so in Annot. The town itself is clustered beside the river and topped by an interesting old town section – from the main square, stroll up the Grand' Rue to the church at the top and return along the Rue Notre-Dame. The carvings and inscriptions on the stone lintels are fascinating. Annot is particularly famous for the huge gritstone boulders (the *grès*) scattered about the town and in the surrounding countryside.

The boulders of Annot

The local explanation for these is that when St Peter failed to convert the town to Christianity, he stormed off shaking the 'dust' of the place from his feet as he went. It was this dust that miraculously clogged together to form the *grès*.

You may think it more likely that those boulders were split from the surrounding cliffs when water froze in the crevasses. At any rate, they are remarkable, and many have been incorporated into local houses. If you have a boulder on hand, you do not need to build a back (or even a side) wall! Several such boulder-houses are visible from the rail line, but if you want to see more, leave the square via the narrow Rue Vers-la-Ville – it is a path worth taking anyway because it is lined with stations of the cross that have beautiful ceramic inserts. The path heads uphill and crosses the railway line to reach the Chapelle de Vers-la-Ville, itself flanked by huge rocks, while across the field on the right is a house taking full advantage of an ivy-covered boulder. The part of the town on the opposite side of the Vaïre seems to have been spared the boulder deluge, but the road along the river bank nevertheless offers a pleasant 15-minute stroll to reach the town's other chapel, the Chapelle de Vérimande, in an attractive setting.

If you would like to see more it is a good idea to spend a day in Annot – and the little Office de Tourisme beside the plane-tree shaded square can suggest some surprisingly good affordable accommodation. This office is also stocked with leaflets of nearby walks, some of which have obligingly been translated into English. The classic 'boulder walk' takes around three hours, is well marked out and requires only stout shoes (good trainers will do) and a little energy to make the initial climb. The route visits the 'Chambre du Roi' with rocks of unimaginable proportions, skirts a cliff-face with strangely human profiles (the path is wide and you do not have to look down) and passes through the famous arch of kissing-stones known as les Portettes – lots of ammunition for the camera!

ANNOT TO DIGNE-LES-BAINS

From Annot the main road (N202) to St André-les-Alpes is a Provençal experience – at the tiny village of Rouaine you could believe you were in the Himalayas. The railway decides to give all this a miss and instead heads north up the Vaïre to the villages of les Fugerets and **Méailles**. The latter perches atop a vertical cliff-face, while the railway holds a position about half-way up, thanks to a series of impressive viaducts. The station of Méailles occupies a rocky niche in the cliff and from there you can choose to ascend to the village by either a many-hair-pinned road or a near-perpendicular footpath.

Méailles is quaint and unspoiled with just one small restaurant catering for locals and visitors. The main point of interest is the Grotte de Méailles, a cave rich in stalactites and stalagmites, but one not afflicted with guides, hourly visits, contrived lighting or cutely-named formations. This natural cave is about 2 miles (3km) north of the village and is reached by an unmarked footpath that leaves the road to la Combe at its first sharp right-hand bend. The path skirts a ravine and then ascends across scrubland marked only by cairns – not a technically difficult walk, but perhaps one better reserved for those with some experience of map-reading (both path and cave are shown on IGN Top 25 – 3541). If you decide to have a shot at it, allow around four hours from the village – and take at least two torches as an insurance measure!

After Méailles the train persists in its climb and then plunges into a long tunnel at its highest point before descending the valley of the Verdon. The next station is **Thorame-Haute** – a place out in the wilderness, but from here buses leave to climb the valley to fortified Colmars and to Allos with its beautiful alpine lake. The train now thankfully trundles its way downhill through a lovely valley to reach **St André-les-Alpes** beside the stunningly blue Lac de Castillon. The lake is artificial, created by a dam on the Verdon, and its colour, like that of the river, is said to be due to the presence of certain algae. St André has developed as a centre for watersports and has added to that a paragliding establishment on the hills above. This is the place to get out if you need a swim (although it is a couple of kilometres to the beach) – otherwise, stay on board for a little longer and follow the valley of the Asse de Moriez (sound the 'z') to Barrême.

At **Barrême** you have finally reached the confines of the geological reserve – in fact, Barrême is one of its main centres. The spare room at the station houses some of the local finds, including some splendid ammonite fossils, and it is just a shame the train does not stop long enough for you to get a quick look. If you do get off in this rather grey little town there is not a lot by way of diversion, although it does offer a good waymarked walk climbing to its hilltop chapel and then going on to visit some of the local geological interest (a sheet of fossils from the eponymous 'Barremian' Age and a reef of small sea-shells known as 'nummulites'). The map of this route is posted on a board in the village square – along with a map showing the huge wartime Resistance presence in this area, known as the Hautes Vallées de l'Asse. Those driving will pass several roadside memorials to these brave men along the way to Digne.

Barrême's other claim to fame is that Napoleon spent the night here on his amazing march to Paris in March 1815. A plaque in the main street points out where he stayed – and the locals even know what he had for dinner (soup, omelette, cod, goat's meat and plenty of wine!). Napoleon left Golfe-Juan (near Cannes) in the early hours of the 2 March, spent the night of the 3rd in Barrême, had lunch next day in Digne and was in Malijai by nightfall. Three days later he entered Grenoble – a remarkable feat in winter conditions with only 12 hours of daylight. Of course the end of it all was at Waterloo – but that is another story.

DIGNE-LES-BAINS

After Barrême it is only another half hour to Digne – and on the way you can enjoy the drama of the Clue de Chabrières and the more gentle approach to the town beside the River Bléone. **Digne-les-Bains** was an important town in Gallo-Roman times and is now the administrative centre of its *département*, Alpes de Haute Provence. From the station it is a mere ten minute walk to the Tourist Information Office (take the second right across the Bléone) where they can help with accommodation and car hire should you wish – and of course there is lots of regional information on offer.

Digne is at the centre of a region growing both fruit and lavender. On the surface it is a quiet unassuming sort of place, but a short stroll around its streets will soon reveal an added extra – the wealth of modern sculptures. The beautiful, the bizarre, the grotesque and the incomprehensible, they are all the result of sculpture competitions held here in the 80s and they adorn every street corner, roundabout or public building. While you are taking them in you can wander through the narrow streets of the old town to the cathedral and carry on to the famous Grande Fontaine, all

Doric columns and vases of moss and lichen. Beyond it is the interesting 13th century cathedral of Notre-Dame du Bourg. When it is open in summer time you can admire the murals in the nave and the 5th century mosaic in the crypt. From here the return to the town centre is made along its main street, the Boulevard Gassendi – a street named, like the town's museum, after Digne's most illustrious son.

Digne's famous son

Pierre Gassendi was born in 1592, and not in fact in Digne, but rather in the nearby village of Champtercier. The son of a humble peasant, he nevertheless became a great mathematician, naturalist, astronomer and humanist – quite an achievement in the 17th century.

Gassendi's life and work are honoured in the Musée Gassendi on the Boulevard of the same name, but there is a lot more to this museum. Among paintings and old scientific instruments are scattered modern art and photography, and miscellaneous passing exhibits such as the 'hoax' fossil of a mermaid (a 'hypopitheque'), given space in the geological reserve.

Leaving the centre of Digne for the suburbs, the first place to visit is the curious Tibetan house named Samten-Dzong, about a kilometre south on the road to Nice. It was once the residence of Alexandra David-Néel, an extraordinary and most talented lady who started life as an opera singer and went on to become a Tibetan explorer and advanced student of Buddhism. She became fluent in seven languages (including Hindi, Sanskrit and Tibetan) and in 1924, at the age of 56, became the first white woman to enter Lhasa, the forbidden capital of Tibet. Her face was blackened for the occasion.

On her return from this particular trip she bought the house at Digne and began filling it with the many souvenirs of her visits, but she could never settle for long. At the age of 80 she would camp in winter beside the frozen Lac d'Allos because it reminded her of Tibet – and at the age of 100, she renewed her passport for another expedition to China. Unfortunately she died before it could take place. The one and a half hour guided tour of her home is entirely free of charge – you are asked only to be quiet and respectful and to take no photographs. Fortunately there is an English translation for most of the visit (headphones and texts) because it is fascinating.

The other attraction just out of town is the splendid geological museum, about a mile (2km) north on the road to Barles. Both this and Samten-Dzong are served by bus routes if you prefer not to walk. The museum is referred to as the 'Musée-Promenade' and its extensive grounds are one of its main attractions, with waterfalls and paths flanked by exhibits. Inside the building are many more exhibits, videos, aquaria and lots of literature – far more than at Tourist Information. You are bound to be inspired by all this and want to get out to see some more, so make sure you get hold of the English version of the leaflet giving just the barest details of the local tours.

Now comes the point where you need to hire a car if you have not one with you. The nearest (and best) route in the geological reserve is that encircling a mountain ridge known

as the Massif du Blayeul. To get the most out of it you will need to do a little walking (and quite a lot for the Vélodrome) so make sure you have a good pair of shoes – and enough food for the day because there is not a lot out there. The route heads towards Barles and begins by passing a roadside sheet of rock clustered with ammonite fossils from 200 million years ago, just to the north of Digne. This site, like all the others on the route, is provided with a suitable marked parking space and an explanation panel in English as well as French.

Five and a half miles (9km) farther on, a track leaves from another parking area to a site in a lonely valley where the fossilised skeleton of an ichthyosaurus has been found (and is now protected by a 'flexiglass' cover). The walk to this spot is lovely and takes around half an hour in each direction. Next comes the site of bird footprints – only a 547yd (500m) walk this time.

But just down the road comes the best hike to the best site of all – the Vélodrome. The path you want is signed to *Vieil Esclangon* and climbs steadily but not too severely to first reach the deserted village surrounded by short-cropped alpine meadows. From here the climb is steeper but briefer, finally reaching the summit of a rock outcrop known as the Serre d'Esclangon. Across the valley the ridges of the Vélodrome swirl and twist before your eyes – it is a welcome diversion to read the explanation board instead. But the view in the opposite direction is more kindly and you can even enjoy a picnic on your rocky perch if you look this way.

Back on the road again (probably some two and a half hours after you left it), further geological treats are the marks of a one-time watercourse beside the River Bès, a mountain spring at constant temperature – and the oppressive rocky sides of the Clue de Barles as you squeeze your vehicle through (in height as well as width). The leaflet completes the route by passing through the village of Barles and continuing to join the D900 heading south. There is not a lot more to see this way (the fossilised forest has restricted access), although the leaflet does suggest a final turn to the village of Draix, stranded amid *robines* of black marl. If you have the mental stamina for a contorted, precipitous 4 mile (7km) drive (meeting others similarly blessed coming the other way), take it. Otherwise, just head home.

For those with a car, there are other worthwhile excursions around Digne, and in summer you will enjoy the heady scents of the lavender fields as you go. Drive west to see the thermal baths and continue to the pretty village of Entrages – from here you can climb the twin-peaked 'Cousson' with a little chapel on its summit ledge (but go soon – that ledge is crumbling). In the opposite direction, the village of Champtercier has a fine view, a chocolate maker, a santon maker and a Rural Park of traditional Provençal buildings. Beyond Champtercier, it is an exciting drive over the Col du Pas de Bonnet to Thoard, a genuine unspoilt perched village with cobbled alleys between its old houses and a lavender distillery. Mathematical minds will appreciate its 'analemma' sundial. On the way back you could walk to Gassendi's birthplace, signed from the top of the col.

Digne has plenty more to offer – but sadly it will soon be time to get back on that train to Nice. This time you could sit on the other side!

Lavender and Digne-les-Bains

Digne is the centre of a lavender growing area and holds its own celebratory fête, the Corso de Lavande, during the first week of August every year. For an informal view of the lavender fields in bloom, drive south-west in the direction of Gréoux-les-Bains some time between mid-June and mid-August.

Two forms of lavender are cultivated commercially in Provence – fine lavender (*lavandula augustifolia*) and the hybrid lavandin (a cross of fine lavender with spike lavender, or aspic). Both display the same brilliant colour, but the hybrid yields five times as much oil as fine lavender and is happy to grow at rather lower altitudes. It now represents more than four-fifths of the region's output. Around Digne the cultivation is generally lavandin, and you will have to travel west to the heights of Mont Ventoux to compare it with fine lavender – which is as superior and costly as its name suggests. The free booklet *Les Routes de la Lavande* (English version *The Lavender Roads*) gives information on tours, fêtes and distilleries.

Offices de Tourisme

Nice
Esplanade Kennedy
06302 NICE
☎ 04.92.14.48.00

St André-les-Alpes
Place Marcel Pastorelli
04170 St ANDRÉ-les-ALPES
☎ 04.92.89.02.39

Puget-Théniers
Maison de Pays RN202
06260 PUGET-THÉNIERS
☎ 04.93.05.05.05

Digne-les-Bains
Place du Tampinet
04000 DIGNE-les-BAINS
☎ 04.92.36.62.62

Annot
Bd. St-Pierre
04240 ANNOT
☎ 04.92.83.32.82

Practical Information

- The Train des Pignes makes four journeys each way between Nice and Digne every day throughout the year. Currently departure times are 6.42, 9.00, 12.43 and 17.00 from Nice and 7.00, 10.33, 13.58 and 17.25 from Digne, but you can always check these on the website (www.trainprovence.com). The whole journey takes just over three hours – and fares are modest by British standards! To see the most dramatic scenery – including the gorges – sit on the right-hand side of the train leaving Nice, although the left has some fine views too.

- Buses for Colmars and Allos generally leave Thorame Gare three times a day during the ski season and in July and August – but some days are exceptional, so check with the website above.

Places of Interest

Entrevaux

Citadel
Accessible via automatic turnstile at any time.

Musée de la Moto
Free guided tours 10am-12noon, 2-7pm May to September. Otherwise, weekends only.

Moulins à huile et à farine (oil and flour mills)
Open July and August 9.30am-7pm; March to June, September and October 9am-12noon, 1.30-5.30pm; November to February 10am-12noon, 2-5pm weekdays only.

Digne-les-Bains

Musée Gassendi
Open April to September 11am-7pm; October to March 3.30-5.30pm. Closed Tuesdays.

Musée Alexandra David-Néel
Visits at 10am, 2pm and 4pm October to June; 10am, 2pm, 3.30pm and 4.30pm July to September.

Réserve Géologique – Musée-Promenade
Open April to October every day 10am-12noon, 2-5.30pm (4.30pm Fridays); rest of year weekends and bank holidays only at same times.

Thermal baths
Open mid-February to end of November. Guided tours at 2 pm every Thursday from March to August and in November.

Champtercier

Atelier de Santons
Open every morning and afternoon in July and August. Otherwise hours may be a bit irregular, but generally closed only on Sundays.

Chocolatier
Rarely open other than by appointment.

Parc Rural de Haute-Provence
Open all year by request only (you could ask at OT in Digne).

Thoard

Distillerie du Siron (lavender distillery)
Free visits on Tuesdays, Thursdays and weekends 9am-5pm in August only.

LOCAL HIGHLIGHTS

Best Walks

- The best of all must be the 4 mile (6km)/3 hour walk through the Grès d'Annot, starting from the railway station. The Tourist Office should be able to offer you a little leaflet in English describing the route – but do not worry, it is very well waymarked on the ground (you follow yellow flashes).

- Walks in the geological reserve. The climb through the old village of Esclangon to the Vélodrome viewpoint is magnificent – but do not miss out on the Ichthyosaurus trail either.

- Seasoned walkers will relish the wild countryside on the way to the Grotte de Méailles.

For cyclists

- You will not have a bike if you arrive by train but you can certainly hire one in Digne. The area prides itself on some fine waymarked VTT circuits with varying degrees of difficulty – ask for a map of these at the Office de Tourisme in Digne.

Watersports

- St. André-les-Alpes is the watersports centre, with a long sandy supervised beach just out of town on the road to Nice. The Tourist Office can also give you details of rafting and canyoning expeditions.

- Canoeing, rafting and canyoning expeditions are also organised from Annot – ☎ 04.92.83.38.09.

For the Palate

- Secca d'Entrevaux. Thin slices of wind-dried salted beef best sprinkled with olive oil and lemon and served with slices of tomato and mozzarella cheese.

- In Provence, anything and everything seems to be cooked with olive oil and herbs. And aïoli, garlic mayonnaise, makes a frequent appearance on regional menus.

- Other Provençal favourites include ratatouille, bouillabaisse (a very exotic form of 'fish stew') and salade niçoise laden with anchovies and olives – and of course you cannot come to Provence without indulging in the wines of the Rhône valley, and quaffing the occasional *pastis.*

And the most memorable

- Walking through the Chambre du Roi above Annot on a sunny autumn morning and thinking we had arrived at a film set from Lord of the Rings.

- Discovering the true meaning of 'Off the Beaten Track' in the station at Touët-sur-Var – cooking smells drifted from the kitchen, a week's washing hung from an upstairs window and a dog with a broken leg lay sunbathing on the platform. Were they expecting any trains?

- The view of that Vélodrome. It simply makes you dizzy.

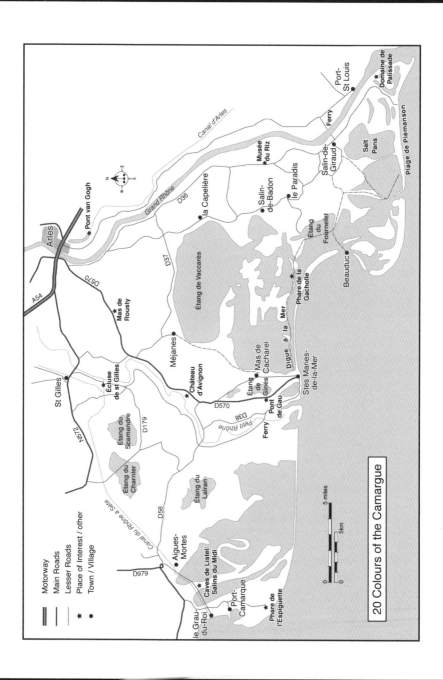

20 Colours of the Camargue

The triangle of land at the mouth of the Rhône was in ancient times an island dedicated to the Egyptian sun god Ra – and well it might be. Here you are at the interface between the land and the sea, a place where a thousand lakes shimmer under a blue Provençal sky, finally merging into the Mediterranean. The light is of an unbelievable intensity and the sweep of the horizon is broken only by the distant tower of a lighthouse or a glistening white cone of salt. In summer the sun burns from a cloudless heaven, while in winter and spring the dreaded mistral periodically scours the land with a force that, according to local lore, can blow the tail (or even the ears) off a donkey. The Camargue is a region of extremes, and its inhabitants are resilient folk, traditionally cattle-rearers whose hardy black animals graze the flat rough ground between dykes and lakes. They are true cowboys (the local name is *gardians*), living in low whitewashed houses backed against the northern wind and managing their herds from the backs of sturdy white Camargue horses.

The Camargue's landscape has changed its character over the years. Enclosed between the arms of the Grand and Petit Rhône, in earliest times this region was alternately flooded by fresh river water and the salty waters of the Mediterranean. The building of sea and river dykes in the middle of the 19th century and the desalination of certain areas rendered the land more hospitable and the northern sector now yields cereals and rice. In the centre, the vast Étang de Vaccarès is maintained as a nature reserve, while in the south the still-saline lakes are home to flocks of pink flamingos and an enormous variety of other birds that come and go with the seasons. And on the low banks

between the lakes, the pink feathery tamarisk and the salt-loving vegetation known as *sansouire* add more colour to the scene. The whole area is quite unique in Europe and since 1970 has been protected as the Parc Naturel Régional de la Camargue.

The Camargue is the only part of France's Mediterranean coast not to be developed and the Park authorities are always striving to protect its delicate ecosystems from the potentially damaging effects of commercialism. Essentially this is a place to appreciate nature in the raw, and there remains only one town within the Park boundaries, Stes-Maries-de-la Mer. Crouching low between the sea and the Étang des Launes, the town derives its name from the story of the 'Two Marys' who landed there in AD 40, having miraculously crossed from the Holy Land without sail or oars. The annual fête-day celebrations commemorating this event must be among the most vivid and exciting in France.

Stes-Maries-de-la-Mer is fascinating in every detail, from the fortified church with its watchpath to the sector of traditional *gardians'* cabins, and from the shops in town offering *Tout pour le Gardian* (everything for the cowboy) to the fishing boats arriving at the harbour on the sea front. The other town in this area meriting a visit, though outside the confines of the Park, is Aigues-Mortes to the west. Fortified by a full mile of ramparts and towers, the town that once kept watch over the sea now looks over salt marshes and has its own seaside sector in le Grau-du-Roi, 5 miles (8km) down the road.

The Camargue is undoubtedly the most different part of France, colourful, rich in history and folklore, a naturalist's paradise – and with some fine beaches thrown in for good measure. But what about the visitors – is it really off the tourist trail? Well, that depends. No part of the south coast of France can truly be said to be 'undiscovered', but in the Camargue, all the visitors go one way – from Arles straight down the D570 to Stes-Maries-de-la-Mer. And most of them go in July and August.

The best time to visit the Camargue is the late spring, when the *sansouire* wears bright colours and on the lagoons, bird-life is teeming with the arrival of summer visitors. Flamingos are nesting, the mistral is in abeyance and the sun is not yet too high in the sky. But at any time of year the eastern side of the Camargue, between the Étang de Vaccarès and the Grand Rhône, receives fewer visitors and is magnificent for just taking a walk or a cycle ride to absorb the atmosphere. You can stride out on the sea dyke (Digue à la Mer), visit a wildlife reserve, take a view out across the salt-pans from the salt town of Salin-de-Giraud or amble through the unchanged wilderness of the south-east corner. Beyond it all, the 15.5 mile (25km) sandy beach of Piémanson is one of the best for miles around.

The only hotels and campsites in this region are not surprisingly to be found around Stes-Maries-de-la-Mer, making it the obvious choice for a holiday base here. The other possibility is Arles, the city at the northern tip of the delta, from which most of the Camargue is accessible in less than three-quarters of an hour.

Arles of course is well on the tourist trail, but if you have not visited it before it is more than worth a few hours (and maybe days) of your time. A Roman capital from which the Amphitheatre and Théâtre Antique are remarkable survivors, it was also for 15 brief and productive months

home to Van Gogh. The former hospital where he became a patient and whose garden he once painted now houses the Espace Van Gogh, open to the public every day. Other sites immortalised by the great man can also be visited, including the famous Pont de Langlois (now called Pont Van Gogh), off the D35 just to the south. The Office de Tourisme in Arles can offer four differently themed itineraries to acquaint visitors with the city, and has helpfully installed ceramic plaques on the pavements to help with direction finding.

STES-MARIES-DE-LA-MER

But back now to the Camargue and **Stes-Maries-de-la-Mer**. This unspoilt little town must be unique on the south coast of France. With a fine sandy beach stretching for miles, there is surprisingly not a high-rise condominium in sight. In fact the white-washed buildings of the town are set at sea-level, and are protected from the waves by a long sea-wall topped by a promenade. On this sea-front, the heights of sophistication are represented only by a handful of restaurants, a small arena where games are held and an old-fashioned carousel. Beyond all these is Port Gardian, home to both pleasure craft and the fishing fleet. On the quayside, the morning's catch is put up for sale as the boats return.

Trip boats offer excursions up the Petit Rhône, enticing aspiring photographers with promises of close-up views of horses and bulls from the safety of the water. Farther on still, between the sea and the Étang des Launes, a collection of traditional *gardians*' cabins has been preserved. White-washed, thatched and with one rounded end topped by a cross, they are even so all different, and one or two can be hired as holiday homes. Other holiday accommodation at Stes-Maries is provided by a few small hotels and two excellent camp-sites on the coast, one with direct access to the beach

Behind the sea-front, the narrow streets of the town contain some interesting shops – and at their heart is the one 'high-rise' building in these parts, the church, which can con-sequently be seen from many miles away across the flat marshlands. A watchpath encircling its roof offers reciprocal views of both marsh and sea. The church was built between the 9th and the 11th centuries, a time when the Camargue was constantly threatened by marauding Saracens and Arabs – its fortifications offered a refuge for the local people. The relics held in the church were discovered somewhat later (1448), and are said to be those of the saints who arrived by boat and remained to evangelise here – in particular, Mary Jacobea (the sister of the Virgin Mary), Mary Salome (the mother of James and John) and Sarah, their black servant who was almost left behind when the boat set out. Stes-Maries may count itself fortunate that she was not, because her presence here is respon-sible for some remarkable festivities.

Sarah has been adopted as the patron saint of the gypsies, thousands of whom flock from all over Europe to celebrate her, along with Saint Mary, on the 24/25 May. Gypsies, guardians on horseback, women dressed in Arlesian costume and droves of onlookers accompany the effigies of the saints from their niches in the church through the streets and into the sea. The whole thing is repeated on a lesser scale in October, when Mary Salome is honoured (and

Saint Sarah stays at home). If you are not here at festival time, at least you can see the figures of the two Marys in their boat in the nave of the church, and in the crypt, the statue of a rather over-dressed Sarah.

Above the door of the church on the outside you can make your first acquaintance with a symbol that has become almost the 'trade-mark' of the Camargue – the Gardiane or Camarguaise Cross. Its three parts represent faith (the cross), hope (the anchor) and charity (the heart) – and the ends of the cross bear the trident of the *gardian*. This cross was designed by the painter Paul Hermann at the request of one Marquis de Baroncelli, a local *manadier* (herdsman) of the early part of last century, who devoted his life to recording and preserving the traditions of the Camargue. Baroncelli's documents along with other material relating to Camarguaise life are housed in the old town hall beside the church (Musée Baroncelli).

HEART OF THE CAMARGUE

Outside the town, it is time to take a look at the Camargue itself. – and the best place to begin is the Centre d'Information de Ginès at **Pont de Gau,** two and a half miles (4km) north on the D570. A panoramic window looks out over the Étang de Ginès and the displays and explanations of the landscape are geared to children (with translations in English). Lots of regional information is on offer, in-cluding an excellent folder of routes for walks and cycle-rides. Next door to the Information Centre is the Parc Ornithologique du Pont de Gau, a lively place where flamingos, egrets, sea-birds and wild-fowl compete noisily for food and water-space on the lagoons. Well-frequented by visitors in summer, you can find both more bird-life and more solitude by leaving the centre and taking the marked path along the lake shore.

The Parc Ornithologique feeds the flamingos and so attracts them in large numbers, but it is far more exciting to come across them yourself in the wild marshes. If you leave Stes-Maries on what is known as the Cacherel road (from the north-east of the town), you will almost certainly see them in the water on both sides. Where this road bends to the left, it is possible to continue ahead on a rough but drivable earthen track – and now you feel you could be on an African safari, out amid the wild-life on the lakes. For cars the journey comes to an end at the first dyke (approx. 1.5 miles [2km]), but cyclists can continue for a further 5 miles (8km) or so to the hamlet of Méjanes.

Méjanes can also be reached by turning off the D570 road to Arles, but whether you arrive this way or by the cycle track, it should be one of your first stops in exploring the Camargue. Paul Ricard (of *pastis* fame) has a farmstead here and for many years has been opening the place to visitors. Today you can take a walk, cycle or ride a white Camargue horse across the marshes to the Étang de Vaccarès, witness the ritual of branding the cattle (the *ferrade*) and watch the games in the bull ring – and there is nothing cruel about this. Quite unlike traditional bull-fights, in *Courses Camarguaises* the idea is to remove a rosette from the horns of the bull using a sort of comb. The only risk is to the white-clad *raseteurs* who attempt it! A cheerful little train carries visitors around the site and two restaurants provide everything from meals to snacks. Méjanes is cert-

ainly popular, but as well as entertaining both children and adults, it also gives a genuine insight into the area and its traditions

More Camarguaise insight is to be had at the nearby Musée Camarguais, one of the eco-museums of the National Park (beside the D570, about 5 miles [8km] south-west of Arles). It is housed in one of the typical low thick-walled farmhouses (*mas*) of this region, the **Mas de Rousty**. Everything about the Camargue is told here with some well-chosen tableaux and exhibits – the history of the landscape, the life of a *gardian*, the traditional practice of sheep-farming and transhumance. After the visit you can amble off alongside the drainage canal to reach an observatory on the marshes, following a waymarked trail.

Returning from Rousty to Stes Maries, you could finish the day with a visit to the **Château d'Avignon** (beside the D570). But admiring 18th century furnishings and tapestries, and even the fine gardens, requires such a mental leap from the wild expanses of the Camargue that it is perhaps best left for another day.

To the West and Aigues-Mortes

Time now to leave Stes Maries-de-la-Mer and explore the area to the west. If you take the road along the sea-front, in a few hundred yards you will pass the turning to Lou Simbeù and 'Tiki III'. Lou Simbeù is one of the many *manades* that offer horses for riding out on the marshes. These excursions will normally be accompanied, and they can provide mounts for all ages and abilities. Beside Lou Simbeù you can see Baroncelli's tomb and memorial. He apparently asked

flamingos, bulls and horses

The name flamingo derives from the Latin *flamma*, a blaze. In Spanish, the word flamenco interestingly denotes both the bird and the dance. In the latter, the lady traditionally wears red and white and the man, black – the colours of the flamingo. Around 10,000 flamingo couples inhabit the Camargue, some staying all year and others leaving to overwinter in Africa. At the beginning of April the female lays a single egg, which hatches three weeks later, and by July the young take to the air for the first time. These young birds are grey in colour, their more colourful adult plumage not developing for a further three to five years. In the wild, the life expectancy for a flamingo is around 34 years, although severe winter weather can cause high mortality in those who choose not to migrate. The birds feed on plankton, sieved by the over-sized bill, which is used to scour the lake bed.

The Camargue bull is an ancient breed that during its evolution has become conditioned to the severity of life on the marshes. Wind, rain, extremes of temperature and poor pasture have produced a race that is tough, wiry and resilient. No more than 4.3ft (1.3m) in height, they weigh around 882lb (400kg) and have particularly long 'lyre-shaped' horns. The best beasts are kept for the games in the arena, while the others find their way to the table.

Legend has it that the Camargue horse was given to the region's inhabitants by Neptune himself – and that he asked them to give it liberty in accordance with its marine and divine nature. So today these beautiful horses wander in semi-freedom between land and sea – and their intelligence and willing nature make them invaluable for managing the herds of bulls. Camargue horses are small (not more than 10 hands), and they are born brown, only achieving their classic creamy-white colour in their fourth or fifth year.

to be buried here where he could look across the marsh to the silhouette of the church at Stes-Maries on the horizon. A few more metres on down the rough road you reach the banks of the Petit Rhône and Tiki III – a brightly painted paddle-boat plying the river, again offering those precious views of the herds and wildlife

On now, up the D38 beside the Petit Rhône – and those wanting to spice up the journey could cross the river by the Bac de Sauvage (a little ferry) and continue up the west bank instead. It all takes you to the same road, the A58 heading west to **Aigues-Mortes.** Before reaching the town you could turn right at a roundabout to the Tour Carbonnière, a 14th century fortified tower that once housed an advance garrison, but now stands isolated in a road across the marshes. The view from the top stretches a long way but it does not include Aigues-Mortes.

That town comes into view just a little way down the road as you cross the bridge over the Canal du Rhône à Sète, and possibly this first glance is the most picturesque. Across the colourful boats of the canal basin, the solid walls of the old town look less severe and their line is broken by the arch of the Porte de la Gardette and the circular Tour de Constance on the right.

A walk around the ramparts is mandatory (and not inexpensive), but, in addition to the wider views, there is something appealing about looking down from the level of the pink-tiled roofs into the jumbled streets and courtyards below. Gateways and towers are passed as you go – note particularly the Burgundians tower (gruesomely filled with dead Burgundians after a battle in 1418); the Wick Tower (*Tour de la Mèche*) where a light was kept burning to ignite the firearms; the Mill Gate (*Porte des Moulins*) with its view over the salt pans; and of course the Constance Tower, used as a prison for Protestant women during the 18th century 'Camisards War'. Its terrace beneath the lantern tower has the most extensive view of all. At ground level, the town within the ramparts is a lattice of crossing streets, centred on a statue of Louis IX in a tree-shaded square. Beside it, the simply-decorated Church of Notre-Dame-des-Sablons has modern stained-glass windows in Provençal colours.

Aigues-Mortes was once on the sea – in fact it was built by Louis IX as a port from which to embark on the crusades, since at that time Marseille and the other Mediterranean ports were outside his kingdom and jurisdiction. Eight hundred years on, the sea has receded, leaving in its place a marsh of salt flats. Continuing out of town on the D979 (the ramparts look their most forbidding from this side),

look for a turning on the left signed to the Salins du Midi and the Caves du Listel. The two seem strange bedfellows – from the same starting point you can choose to take a train (or 'bus) tour of the salt works or stroll around the museum relating to the production of the fine Listel wines. Of course no-one is barred from the wine shop at the end of the day.

A few more kilometres down the road, the sea is finally reached at **le Grau-du-Roi**. Although there is a good beach here, the town and sea-front are not attractive in the way of Stes-Maries – probably because it is outside the Natural Regional Park. The most interesting area is that beside the canal connecting the town to Aigues-Mortes, where there are pleasure craft, fishing boats, bustling cafés and a lighthouse at the end of the quay. Le Grau-du-Roi has room for only a few boats, but just along the road is a purpose-built extension – **Port Camargue**. If you want to see some of the Mediterranean's floating palaces, get down to the *Capitainerie* and from there wander along the quays.

Beyond Port-Camargue, the road continues past campsites and horse-riding establishments to the **Phare de l'Espiguette**, a tiny lighthouse above an unimaginably vast sandy beach – walk out along those sandy dunes for an hour and the view is just the same. It is awe-inspiring, but at least there is room for all those campers. On the way back it is worth a pause at the Maison Méditerranéene (less than a mile and a half [2km] from the light-house) for a selection of some of the best quality Provençal souvenirs to take home.

THE NORTH OF THE CAMARGUE

Another day now and you could return north via the same route (maybe varied with that ferry) and this time turn off the D58 to another excellent eco-museum, the Centre du Scamandre on the banks of the *étang* of the same name. On the D179 you pass through some of the Camargue's most famous vineyards at Montcalm, and continue on a narrow road set alarmingly above one of the main drainage channels. Having negotiated this one, you will be pleased to arrive at the **Centre de Découverte du Scamandre**, right beside the road junction – and again there is lots of information along with an interesting trail into the wilds.

From here, the D179 heading east to St Gilles will take you first to the **Écluse de St Gilles**, a lock of impressive proportions, set where the Canal du Rhône à Sète connects with the Petit Rhône. Well provided with picnic tables, this is obviously a spot from which to enjoy the antics of the holiday boaters. Farther on, **St Gilles** itself is a lovely little town whose centrepiece is an abbey dating from the 11th century.

The ornate West Front of the abbey is said to be one of the finest examples of Romanesque sculpture in the south of France. The church behind this façade is the result of repairs and alterations in the 17th century and is a mere fraction of the size of the original. Tickets are needed for the beautifully vaulted crypt, part of the original abbey, where St Gilles tomb is overlooked by a keystone carving of the smiling Christ. St Gilles was the first stop on the route from Arles to Santiago de Compostela, and

you can see the old staircase from which the tomb was revered by generations of passing pilgrims. Behind the church are the ruins of the abbey and among them a tower housing a remarkable stone staircase. The craftwork of the Vis de St-Gilles has always attracted stonemasons from far and wide (some of whom left graffiti) – the carved blocks have both concave and convex faces and, fitting together without mortar, form a perfect spiral vault. Outside among the ruins, look out for the tiny carving of a man whose leg is trapped, slumped at the base of a broken pillar. It is thought to commemorate an accident during the building of the abbey.

THE EASTERN WILDERNESS

The final excursion from Stes. Maries must be to the eastern side of the Camargue – and there is so much here that you may want to return a second day. As the crow flies it is not a great distance from Stes-Maries to the Phare de Gachole and the reserves of Salon de Badon and la Capelière, but terrestrial travellers must circumnavigate the vast Ètang de Vaccarès. Nevertheless, taking the D37 along the north of the lake between the towering reeds and the shore gives some idea of its dimensions – you cannot actually see the other side. Turning south on the road to la Capelière, a roadside platform offers a more elevated view and lots of explanation (in English, too).

La Capelière is one of the main reserves of the Regional Park. From the displays and texts of the centre you are led on to a 1 mile (1.5km) path around the wetlands, punctuated by four waterside hides. What you see will depend on the seasons – and on whether or not you have binoculars with you. A further modest entry fee paid at la Capelière will admit you to the wilder reserve at Salon-de-Badon to the south. Taking the *Foulques* (Coot) and *Flamants Roses* (Flamingo) trails here will get you farther out into the marshes than you are likely to get anywhere else – and whatever you see or do not see, your own silent journey will be made to a background of squawks, caws and flaps from the hidden feathered locals.

From Salon de Badon the road heads south to Salin-de-Giraud – and you could divert to visit the curious little Rice Museum on the D36 on the way (most information comes from a video in French only). **Salin-de-Giraud** is a town created at the end of the 19th century by two salt companies, Péchiney and Solvay. Each built houses and provided facilities for a workforce drawn largely from outside France – hard manual labour in such a sun-baked desolate place could attract only Greeks, Italians and Armenians. Later the two communities were connected and a central square and town hall were added. Today, plane and palm trees shade the streets of Salin-de-Giraud and the salt works is managed by Pechiney's successor, Salins. The rows of houses, though much improved, still bear witness to the settlement's origins. Even if you only drive down the main road past the town you can see the gradation from the managerial to the humblest workers.

At the centre of town, the Office de Tourisme can point you to a garage hiring cycles and can suggest some interesting local routes. From Salin-de-Giraud, both bikes and cars can be taken across the Grand Rhône on a ferry (the Bac de Barcarin). Cyclists could head then south to explore the river banks, while car travellers might turn north to the nature reserve of the Marais de Vigueirat and continue past Van Gogh's famous Pont de Langlois to return through Arles.

Back to Salin-de-Giraud now – and south of here you are reaching the end of the world. Salt heaps line the road and beside a viewpoint, a little train calls at intervals to take visitors out among them. Beyond the salt heaps the road swings to the right – and the **Domaine de Palissade** offers final contact with the land.

Nature walks

There are some lovely walks in the far-flung reserve of the Domaine de Palissade, and it is here that many migratory birds make their first landing. Flamingos strut on the marsh, coypu plop silently into the water at your side and pink tamarisk shimmers in the bright light.

Take time to walk here if you can – and then back in the car, continue on a causeway that seemingly leads out into the sea. Its end is the **Plage de Piémanson,** a vast stretch of sand so firm that bikes, cars, and even caravans roll out along it. This remote beach is surprisingly popular. Supervised in summer, it provides safe bathing, and is more attractive on its west side, where dunes rather than the industrial installations of Port St Louis form the backdrop.

No-one should leave this side of the Camargue without visiting the **Phare de Gachole** (lighthouse) – and, in springtime, the Ètang de Fangassier where the flamingos breed. But as an alternative, both can be reached from Stes-Maries by cycling across the seven and a half mile (12km) Digue à la Mer (Sea-Dyke).

To get there by car, follow the signs from le Paradis, just south of Salon-de-Badon. Towards the end, the road becomes a gravelled track and most motorists will prefer to park at the pumping station two and a half miles (4km) short of the lighthouse as the causeway thereafter becomes very potholed. But walking that 4 km can be quite gruelling under the hot sun. Apart from its obvious function, the lighthouse is a base for local ornithologists who man the station at weekends and welcome all who arrive. Their intimate knowledge and high-powered telescopes will probably reveal more wild-life than you have yet seen on the Camargue. Back at the pumping station, you can continue on foot to a viewpoint over the island in the Ètang de Fangassier that is the flamingos' breeding place. Between April and June a pink mass can be seen in the distance across the bright blue water – yet another of the colourful sights of the Camargue.

OFFICES DE TOURISME

Arles
Boulevard de Craponne
13200 ARLES
☎ 04.90.18.41.20

Stes-Maries-de-la-Mer
5, Ave. Van Gogh BP 73
13732 SAINTES-MARIES-de-la-MER
☎ 04.90.97.82.55

Aigues-Mortes
Porte de la Gardette
30220 AIGUES-MORTES
☎ 04.66.53.73.00

PLACES OF INTEREST

Saintes-Maries-de-la-Mer

Church
Open throughout the year.

Watchpath
Open July and August 10am-8pm; March to June, September and October 10am-12.30pm, 2-6.30pm (no lunchbreak at weekends); November to March 10am-12noon, 2-5pm Wednesdays, Saturdays, Sundays and school holidays only.

Musée Baroncelli
Open April to October 10am-12noon, 2-6pm every day except Tuesday (Tuesday opening July and August only).

Boat trips
Boat trips up the Petit Rhône (starting from either Port Gardian or the banks of river itself) generally operate between mid-March and the end of October and there are several departures each day. All offer the photo opportunities –

some offer commentary and an 'English translation'. More boat trips start from Aigues-Mortes.

Horse-riding
Excursions on horseback are widely available throughout the Camargue. Ask at any OT for details.

Pont de Gau

Centre d'Information du Parc Naturel Régional de Camargue
Open April to September 10am-6pm every day, October to March 9.30am-5pm every day except Friday.

Parc Ornithologique
Open April to September 9am-sunset; October to March 10am-sunset every day.

Méjanes

Domaine de Méjanes
Discovery walks, horse-riding and bike-hire available throughout the year, other activities from Easter onwards. Games in the arena on certain afternoons in May, June and September according to demand (it is too hot in July and August) – but consult an Office de Tourisme for details at the time.

Mas de Rousty

Musée Camarguais
Open April to September 9.15am-5.45pm (6.45pm July and August) every day: October to March 10.15am-4.45pm every day except Tuesday.

Château d'Avignon
Park open from April to October every day except Tuesday 9.45am-5.45pm. Guided visits to the château between 10am and 5pm.

Aigues-Mortes

Ramparts and Tour de Constance
Open May to August 10am-7pm; September to April 10am-1pm, 2-5.30pm (last entry 1 hour before closing).

Salins du Midi
Train and/or sightseeing bus departs several times daily June to August 10am-12noon, 1.30-6.45pm; April to June, September and October 10am-12noon, 1.30-5.15pm.

Caves Listel
Museum open from April to October.

Maison Méditerranéene
Open from 9.30am every day throughout the year.

Centre de Découverte du Scamandre
Open 9am-5pm Wednesday to Friday throughout the year, and Saturdays also from April to October.

St. Gilles

Ancient ruins, crypt and Vis de St-Gilles
Open 9am-12noon, 2-5pm (later in summer) every day except Sundays throughout the year.

La Capelière and Salon-de-Badon Reserves
Open April to September 9am-1pm, 2-6pm every day; October to March 9am-1pm, 2-5pm every day except Tuesday.

Musée du Riz
Open weekdays only throughout
the year.

Domaine de la Palissade
Open every day throughout the
year 9am-5pm with the exception
of bank holidays.

LOCAL HIGHLIGHTS

Best Walks

· Take the walk out on the Digue à la Mer or along the edge of the Étang de Fangassier from the pumping station for the curious experience of 'walking on water'. But make sure you are well protected from the sun!

· There are signed footpaths at the reserves of Scamandre, la Capelière, Salon-de-Badon and Domaine de la Palissade. The latter is probably the most peaceful, and offers a choice of routes up to 4 miles (6km) in length.

Cycle rides

· From Stes-Maries-de-la-Mer there are, among others, two classic rides – along the Digue à la Mer to the Gachole lighthouse (6 miles [10km] each way) and along the Cacherel road to Méjanes (11 miles [18km] approx. each way). A leaflet is obtainable from OT.

· For more suggestions, look out for the folder entitled *Randonnées dans le Parc naturel régional de Camargue et ses environs* at the Park HQ or any of the eco-museums. It offers routs for road-bikes (vélos) and all-terrain bikes (VTTs).

Watersports

· Stes-Maries-de-la-Mer has a long sandy beach divided by breakwaters, ideal for families.

· The other supervised beach is that of Piémanson, at the south-east corner – vast, sandy and backed by dunes.

· Canoes suitable for all the family can be hired from the Mas de Sylvéréal on the Petit Rhône between Stes-Maries and Aigues-Mortes. Several waterways are accessible. Contact OT at Aigues-Mortes or Stes-Maries.

For the Palate

· Bull meat. The classic dish is Gardianne de Taureau, a sort of dark grey stew, whose taste is happily far more attractive than its looks.

· Seafood. Fresh fish and *moules* are widely available, but look out for *tellines*. These tiny bivalves collected along the shore can be cooked in garlic to make a delicious 'starter'.

- The local popular wines are from the *caves* of Listel. In particular, try the *gris de gris* (grey of grey – actually pale pink).

And the most memorable

- Flamingos in flight – something you can never see in ornithological parks at home. Necks are longer than legs, and the underwing is bright salmon pink edged with black. Stunning.

- Walking out to the Phare de Gachole on one of the Camargue's rare rainy days. Being completely surrounded by water!

- The classic sight of white Camarguaise horses galloping across the empty marshland in a shower of spray.

How to get there

Options from the UK are by land, sea and air

By land

This means Eurostar for those who are not taking a vehicle, and le Shuttle for everyone else.

Eurostar: There are at least a dozen trains every day from London-Waterloo to Paris-Gare du-Nord (2h 45min approx.), and a similar number to Lille (1h 45min) approx.. Onward travel from both cities can be made by high-speed TGV or the regular SNCF network. Information for services throughout France can be obtained by phoning Rail Europe (08705 848848) or on the website www.sncf-voyages.com. But to take full advantage of the recommendations of this book, you are probably at some time going to need your own transport.

Le Shuttle: Staying with your vehicle all the time, this is probably the 'least hassle' way of getting to France, and almost a must for those who are seasick, in a hurry or have pets with them. With several departures every hour, only in high season do you need to purchase your ticket ahead of time. Nevertheless, you may be able to take advantage of offers by doing this – and should you arrive at the check-in early, you have a pretty good chance of getting an earlier train. Crossing time is about 35 minutes and both loading and unloading are carried out with admirable efficiency.

By sea

This is the leisurely way to travel, and most people still feel it marks the start to the family holiday. At least it gets everyone out of the car for a while! A wide choice of crossings is on offer.

Eastern crossings: Dover-Calais is the shortest and quickest crossing of the channel. Regular ferry services are offered by Sea France, P&O and Norfolk line with a crossing time of about 90 minutes. Taking the slightly more expensive Hoverspeed can cut this time to about an hour. A new arrival on the scene is Speed Ferries, operating a '3rd generation wave-piercing catamaran' between Dover and Boulogne. With the fastest crossing time (50 mins) and competitive rates, it is worth consideration.

Western crossings: The western crossings are all longer and generally a little more expensive – but, depending on your home and destination, consider the mileage (and time) you might save on both sides of the channel. All the western crossings have overnight options, which can be helpful if you have a long journey through France the next day. Reveille always tends to be on the early side and it is surprising how far you can get before lunch! Brittany Ferries have crossings from Portsmouth to Caen (5h 45min), Poole to Cherbourg (4h 30min), Portsmouth to Cherbourg (5h 30min), Portsmouth to St Malo (8h 15min), and Plymouth to

Roscoff(6 hours). All except the last two crossings have high-speed options in summertime that can reduce times by about 50 per cent. A new name on the scene is LD Lines, operating from Portsmouth to le Havre, with some attractive offers.

By air

This may well be preferable if there are not too many of you, and you are heading for the south. As a rough guide, Calais to Marseille is a journey of 666 miles (1072km), around 12 hours' driving, while the flight from Stansted to Marseille takes 2h 30min.

British Airways, Air France and others offer flights to several destinations in France, but are finding it difficult to cope with the success of the budget airlines. Anyone living in the north of England will generally find it cheaper to fly to Nice than to take a train to London! Easyjet flies from Liverpool and Bristol to Nice and Paris, while from 'London' (Luton, Stansted and Gatwick) the destinations are extended to include Lyon, Marseille and Toulouse. Ryanair, operating its French flights mainly from Stansted (with one or two from Liverpool or Luton), has so many 'off-the-beaten-track' destinations that it is impossible to list them all – instead, try the website www.ryanair.com.

Car hire is always available from the airports, but it would be as well to arrange this in advance (possibly in a package with the flight). Expect to spend the first couple of hours reaching for the gear lever and/or handbrake with the wrong hand!

Onward travel in France

Before you leave home, make sure you have your **passport, driving licence, insurance certificate and registration document** (including a letter of authorisation from the owner if the vehicle is not registered in your name), and keep them all with you whenever you are out in the car. The French police are very keen on spot checks, and being on the road without these documents is an offence.

It goes without saying that you **drive on the right**! This sounds simple enough, but your weakest moments are first thing in the morning, and when turning out of a car park or one-way street into an empty two-way road. Known precautionary measures include putting a red spot on your windscreen and wearing your watch on the other wrist while in France – perhaps you can think of something better!

It is compulsory to carry a **red warning triangle** unless your vehicle has hazard flashers fitted – either triangle or flashers must be used if you break down on the road. Anyone towing must carry a red triangle at all times.

Car headlights must be fitted with appropriate beam deflectors – it is an offence to drive without these even in daylight. And dipped beams must be used when the visibility is poor.

Carrying a **spare set of lightbulbs** for your vehicle is compulsory.

Seat belts must be worn by front and rear seat passengers, and children under 10 years of age may not travel in the front seat. As in the UK, young children must be belted into seats that are appropriate for their weight and age.

Speed limits are 130kph/81mph on motorways in good weather conditions, 110kph/68mph on dual carriageways and on motorways in bad weather, 90kph/56mph on all other roads. In towns and villages, the speed limit is 51kph/31mph from the name sign at the entrance to the sign where the name is crossed out at the end, even though no limits may be displayed. And added to all that, there are many sections of road marked with their own peculiar limits, which you need to remember. Police are empowered to impose on-the-spot fines for speeding, and to confiscate the driver's licence if the limit was exceeded by more than 25kph.

France has had to crack down very hard on **drunken drivers** – limits are now much more strict than in the UK and punishments are severe. Do not touch even a drop before getting behind the wheel!

The old rule of ***priorité à droite*** (you should give priority to any vehicle arriving from the right) lingers in some town centres – and also in the minds of some older drivers. Since the rule is not yet extinct, look out for signs telling you who has priority at junctions and roundabouts – and if you do not know, err on the safe side. *Cédez le passage* means Give Way!

***Autoroutes* (motorways)** are generally the choice for getting anywhere in a hurry. They have a generous provision of pull-offs known as *aires*, which at their most basic have picnic tables and toilets, and at their most sophisticated have petrol stations, top class restaurants, fitness courses and even regional museums to take your mind off the road for a while. Most *autoroutes* carry tolls (although not while skirting big cities), which vary with the operating company. Traffic volume too varies, and while many *autoroutes* are almost empty by our standards, there are a few that carry a less than agreeable quota of heavy transport on two-lane carriageways.

ACCOMMODATION

This can be divided into hotels, *chambres d'hôtes* (bed and breakfast), *gîtes* (country cottages) and campsites (with hostel accommodation in *auberges de jeunesse* and *gîtes d'étapes* for the young at heart on a budget). Any tourist office will be able to supply you with lists of what is available in their area. For peace of mind, it is advisable to book ahead all accommodation needed in high season, even in these 'undiscovered' areas.

Hotels

Nationally, these are graded from 0 to 5 stars, and usually perform as their grade would lead you to expect. The most highly favoured guide is the *Michelin Red Hotel and Restaurant Guide* (in English) – which also rates a few thousand restaurants as well. Hotels listed in the *Logis de France* catalogue (available to order from the

Fact File

website logis-de-france.fr) are of guaranteed quality and not necessarily expensive. Ratings here vary from 1 to 3 'hearths' and whatever the grade, you are likely to find a good standard of regional cuisine.

For overnight stops, you could consider one of the motel chains (Campanile, Ibis, Novotel are the most upmarket) to be found near most big towns. In contrast to their British counterparts, these motels generally serve high quality imaginative food, again with regional emphasis, and are more than generous with the buffet parts of set menus. If you are staying for several nights in a hotel and thinking of eating in, look for their *demi-pension* (half-board) rates. These usually represent an overall saving (not invariably, so look hard!), but you are generally expected to eat from the humblest of the menus on offer.

Chambres d'hôtes — B&B

Many of them also offer an optional evening meal *en famille* – an opportunity to meet people and try out your French in an informal setting. *Fermes auberges* offer something of the same. *Gîtes-de-France* catalogues also contain information on *Chambres d'hôtes* (see below for details)

Gîtes Ruraux

These are country cottages (not to be confused with *gîtes d'étapes*, which are more like youth hostels). There are probably going to be quite a lot of these available in the area you have selected. British owners of properties in France generally advertise with Brittany Ferries (The French Collection), Chez Nous or Owners in France (among others); French owners seem to prefer to deal directly with *Gîtes de France*, who have a vast number of properties listed and catalogued by *département*. Go to their website (www.gites-de-france.fr – there is an English version), order a catalogue and browse. All the facts are there, the only thing you cannot predict is the owner. A few will give you a brief tour, meet you at the end and add up the electricity bill; most go well beyond that and some will lavish wine, regional gifts and free fire wood upon you and spend as much time as you care to give them extolling the virtues of their region, thus providing you with a wonderful opportunity of improving your French whatever its standard. This is definitely the off-the-beaten-track option, although satisfaction cannot be entirely guaranteed.

Camping

The French love camping and you will probably see three-generation families that have evidently moved under canvas for the duration of summer, taking with them what appears to be the entire contents of their house and assorted livestock as well. Campsites in France are plentiful and of varying quality – municipal sites usually represent good value for money and are of a high standard. The catalogue of choice is probably Michelin's *Camping France*, obtainable at bookshops in the UK, with a new edition released each spring. Nevertheless, there is virtually no descriptive text in the Michelin book (and a few sites of perfectly reasonable quality are unaccountably absent) so you might like to equip yourself also with the AA *Camping and Caravanning France*, or even the French *Camping Caravaning Guide Officiel*, which lists everything that could with abundant imagination be deemed an outdoor place to spend the night, and needs reading with care (in French). Occasionally, campsites that are outstanding for either their location or their facilities have been mentioned in this book – they are all ones that have been seen personally.

EATING OUT

Eating out is very popular in France and even small villages that have no shops may have their own restaurant. If you are in a place where there is a choice of restaurants, go for one that is full – the locals are in the know.

Have no doubts about taking the **children** – they are always very welcome, and restaurants are usually happy to adapt to their needs, dividing a meal, or bringing an extra plate, if there is no children's menu.

Fixed menus are usually the best value and there are particularly good bargain feasts to be had at lunchtime – but of course you may put yourself out of action for the rest of the afternoon!

Take note that the **cheese course** comes before the desert in France (i.e. don't leave as soon as you have had it), and a tiny cup of coffee (not usually included in the meal price) rounds everything off very nicely.

If you want to study form before you venture out, the *Michelin Red Guide* is the generally recognised authority, but also useful is the *Guide du Routard – Hotels and Restaurants*, of which there is an English version, and Dorling Kindersley have thrown in a glossy tome (*France – Best Places to Eat and Stay*) which interestingly details the regional specialities to look out for, as well as where to eat them.

And on leaving the restaurant **tips** are not strictly necessary, although 2 or 3 euros does register appreciation of a particularly good meal or service.

ELECTRICITY

The electric current is 220 volts and two pin circular plugs are the norm. If you are going to use your own electrical devices, make sure you get an adaptor before you leave home (or at the ferry terminal) because they are not so easy to come by once you are in France

HISTORY

No one wants a history lesson before going on holiday, and a long rigmarole is not easy to remember anyway. Nevertheless, just a few time markers might help you make more sense of what you see, so let us be cavalier and – with apologies to the French – slash all Gallic history to seven salient points (not forgetting a confusing Five Republics!)

1. Prehistory

Tautavel, on the eastern side of the Pyrenees has yielded human remains dating from around 450,000BC, thought to be older than any outside Africa. It is a giant leap in time to 15,000BC, when Cromagnon man was painting the walls of his caves in the Dordogne. And the multitude of megaliths in the west of France are fairly recent additions, having been fashioned somewhere in the immediate 5,000 years before the birth of Christ.

2. The Romans

They arrived in Provence around 125BC and by 51BC had subdued the resident Gallic (Celtic) tribes and conquered the whole of France. Remains of their buildings can be found almost everywhere, but Provence, and in particular the Rhône valley, has the greatest wealth. The Romans were finally driven out by the barbaric Franks in the 5th century AD.

3. An auspicious marriage

The union (in 1152) of wealthy land-owning Eleanor of Aquitaine and Henry of Anjou, otherwise known as Henry Plantagenet, certainly had far-reaching effects for both England and France. Two years later, on the death of his mother's cousin King Stephen, Henry became Henry II of England, and so at this time England ruled all the territory between 'the Arctic Ocean and the Pyrenees'.

4. The Hundred Years War and Joan of Arc

When Charles IV died without male heirs in 1328, the crown was given to his cousin Philip of Valois as a result of the recently established Salic Law in which no female could accede to the throne of France. Edward III of England thought that he had a greater claim through his mother (the sister of Charles IV), and thus began the so-called Hundred Years War (1337-1453). The English were victorious at Sluys, Crécy and Poitiers before the tide turned and the French regained territory. England gained the upper hand again after Agincourt (1415) and held Brittany, Normandy, Maine, Champagne and Guienne (the south-west corner).

In 1439, a peasant girl from Lorraine heard voices telling her she could oust the English from France. Amazingly she secured an audience with the Dauphin and was given an army with which she quickly managed to relieve the siege of Orléans. Other victories followed before Joan of Arc was captured by the Burgundians, handed over to the English and burnt at the stake in Rouen in 1431. The war dragged on for another 20 years, but there is no doubt that Joan's brief campaign was its turning point. Very soon, Calais was the only French territory remaining in English hands.

Fact File

5. The Wars of Religion (1562-98)

In the 16th century the Catholic aristocracy were beginning to feel that the Protestants (Huguenots) were threatening their powers. In the notorious St Bartholomew's day massacre of 1572, 30,000 French Huguenots were massacred, 3,000 of them in Paris. Persecution of Huguenots continued until the Protestant Henry IV acceded to the throne in 1594. He promptly converted to Catholicism (with the famous quote *Paris vaut bien une messe* – Paris is well worth a Mass) and four years later issued the Edict of Nantes ensuring religious toleration for both sides. This state of truce lasted until 1685 when the Edict of Nantes was revoked by the extravagant, flamboyant and personally powerful Louis XIV.

6. The Revolution (1789) and its aftermath

France had flourished economically under Louis XIV, even though he himself spent a lot of its wealth. Under Louis XV and then Louis XVI it became poorer, taxation was high and the gulf between rich and poor ever widening. The Estates General, a committee of representatives from the nobles, clergy and commons, was called in to help resolve the crisis. The Third Estate (the commons) decided they constituted a national assembly, whereupon the king's troops moved in to disperse them, and the people of Paris famously stormed the Bastille, the prison that they took to be the symbol of the king's authority. The new National Assembly soon came up with its Declaration of the Rights of Man and the democratic ethic of *Liberté, Égalité, Fraternité.* A constitutional monarchy was declared, but Louis XVI, although imprisoned, was soon deemed to represent a threat.

A First Republic was proclaimed instead and both the king and Queen Marie-Antoinette were executed. The radical Jacobins seized power at this point and the period known as the Reign of Terror (*la Terreur*) ensued, with almost a year of horrendous bloodshed. Eventually, the Jacobin leader himself (the renowned Robespierre) went to the guillotine and government passed into the hands of the Directory, a group who aimed to steer a middle course.

Meanwhile France had been waging war abroad under the command of Napoleon. In 1799 he returned to France and overthrew the Directory to establish his own dictatorship, which (bar a little period in exile) lasted until his defeat at Waterloo in 1815. France then became a monarchy again, with Louis XVIII being succeeded by Charles X and Louis-Philippe. A further revolution in 1848 forced Louis-Philippe to abdicate and the Second Republic was declared. Its leader, elected the first President of France, was Louis-Napoleon (known as Napoleon III), a nephew of the emperor. Four years later he ended the republic by proclaiming himself 'Emperor' and ruled in this way until France's defeat by the Prussians in 1870 brought about the Third Republic.

7. Wars of the 20th century

In World War I the north-east of France saw terrible fighting for little gain. France lost almost a quarter of her youth (men aged between 18 and 30). In World War II, once the troops had been evacuated from Dunkerque, Paris fell very quickly. France was divided into an 'occupied' north and a southern 'Vichy France' under the collaborating 84-year-old Maréchal Pétain. France is deeply ashamed of the part this latter government played in the deportation of the Jews. Men who managed to escape from the country fought as the Free French Forces under the command of Général de Gaulle, based in London.

Of those who remained, France is hugely and justly proud of its brave *Résistance* (also known as the *Maquis*). The latter, informed by coded messages, played their part in the events of D-Day (6 June1944), the allied invasion that only just succeeded in gaining a first foothold, but went on to liberate Paris on 25 August that year. France was in ruins, both physically and economically, but began the process of regeneration with enthusiasm under de Gaulle, who proposed a constitution for the Fourth Republic. After the ups-and-downs of the Post-war years, it was the Algerian crisis that in 1962 resulted in yet another constitution, the Fifth Republic, in which the president has supreme power.

HOLIDAY PURSUITS

Museums

Published opening hours for museums are given in the information section at the end of each chapter – some establishments prefer to keep things more general by saying that they are open in the 'morning' or the 'afternoon'. And, of course, even where times are stated, they can change (although not usually radically) over the years. You could always phone the appropriate OT to check when timing is critical. Generally speaking, museums are quite likely to be closed on either a Monday or a Tuesday out of season and when open they may well take a longish lunch-break. In many places museum entry is free on the first Sunday of the month. And most museums are open all day every day in July and August.

Festivals

Local festivals can be wonderful entertainment. If you are in Brittany, try to take in at least one *pardon* – a religious festival that usually includes singing and dancing and lots of national costumes. The one at le Folgoët on the first Sunday in September is possibly the biggest and best. Other festivals worth moving heaven and earth to get to include the colourful Mardi Gras at Nice (the week before Lent) and the exuberant Gypsy Festival at Stes Maries de-la-Mer (24/25 May)

329

Walking

This is another popular French pastime, and almost every Office de Tourisme will be able to offer you maps of short circular walks in their area. These *Petites Randonnées* are usually waymarked with flashes of paint (yellow is the most common) on rocks, trees, walls etc, making them relatively easy to follow. A painted X indicates that you have taken the wrong way.

The other type of path that you will commonly meet is the long-distance route, the *Grande Randonnée*. There are many of these criss-crossing the country and they are marked with bars of white on red. Following one can be a great adventure, but first of all equip yourself with the appropriate map and decide how you are going to get back at the end of the day (e.g. with the help of OT, for bus routes and taxis).

Anyone with really serious intent should get on to the website of the French walking organisation, the *Fédération Française de la Randonnée Pédestre* (www. ffrandonnee.fr) who produce truly excellent *Topoguides* covering most of France. Attractive, colourful and with maps good enough to compensate for the lack of English translation, they describe both short local routes (PR) and long-distance trails (GR) and can be obtained by post from the FFRP headquarters in Paris.

Cycling

This is almost the French national sport – witness the popularity of the Tour de France (held the first three weeks in July, routes from the website www.letour.fr if you want to see it or avoid it). Routes for road bikers wanting to explore the local countryside can usually be obtained from any tourist office – although their idea of what constitutes a quiet country road might not entirely agree with your own. But, as in Britain, there are miles of designated safe family cycle track using, for example, disused railways and canal towpaths.

A mountain bike is known as a VTT (*Vélo Tout Terrain*) and the popularity of these has really taken off in recent years. Regions sometimes have as many waymarked bike circuits as they do circular walks – the logo is two wheels topped by a triangle pointing the direction. Tourist Offices should have all the necessary maps and information on bike hire.

Watersports

You do not have to go to the seaside to swim in a pleasant outdoor environment in France – a *Plan d'eau* will do just as well. The latter may refer to a section of a river or lake reserved for swimming and watersports, or most commonly, it denotes a small man-made lake with recreation facilities – usually a beach of imported sand, children's play equipment nearby and possibly pedalos or other boats for hire. In many ways a *plan d'eau* is much safer for young children – it is easier to keep eyes on them for a start and the swimming area is usually supervised in the summer months.

Other popular French pursuits are canoeing and kayaking, and there is almost certain to be a hire base somewhere near where you are staying. Organised excursions suitable for all the family are possible on many of the larger rivers. More possibilities include sailing and white-water rafting. Brief information about what is available in each area is given at the end of the appropriate chapter, but any Office de Tourisme should be able to fill in the finer details.

MEDICAL TREATMENT

Before you leave, make sure you have an EHIC card (obtainable online, by phone or by post. Enquire at your local Post Office in the UK) – and you would be ill-advised to travel without extra medical insurance. The EHIC replaces the E111 form from January 2006.

If you consult a doctor or dentist, you will be expected to pay and then be given a *feuille de soins* (medical treatment form) and a prescription, both of which should be taken to the chemist. To reclaim a proportion of costs, the *feuille de soins*, the sticky labels from drugs prescribed and your passport should be taken to a Caisse Primaire Assurance Maladie (CPAM) – the local OT should be able to direct you (the items can be sent later with the passport photocopied if you prefer). It is sometimes possible to get a refund immediately, although more usually it will be sent to your UK address in about six weeks.

In France, pharmacists are very used to dealing with minor ailments – coughs, colds, sprained ankles and more. It might well be worth consulting a pharmacist first to see if he can help – but you will not get the cost of his treatments reimbursed.

MONEY MATTERS

The euro in your pocket

For a quick calculation, £1 is approximately equal to 1.5 euros, or 1 euro = two thirds of a pound (67p). Money can usually be exchanged without commission in the UK before you leave, and top-ups can be obtained from any ATM with the appropriate logo for your card. In practice, holders of the major cards will have no problem at all, but note that, in addition to the commission on the exchange, a fee is usually charged even for debit card withdrawals, and taking out small amounts is therefore relatively costly. If you cannot find a bank, larger post offices will always have a cash-point (*distributeur de billets*).

The other option is travellers' cheques, and you may be lucky enough to obtain them without commission – but of course they can only be cashed during banking hours. These are something like Monday to Friday, 9am-5pm but – some banks close for two hours in the middle of the day, some close on Mondays, some open on Saturday mornings, all close for designated public holi-

Fact File

days, and if the latter fall within one day of a weekend, many will not miss the obvious opportunity have an extended holiday.

Card purchases

Major credit cards are widely accepted in hotels, restaurants, supermarkets and petrol stations. At the time of writing, British cards are gradually being changed over from the magnetic-strip type to chip-and-PIN, a system that has been used for several years in France. It will normally be possible to use the new British chip-and-PIN cards in French machines, but success will depend on whether the individual merchant is using the same system. If not, he should nevertheless be able to swipe the card as it will still have a magnetic strip. It should be said that, particularly in off-the-beaten-track areas, some supermarkets seem to have trouble with this swiping, but it is usually successful eventually, if everyone remains patient (including the lengthening queue). The new chip-and-PIN cards should be especially useful in supermarket petrol stations (normally the cheapest place to fill up), which are commonly left unmanned over a generous two-hour lunch break.

PUBLIC HOLIDAYS

The French year is scattered with public holidays and even more festivals that require ritual observance. On Rameaux (Palm Sunday) you will see people carrying palm fronds (or, in the north, other stand-ins for the same); on Toussaint (All Saints' – 1 November) they are carrying huge pots of chrysanthemums to put on the graves of their loved one; on the longest day (21 June), music is celebrated and there will be singing and dancing in town; at Carnaval (Carnival – the days immediately before Lent) – well, anything can happen, and on Bastille Day (14 July), every town will be brought to a halt for the triumphant procession. And that is not even a fraction of it! But, for practical purposes, expect everything to be closed on the 12 official public holidays – 1 January, Easter Sunday, Easter Monday, 1 May, 8 May (Armistice 1945), Ascension Day, Whit Monday, 14 July (Bastille Day), 15 August (the Assumption), 1 November (All Saints), 11 November (Armistice 1918) and 25 December. And where these fall on a Sunday, the Monday following will also be taken as a holiday.

SHOPPING

Markets

When in France, do as the French do (at least traditionally) and buy your fresh produce from the market. Almost every small town holds one at least once a week, and it is almost always all over by mid-day. But markets are by no means just a source of fruit and vegetables – almost anything, animal, vegetable or mineral, can be found in some of the larger ones. All French life is here, and

Provençal markets are best of all with their colourful cotton prints and rich aromas of herbs and spices.

Supermarkets

At the other end of the scale are the supermarkets, which are becoming more popular with the busy housewives of today. Worst scenario opening hours are 9am-12noon, 2-6pm Tuesday to Saturday. Many, though not all, now open on Mondays, some open on Sunday mornings, but not one opens on a Sunday afternoon.

High Street shops

These have hours similar to supermarkets, give or take a bit. Bread at least is usually obtainable on a Sunday morning, and even on public holidays – to find it, you have only to look where all those carrying their breakfast bundles are coming from.

TELEPHONING

Card-operated telephones are far more common than those that will take cash. Telecartes can be obtained from any Post Office or from any shop displaying the sign 'Tabac' and come in two different sizes, 50 and 120 units. Many phones will now also accept the major credit cards.

You may be able to use your **mobile phone** in France if you have made arrangements in advance, but both calls and texts can be costly (texts are usually double the internal cost).

To call the UK from France, begin with the international code 0044, followed by the required number with the first zero omitted.

Emergency numbers are:
15   Ambulance (SAMU – paramedics)
17   Police
18   Fire-brigade (*sapeurs-pompiers*), who will deal with just about anything
112 A number that can be used throughout the EEC covering all three emergency services. You can expect to be connected to someone who speaks English

Index

Published in the UK by
Landmark Publishing Ltd,
Ashbourne Hall, Cokayne Avenue, Ashbourne, Derbyshire DE6 1EJ England
Tel: (01335) 347349 Fax: (01335) 347303
e-mail: sales@landmarkpublishing.co.uk
website: landmarkpublishing.co.uk

Published in the USA by
Hunter Publishing Inc,
130 Campus Drive, Edison NJ 08818
Tel: (732) 225 1900, (800) 255 0343 Fax: (732) 417 0482
website: www.hunterpublishing.com

ISBN 1 84306 161 9

British Library Cataloguing in Publication Data: a catalogue record for this book is available
from the British Library.

Print: Cromwell Press
Design & Cartography: Mark Titterton

Front cover: Medieval town of Vitré.
Back cover, top: Cathedral at Amiens.
Back cover, bottom: Lavender fields in the Diois.

All photographs supplied by the author